Library of Congress Cataloging-in-Publication Data

Dunham, Margaret H.
Data mining introductory and advanced topics / Margaret H. Dunham.
p. cm.
Includes bibliographical references and index.
ISBN 0-13-088892-3
1. Data mining. I. Title

QA76.9.D343 D86 2002
006.3–dc21   2002075976

Vice President and Editorial Director, ECS: *Marcia J. Horton*
Publisher: *Alan R. Apt*
Associate Editor: *Toni D. Holm*
Editorial Assistant: *Patrick Lindner*
Vice President and Director of Production and Manufacturing, ESM: *David W. Riccardi*
Executive Managing Editor: *Vince O'Brien*
Assistant Managing Editor: *Camille Trentacoste*
Production Editor: *Joan Wolk*
Director of Creative Services: *Paul Belfanti*
Creative Director: *Carole Anson*
Art director: *Jayne Conte*
Cover Designer: *Bruce Kenselaar*
Art Editor: *Greg Dulles*
Manufacturing Manager: *Trudy Pisciotti*
Manufacturing Buyer: *Lynda Castillo*
Marketing Manager: *Pamela Shaffer*
Marketing Assistant: *Barrie Reinhold*

© 2003 by Pearson Education, Inc.
Pearson Education, Inc.
Upper Saddle River, New Jersey 07458

The author and publisher of this book have used their best efforts in preparing this book. These efforts include the development, research, and testing of the theories and programs to determine their effectiveness. The author and publisher make no warranty of any kind, expressed or implied, with regard to these programs or the documentation contained in this book. The author and publisher shall not be liable in any event for incidental or consequential damages in connection with, or arising out of, the furnishing, performance, or use of these programs.

Printed in the United States of America
10 9 8 7 6 5 4 3 2 1

ISBN 0-13-088892-3

Pearson Education LTD., *London*
Pearson Education Australia PTY, Limited, *Sydney*
Pearson Education Singapore, Pte. Ltd
Pearson Education North Asia Ltd, *Hong Kong*
Pearson Education Canada, Inc., *Toronto*
Pearson Educación de Mexico, S.A. de C.V.
Pearson Education—Japan, *Tokyo*
Pearson Education Malaysia, Pte. Ltd
Pearson Education, Inc., *Upper Saddle River, New Jersey*

Data Mining
Introductory and Advanced
Topics

Margaret H. Dunham
Southern Methodist University

 *An Alan R. Apt Book*

PEARSON EDUCATION INC.
Upper Saddle River, New Jersey 07458

to
Boom Boom and Gakin,
Jim,
Stephanie and Kristina.
You are my past, present, and future.
I LOVE YOU.

Contents

APPENDICES

Preface

Data doubles about every year, but useful information seems to be decreasing. The area of data mining has arisen over the last decade to address this problem. It has become not only an important research area, but also one with large potential in the real world. Current business users of data mining products achieve millions of dollars a year in savings by using data mining techniques to reduce the cost of day to day business operations. Data mining techniques are proving to be extremely useful in detecting and predicting terrorism.

The purpose of this book is to introduce the reader to various data mining concepts and algorithms. The book is concise yet thorough in its coverage of the many data mining topics. Clearly written algorithms with accompanying pseudocode are used to describe approaches. A database perspective is used throughout. This means that I examine algorithms, data structures, data types, and complexity of algorithms and space. The emphasis is on the use of data mining concepts in real-world applications with large database components.

Data mining research and practice is in a state similar to that of databases in the 1960s. At that time applications programmers had to create an entire database environment each time they wrote a program. With the development of the relational data model, query processing and optimization techniques, transaction management strategies, and ad hoc query languages (SQL) and interfaces, the current environment is drastically different. The evolution of data mining techniques may take a similar path over the next few decades, making data mining techniques easier to use and develop. The objective of this book is to help in this process.

The intended audience of this book is either the experienced database professional who wishes to learn more about data mining or graduate level computer science students who have completed at least an introductory database course. The book is meant to be used as the basis of a one-semester graduate level course covering the basic data mining concepts. It may also be used as reference book for computer professionals and researchers.

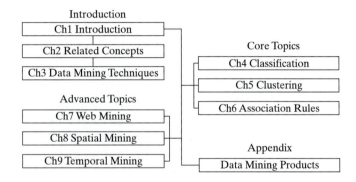

The book is divided into four major parts: Introduction, Core Topics, Advanced Topics, and Appendix. The introduction covers background information needed to understand the later material. In addition, it examines topics related to data mining such as OLAP, data warehousing, information retrieval, and machine learning. In the first chapter of the introduction I provide a very cursory overview of data mining and how it relates to the complete KDD process. The second chapter surveys topics related to data mining. While this is not crucial to the coverage of data mining and need not be read to understand later chapters, it provides the interested reader with an understanding and appreciation of how data mining concepts relate to other areas. To thoroughly understand and appreciate the data mining algorithms presented in subsequent chapters, it is important that the reader realize that data mining is not an isolated subject. It has its basis in many related disciplines that are equally important on their own. The third chapter in this part surveys some techniques used to implement data mining algorithms. These include statistical techniques, neural networks, and decision trees. This part of the book provides the reader with an understanding of the basic data mining concepts. It also serves as a standalone survey of the entire data mining area.

The Core Topics covered are classification, clustering, and association rules. I view these as the major data mining functions. Other data mining concepts (such as prediction, regression, and pattern matching) may be viewed as special cases of these three. In each of these chapters I concentrate on coverage of the most commonly used algorithms of each type. Our coverage includes pseudocode for these algorithms, an explanation of them and examples illustrating their use.

The advanced topics part looks at various concepts that complicate data mining applications. I concentrate on temporal data, spatial data, and Web mining. Again, algorithms and pseudocode are provided.

In the appendix, production data mining systems are surveyed. I will keep a more up to data list on the Web page for the book. I thank all the representatives of the various companies who helped me correct and update my descriptions of their products.

All chapters include exercises covering the material in that chapter. In addition to conventional types of exercises that either test the student's understanding of the material or require him to apply what he has learned. I also include some exercises that require implementation (coding) and research. A one-semester course would cover the core topics and one or more of the advanced ones.

ACKNOWLEDGMENTS

Many people have helped with the completion of this book. Tamer Özsu provided initial advice and inspiration. My dear friend Bob Korfhage introduced me to much of computer science, including pattern matching and information retrieval. Bob, I think of you often.

I particularly thank my graduate students for contributing a great deal to some of the original wording and editing. Their assistance in reading and commenting on earlier drafts has been invaluable. Matt McBride helped me prepare most of the original slides, many of which are still available as a companion to the book. Yongqiao Xiao helped write much of the material in the Web mining chapter. He also meticulously reviewed an earlier draft of the book and corrected many mistakes. Le Gruenwald, Zahid Hossain, Yasemin Seydim, and Al Xiao performed much of the research that provided information found concerning association rules. Mario Nascimento introduced me to the world of temporal databases, and I have used some of the information from his dissertation in the temporal mining chapter. Nat Ayewah has been very patient with his explanations of hidden Markov models and helped improve the wording of that section. Zhigang Li has introduced me to the complex world of time series and helped write the solutions manual. I've learned a lot, but still feel a novice in many of these areas.

The students in my CSE8331 class (Spring 1999, Fall 2000, and Spring 2002) at SMU have had to endure a great deal. I never realized how difficult it is to clearly word algorithm descriptions and exercises until I wrote this book. I hope they learned something even though at times the continual revisions necessary were, I'm sure, frustrating. Torsten Staab wins the prize for finding and correcting the most errors. Students in my CSE8331 class during Spring 2002 helped me prepare class notes and solutions to the exercises. I thank them for their input.

My family has been extremely supportive in this endeavor. My husband, Jim, has been (as always) understanding and patient with my odd work hours and lack of sleep. A more patient and supportive husband could not be found. My daughter Stephanie has put up with my moodiness caused by lack of sleep. Sweetie, I hope I haven't been too short-tempered with you (ILYMMTYLM). At times I have been impatient with Kristina but you know how much I love you. My Mom, sister Martha, and brother Dave as always are there to provide support and love.

Some of the research required for this book was supported by the National Science Foundation under Grant No. IIS-9820841. I would finally like to thank the reviewers (Michael Huhns, Julia Hodger, Bob Cimikowski, Greg Speegle, Zoran Obradovic, T.Y. Lin, and James Buckly) for their many constructive comments. I tried to implement as many of these I could.

PART ONE
INTRODUCTION

C H A P T E R 1

Introduction

The amount of data kept in computer files and databases is growing at a phenomenal rate. At the same time, the users of these data are expecting more sophisticated information from them. A marketing manager is no longer satisfied with a simple listing of marketing contacts, but wants detailed information about customers' past purchases as well as predictions of future purchases. Simple structured/query language queries are not adequate to support these increased demands for information. Data mining steps in to solve these needs. *Data mining* is often defined as finding hidden information in a database. Alternatively, it has been called exploratory data analysis, data driven discovery, and deductive learning.

Traditional database queries (Figure 1.1), access a database using a well-defined query stated in a language such as SQL. The output of the query consists of the data from the database that satisfies the query. The output is usually a subset of the database, but it may also be an extracted view or may contain aggregations. Data mining access of a database differs from this traditional access in several ways:

- **Query:** The query might not be well formed or precisely stated. The data miner might not even be exactly sure of what he wants to see.

- **Data:** The data accessed is usually a different version from that of the original operational database. The data have been cleansed and modified to better support the mining process.

- **Output:** The output of the data mining query probably is not a subset of the database. Instead it is the output of some analysis of the contents of the database.

The current state of the art of data mining is similar to that of database query processing in the late 1960s and early 1970s. Over the next decade there undoubtedly will be great

FIGURE 1.1: Database access.

strides in extending the state of the art with respect to data mining. We probably will see the development of "query processing" models, standards, and algorithms targeting the data mining applications. We probably will also see new data structures designed for the storage of databases being used for data mining applications. Although data mining is currently in its infancy, over the last decade we have seen a proliferation of mining algorithms, applications, and algorithmic approaches. Example 1.1 illustrates one such application.

EXAMPLE 1.1

Credit card companies must determine whether to authorize credit card purchases. Suppose that based on past historical information about purchases, each purchase is placed into one of four classes: (1) authorize, (2) ask for further identification before authorization, (3) do not authorize, and (4) do not authorize but contact police. The data mining functions here are twofold. First the historical data must be examined to determine how the data fit into the four classes. Then the problem is to apply this model to each new purchase. Although the second part indeed may be stated as a simple database query, the first part cannot be.

Data mining involves many different algorithms to accomplish different tasks. All of these algorithms attempt to fit a model to the data. The algorithms examine the data and determine a model that is closest to the characteristics of the data being examined. Data mining algorithms can be characterized as consisting of three parts:

- *Model*: The purpose of the algorithm is to fit a model to the data.

- *Preference*: Some criteria must be used to fit one model over another.

- *Search*: All algorithms require some technique to search the data.

In Example 1.1 the data are modeled as divided into four classes. The search requires examining past data about credit card purchases and their outcome to determine what criteria should be used to define the class structure. The preference will be given to criteria that seem to fit the data best. For example, we probably would want to authorize a credit card purchase for a small amount of money with a credit card belonging to a long-standing customer. Conversely, we would not want to authorize the use of a credit card to purchase anything if the card has been reported as stolen. The search process requires that the criteria needed to fit the data to the classes be properly defined.

As seen in Figure 1.2, the model that is created can be either predictive or descriptive in nature. In this figure, we show under each model type some of the most common data mining tasks that use that type of model.

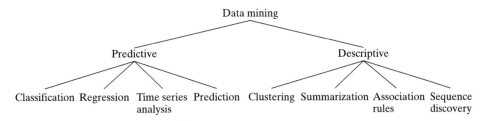

FIGURE 1.2: Data mining models and tasks.

A *predictive model* makes a prediction about values of data using known results found from different data. Predictive modeling may be made based on the use of other historical data. For example, a credit card use might be refused not because of the user's own credit history, but because the current purchase is similar to earlier purchases that were subsequently found to be made with stolen cards. Example 1.1 uses predictive modeling to predict the credit risk. Predictive model data mining tasks include classification, regression, time series analysis, and prediction. Prediction may also be used to indicate a specific type of data mining function, as is explained in section 1.1.4.

A *descriptive model* identifies patterns or relationships in data. Unlike the predictive model, a descriptive model serves as a way to explore the properties of the data examined, not to predict new properties. Clustering, summarization, association rules, and sequence discovery are usually viewed as descriptive in nature.

1.1 BASIC DATA MINING TASKS

In the following paragraphs we briefly explore some of the data mining functions. We follow the basic outline of tasks shown in Figure 1.2. This list is not intended to be exhaustive, but rather illustrative. Of course, these individual tasks may be combined to obtain more sophisticated data mining applications.

1.1.1 Classification

Classification maps data into predefined groups or *classes*. It is often referred to as supervised learning because the classes are determined before examining the data. Two examples of classification applications are determining whether to make a bank loan and identifying credit risks. Classification algorithms require that the classes be defined based on data attribute values. They often describe these classes by looking at the characteristics of data already known to belong to the classes. *Pattern recognition* is a type of classification where an input pattern is classified into one of several classes based on its similarity to these predefined classes. Example 1.1 illustrates a general classification problem. Example 1.2 shows a simple example of pattern recognition.

EXAMPLE 1.2

An airport security screening station is used to determine if passengers are potential terrorists or criminals. To do this, the face of each passenger is scanned and its basic pattern (distance between eyes, size and shape of mouth, shape of head, etc.) is identified.

This pattern is compared to entries in a database to see if it matches any patterns that are associated with known offenders.

1.1.2 Regression

Regression is used to map a data item to a real valued prediction variable. In actuality, regression involves the learning of the function that does this mapping. Regression assumes that the target data fit into some known type of function (e.g., linear, logistic, etc.) and then determines the best function of this type that models the given data. Some type of error analysis is used to determine which function is "best." Standard linear regression, as illustrated in Example 1.3, is a simple example of regression.

EXAMPLE 1.3

A college professor wishes to reach a certain level of savings before her retirement. Periodically, she predicts what her retirement savings will be based on its current value and several past values. She uses a simple linear regression formula to predict this value by fitting past behavior to a linear function and then using this function to predict the values at points in the future. Based on these values, she then alters her investment portfolio.

1.1.3 Time Series Analysis

With *time series analysis*, the value of an attribute is examined as it varies over time. The values usually are obtained as evenly spaced time points (daily, weekly, hourly, etc.). A time series plot (Figure 1.3), is used to visualize the time series. In this figure you can easily see that the plots for Y and Z have similar behavior, while X appears to have less volatility. There are three basic functions performed in time series analysis. In one case, distance measures are used to determine the similarity between different time series. In the second case, the structure of the line is examined to determine (and perhaps classify) its behavior. A third application would be to use the historical time series plot to predict future values. A time series example is given in Example 1.4.

EXAMPLE 1.4

Mr. Smith is trying to determine whether to purchase stock from Companies X, Y, or Z. For a period of one month he charts the daily stock price for each company. Figure 1.3 shows the time series plot that Mr. Smith has generated. Using this and similar information available from his stockbroker, Mr. Smith decides to purchase stock X because it is less volatile while overall showing a slightly larger relative amount of growth than either of the other stocks. As a matter of fact, the stocks for Y and Z have a similar behavior. The behavior of Y between days 6 and 20 is identical to that for Z between days 13 and 27.

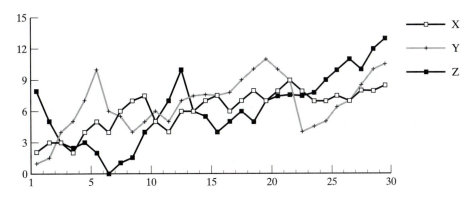

FIGURE 1.3: Time series plots.

1.1.4 Prediction

Many real-world data mining applications can be seen as predicting future data states based on past and current data. *Prediction* can be viewed as a type of classification. (Note: This is a data mining task that is different from the prediction model, although the prediction task is a type of prediction model.) The difference is that prediction is predicting a future state rather than a current state. Here we are referring to a type of application rather than to a type of data mining modeling approach, as discussed earlier. Prediction applications include flooding, speech recognition, machine learning, and pattern recognition. Although future values may be predicted using time series analysis or regression techniques, other approaches may be used as well. Example 1.5 illustrates the process.

EXAMPLE 1.5

Predicting flooding is a difficult problem. One approach uses monitors placed at various points in the river. These monitors collect data relevant to flood prediction: water level, rain amount, time, humidity, and so on. Then the water level at a potential flooding point in the river can be predicted based on the data collected by the sensors upriver from this point. The prediction must be made with respect to the time the data were collected.

1.1.5 Clustering

Clustering is similar to classification except that the groups are not predefined, but rather defined by the data alone. Clustering is alternatively referred to as unsupervised learning or segmentation. It can be thought of as partitioning or segmenting the data into groups that might or might not be disjoint. The clustering is usually accomplished by determining the similarity among the data on predefined attributes. The most similar data are grouped into clusters. Example 1.6 provides a simple clustering example. Since the clusters are not predefined, a domain expert is often required to interpret the meaning of the created clusters.

EXAMPLE 1.6

A certain national department store chain creates special catalogs targeted to various demographic groups based on attributes such as income, location, and physical characteristics of potential customers (age, height, weight, etc.). To determine the target mailings of the various catalogs and to assist in the creation of new, more specific catalogs, the company performs a clustering of potential customers based on the determined attribute values. The results of the clustering exercise are then used by management to create special catalogs and distribute them to the correct target population based on the cluster for that catalog.

A special type of clustering is called *segmentation*. With segmentation a database is partitioned into disjointed groupings of similar tuples called *segments*. Segmentation is often viewed as being identical to clustering. In other circles segmentation is viewed as a specific type of clustering applied to a database itself. In this text we use the two terms, *clustering* and *segmentation*, interchangeably.

1.1.6   Summarization

Summarization maps data into subsets with associated simple descriptions. Summarization is also called *characterization* or *generalization*. It extracts or derives representative information about the database. This may be accomplished by actually retrieving portions of the data. Alternatively, summary type information (such as the mean of some numeric attribute) can be derived from the data. The summarization succinctly characterizes the contents of the database. Example 1.7 illustrates this process.

EXAMPLE 1.7

One of the many criteria used to compare universities by the *U.S. News & World Report* is the average SAT or ACT score [GM99]. This is a summarization used to estimate the type and intellectual level of the student body.

1.1.7   Association Rules

Link analysis, alternatively referred to as *affinity analysis* or *association*, refers to the data mining task of uncovering relationships among data. The best example of this type of application is to determine association rules. An *association rule* is a model that identifies specific types of data associations. These associations are often used in the retail sales community to identify items that are frequently purchased together. Example 1.8 illustrates the use of association rules in market basket analysis. Here the data analyzed consist of information about what items a customer purchases. Associations are also used in many other applications such as predicting the failure of telecommunication switches.

EXAMPLE 1.8

A grocery store retailer is trying to decide whether to put bread on sale. To help determine the impact of this decision, the retailer generates association rules that show what other products are frequently purchased with bread. He finds that 60% of the time that bread is sold so are pretzels and that 70% of the time jelly is also sold. Based on these facts, he tries to capitalize on the association between bread, pretzels, and jelly by placing some pretzels and jelly at the end of the aisle where the bread is placed. In addition, he decides not to place either of these items on sale at the same time.

Users of association rules must be cautioned that these are not causal relationships. They do not represent any relationship inherent in the actual data (as is true with functional dependencies) or in the real world. There probably is no relationship between bread and pretzels that causes them to be purchased together. And there is no guarantee that this association will apply in the future. However, association rules can be used to assist retail store management in effective advertising, marketing, and inventory control.

1.1.8 Sequence Discovery

Sequential analysis or *sequence discovery* is used to determine sequential patterns in data. These patterns are based on a time sequence of actions. These patterns are similar to associations in that data (or events) are found to be related, but the relationship is based on time. Unlike a market basket analysis, which requires the items to be purchased at the same time, in sequence discovery the items are purchased over time in some order. Example 1.9 illustrates the discovery of some simple patterns. A similar type of discovery can be seen in the sequence within which data are purchased. For example, most people who purchase CD players may be found to purchase CDs within one week. As we will see, temporal association rules really fall into this category.

EXAMPLE 1.9

The Webmaster at the XYZ Corp. periodically analyzes the Web log data to determine how users of the XYZ's Web pages access them. He is interested in determining what sequences of pages are frequently accessed. He determines that 70 percent of the users of page A follow one of the following patterns of behavior: $\langle A, B, C \rangle$ or $\langle A, D, B, C \rangle$ or $\langle A, E, B, C \rangle$. He then determines to add a link directly from page A to page C.

1.2 DATA MINING VERSUS KNOWLEDGE DISCOVERY IN DATABASES

The terms *knowledge discovery in databases (KDD)* and *data mining* are often used interchangeably. In fact, there have been many other names given to this process of discovering useful (hidden) patterns in data: knowledge extraction, information discovery, exploratory data analysis, information harvesting, and unsupervised pattern recognition. Over the last few years KDD has been used to refer to a process consisting of many steps, while data mining is only one of these steps. This is the approach taken in this book. The following definitions are modified from those found in [FPSS96c, FPSS96a].

> **Definition 1.1. Knowledge discovery in databases (KDD)** is the process of finding useful information and patterns in data.

> **Definition 1.2. Data mining** is the use of algorithms to extract the information and patterns derived by the KDD process.

The KDD process is often said to be nontrivial; however, we take the larger view that KDD is an all-encompassing concept. A traditional SQL database query can be viewed as the data mining part of a KDD process. Indeed, this may be viewed as somewhat simple and trivial. However, this was not the case 30 years ago. If we were to advance 30 years into the future, we might find that processes thought of today as nontrivial and complex will be viewed as equally simple. The definition of KDD includes the keyword *useful*. Although some definitions have included the term "potentially useful," we believe that if the information found in the process is not useful, then it really is not information. Of course, the idea of being useful is relative and depends on the individuals involved.

KDD is a process that involves many different steps. The input to this process is the data, and the output is the useful information desired by the users. However, the objective may be unclear or inexact. The process itself is interactive and may require much elapsed time. To ensure the usefulness and accuracy of the results of the process, interaction throughout the process with both domain experts and technical experts might be needed. Figure 1.4 (modified from [FPSS96c]) illustrates the overall KDD process.

The KDD process consists of the following five steps [FPSS96c]:

- **Selection:** The data needed for the data mining process may be obtained from many different and heterogeneous data sources. This first step obtains the data from various databases, files, and nonelectronic sources.

- **Preprocessing:** The data to be used by the process may have incorrect or missing data. There may be anomalous data from multiple sources involving different data types and metrics. There may be many different activities performed at this time. Erroneous data may be corrected or removed, whereas missing data must be supplied or predicted (often using data mining tools).

- **Transformation:** Data from different sources must be converted into a common format for processing. Some data may be encoded or transformed into more usable formats. Data reduction may be used to reduce the number of possible data values being considered.

- **Data mining:** Based on the data mining task being performed, this step applies algorithms to the transformed data to generate the desired results.

- **Interpretation/evaluation:** How the data mining results are presented to the users is extremely important because the usefulness of the results is dependent on it. Various visualization and GUI strategies are used at this last step.

Transformation techniques are used to make the data easier to mine and more useful, and to provide more meaningful results. The actual distribution of the data may be

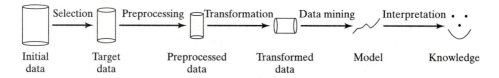

FIGURE 1.4: KDD process (modified from [FPSS96c]).

modified to facilitate use by techniques that require specific types of data distributions. Some attribute values may be combined to provide new values, thus reducing the complexity of the data. For example, current date and birth date could be replaced by age. One attribute could be substituted for another. An example would be replacing a sequence of actual attribute values with the differences between consecutive values. Real valued attributes may be more easily handled by partitioning the values into ranges and using these discrete range values. Some data values may actually be removed. Outliers, extreme values that occur infrequently, may actually be removed. The data may be transformed by applying a function to the values. A common transformation function is to use the log of the value rather than the value itself. These techniques make the mining task easier by reducing the dimensionality (number of attributes) or by reducing the variability of the data values. The removal of outliers can actually improve the quality of the results. As with all steps in the KDD process, however, care must be used in performing transformation. If used incorrectly, the transformation could actually change the data such that the results of the data mining step are inaccurate.

Visualization refers to the visual presentation of data. The old expression "a picture is worth a thousand words" certainly is true when examining the structure of data. For example, a line graph that shows the distribution of a data variable is easier to understand and perhaps more informative than the formula for the corresponding distribution. The use of visualization techniques allows users to summarize, extract, and grasp more complex results than more mathematical or text type descriptions of the results. Visualization techniques include:

- **Graphical:** Traditional graph structures including bar charts, pie charts, histograms, and line graphs may be used.

- **Geometric:** Geometric techniques include the box plot and scatter diagram techniques.

- **Icon-based:** Using figures, colors, or other icons can improve the presentation of the results.

- **Pixel-based:** With these techniques each data value is shown as a uniquely colored pixel.

- **Hierarchical:** These techniques hierarchically divide the display area (screen) into regions based on data values.

- **Hybrid:** The preceding approaches can be combined into one display.

Any of these approaches may be two-dimensional or three-dimensional. Visualization tools can be used to summarize data as a data mining technique itself. In addition, visualization can be used to show the complex results of data mining tasks.

The data mining process itself is complex. As we will see in later chapters, there are many different data mining applications and algorithms. These algorithms must be carefully applied to be effective. Discovered patterns must be correctly interpreted and properly evaluated to ensure that the resulting information is meaningful and accurate.

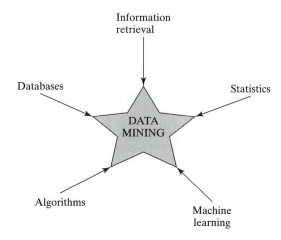

FIGURE 1.5: Historical perspective of data mining.

1.2.1 The Development of Data Mining

The current evolution of data mining functions and products is the result of years of influence from many disciplines, including databases, information retrieval, statistics, algorithms, and machine learning (Figure 1.5). Another computer science area that has had a major impact on the KDD process is multimedia and graphics. A major goal of KDD is to be able to describe the results of the KDD process in a meaningful manner. Because many different results are often produced, this is a nontrivial problem. Visualization techniques often involve sophisticated multimedia and graphics presentations. In addition, data mining techniques can be applied to multimedia applications.

Unlike previous research in these disparate areas, a major trend in the database community is to combine results from these seemingly different disciplines into one unifying data or algorithmic approach. Although in its infancy, the ultimate goal of this evolution is to develop a "big picture" view of the area that will facilitate integration of the various types of applications into real-world user domains.

Table 1.1 shows developments in the areas of artificial intelligence (AI), information retrieval (IR), databases (DB), and statistics (Stat) leading to the current view of data mining. These different historical influences, which have led to the development of the total data mining area, have given rise to different views of what data mining functions actually are [RG99]:

- *Induction* is used to proceed from very specific knowledge to more general information. This type of technique is often found in AI applications.

- Because the primary objective of data mining is to describe some characteristics of a set of data by a general model, this approach can be viewed as a type of *compression*. Here the detailed data within the database are abstracted and compressed to a smaller description of the data characteristics that are found in the model.

- As stated earlier, the data mining process itself can be viewed as a type of *querying* the underlying database. Indeed, an ongoing direction of data mining research is

TABLE 1.1: Time Line of Data Mining Development

Time	Area	Contribution	Reference
Late 1700s	Stat	Bayes theorem of probability	[Bay63]
Early 1900s	Stat	Regression analysis	
Early 1920s	Stat	Maximum likelihood estimate	[Fis21]
Early 1940s	AI	Neural networks	[MP43]
Early 1950s		Nearest neighbor	[FJ51]
Early 1950s		Single link	[FLP$^+$51]
Late 1950s	AI	Perceptron	[Ros58]
Late 1950s	Stat	Resampling, bias reduction, jackknife estimator	
Early 1960s	AI	ML started	[FF63]
Early 1960s	DB	Batch reports	
Mid 1960s		Decision trees	[HMS66]
Mid 1960s	Stat	Linear models for classification	[Nil65]
	IR	Similarity measures	
	IR	Clustering	
	Stat	Exploratory data analysis (EDA)	
Late 1960s	DB	Relational data model	[Cod70]
Early 1970s	IR	SMART IR systems	[Sal71]
Mid 1970s	AI	Genetic algorithms	[Hol75]
Late 1970s	Stat	Estimation with incomplete data (EM algorithm)	[DLR77]
Late 1970s	Stat	K-means clustering	
Early 1980s	AI	Kohonen self-organizing map	[Koh82]
Mid 1980s	AI	Decision tree algorithms	[Qui86]
Early 1990s	DB	Association rule algorithms	
		Web and search engines	
1990s	DB	Data warehousing	
1990s	DB	Online analytic processing (OLAP)	

how to define a data mining query and whether a query language (like SQL) can be developed to capture the many different types of data mining queries.

- Describing a large database can be viewed as using ***approximation*** to help uncover hidden information about the data.

- When dealing with large databases, the impact of size and efficiency of developing an abstract model can be thought of as a type of ***search*** problem.

It is interesting to think about the various data mining problems and how each may be viewed in several different perspectives based on the viewpoint and background of the researcher or developer. We mention these different perspectives only to give the reader the "full picture" of data mining. Often, due to the varied backgrounds of the data mining participants, we find that the same problems (and perhaps even the same solutions) are described differently. Indeed, different terminologies can lead to misunderstandings and apprehension among the different players. You can see statisticians voice concern over the compounded use of estimates (approximation) with results being generalized when they should not be. Database researchers often voice concern about the inefficiency of many proposed AI algorithms, particularly when used on very large databases. IR and those interested in data mining of textual databases might be concerned about the fact that many algorithms are targeted only to numeric data. The approach taken in this book is to examine data mining contributions from all these different disciplines together.

There are at least two issues that characterize a database perspective of examining data mining concepts: efficiency and scalability. Any solutions to data mining problems must be able to perform well against real-world databases. As part of the efficiency, we are concerned about both the algorithms and the data structures used. Parallelization may be used to improve efficiency. In addition, how the proposed algorithms behave as the associated database is updated is also important. Many proposed data mining algorithms may work well against a static database, but they may be extremely inefficient as changes are made to the database. As database practitioners, we are interested in how algorithms perform against very large databases, not "toy" problems. We also usually assume that the data are stored on disk and may even be distributed.

1.3   DATA MINING ISSUES

There are many important implementation issues associated with data mining:

1. **Human interaction:** Since data mining problems are often not precisely stated, interfaces may be needed with both domain and technical experts. Technical experts are used to formulate the queries and assist in interpreting the results. Users are needed to identify training data and desired results.

2. **Overfitting:** When a model is generated that is associated with a given database state, it is desirable that the model also fit future database states. Overfitting occurs when the model does not fit future states. This may be caused by assumptions that are made about the data or may simply be caused by the small size of the training database. For example, a classification model for an employee database may be developed to classify employees as short, medium, or tall. If the training database is quite small, the model might erroneously indicate that a short person is anyone under five feet eight inches because there is only one entry in the training database under five feet eight. In this case, many future employees would be erroneously classified as short. Overfitting can arise under other circumstances as well, even though the data are not changing.

3. **Outliers:** There are often many data entries that do not fit nicely into the derived model. This becomes even more of an issue with very large databases. If a model is developed that includes these outliers, then the model may not behave well for data that are not outliers.

4. **Interpretation of results:** Currently, data mining output may require experts to correctly interpret the results, which might otherwise be meaningless to the average database user.

5. **Visualization of results:** To easily view and understand the output of data mining algorithms, visualization of the results is helpful.

6. **Large datasets:** The massive datasets associated with data mining create problems when applying algorithms designed for small datasets. Many modeling applications grow exponentially on the dataset size and thus are too inefficient for larger datasets. Sampling and parallelization are effective tools to attack this scalability problem.

7. **High dimensionality:** A conventional database schema may be composed of many different attributes. The problem here is that not all attributes may be needed to solve a given data mining problem. In fact, the use of some attributes may interfere with the correct completion of a data mining task. The use of other attributes may simply increase the overall complexity and decrease the efficiency of an algorithm. This problem is sometimes referred to as the *dimensionality curse*, meaning that there are many attributes (dimensions) involved and it is difficult to determine which ones should be used. One solution to this high dimensionality problem is to reduce the number of attributes, which is known as *dimensionality reduction*. However, determining which attributes not needed is not always easy to do.

8. **Multimedia data:** Most previous data mining algorithms are targeted to traditional data types (numeric, character, text, etc.). The use of multimedia data such as is found in GIS databases complicates or invalidates many proposed algorithms.

9. **Missing data:** During the preprocessing phase of KDD, missing data may be replaced with estimates. This and other approaches to handling missing data can lead to invalid results in the data mining step.

10. **Irrelevant data:** Some attributes in the database might not be of interest to the data mining task being developed.

11. **Noisy data:** Some attribute values might be invalid or incorrect. These values are often corrected before running data mining applications.

12. **Changing data:** Databases cannot be assumed to be static. However, most data mining algorithms do assume a static database. This requires that the algorithm be completely rerun anytime the database changes.

13. **Integration:** The KDD process is not currently integrated into normal data processing activities. KDD requests may be treated as special, unusual, or one-time needs. This makes them inefficient, ineffective, and not general enough to be used on an ongoing basis. Integration of data mining functions into traditional DBMS systems is certainly a desirable goal.

14. **Application:** Determining the intended use for the information obtained from the data mining function is a challenge. Indeed, how business executives can effectively use the output is sometimes considered the more difficult part, not the running of the algorithms themselves. Because the data are of a type that has not previously been known, business practices may have to be modified to determine how to effectively use the information uncovered.

These issues should be addressed by data mining algorithms and products.

1.4   DATA MINING METRICS

Measuring the effectiveness or usefulness of a data mining approach is not always straightforward. In fact, different metrics could be used for different techniques and also based on the interest level. From an overall business or usefulness perspective, a measure such as *return on investment (ROI)* could be used. ROI examines the difference between what the data mining technique costs and what the savings or benefits from its use are. Of course, this would be difficult to measure because the return is hard to quantify. It could be measured as increased sales, reduced advertising expenditure, or both. In a specific advertising campaign implemented via targeted catalog mailings, the percentage of catalog recipients and the amount of purchase per recipient would provide one means to measure the effectiveness of the mailings.

In this text, however, we use a more computer science/database perspective to measure various data mining approaches. We assume that the business management has determined that a particular data mining application be made. They subsequently will determine the overall effectiveness of the approach using some ROI (or related) strategy. Our objective is to compare different alternatives to implementing a specific data mining task. The metrics used include the traditional metrics of space and time based on complexity analysis. In some cases, such as accuracy in classification, more specific metrics targeted to a data mining task may be used.

1.5 SOCIAL IMPLICATIONS OF DATA MINING

The integration of data mining techniques into normal day-to-day activities has become commonplace. We are confronted daily with targeted advertising, and businesses have become more efficient through the use of data mining activities to reduce costs. Data mining adversaries, however, are concerned that this information is being obtained at the cost of reduced privacy. Data mining applications can derive much demographic information concerning customers that was previously not known or hidden in the data. The unauthorized use of such data could result in the disclosure of information that is deemed to be confidential.

We have recently seen an increase in interest in data mining techniques targeted to such applications as fraud detection, identifying criminal suspects, and prediction of potential terrorists. These can be viewed as types of classification problems. The approach that is often used here is one of "profiling" the typical behavior or characteristics involved. Indeed, many classification techniques work by identifying the attribute values that commonly occur for the target class. Subsequent records will be then classified based on these attribute values. Keep in mind that these approaches to classification are *imperfect*. Mistakes can be made. Just because an individual makes a series of credit card purchases that are similar to those often made when a card is stolen does not mean that the card is stolen or that the individual is a criminal.

Users of data mining techniques must be sensitive to these issues and must not violate any privacy directives or guidelines.

1.6 DATA MINING FROM A DATABASE PERSPECTIVE

Data mining can be studied from many different perspectives. An IR researcher probably would concentrate on the use of data mining techniques to access text data; a statistician might look primarily at the historical techniques, including time series analysis, hypothesis testing, and applications of Bayes theorem; a machine learning specialist might be interested primarily in data mining algorithms that learn; and an algorithms researcher would be interested in studying and comparing algorithms based on type and complexity.

The study of data mining from a database perspective involves looking at all types of data mining applications and techniques. However, we are interested primarily in those that are of practical interest. While our interest is not limited to any particular type of algorithm or approach, we are concerned about the following implementation issues:

- **Scalability:** Algorithms that do not scale up to perform well with massive real-world datasets are of limited application. Related to this is the fact that techniques should work regardless of the amount of available main memory.

- **Real-world data:** Real-world data are noisy and have many missing attribute values. Algorithms should be able to work even in the presence of these problems.

- **Update:** Many data mining algorithms work with static datasets. This is not a realistic assumption.

- **Ease of use:** Although some algorithms may work well, they may not be well received by users if they are difficult to use or understand.

These issues are crucial if applications are to be accepted and used in the workplace. Throughout the text we will mention how techniques perform in these and other implementation categories.

Data mining today is in a similar state as that of databases in the early 1960s. At that time, each database application was implemented independently even though there were many similarities between different applications. In the mid 1960s, an abundance of database management systems (DBMS) like tools (such as bill of material systems including DBOMP and CFMS) emerged. While these made the development of applications easier, there were still different tools for different applications. The rise of DBMS occurred in the early 1970s. Their success has been due partly to the abstraction of data definition and access primitives to a small core of needed requirements. This abstraction process has yet to be performed for data mining tasks. Each task is treated separately. Most data mining work (to date) has focused on specific algorithms to realize each individual data mining task. There is no accepted abstraction to a small set of primitives. One goal of some database researchers is the development of such an abstraction.

One crucial part of the database abstraction is query processing support. One reason relational databases are so popular today is the development of SQL. It is easy to use (at least when compared with earlier query languages such as the DBTG or IMS DML) and has become a standard query language implemented by all major DBMS vendors. SQL also has well-defined optimization strategies. Although there currently is no corresponding data mining language, there is ongoing work in the area of extending SQL to support data mining tasks.

1.7   THE FUTURE

The advent of the relational data model and SQL were milestones in the evolution of database systems. Currently, data mining is little more than a set of tools that can be used to uncover previously hidden information in a database. While there are many tools to aid in this process, there is no all-encompassing model or approach. Over the next few years, not only will there be more efficient algorithms with better interface techniques, but also steps will be taken to develop an all-encompassing model for data mining. While it may not look like the relational model, it probably will include similar items: algorithms, data model, and metrics for goodness (like normal forms). Current data mining tools require much human interaction not only to define the request, but also to interpret the results. As the tools become better and more integrated, this extensive human interaction is likely to decrease. The various data mining applications are of many diverse types, so the development of a complete data mining model is desirable. A major development will be the creation of a sophisticated "query language" that includes traditional SQL functions as well as more complicated requests such as those found in OLAP (online analytic processing) and data mining applications.

A *data mining query language (DMQL)* based on SQL has been proposed. Unlike SQL, where the access is assumed to be only to relational databases, DMQL allows access to background information such as concept hierarchies. Another difference is that the retrieved data need not be a subset or aggregate of data from relations. Thus, a DMQL statement must indicate the type of knowledge to be mined. Another difference is that a DMQL statement can indicate the necessary importance or threshold that any mined information should obey. A BNF statement of DMQL (from [Zaï99]) is:

```
⟨DMQL⟩ ::=
    USE DATABASE ⟨database_name⟩
    {USE HIERARCHY ⟨hierarchy_name⟩ FOR ⟨attribute⟩}
    ⟨rule_spec⟩
    RELATED TO ⟨attr_or_agg_list⟩
    FROM ⟨relation(s)⟩
    [WHERE ⟨condition⟩]
    [ORDER BY ⟨order_list⟩]
    {WITH [⟨kinds_of⟩] THRESHOLD = ⟨threshold_value⟩
                                [FOR ⟨attribute(s)⟩]}
```

The heart of a DMQL statement is the rule specification portion. This is where the true data mining request is made. The data mining request can be one of the following [HFW+96]:

- A *generalized relation* is obtained by generalizing data from input data.

- A *characteristic rule* is a condition that is satisfied by almost all records in a target class.

- A *discriminate rule* is a condition that is satisfied by a target class but is different from conditions satisfied in other classes.

- A *classification rule* is a set of rules that are used to classify data.

The term *knowledge and data discovery management system (KDDMS)* has been coined to describe the future generation of data mining systems that include not only data mining tools but also techniques to manage the underlying data, ensure its consistency, and provide concurrency and recovery features. A KDDMS will provide access via ad hoc data mining queries that have been optimized for efficient access.

A new KDD process model, *CRISP-DM (CRoss-Industry Standard Process for Data Mining)*, has arisen and is applicable to many different applications. The model addresses all steps in the KDD process, including the maintenance of the results of the data mining step. The CRISP-DM life cycle contains the following steps: business understanding, data understanding, data preparation, modeling, and evaluation deployment. The steps involved in the CRISP-DM model can be summarized as the "the 5As:" assess, access, analyze, act, and automate.

1.8 EXERCISES

1. Identify and describe the phases in the KDD process. How does KDD differ from data mining?

2. Gather temperature data at one location every hour starting at 8:00 A.M. for 12 straight hours on 3 different days. Plot the three sets of time series data on the same graph. Analyze the three curves. Do they behave in the same manner? Does there appear to be a trend in the temperature during the day? Are the three plots similar? Predict what the next temperature value would have been for the next hour in each of the 3 days. Compare your prediction with the actual value that occurred.

3. Identify what work you performed in each step of the KDD process for exercise 2. What were the data mining activities you completed?

4. Describe which of the data mining issues you encountered while completing exercise 2.

5. Describe how each of the data mining issues discussed in section 1.3 are compounded by the use of real production databases.

6. (**Research**) Find two other definitions for data mining. Compare these definitions with the one found in this chapter.

7. (**Research**) Find at least three examples of data mining applications that have appeared in the business section of your local newspaper or other news publication. Describe the data mining applications involved.

1.9 BIBLIOGRAPHIC NOTES

Although many excellent books have been published that examine data mining and knowledge discovery in databases, most are high-level books that target users of data mining techniques and business professionals. There have been, however, some other technical books that examine data mining approaches and algorithms. An excellent text that is written by one of the foremost experts in the area is *Data Mining Concepts and Techniques* by Jiawei Han and Micheline Kamber [HK01]. This book not only examines data mining algorithms, but also includes a thorough coverage of data warehousing, OLAP, preprocessing, and data mining language developments. Other books that provide a technical survey of portions of data mining algorithms include [Ada00] and [HMS01].

There have been several recent surveys and overviews of data mining, including special issues of the *Communications of the ACM* in November 1996 and November 1999, *IEEE Transactions on Knowledge and Data Engineering* in December 1996, and *Computer* in August 1999. Other survey articles can be found: [FPSS96c], [FPSS96b], [GGR99a], [Man96], [Man97], and [RG99]. A popular tutorial booklet has been produced by Two Crows Corporation [Cor99]. A complete discussion of the KDD process is found in [BA96]. Articles that examine the intersection between databases and data mining include [Cha97], [Cha98], [CHY96], [Fay98], and [HKMT95]. There have also been several tutorials surveying data mining concepts: [Agr94], [Agr95], [Han96], and [RS99]. A recent tutorial [Kei97] provided a thorough survey of visualization techniques as well as a comprehensive bibliography.

The aspect of parallel and distributed data mining has become an important research topic. A workshop on Large-Scale Parallel KDD Systems was held in 1999 [ZH00].

The idea of developing an approach to unifying all data mining activities has been proposed in [FPSS96b], [Man96], and [Man97]. The term *KDDMS* was first proposed in [IM96]. A recent unified model and algebra that supports all major data mining tasks has been proposed [JLN00]. The *3W model* views data as being divided into three dimensions. An algebra, called the *dimension algebra*, has been proposed to access this three-dimensional world.

DMQL was developed at Simon Fraser University [HFW$^+$96].

There are several KDD and data mining resources. The ACM (Association for Computing Machinery) has a special interest group, SIGKDD, devoted to the promotion and dissemination of KDD information. *SIGKDD Explorations* is a free newsletter produced by ACM SIGKDD. The ACM SIGKDD home page contains a wealth of resources concerning KDD and data mining (www.acm.org/sigkdd).

A vendor-led group, *Data Mining Group (DMG)*, is active in the development of data mining standards. Information about DMG can be found at www.dmg.org. The ISO/IEC standards group has created a final committee draft for an SQL standard including data mining extensions [Com01]. In addition, a project begun by a consortium of data mining vendors and users resulted in the development of the data mining process model, *CRISP-DM* (see: www.crisp-dm.org).

There currently are several research journals related to data mining. These include *IEEE Transactions on Knowledge and Data Engineering* published by IEEE Computer Society and *Data Mining and Knowledge Discovery* from Kluwer Academic Publishers. International KDD conferences include the ACM SIGKDD International Conference on Knowledge Discovery and Data Mining (KDD), the Conference on Information and Knowledge Management (CIKM), the IEEE International Conference on Data Mining (ICDM), the European Conference on Principles of Data Mining and Knowledge Discovery (PKDD), and the Pacific–Asia Conference on Knowledge Discovery and Data Mining (PAKDD). *KDnuggets News* is an e-mail newsletter that is produced biweekly. It contains a wealth of KDD and data mining information for practitioners, users, and researchers. Subscriptions are free at www.kdnuggets.com. Additional KDD resources can be found at Knowledge Discovery Central (www.kdcentral.com).

C H A P T E R 2

Related Concepts

Data mining applications have existed for thousands of years. For example, the classification of plants as edible or nonedible is a data mining task. The development of the data mining discipline has its roots in many other areas. In this chapter we examine many concepts related to data mining. We briefly introduce each concept and indicate how it is related to data mining.

2.1 DATABASE/OLTP SYSTEMS

A *database* is a collection of data usually associated with some organization or enterprise. Unlike a simple set, data in a database are usually viewed to have a particular structure or *schema* with which it is associated. For example, (*ID, Name, Address, Salary, JobNo*) may be the schema for a personnel database. Here the schema indicates that each record (or tuple) in the database has a value for each of these five attributes. Unlike a file, a database is independent of the physical method used to store it on disk (or other media). It also is independent of the applications that access it. A *database management system (DBMS)* is the software used to access a database.

Data stored in a database are often viewed in a more abstract manner or data model. This *data model* is used to describe the data, attributes, and relationships among them. A data model is independent of the particular DBMS used to implement and access the database. In effect, it can be viewed as a documentation and communication tool to convey the type and structure of the actual data. A common data model is the

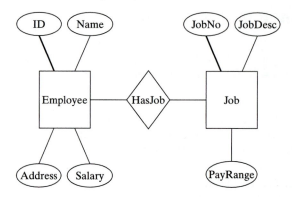

FIGURE 2.1: ER model example.

ER (*entity-relationship*) data model. Although originally proposed in 1976, the *ER data model* is still used today with many extensions and improvements to the first design. Example 2.1 illustrates the use of an ER model with an associated *ER diagram* seen in Figure 2.1. The basic components of an ER model are the entities and the relationships. An *entity* is associated with a real-world object and has a *key* that uniquely identifies it. A *relationship* is used to describe as association that exists between entities.

EXAMPLE 2.1

An employee database consists of employees and information concerning the jobs that they perform. An entity would be an Employee and the key could be the ID. Similarly, different jobs can be associated with a job number so that we can think of the Job as an entity with key JobNo. In Figure 2.1, there is a rectangle for each entity. The diamond is used to represent the relationship between the two entities. Here the relationship HasJob indicates that a specific employee with key ID has a particular job with key JobNo. The attributes associated with Employee are {ID, Name, Address, Salary} and the attributes for Job are {JobNo, NobDesc, PayRange}.

The ER model is often used to abstractly view the data independent of DBMS. DBMS systems often view the data in a structure more like a table. This gives rise to the *relational model*, where data are viewed as being composed of relations. Taking a mathematical perspective, a *relation* is a subset of a Cartesian product. Imagine looking at the *domain*, or set of values, associated with each attribute in the Employee example. A relation R could then be viewed as a subset of the product of the domains:

$$R \subseteq \text{dom}(ID) \times \text{dom}(Name) \times \text{dom}(Address) \times \text{dom}(Salary) \times \text{dom}(JobNo) \quad (2.1)$$

Access to a relation can be performed based on operations in the traditional set algebra such as union and intersection. This extended group of set operations is referred to as *relational algebra*. An equivalent set based on first-order predicate calculus is called *relational calculus*. Access to databases is usually achieved via a *query language*. This query language may be based on relational algebra or calculus. Although many query languages have been proposed, the standard language used by most DBMSs is SQL.

SELECT Name
FROM R
WHERE Salary > 100,000

FIGURE 2.2: SQL example.

Figure 2.2 shows a sample SQL statement issued against the relation R, which lists the names of all employees with a salary greater than $100,000.

Users' expectations for queries have increased, as have the amount and sophistication of the associated data. In the early days of *database (DB)* and *online transaction processing (OLTP)* systems, simple selects were enough. Now queries are complex, involving data distributed over many sites, and they use complicated functions such as joins, aggregates, and views. Traditional database queries usually involve retrieving data from a database based on a well-defined query. As shown in Figure 2.2, a user may ask to find all employees who earn over $100,000. This could be viewed as a type of classification application as we segment the database into two classes: those who have salaries satisfying the predicate and those who do not. A simple database application is not thought of as a data mining task, however, because the queries are well defined with precise results. Data mining applications, conversely, are often vaguely defined with imprecise results. Users might not even be able to precisely define what they want, let alone be able to tell if the results of their request are accurate. A database user usually can tell if the results of his query are not correct. Thus, it is usually assumed that a DBMS returns the correct results for a query. Metrics (instead of quality) often include such things as response time and throughput.

When viewed as a query system, data mining queries extend database concepts. Data mining problems are often ill-posed with many different solutions. Judging the effectiveness of the result of a data mining request is often difficult. A major difference between data mining queries and those of database systems is the output. Basic database queries always output either a subset of the database or aggregates of the data. A data mining query outputs a KDD object. A *KDD object* is either a rule, a classification, or a cluster. These objects do not exist before executing the query, and they are not part of the database being queried. Aggregation operators have existed in SQL for years. They do not return objects existing in the database, but return a model of the data. For example, an average operator returns the average of a set of attribute values rather than the values themselves. This is a simple type of data mining operator.

2.2   FUZZY SETS AND FUZZY LOGIC

A *set* is normally thought of as a collection of objects. It can be defined by enumerating the set

$$F = \{1, 2, 3, 4, 5\} \tag{2.2}$$

or by indicating the set membership requirement

$$F = \{x \mid x \in Z^+ \text{ and } x \leq 5\} \tag{2.3}$$

A *fuzzy set* is a set, F, in which the set membership function, f, is a real valued (as opposed to boolean) function with output in the range [0, 1]: An element x is said to belong to F with probability $f(x)$ and simultaneously to be in $\neg F$ with probability $1-f(x)$. In actuality, this is not a true probability, but rather the degree of truth associated with the statement that x is in the set. To show the difference, let us look at a fuzzy set operation. Suppose the membership value for Mary being tall is 0.7 and the value for her being thin is 0.4. The membership value for her being both is 0.4, the minimum of the two values. If these were really probabilities, we would look at the product of the two values.

Fuzzy sets have been used in many computer science and database areas. In the classification problem, all records in a database are assigned to one of the predefined classification areas. A common approach to solving the classification problem is to assign a set membership function to each record for each class. The record is then assigned to the class that has the highest membership function value. Similarly, fuzzy sets may be used to describe other data mining functions. Association rules are generated given a confidence value that indicates the degree to which it holds in the entire database. This can be thought of as a membership function.

Queries can be thought of as defining a set. With traditional database queries, however, the set membership function is boolean. The set of tuples in relation R that satisfy the SQL statement in Figure 2.2 can be defined as

$$\{x \mid x \in R \text{ and } x.Salary > 100,000\} \tag{2.4}$$

Here $x.Salary$ refers to the Salary attribute within the tuple x. Some queries, however, do not have a membership function that is boolean. For example, suppose that we wished to find the names of employees who are tall:

$$\{x \mid x \in R \text{ and } x \text{ is tall}\} \tag{2.5}$$

This membership function is not boolean, and thus the results of this query are fuzzy. A good example of queries of this type are searches performed on the Web.

Figure 2.3 shows the real difference between traditional and fuzzy set membership. Suppose there are three sets (short, medium, and tall) to which a person can be classified based on his height. In Figure 2.3(a) the traditional (or crisp) set membership values are shown. Part (b) shows the triangular view of set membership values. Notice that there is a gradual decrease in the set membership value for short; there is a gradual increase and decrease for set membership in the medium set; there is a gradual increase in the set membership value for tall.

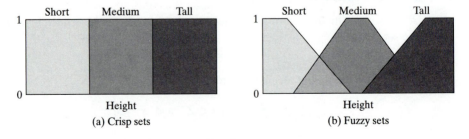

FIGURE 2.3: Fuzzy vs. traditional set membership.

Fuzzy logic is reasoning with uncertainty. That is, instead of a two valued logic (true and false), there are multiple values (true, false, maybe). Fuzzy logic has been used in database systems to retrieve data with imprecise or missing values. In this case, the membership of records in the query result set is fuzzy. As with traditional boolean logic, fuzzy logic uses operators such as $\neg$, $\wedge$, and $\vee$. Assuming that x and y are fuzzy logic statements and that $mem(x)$ defines the membership value, the following values are commonly used to define the results of these operations:

$$\text{mem}(\neg x) \quad = \quad 1 - \text{mem}(x) \tag{2.6}$$

$$\text{mem}(x \wedge y) \quad = \quad \min(\text{mem}(x), \text{mem}(y)) \tag{2.7}$$

$$\text{mem}(x \vee y) \quad = \quad \max(\text{mem}(x), \text{mem}(y)) \tag{2.8}$$

Fuzzy logic uses rules and membership functions to estimate a continuous function. Fuzzy logic is a valuable tool to develop control systems for such things as elevators, trains, and heating systems. In these cases, instead of providing a crisp on-off environment, the fuzzy controller provides a more continuous adjustment.

Most real-world classification problems are fuzzy. This is illustrated by Figure 2.4. In this figure we graphically show the threshold for approving a loan based on the income of the individual and the loan amount requested. A loan officer may make the loan decision by simply approving any loan requests on or above the line and rejecting any requests that fall below the line [Figure 2.4(a)]. This type of decision would not be fuzzy. However, this type of decision could lead to erroneous and perhaps costly decisions by the loan officer. From a data mining perspective, this application is a classification problem; that is, classify a loan application into the approval or reject class. There are many other factors (other than income) that should be used to predict the classification problem (such as net worth and credit rating). Even if all the associated predictors could be identified, the classification problem is not a black-and-white issue. It is possible that two individuals with exactly the same predictor values should be placed in two different classes. This is due to the fuzzy nature of this classification. This is shown by the shading around the line in Figure 2.4(b). We could perhaps classify

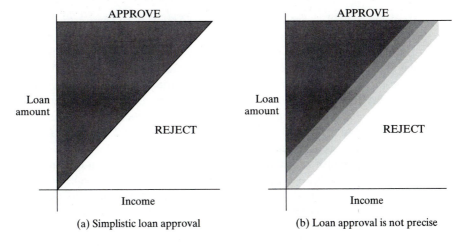

FIGURE 2.4: Fuzzy classification.

the individuals into multiple classes: approve, reject, unknown, probably approve, and probably reject. This approach attacks the fuzzy nature of the classification by flagging the applications requiring more analysis into the three new fuzzy classes. Procedural policies could then be used to determine the ultimate classification of these cases into the final approve or reject classes. This is one of many possible approaches to defuzzify the classification problem.

2.3 INFORMATION RETRIEVAL

Information retrieval (IR) (and more recently digital libraries and Internet searching) involves retrieving desired information from textual data. The historical development of IR was based on effective use of libraries. So a typical IR request would be to find all library documents related to a particular subject, for example "data mining." This is, in fact, a classification task because the set of documents in the library is divided into classes based on the keywords involved. In IR systems, documents are represented by document surrogates consisting of data, such as identifiers, title, authors, dates, abstracts, extracts, reviews, and keywords. As can be seen, the data consist of both formatted and unformatted (text) data. The retrieval of documents is based on calculation of a *similarity measure* showing how close each document is to the desired results (i.e., the stated query). Similarity measures are also used in classification and clustering problems.

An IR system consists of a set of documents $D = \{D_1, \ldots, D_n\}$. The input is a query, q, often stated as a list of keywords. The similarity between the query and each document is then calculated: $sim(q, D_i)$. This similarity measure is a set membership function describing the likelihood that the document is of interest (relevant) to the user based on the user's interest as stated by the query. The effectiveness of the system in processing the query is often measured by looking at *precision* and *recall*:

$$\text{Precision} \quad = \quad \frac{\mid \text{Relevant and Retrieved} \mid}{\mid \text{Retrieved} \mid} \qquad (2.9)$$

$$\text{Recall} \quad = \quad \frac{\mid \text{Relevant and Retrieved} \mid}{\mid \text{Relevant} \mid} \qquad (2.10)$$

Precision is used to answer the question: "Are all documents retrieved ones that I am interested in?" Recall answers: "Have all relevant documents been retrieved?" Here a document is *relevant* if it should have been retrieved by the query. Figure 2.5 illustrates the four possible query results available with IR queries. Of these four quadrants, two represent desirable outcomes: relevant and retrieved or not relevant and not retrieved. The other two quadrants represent error situations. Documents that are relevant and not retrieved should have been retrieved but were not. Documents that are not relevant and retrieved should not have been retrieved but were. Figure 2.6 illustrates the basic structure of a conventional information retrieval query.

Many similarity measures have been proposed for use in information retrieval. As stated earlier, $sim(q, D_i)$ $1 \le i \le n$ is used to determine the results of a query q applied to a set of documents $D = \{D_1, \ldots, D_n\}$. Similarity measures may also be used to cluster or classify documents by calculating $sim(D_i, D_j)$ for all documents in the database. Thus, similarity can be used for document-document, query-query, and query-document measurements. The *inverse document frequency (IDF)* is often used by similarity measures. IDF assumes that the importance of a keyword in calculating similarity measures is

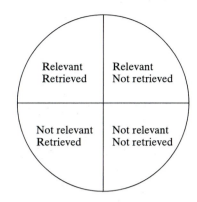

FIGURE 2.5: IR query result measures.

FIGURE 2.6: Information retrieval query.

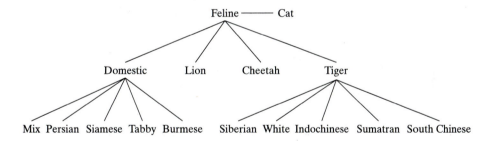

FIGURE 2.7: Concept hierarchy.

inversely proportional to the total number of documents that contain it. Given a keyword, k, and n documents, IDF can be defined as

$$\text{IDF}_k = lg \frac{n}{\mid \text{documents containing } k \mid} + 1 \qquad (2.11)$$

Concept hierarchies are often used in information retrieval systems to show the relationships between various keywords (concepts) as related to documents. Suppose you wish to find all documents about cats. Figure 2.7 illustrates a *concept hierarchy* that could be used to answer this query. This figure shows that *feline* and *cat* are similar terms. In addition, a cat may be domestic or tiger or lion or cheetah. In turn, a tiger may be a Siberian, White, Indochinese, Sumatran, or South Chinese. Nodes lower in the tree represent more specific groups of tigers. When a user requests a book on tigers, this query could be modified by replacing the keyword "tiger" with a keyword at a higher

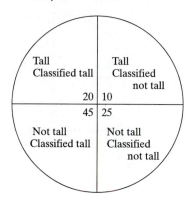

FIGURE 2.8: Precision and recall applied to classification.

level in the tree, such as "cat." Although this would result in a higher recall, the precision would decrease. A concept hierarchy may actually be a *DAG (directed acyclic graph)* rather than a tree.

IR has had a major impact on the development of data mining. Much of the data mining classification and clustering approaches had their origins in the document retrieval problems of library science and information retrieval. Many of the similarity measures developed for information retrieval have been applied to more general data mining applications. Similarly, the precision and recall measures are often applied to data mining applications, as illustrated in Example 2.2. Concept hierarchies are frequently used in spatial data mining applications. Data mining consists of many more types of applications than are found in traditional information retrieval. The linking and predictive tasks have no real counterpart in IR, for example.

EXAMPLE 2.2

The accuracy of a predictive modeling technique can be described based on precision and recall. Suppose 100 college students are to be classified based on height. In actuality, there are 30 tall students and 70 who are not tall. A classification technique classifies 65 students as tall and 35 as not tall. The precision and recall applied to this problem are shown in Figure 2.8. The precision is 20/65, while the recall is 20/30. The precision is low because so many students who are not tall are classified as such.

2.4   DECISION SUPPORT SYSTEMS

Decision support systems (DSS) are comprehensive computer systems and related tools that assist managers in making decisions and solving problems. The goal is to improve the decision-making process by providing specific information needed by management. These systems differ from traditional database management systems in that more ad hoc queries and customized information may be provided. Recently, the terms *executive information systems (EIS)* and *executive support systems (ESS)* have evolved as well. These systems all aim at developing the business structure and computer techniques to better provide information needed by management to make effective business decisions. Data mining can be thought of as a suite of tools that assist in the overall DSS process; that is, DSS may use data mining tools.

In many ways the term *DSS* is much more broad than the term *data mining*. While a DSS usually contains data mining tools, this need not be so. Likewise, a data mining tool need not be contained in a DSS system. A decision support system could be enterprise-wide, thus allowing upper-level managers the data needed to make intelligent business decisions that impact the entire company. A DSS typically operates using data warehouse data. Alternatively, a DSS could be built around a single user and a PC. The bottom line is that the DSS gives managers the tools needed to make intelligent decisions.

2.5 DIMENSIONAL MODELING

Dimensional modeling is a different way to view and interrogate data in a database. This view may be used in a DSS in conjunction with data mining tasks. Although not required, for efficiency purposes the data may be stored using different data structures as well. Decision support applications often require that information be obtained along many dimensions. For example, a sales manager may want to obtain information about the amount of sales in a geographic region, particular time frame, and by-product type. This query requires three dimensions. A *dimension* is a collection of logically related attributes and is viewed as an axis for modeling the data. The time dimension could be divided into many different granularities: millennium, century, decade, year, month, day, hour, minute, or second. Within each dimension, these entities form levels on which various DSS questions may be asked. The specific data stored are called the *facts* and usually are numeric data. Facts consist of measures and context data. The measures are the numeric attributes about the facts that are queried. DSS queries may access the facts from many different dimensions and levels. The levels in each dimension facilitate the retrieval of facts at different levels. For example, the sales information could be obtained for the year 1999, for the month of February in the year 2000, or between the times of 10 and 11 A.M. on March 1, 2000. The same query could be formulated for a more general level, *roll up*, or for a more specific level, *drill down*.

Table 2.1 shows a relation with three dimensions: Products, Location, and Date. Determining a key for this relation could be difficult because it is possible for the same product to be sold multiple times on the same day. In this case, product 150 was sold at two different times in Dallas on the same day. A finer granularity on the time (perhaps down to the minute rather than date as is here) could make a key. However, this illustrates that choice of key may be difficult. The same multidimensional data may also be viewed as a cube. Figure 2.9 shows a view of the data from Table 2.1 as a cube. Each dimension is seen as an axis for the cube. This cube has one fact for each unique combination of dimension values. In this case, we could have $8 * 7 * 5 = 280$ facts stored (even though the relation showed only 10 tuples). Obviously, this sparse amount of data would need to be stored efficiently to reduce the amount of space required.

The levels of a dimension may support a partial order or a total order and can be viewed via a directed path, a hierarchy, or a lattice. To be consistent with earlier uses of the term, we use *aggregation hierarchy*, even though it may be a lattice, to refer to the order relationship among different levels in a dimension. We use $<$ to represent this order relationship. $X < Y$ if X and Y are levels in the same dimension and X is contained

TABLE 2.1: Relational View of Multidimensional Data

ProdID	LocID	Date	Quantity	UnitPrice
123	Dallas	022900	5	25
123	Houston	020100	10	20
150	Dallas	031500	1	100
150	Dallas	031500	5	95
150	Fort Worth	021000	5	80
150	Chicago	012000	20	75
200	Seattle	030100	5	50
300	Rochester	021500	200	5
500	Bradenton	022000	15	20
500	Chicago	012000	10	25

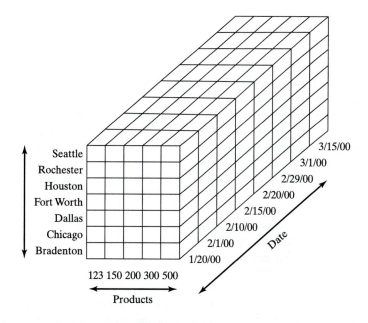

FIGURE 2.9: Cube.

in Y. Figure 2.10(a) shows a total order relationship among levels in the Product dimension from Figure 2.9. Here Product < Type < Company. The two facts that we are using in this example are Quantity and UnitPrice. When this order relationship is satisfied between two levels, there is an aggregate type of relationship among the facts. Here the Quantity of products sold of a particular type is the sum of the quantities for all products within that type. Similarly, the quantity of products sold for a company is the sum of all products sold across all product types. The aggregate operation is not always the sum, however. When looking at the unit price, it would be reasonable to look at

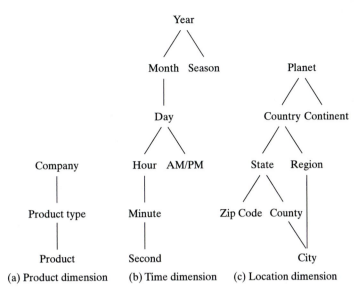

FIGURE 2.10: Aggregation hierarchies.

such aggregate operations as average, maximum, and minimum prices. Figure 2.10(b) shows a hierarchical relationship among levels in the time dimension, and Figure 2.10(c) shows a lattice for the location dimension. Here Day $<$ Month but Day $\not<$ Season. The aggregation can be applied only to levels that can be found in the same path as defined by the $<$ relationship. When levels for a dimension satisfy this structure, the facts along these dimensions are said to be *additive*. If we add the sales data for all 24 hours in a day, we get the sales data for that day. This is not always the case. Looking at the location dimension, if we were to sum up the sales data for all zip codes in a given county, however, we would not get the sales data for the county. Thus, these dimensions are not additive. This is due to the fact that zip codes may span different counties. The use of nonadditive dimensions complicate the roll up and drill down applications.

2.5.1 Multidimensional Schemas

Specialized schemas have been developed to portray multidimensional data. These include star schema, snowflake schema, and fact constellation schema.

A *star schema* shows data as a collection of two types: facts and dimensions. Unlike a relational schema, which is flat, a star schema is a graphical view of the data. At the center of the star, the data being examined, the facts, are shown in *fact tables* (sometimes called *major tables*). On the outside of the facts, each dimension is shown separately in *dimension tables* (sometimes called *minor tables*). The simplest star schema has one fact table with multiple dimension tables. In this case each fact points to one tuple in each of the dimensions. The actual data being accessed are stored in the fact tables and thus tend to be quite large. Descriptive information about the dimensions is stored in the dimensions tables, which tend to be smaller. Figure 2.11 shows a star schema based on the data in Figure 2.9. Here one extra dimension, division, is shown. The facts include the quantity and price, while the dimensions are the product, time,

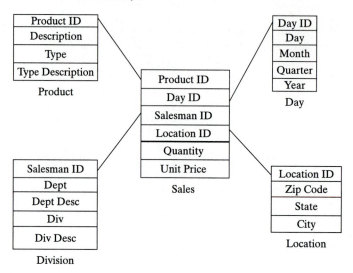

FIGURE 2.11: Star schema.

location, and division. Descriptive information about a product includes the description, type, and type description. Access to the fact table from a dimension table can be accomplished via a join between a dimension table and the fact table on particular dimension values. For example, we could access all locations in Dallas by doing the following SQL query:

```
SELECT Quantity, Price
FROM Facts, Location
Where (Facts.LocationID = Location.LocationID)
and
(Location.City = ''Dallas'')
```

Here the LocationID is a foreign key from the fact table to the Location dimension table. The primary key for the fact table is a collection of foreign keys that point to the dimension tables. Although this example shows only one fact table, there may be several. In addition, a dimension table may itself point to another dimension table.

A star schema view can be obtained via a relational system where each dimension is a table and the facts are stored in a fact table. The facts can be accessed relatively efficiently through the creation of indices for the dimensions. However, the sheer volume of the data involved, exacerbated by the need to summarize the fact information at different levels across all the dimensions, complicates the process. For example, we may wish to see all sales in all regions for a particular day. Or we may want to see all sales in May 2000 for the salesmen in a specific department. To ensure efficiency of access, facts may be stored for all possible aggregation levels. The fact data would then be extended to include a level indicator.

We assume that the data are stored as both fact tables and dimension tables. Data in the fact table can be viewed as a regular relation with an attribute for each fact to be stored and the key being the values for each dimension. There are four basic approaches to the storage of data in dimension tables [PB99]. Each dimension table can be stored in one of these four manners. Figure 2.12 illustrates these four approaches with the sales data. The first technique, the *flattened* technique, stores the data for each dimension in exactly one table. There is one row in the table for each row in the lowest level in the dimensional model. The key to the data are the attributes for all levels in that dimension. With the flattened approach, a roll up is accomplished by a SUM aggregation operation over the appropriate tuples. Even though this approach suffers from space problems as the

```
Sales(Product ID, Day ID, Salesman ID, Location ID, Quantity, Unit Price)
Product(Product ID, Description, Type, Type Description)
Day(Day ID, Month, Quarter, Year)
Division(Salesman ID, Dept, Dept Desc, Div, Div Desc)
Location(Location ID, Zip Code, State, City)
```

(a) Flattened

```
Sales(Product ID, Day ID, Salesman ID, Location ID, Quantity, Unit Price)
Product(Product ID, Description, Type)
Types(Type, Type Description)
Day(Day ID, Month)
Months(Month, Quarter)
Quarters(Quarter, Year)
Years(Year)
Salesman(Salesman ID, Dept)
Depts(Dept, Dept Desc, Div)
Divs(Div, Div Desc)
Location(Location ID, Zip Code)
Zip(Zip Code, City)
Cities(State, City)
States(State)
```

(b) Normalized

```
Sales(Product ID, Day ID, Salesman ID, Location ID, Quantity, Unit Price)
Product(Product ID, Description, Type, Type Description)
Types(Type, Type Description)
Day(Day ID, Month, Quarter, Year)
Months(Month, Quarter, Year)
Quarters(Quarter, Year)
Years(Year)
Salesman(Salesman ID, Dept, Dept Desc, Div, Div Desc)
Depts(Dept, Dept Desc, Div, Div Desc)
Divs(Div, Div Desc)
Location(Location ID, Zip Code, State, City)
Zip(Zip Code, State, City)
Cities(State, City)
States(State)
```

(c) Expanded

```
Sales(Product ID, Day ID, Salesman ID, Location ID, Quantity, Unit Price)
Product(Product ID, Description, Type, Type Description, Level No)
Day(Day ID, Month, Quarter, Year, Level No)
Division(Salesman ID, Dept, Dept Desc, Div, Div Desc, Level No)
Location(Location ID, Zip Code, State, City, Level No)
```

(d) Levelized

FIGURE 2.12: Options to implement star schema.

number of attributes grows with the number of levels, it does facilitate the simple implementation of many DSS applications via the use of traditional SQL aggregation operations.

The second technique to store a dimension table is called the *normalized* technique, where a table exists for each level in each dimension. Each table has one tuple for every occurrence at that level. As with traditional normalization, duplication is removed at the expense of creating more tables and potentially more expensive access to factual data due to the requirement of more joins. Each lower level dimension table has a foreign key pointing to the next higher level table.

Using *expanded* dimension tables achieves the operational advantages of both the flattened and the normalized views, while actually increasing the space requirements beyond that of the flattened approach. The number of dimension tables is identical to that in the normalized approach, and the structure of the lowest level dimension table is identical to that in the flattened technique. Each higher level dimension table has, in addition to the attributes existing for the normalized structure, attributes from all higher level dimensions.

The *levelized* approach has one dimension table as does the flattened technique. However, the aggregations have already been performed. There is one tuple for each instance of each level in the dimension, the same number existing in all normalized tables combined. In addition, attributes are added to show the level number.

An extension of the star schema, the *snowflake schema* facilitates more complex data views. In this case, the aggregation hierarchy is shown explicitly in the schema itself. An example of a snowflake schema based on the sales data is shown in Figure 2.13. A snowflake schema can be viewed as a partially normalized version of the corresponding star schema. The division and location dimension tables have been normalized in this figure.

2.5.2 Indexing

With multidimensional data, indices help to reduce the overhead of scanning the extremely large tables. Although the indices used are not defined specifically to support multidimensional data, they do have inherent advantages in their use for these types of data.

With *bitmap indices* each tuple in the table (fact table or dimension table) is represented by a predefined bit so that a table with n tuples would be represented by a vector of n bits. The first tuple in the table is associated with the first bit, the second with the second bit, and so on. There is a unique bit vector for each value in the domain. This vector indicates which associated tuples in the table have that domain value. To find the precise tuples, an address or pointer to each tuple would also have to be associated with each bit position, not each vector. Bitmap indices facilitate easy functions such as join and aggregation through the use of bit arithmetic operations. Bitmap indices also save space over more traditional indices where pointers to records are maintained.

Join indices support joins by precomputing tuples from tables that join together and pointing to the tuples in those tables. When used for multidimensional data, a common approach is to create a join index between a dimension table and a fact table. This facilitates the efficient identification of facts for a specific dimension level and/or value. Join indices can be created for multiway joins across multiple dimension tables. Join indices can be constructed using bitmaps as opposed to pointers.

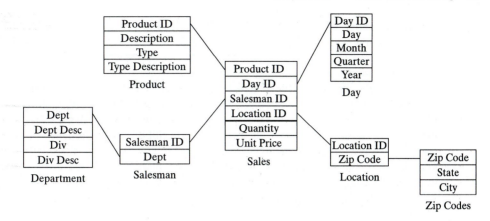

FIGURE 2.13: Snowflake schema.

Traditional *B-tree* indices may be constructed to access each entry in the fact table. Here the key would be the combination of the foreign keys to the dimension tables.

2.6 DATA WAREHOUSING

Decision support systems (DSS) are subject-oriented, integrated, time-variant, and nonvolatile. The term *data warehouse* was first used by William Inmon in the early 1980s. He defined *data warehouse* to be a set of data that supports DSS and is "subject-oriented, integrated, time-variant, nonvolatile" [Inm95]. With data warehousing, corporate-wide data (current and historical) are merged into a single repository. Traditional databases contain *operational data* that represent the day-to-day needs of a company. Traditional business data processing (such as billing, inventory control, payroll, and manufacturing support) support online transaction processing and batch reporting applications. A data warehouse, however, contains *informational data*, which are used to support other functions such as planning and forecasting. Although much of the content is similar between the operational and informational data, much is different. As a matter of fact, the operational data are transformed into the informational data. Example 2.3 illustrates the difference between the two.

EXAMPLE 2.3

The ACME Manufacturing Company maintains several operational databases: sales, billing, employee, manufacturing, and warehousing. These are used to support the day-to-day functions such as writing paychecks, placing orders for supplies needed in the manufacturing process, billing customers, and so on. The president of ACME, Stephanie Eich, wishes to streamline manufacturing to concentrate production on the most profitable products. To perform this task, she asks several "what if" questions, does a projection of current sales into the future, and examines data at different geographic and time dimensions. All the data that she needs to perform this task can be found in one or more of the existing databases. However, it is not easily retrieved in the exact format that she desires. A data warehouse is created with exactly the sales information she needs by location and time. OLAP retrieval tools are provided to facilitate quick response to her questions at any and all dimension granularities.

The data warehouse market supports such diverse industries as manufacturing, retail, telecommunications, and health care. Think of a personnel database for a company that is continually modified as personnel are added and deleted. A personnel database that contains information about the current set of employees is sufficient. However, if management wishes to analyze trends with respect to employment history, more data are needed. They may wish to determine if there is a problem with too many employees quitting. To analyze this problem, they would need to know which employees have left, when they left, why they left, and other information about their employment. For management to make these types of high-level business analyses, more historical data (not just the current snapshot that is typically stored) and data from other sources (perhaps employment applications and results of exit interviews) are required. In addition, some of the data in the personnel database, such as address, may not be needed. A data warehouse provides just this information. In a nutshell, a *data warehouse* is a data repository used to support decision support systems.

The basic motivation for this shift to the strategic use of data is to increase business profitability. Traditional data processing applications support the day-to-day clerical and administrative decisions, while data warehousing supports long-term strategic decisions. A 1996 report by International Data Corporation (IDC) stated that an average *return on investment (ROI)* in data warehousing reached 401% [BS97, 292].

Figure 2.14, adapted from [BS97, Figure 6.1] shows a simple view of a data warehouse. The basic components of a data warehousing system include data migration, the warehouse, and access tools. The data are extracted from operational systems, but must be reformatted, cleansed, integrated, and summarized before being placed in the warehouse. Much of the operational data are not needed in the warehouse (such as employee addresses in Example 2.3) and are removed during this conversion process. This migration process is similar to that needed for data mining applications except that data mining applications need not necessarily be performed on summarized or business-wide data. The applications that are shown in Figure 2.14 to access a warehouse include traditional querying, OLAP, and data mining. Since the warehouse is stored as a database, it can be accessed by traditional query languages.

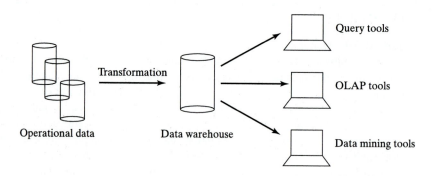

FIGURE 2.14: Data warehouse.

TABLE 2.2: Comparing Operational Database to Data Warehouse

	Operational Data	Data Warehouse
Application	OLTP	OLAP
Use	Precise queries	Ad hoc
Temporal	Snapshot	Historical
Modification	Dynamic	Static
Orientation	Application	Business
Data	Operational values	Integrated
Size	Gigabits	Terabits
Level	Detailed	Summarized
Access	Often	Less often
Response	Few seconds	Minutes
Data schema	Relational	Star/snowflake

Table 2.2 summarizes the differences between operational data stored in traditional databases and the data stored in a data warehouse. The traditional database applications are related to OLTP where the users' requests are stated in a high-level query language (such as SQL) and the results are subsets of the relationships. Data warehouse applications are directly related to business decisions and analysis of the data, OLAP. While operational data usually represent facts concerning a snapshot in time (the current time), a warehouse has historical data as well. Data in the warehouse are not modified as frequently as data in a conventional database. Updates are batched and merged into the warehouse at weekly or monthly intervals. Although this means that the warehouse data are not completely up-to-date, this usually is not a problem with the normal decision support applications. A conventional database usually is related to one application type. This is a fallout of the normalization design process used. The warehouse is associated with the business enterprise, not with an application. Traditional databases may be on the order of megabytes or gigabytes, whereas a warehouse may be terabytes in size. The fact that conventional data are stored in many diverse formats and locations makes it inefficient to support decision support applications. OLTP users expect to get a response in a few seconds. As a result of the complexity of OLAP application, their users may have to wait minutes for a response to their query.

The data transformation process required to convert operational data to informational involves many functions including:

- Unwanted data must be removed.

- Converting heterogeneous sources into one common schema. This problem is the same as that found when accessing data from multiple heterogeneous sources. Each operational database may contain the same data with different attribute names. For example, one system may use "Employee ID," while another uses "EID" for the same attribute. In addition, there may be multiple data types for the same attribute.

- As the operational data is probably a snapshot of the data, multiple snapshots may need to be merged to create the historical view.

- Summarizing data is performed to provide a higher level view of the data. This summarization may be done at multiple granularities and for different dimensions.

- New derived data (e.g., using age rather than birth date) may be added to better facilitate decision support functions.

- Handling missing and erroneous data must be performed. This could entail replacing them with predicted or default values or simply removing these entries.

The portion of the transformation that deals with ensuring valid and consistent data is sometimes referred to as *data scrubbing* or *data staging*.

There are many benefits to the use of a data warehouse. Because it provides an integration of data from multiple sources, its use can provide more efficient access of the data. The data that are stored often provide different levels of summarization. For example, sales data may be found at a low level (purchase order), at a city level (total of sales for a city), or at higher levels (county, state, country, world). The summary can be provided for different types of granularity. The sales data could be summarized by both salesman and department. These summarizations are provided by the conversion process instead of being calculated when the data are accessed. Thus, this also speeds up the processing of the data for decision support applications.

The data warehouse may appear to increase the complexity of database management because it is a replica of the operational data. But keep in mind that much of the data in the warehouse are not simply a replication but an extension to or aggregation of the data. In addition, because the data warehouse contains historical data, data stored there probably will have a longer life span than the snapshot data found in the operational databases. The fact that the data in the warehouse need not be kept consistent with the current operational data also simplifies its maintenance. The benefits obtained by the capabilities (e.g., DSS support) provided usually are deemed to outweigh any disadvantages.

A subset of the complete data warehouse, *data mart*, may be stored and accessed separately. The level is at a departmental, regional, or functional level. These separate data marts are much smaller, and they more efficiently support narrower analytical types of applications.

A *virtual warehouse* is a warehouse implemented as a view from the operational data. While some of this view may actually be materialized for efficiency, it need not all be.

There are several ways to improve the performance of data warehouse applications.

- **Summarization:** Because many applications require summary-type information, data that are known to be needed for consolidation queries should be presummarized before storage. Different levels of summarization should be included to improve performance. With a 20 to 100% increase in storage space, an increase in performance of 2 to 10 times can be achieved [Sin98, p. 302].

- **Denormalization:** Traditional normalization reduces such problems as redundancy as well as insert, update, and deletion anomalies. However, these improvements are achieved at the cost of increased processing time due to joins. With a data warehouse, improved performance can be achieved by storing denormalized data.

Since data warehouses are not usually updated as frequently as operational data are, the negatives associated with update operations are not an issue.

- **Partitioning:** Dividing the data warehouse into smaller fragments may reduce processing time by allowing queries to access small data sets.

The relationship between data mining and data warehousing can be viewed as symbiotic [Inm96]. Data used in data mining applications are often slightly modified from that in the databases where the data permanently reside. The same is true for data in a data warehouse. When data are placed in a warehouse, they are extracted from the database, cleansed, and reformatted. The fact that the data are derived from multiple sources with heterogeneous formats complicates the problem. In addition, the fact that the source databases are updated requires that the warehouse be updated periodically or work with stale data. These issues are identical to many of those associated with data mining and KDD (see Figure 1.4). While data mining and data warehousing are actually orthogonal issues, they are complementary. Due to the types of applications and massive amount of data in a data warehouse, data mining applications can be used to provide meaningful information needed for decision support systems. For example, management may use the results of classification or association rule applications to help determine the target population for an advertising campaign. In addition, data mining activities can benefit from the use of data in a data warehouse. However, its use is not required. Data warehousing and data mining are sometimes thought of as the same thing. Even though they are related, they are different and each can be used without the other.

2.7 OLAP

Online analytic processing (OLAP) systems are targeted to provide more complex query results than traditional OLTP or database systems. Unlike database queries, however, OLAP applications usually involve analysis of the actual data. They can be thought of as an extension of some of the basic aggregation functions available in SQL. This extra analysis of the data as well as the more imprecise nature of the OLAP queries is what really differentiates OLAP applications from traditional database and OLTP applications. OLAP tools may also be used in DSS systems.

OLAP is performed on data warehouses or data marts. The primary goal of OLAP is to support ad hoc querying needed to support DSS. The multidimensional view of data is fundamental to OLAP applications. OLAP is an application view, not a data structure or schema. The complex nature of OLAP applications requires a multidimensional view of the data. The type of data accessed is often (although not a requirement) a data warehouse.

OLAP tools can be classified as ROLAP or MOLAP. With *MOLAP (multidimensional OLAP)*, data are modeled, viewed, and physically stored in a *multidimensional database (MDD)*. MOLAP tools are implemented by specialized DBMS and software systems capable of supporting the multidimensional data directly. With MOLAP, data are stored as an *n*-dimensional array (assuming there are *n* dimensions), so the cube view is stored directly. Although MOLAP has extremely high storage requirements, indices are used to speed up processing. With *ROLAP (relational OLAP)*, however, data are stored in a relational database, and a ROLAP server (middleware) creates the multidimensional view for the user. As one would think, the ROLAP tools tend to be less

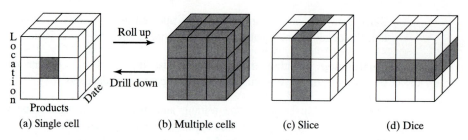

(a) Single cell   (b) Multiple cells   (c) Slice   (d) Dice

FIGURE 2.15: OLAP operations.

complex, but also less efficient. MDD systems may presummarize along all dimensions. A third approach, *hybrid OLAP (HOLAP)*, combines the best features of ROLAP and MOLAP. Queries are stated in multidimensional terms. Data that are not updated frequently will be stored as MDD, whereas data that are updated frequently will be stored as RDB.

As seen in Figure 2.15, there are several types of OLAP operations supported by OLAP tools:

- A simple query may look at a single cell within the cube [Figure 2.15(a)].

- **Slice:** Look at a subcube to get more specific information. This is performed by selecting on one dimension. As seen in Figure 2.15(c), this is looking at a portion of the cube.

- **Dice:** Look at a subcube by selecting on two or more dimensions. This can be performed by a slice on one dimension and then rotating the cube to select on a second dimension. In Figure 2.15(d), a dice is made because the view in (c) is rotated from all cells for one product to all cells for one location.

- **Roll up** (dimension reduction, aggregation): Roll up allows the user to ask questions that move up an aggregation hierarchy. Figure 2.15(b) represents a roll up from (a). Instead of looking at one single fact, we look at all the facts. Thus, we could, for example, look at the overall total sales for the company.

- **Drill down:** Figure 2.15(a) represents a drill down from (b). These functions allow a user to get more detailed fact information by navigating lower in the aggregation hierarchy. We could perhaps look at quantities sold within a specific area of each of the cities.

- **Visualization:** Visualization allows the OLAP users to actually "see" results of an operation.

To assist with roll up and drill down operations, frequently used aggregations can be precomputed and stored in the warehouse. There have been several different definitions for a dice. In fact, the term *slice* and *dice* is sometimes viewed together as indicating that the cube is subdivided by selecting on multiple dimensions.

2.8   WEB SEARCH ENGINES

As a result of the large amount of data on the Web and the fact that it is continually growing, obtaining desired information can be challenging. Web search engines are used to access the data and can be viewed as query systems much like IR systems. As with IR queries, search engine queries can be stated as keyword, boolean, weighted, and so on. The difference is primarily in the data being searched, pages with heterogeneous data and extensive hyperlinks, and the architecture involved.

Conventional search engines suffer from several problems [RS99]:

- **Abundance:** Most of the data on the Web are of no interest to most people. In other words, although there is a lot of data on the Web, an individual query will retrieve only a very small subset of it.

- **Limited coverage:** Search engines often provide results from a subset of the Web pages. Because of the extreme size of the Web, it is impossible to search the entire Web any time a query is requested. Instead, most search engines create indices that are updated periodically. When a query is requested, often only the index is directly accessed.

- **Limited query:** Most search engines provide access based only on simple keyword-based searching. More advanced search engines may retrieve or order pages based on other properties such as the popularity of pages.

- **Limited customization:** Query results are often determined only by the query itself. However, as with traditional IR systems, the desired results are often dependent on the background and knowledge of the user as well. Some more advanced search engines add the ability to do customization using user profiles or historical information.

Traditional IR systems (such as Lexis-Nexis) may actually be tailored to a specific domain. The Web, however, has information for everyone.

As discussed in Chapter 7, True Web mining consists of content, structure, and usage mining. Web search engines are very simplistic examples of Web content mining.

2.9   STATISTICS

Such simple statistical concepts as determining a data distribution and calculating a mean and a variance can be viewed as data mining techniques. Each of these is, in its own right, a descriptive model for the data under consideration.

Part of the data mining modeling process requires searching the actual data. An equally important part requires inferencing from the results of the search to a general model. A current database state may be thought of as a sample (albeit large) of the real data that may not be stored electronically. When a model is generated, the goal is to fit it to the entire data, not just that which was searched. Any model derived should be statistically significant, meaningful, and valid. This problem may be compounded by the preprocessing step of the KDD process, which may actually remove some of the data. Outliers compound this problem. The fact that most database practitioners and users are not probability experts also complicates the issues. The tools needed to make the computationally difficult problems tractable may actually invalidate the results. Assumptions often made about independence of data may be incorrect, thus leading to errors in the resulting model.

An often-used tool in data mining and machine learning is that of sampling. Here a subset of the total population is examined, and a generalization (model) about the entire population is made from this subset. In statistics this approach is referred to as *statistical inference*. Of course, this generalization may lead to errors in the final model caused by the sampling process.

The term *exploratory data analysis* was actually coined by statisticians to describe the fact that the data can actually drive the creation of the model and any statistical characteristics. This seems contradictory to the traditional statistical view that one should not be corrupted or influenced by looking at the data before creating the model. This would unnecessarily bias any resulting hypothesis. Of course, database practitioners would never think of creating a model of the data without looking at the data in detail first and then creating a schema to describe it.

Some data mining applications determine correlations among data. These relationships, however, are not causal in nature. A discovered association rule may show that 60 percent of the time when customers purchased hot dogs they also bought beer. Care must be taken when assigning any significance to this relationship. We do not know why these items were purchased together. Perhaps the beer was on sale or it was an extremely hot day. There may be no relationship between these two data items except that they were often purchased together. There need not be any probabilistic inference that can be deduced.

Statistics research has produced many of the proposed data mining algorithms. The difference lies in the goals, the fact that statisticians may deal with smaller and more formatted data sets, and the emphasis of data mining on the use of machine learning techniques. However, it is often the case that the term *data mining* is used in a derogatory manner by statisticians as data mining is "analysis without any clearly formulated hypotheses" [Man96]. Indeed, this may be the case because data itself, not a predefined hypothesis, is the guide.

Probability distributions can be used to describe the domains found for different data attributes. Statistical inference techniques can be viewed as special estimators and prediction methods. Use of these approaches may not always be applicable because the precise distribution of real data values may not actually follow any specific probability distribution, assumptions on the independence of attributes may be invalid, and some heuristic-based estimator techniques may never actually converge.

It has been stated that "the main difference between data mining and statistics is that data mining is meant to be used by the business user—not the statistician" [BS97, 292]. As such, data mining (particularly from a database perspective) involves not only modeling but also the development of effective and efficient algorithms (and data structures) to perform the modeling on large data sets.

2.10 MACHINE LEARNING

Artificial intelligence (AI) includes many DM techniques such as neural networks and classification. However, AI is more general and involves areas outside traditional data mining. AI applications also may not be concerned with scalability as data sets may be small.

Machine learning is the area of AI that examines how to write programs that can learn. In data mining, machine learning is often used for prediction or classification. With machine learning, the computer makes a prediction and then, based on feedback as to whether it is correct, "learns" from this feedback. It learns through examples, domain knowledge, and feedback. When a similar situation arises in the future, this feedback is used to make the same prediction or to make a completely different prediction. Statistics are very important in machine learning programs because the results of the predictions must be statistically significant and must perform better than a naive prediction. Applications that typically use machine learning techniques include speech recognition, training moving robots, classification of astronomical structures, and game playing.

When machine learning is applied to data mining tasks, a model is used to represent the data (such as a graphical structure like a neural network or a decision tree). During the learning process, a sample of the database is used to train the system to properly perform the desired task. Then the system is applied to the general database to actually perform the task. This predictive modeling approach is divided into two phases. During the training phase, historical or sampled data are used to create a model that represents those data. It is assumed that this model is representative not only for this sample data, but also for the database as a whole and for future data as well. The testing phase then applies this model to the remaining and future data.

A basic machine learning application includes several major aspects. First, an appropriate training set must be chosen. The quality of the training data determines how well the program learns. In addition, the type of feedback available is important. Direct feedback entails specific information about the results and impact of each possible move or database state. Indirect feedback is at a higher level, with no specific information about individual moves or predictions. An important aspect is whether the learning program can actually propose new moves or database states. Another major feature that impacts the quality of learning is how representative the training set is of the overall final system to be examined. If a program is to be designed to perform speech recognition, it is hoped that the system is allowed to learn with a large sample of the speech patterns it will encounter during its actually processing.

There are two different types of machine learning: *supervised learning* and *unsupervised learning*. A supervised approach learns by example. Given a training set of data plus correct answers, the computational model successively applies each entry in the training set. Based on its ability to correctly handle each of these entries, the model is changed to ensure that it works better with this entry if it were applied again. Given enough input values, the model will learn the correct behavior for any potential entry. With unsupervised data, data exist but there is no knowledge of the correct answer of applying the model to the data.

Although machine learning is the basis for many of the core data mining research topics, there is a major difference between the approaches taken by the AI and database disciplines. Much of the machine learning research has focused on the learning portion rather than on the creation of useful information (prediction) for the user. Also, machine learning looks at things that may be difficult for humans to do or concentrates on how to develop learning techniques that can mimic human behavior. The objective for data

TABLE 2.3: Relationship Between Topics [FPSM91]

Database Management	Machine Learning
Database is an active, evolving entity	Database is static
Records may contain erroneous or missing data	Databases are complete and noise-free
Typical field is numeric	Typical feature is binary
Database contains millions of records	Database contains hundreds of instances
AI should get down to reality	All database problems have been solved

mining is to uncover information that can be used to provide information to humans (not take their place). These two conflicting views are summarized in Table 2.3, which originally appeared in [FPSM91]. The items listed in the first column indicate the concerns and views that are taken in this book. Many of the algorithms introduced in this text were created in the AI community and are now being exported into more realistic data mining activities. When applying these machine learning concepts to databases, additional concerns and problems are raised: size, complex data types, complex data relationships, noisy and missy data, and databases that are frequently updated.

2.11 PATTERN MATCHING

Pattern matching or *pattern recognition* finds occurrences of a predefined pattern in data. Pattern matching is used in many diverse applications. A text editor uses pattern matching to find occurrences of a string in the text being edited. Information retrieval and Web search engines may use pattern matching to find documents containing a predefined pattern (perhaps a keyword). Time series analysis examines the patterns of behavior in data obtained from two different time series to determine similarity. Pattern matching can be viewed as a type of classification where the predefined patterns are the classes under consideration. The data are then placed in the correct class based on a similarity between the data and the classes.

2.12 SUMMARY

When viewed as a query system, data mining queries extend both database and IR concepts. Data mining problems are often ill-posed, with many different solutions. Judging the effectiveness of the result of a data mining request is often difficult. A major difference between data mining queries and those of earlier types is the output. Basic database queries always output either a subset of the database or aggregates of the data. A data mining query outputs a KDD object. A KDD object is either a rule, classifier, or clustering [IM96]. These objects do not exist before executing the query and they are not part of the database being queried. Table 2.4 compares the different query systems. Aggregation operators have existed in SQL for years. They do not return objects existing

TABLE 2.4: Relationship Between Topics

Area	Query	Data	Results	Output
DB/OLTP	Precise	Database	Precise	DB objects or aggregation
IR	Precise	Documents	Vague	Documents
OLAP	Analysis	Multidimensional	Precise	DB objects or aggregation
DM	Vague	Preprocessed	Vague	KDD objects

in the database, but return a model of the data. For example, an average operator returns the average of a set of attribute values rather than the values themselves. This is a simple type of data mining operator.

2.13   EXERCISES

1. Compare and contrast database, information retrieval, and data mining queries. What metrics are used to measure the performance of each type of query?

2. What is the relationship between a fuzzy set membership function and classification? Illustrate this relationship using the problem of assigning grades to students in classes where outliers (extremely high and low grades) exist.

3. (**Research**) Data warehouses are often viewed to contain relatively static data. Investigate techniques that have been proposed to provide updates to this data from the operational data. How often should these updates occur?

2.14   BIBLIOGRAPHIC NOTES

There are many excellent database books, including [Dat00], [EN00], [GMUW02], and [OO01]. There are several books that provide introductions to database query processing and SQL, including [DD97] and [YM98].

Fuzzy sets were first examined by Lotfi Zadeh in [Zad65]. They continue to be an important research topic in all areas of computer science, with many introductory texts available such as [KY95], [NW99], and [San98]. Some texts explore the relationship between fuzzy sets and various data mining applications. Pedrycz and Gomide examine fuzzy neural networks and fuzzy genetic algorithms. [PG98]

There are several excellent information retrieval texts, including [BYRN99] and [SM83]. The *ER (entity-relationship) data model* was first proposed by Chen in 1976 [Che76].

An examination of the relationship between statistics and KDD can be found in [IP96]. This article provides an historical perspective of the development of statistical techniques that have influenced data mining. Much of the research concerning outliers has been performed in the statistics community [BL94] and [Haw80].

There is an abundance of books covering of DSS, OLAP, dimensional modeling, multidimensional schemas, and data warehousing, including [BE97], [PKB98], [Sin98], and [Sin99].

An excellent textbook on machine learning is [Mit97]. The relationships between machine learning and data mining are investigated in [MBK99].

CHAPTER 3

Data Mining Techniques

3.1 INTRODUCTION

There are many different methods used to perform data mining tasks. These techniques not only require specific types of data structures, but also imply certain types of algorithmic approaches. In this chapter we briefly introduce some of the common data mining techniques. These will be examined in more detail in later chapters of the book as they are used to perform specific data mining tasks.

Parametric models describe the relationship between input and output through the use of algebraic equations where some parameters are not specified. These unspecified parameters are determined by providing input examples. Even though parametric modeling is a nice theoretical topic and can sometimes be used, often it is either too simplistic or requires more knowledge about the data involved than is available. Thus, for real-world problems, these parametric models may not be useful.

Nonparametric techniques are more appropriate for data mining applications. A *nonparametric model* is one that is data-driven. No explicit equations are used to determine the model. This means that the modeling process adapts to the data at hand. Unlike parametric modeling, where a specific model is assumed ahead of time, the nonparametric techniques create a model based on the input. While the parametric methods require more knowledge about the data before the modeling process, the nonparametric technique requires a large amount of data as input to the modeling process itself. The modeling process then creates the model by sifting through the data. Recent nonparametric methods have employed machine learning techniques to be able to learn dynamically as data are added to the input. Thus, the more data, the better the model created. Also, this dynamic learning process allows the model to be created continuously as the data is input. These features make nonparametric techniques particularly suitable to database applications with large amounts of dynamically changing data. Nonparametric techniques include neural networks, decision trees, and genetic algorithms.

3.2   A STATISTICAL PERSPECTIVE ON DATA MINING

There have been many statistical concepts that are the basis for data mining techniques. We briefly review some of these concepts.

3.2.1   Point Estimation

Point estimation refers to the process of estimating a population parameter, Θ, by an estimate of the parameter, $\hat{\Theta}$. This can be done to estimate mean, variance, standard deviation, or any other statistical parameter. Often the estimate of the parameter for a general population may be made by actually calculating the parameter value for a population sample. An estimator technique may also be used to estimate (predict) the value of missing data. The *bias* of an estimator is the difference between the expected value of the estimator and the actual value:

$$\text{Bias} = E(\hat{\Theta}) - \Theta \tag{3.1}$$

An *unbiased* estimator is one whose bias is 0. While point estimators for small data sets may actually be unbiased, for larger database applications we would expect that most estimators are biased.

One measure of the effectiveness of an estimate is the *mean squared error (MSE)*, which is defined as the expected value of the squared difference between the estimate and the actual value:

$$\text{MSE}(\hat{\Theta}) = E(\hat{\Theta} - \Theta)^2 \tag{3.2}$$

The *squared error* is often examined for a specific prediction to measure accuracy rather than to look at the average difference. For example, if the true value for an attribute was 10 and the prediction was 5, the squared error would be $(5 - 10)^2 = 25$. The squaring is performed to ensure that the measure is always positive and to give a higher weighting to the estimates that are grossly inaccurate. As we will see, the MSE is commonly used in evaluating the effectiveness of data mining prediction techniques. It is also important in machine learning. At times, instead of predicting a simple point estimate for a parameter, one may determine a range of values within which the true parameter value should fall. This range is called a *confidence interval*.

The *root mean square (RMS)* may also be used to estimate error or as another statistic to describe a distribution. Calculating the mean does not indicate the magnitude of the values. The RMS can be used for this purpose. Given a set of n values $X = \{x_1, \ldots, x_n\}$, the RMS is defined by

$$\text{RMS} = \sqrt{\frac{\sum_{j=1}^{n} x_j^2}{n}} \tag{3.3}$$

An alternative use is to estimate the magnitude of the error. The *root mean square error (RMSE)* is found by taking the square root of the MSE.

A popular estimating technique is the *jackknife estimate*. With this approach, the estimate of a parameter, $\hat{\theta}$, is obtained by omitting one value from the set of observed values. Suppose that there is a set of n values $X = \{x_1, \ldots, x_n\}$. An estimate for the mean would be

$$\hat{\mu}_{(i)} = \frac{\sum_{j=1}^{i-1} x_j + \sum_{j=i+1}^{n} x_j}{n-1} \tag{3.4}$$

Here the subscript (i) indicates that this estimate is obtained by omitting the ith value. Given a set of jackknife estimates, $\hat{\theta}_{(i)}$, these can in turn be used to obtain an overall estimate

$$\hat{\theta}_{(.)} = \frac{\sum_{j=1}^{n} \hat{\theta}_{(j)}}{n} \tag{3.5}$$

EXAMPLE 3.1

Suppose that a coin is tossed in the air five times with the following results (1 indicates a head and 0 indicates a tail): $\{1, 1, 1, 1, 0\}$. If we assume that the coin toss follows the Bernoulli distribution, we know that

$$f(x_i \mid p) = p^{x_i}(1-p)^{1-x_i} \tag{3.6}$$

Assuming a perfect coin when the probability of 1 and 0 are both $1/2$, the likelihood is then

$$L(p \mid 1, 1, 1, 1, 0) = \prod_{i=1}^{5} 0.5 = 0.03 \tag{3.7}$$

However, if the coin is not perfect but has a bias toward heads such that the probability of getting a head is 0.8, the likelihood is

$$L(p \mid 1, 1, 1, 1, 0) = 0.8 \times 0.8 \times 0.8 \times 0.8 \times 0.2 = 0.08 \tag{3.8}$$

Here it is more likely that the coin is biased toward getting a head than that it is not biased. The general formula for likelihood is

$$L(p \mid x_1, \ldots, x_5) = \prod_{i=1}^{5} p^{x_i}(1-p)^{1-x_i} = p^{\sum_{i=1}^{5} x_i}(1-p)^{5-\sum_{i=1}^{5} x_i} \tag{3.9}$$

By taking the log we get

$$l(p) = \log L(p) = \sum_{i=1}^{5} x_i \log(p) + \left(5 - \sum_{i=1}^{5} x_i\right) \log(1-p) \tag{3.10}$$

and then we take the derivative with respect to p

$$\frac{\partial l(p)}{\partial p} = \sum_{i=1}^{5} \frac{x_i}{p} - \frac{5 - \sum_{i=1}^{5} x_i}{1-p} \tag{3.11}$$

Setting equal to zero we finally obtain

$$p = \frac{\sum_{i=1}^{5} x_i}{5} \tag{3.12}$$

For this example, the estimate for p is then $\hat{p} = \frac{4}{5} = 0.8$. Thus, 0.8 is the value for p that maximizes the likelihood that the given sequence of heads and tails would occur.

Another technique for point estimation is called the *maximum likelihood estimate (MLE)*. *Likelihood* can be defined as a value proportional to the actual probability that with a specific distribution the given sample exists. So the sample gives us an estimate for a parameter from the distribution. The higher the likelihood value, the more likely the underlying distribution will produce the results observed. Given a sample set of values $X = \{x_1, \ldots, x_n\}$ from a known distribution function $f(x_i \mid \Theta)$, the MLE can estimate parameters for the population from which the sample is drawn. The approach obtains parameter estimates that maximize the probability that the sample data occur for the specific model. It looks at the joint probability for observing the sample data by multiplying the individual probabilities. The likelihood function, L, is thus defined as

$$L(\Theta \mid x_1, \ldots, x_n) = \prod_{i=1}^{n} f(x_i \mid \Theta) \tag{3.13}$$

The value of Θ that maximizes L is the estimate chosen. This can be found by taking the derivative (perhaps after finding the log of each side to simplify the formula) with respect to Θ. Example 3.1 illustrates the use of MLE.

ALGORITHM 3.1

```
Input:
    Θ = {θ₁,...,θₚ}          //Parameters to be estimated
    Xobs = {x₁,...,xₖ}       //Input database values observed
    Xmiss = {xₖ₊₁,...,xₙ}    //Input database values missing
Output:
    Θ̂                        //Estimates for Θ
EM algorithm:
    i := 0;
    Obtain initial parameter MLE estimate, Θ̂ⁱ;
    repeat
        Estimate missing data, X̂ⁱmiss;
        i++
        Obtain next parameter estimate, θ̂ⁱ to
            maximize likelihood;
    until estimate converges;
```

The *expectation-maximization (EM)* algorithm is an approach that solves the estimation problem with incomplete data. The EM algorithm finds an MLE for a parameter (such as a mean) using a two-step process: estimation and maximization. The basic EM algorithm is shown in Algorithm 3.1. An initial set of estimates for the parameters is obtained. Given these estimates and the training data as input, the algorithm then calculates a value for the missing data. For example, it might use the estimated mean to predict a missing value. These data (with the new value added) are then used to determine an estimate for the mean that maximizes the likelihood. These steps are applied iteratively until successive parameter estimates converge. Any approach can be used to find the initial parameter estimates. In Algorithm 3.1 it is assumed that the input database has actual observed values $X_{obs} = \{x_1, \ldots, x_k\}$ as well as values that are missing $X_{miss} = \{x_{k+1}, \ldots, x_n\}$. We assume that the entire database is actually $X = X_{obs} \cup X_{miss}$. The parameters to be estimated are $\Theta = \{\theta_1, \ldots, \theta_p\}$. The likelihood function is defined by

$$L(\Theta \mid X) = \prod_{i=1}^{n} f(x_i \mid \Theta) \tag{3.14}$$

We are looking for the Θ that maximizes L. The MLE of Θ are the estimates that satisfy

$$\frac{\partial \ln L(\Theta \mid X)}{\partial \theta_i} = 0 \tag{3.15}$$

The expectation part of the algorithm estimates the missing values using the current estimates of Θ. This can initially be done by finding a weighted average of the observed data. The maximization step then finds the new estimates for the Θ parameters that maximize the likelihood by using those estimates of the missing data. An illustrative example of the EM algorithm is shown in Example 3.2.

EXAMPLE 3.2

We wish to find the mean, μ, for data that follow the normal distribution where the known data are $\{1, 5, 10, 4\}$ with two data items missing. Here $n = 6$ and $k = 4$. Suppose that we initially guess $\hat{\mu}^0 = 3$. We then use this value for the two missing values. Using this, we obtain the MLE estimate for the mean as

$$\hat{\mu}^1 = \frac{\sum_{i=1}^{k} x_i}{n} + \frac{\sum_{i=k+1}^{n} x_i}{n} = 3.33 + \frac{3+3}{6} = 4.33 \tag{3.16}$$

We now repeat using this as the new value for the missing items, then estimate the mean as

$$\hat{\mu}^2 = \frac{\sum_{i=1}^{k} x_i}{n} + \frac{\sum_{i=k+1}^{n} x_i}{n} = 3.33 + \frac{4.33 + 4.33}{6} = 4.77 \tag{3.17}$$

Repeating we obtain

$$\hat{\mu}^3 = \frac{\sum_{i=1}^{k} x_i}{n} + \frac{\sum_{i=k+1}^{n} x_i}{n} = 3.33 + \frac{4.77 + 4.77}{6} = 4.92 \tag{3.18}$$

and then

$$\hat{\mu}^4 = \frac{\sum_{i=1}^{k} x_i}{n} + \frac{\sum_{i=k+1}^{n} x_i}{n} = 3.33 + \frac{4.92 + 4.92}{6} = 4.97 \qquad (3.19)$$

We decide to stop here because the last two estimates are only 0.05 apart. Thus, our estimate is $\hat{\mu} = 4.97$.

One of the basic guidelines in estimating is *Ockham's Razor*,[1] which basically states that simpler models generally yield the best results.

3.2.2 Models Based on Summarization

There are many basic concepts that provide an abstraction and summarization of the data as a whole. The basic well-known statistical concepts such as *mean, variance, standard deviation, median,* and *mode* are simple models of the underlying population. Fitting a population to a specific *frequency distribution* provides an even better model of the data. Of course, doing this with large databases that have multiple attributes, have complex and/or multimedia attributes, and are constantly changing is not practical (let alone always possible).

There are also many well-known techniques to display the structure of the data graphically. For example, a *histogram* shows the distribution of the data. A *box plot* is a more sophisticated technique that illustrates several different features of the population at once. Figure 3.1 shows a sample box plot. The total *range* of the data values is divided into four equal parts called *quartiles*. The box in the center of the figure shows the range between the first, second, and third quartiles. The line in the box shows the median. The lines extending from either end of the box are the values that are a distance of 1.5 of the interquartile range from the first and third quartiles, respectively. Outliers are shown as points beyond these values.

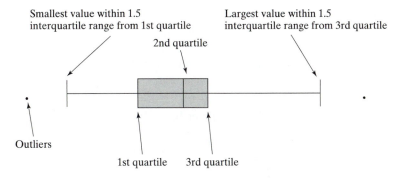

FIGURE 3.1: Box plot example.

---

[1] Sometimes this is spelled Occum or Occam. It is named after William Ockham, who was a monk in the late thirteenth and early fourteenth centuries. However, it was first used by Durand de Saint-Pourcain an earlier French theologian.

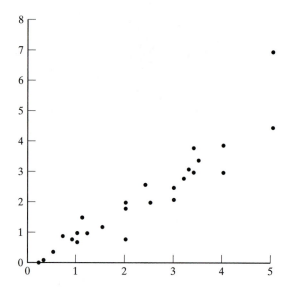

FIGURE 3.2: Scatter diagram example.

Another visual technique to display data is called a *scatter diagram*. This is a graph on a two-dimensional axis of points representing the relationships between x and y values. By plotting the actually observable (x, y) points as seen in a sample, a visual image of some derivable functional relationship between the x and y values in the total population may be seen. Figure 3.2 shows a scatter diagram that plots some observed values. Notice that even though the points do not lie on a precisely linear line, they do hint that this may be a good predictor of the relationship between x and y.

3.2.3 Bayes Theorem

With statistical inference, information about a data distribution are inferred by examining data that follow that distribution. Given a set of data $X = \{x_1, \ldots, x_n\}$, a data mining problem is to uncover properties of the distribution from which the set comes. Bayes rule, defined in Definition 3.1, is a technique to estimate the likelihood of a property given the set of data as evidence or input. Suppose that either hypothesis h_1 or hypothesis h_2 must occur, but not both. Also suppose that x_i is an observable event.

DEFINITION 3.1. Bayes Rule or **Bayes Theorem** is

$$P(h_1 \mid x_i) = \frac{P(x_i \mid h_1)P(h_1)}{P(x_i \mid h_1)P(h_1) + P(x_i \mid h_2)P(h_2)} \qquad (3.20)$$

Here $P(h_1 \mid x_i)$ is called the **posterior probability**, while $P(h_1)$ is the **prior probability** associated with hypothesis h_1. $P(x_i)$ is the probability of the occurrence of data value x_i and $P(x_i \mid h_1)$ is the conditional probability that, given a hypothesis, the tuple satisfies it.

TABLE 3.1: Training Data for Example 3.3

ID	Income	Credit	Class	x_i
1	4	Excellent	h_1	x_4
2	3	Good	h_1	x_7
3	2	Excellent	h_1	x_2
4	3	Good	h_1	x_7
5	4	Good	h_1	x_8
6	2	Excellent	h_1	x_2
7	3	Bad	h_2	x_{11}
8	2	Bad	h_2	x_{10}
9	3	Bad	h_3	x_{11}
10	1	Bad	h_4	x_9

Where there are m different hypotheses we have:

$$P(x_i) = \sum_{j=1}^{m} P(x_i \mid h_j)P(h_j) \tag{3.21}$$

Thus, we have

$$P(h_1 \mid x_i) = \frac{P(x_i \mid h_1)P(h_1)}{P(x_i)} \tag{3.22}$$

Bayes rule allows us to assign probabilities of hypotheses given a data value, $P(h_j \mid x_i)$. Here we discuss tuples when in actuality each x_i may be an attribute value or other data label. Each h_i may be an attribute value, set of attribute values (such as a range), or even a combination of attribute values.

Example 3.3 uses the training data in Table 3.1 to illustrate the use of Bayes rule. Example 3.3 also illustrates that we may take advantage of other probability laws to determine combinations of probabilities. For example, we may find $P(h_1) = P(I < \$10,000 \land \text{Good})$ by instead finding $P(I < \$10,000)P(\text{Good} \mid I < \$10,000)$.

EXAMPLE 3.3

Suppose that a credit loan authorization problem can be associated with four hypotheses: $H = \{h_1, h_2, h_3, h_4\}$ where $h_1 = $ authorize purchase, $h_2 = $ authorize after further identification, $h_3 = $ do not authorize, and $h_4 = $ do not authorize but contact police. The training data for this example are shown in Table 3.1. From training data, we find that $P(h_1) = 60\%$, $P(h_2) = 20\%$, $P(h_3) = 10\%$, and $P(h_4) = 10\%$. To make our predictions, a domain expert has determined that the attributes we should be looking at are income and credit category. Assume that income, I, has been categorized by ranges $[0, \$10,000)$, $[\$10,000, \$50,000)$, $[\$50,000, \$100,000)$, and $[\$100,000, \infty)$. These ranges are encoded and are shown in Table 3.1 as 1, 2, 3, and 4, respectively. Suppose that credit is categorized as excellent, good, or bad. By combining these, we then have 12 values in the data space: $D = \{x_1, \ldots, x_{12}\}$. The relationship between

TABLE 3.2: x_i Assignments for Example 3.3

	1	2	3	4
Excellent	x_1	x_2	x_3	x_4
Good	x_5	x_6	x_7	x_8
Bad	x_9	x_{10}	x_{11}	x_{12}

these x_i values and the two attributes is shown in Table 3.2. Using these values, the last column in Table 3.1 shows the x_i group into which that tuple falls. Given these, we can then calculate $P(x_i \mid h_j)$ and $P(x_i)$. We illustrate how this is done with h_1. There are six tuples from the training set that are in h_1; we use the distribution of these across the x_i to obtain: $P(x_7 \mid h_1) = 2/6$, $P(x_4 \mid h_1) = 1/6$, $P(x_2 \mid h_1) = 2/6$, $P(x_8 \mid h_1) = 1/6$, and $P(x_i \mid h_1) = 0$ for all other values of i. Suppose we wanted to predict the class for x_4. We thus need to find $P(h_j \mid x_4)$ for each h_j. We would then classify x_4 to the class with the largest value for h_1. We find $P(h_1 \mid x_4) = \frac{(P(x_4|h_1))(P(h_1))}{P(x_4)} = \frac{(1/6)(0.6)}{0.1} = 1$. We would thus classify x_4 to the h_1 class.

This example illustrates some issues associated with sampling. First note that Table 3.1 has no entries for x_1, x_3, x_5, x_6, or x_{12}. This makes it impossible to use this training sample to determine how to make predictions for this combination of input data. If indeed these combinations never occur, this would not be a problem. However, in this case we certainly do not know this to be true. Another issue with this sample is its size. Of course, a sample of this size is too small. But what constitutes a good sample? Size certainly is not the only criterion. This is a crucial issue that impacts the quality of any data mining technique that uses sampling. There is much work in the statistics community on good sampling strategies, so we do not cover that topic in this text.

3.2.4 Hypothesis Testing

Hypothesis testing attempts to find a model that explains the observed data by first creating a hypothesis and then testing the hypothesis against the data. This is in contrast to most data mining approaches, which create the model from the actual data without guessing what it is first. The actual data itself drive the model creation. The hypothesis usually is verified by examining a data sample. If the hypothesis holds for the sample, it is assumed to hold for the population in general. Given a population, the initial (assumed) hypothesis to be tested, H_0, is called the *null hypothesis*. Rejection of the null hypothesis causes another hypothesis, H_1, called the *alternative hypothesis*, to be made.

One technique to perform hypothesis testing is based on the use of the chi-squared statistic. Actually, there is a set of procedures referred to as chi squared. These procedures can be used to test the association between two observed variable values and to determine if a set of observed variable values is statistically significant (i.e., if it differs from the expected case). A hypothesis is first made, and then the observed values are compared based on this hypothesis. Assuming that O represents the observed data and E is the expected values based on the hypothesis, the *chi-squared statistic*, χ^2, is defined as:

$$\chi^2 = \sum \frac{(O - E)^2}{E} \qquad (3.23)$$

When comparing a set of observed variable values to determine statistical significance, the values are compared to those of the expected case. This may be the uniform distribution. Example 3.4 illustrates this process. We could look at the ratio of the difference of each observed score from the expected value over the expected value. However, since the sum of these scores will always be 0, this approach cannot be used to compare different samples to determine how they differ from the expected values. The solution to this is the same as we saw with the mean square error—square the difference. Here, if all scores are as expected, the result would be 0. Statistical tables (found in most statistics books) allow the actual value to be evaluated to determine its significance.

EXAMPLE 3.4

Suppose that there are five schools being compared based on students' results on a set of standardized achievement tests. The school district expects that the results will be the same for each school. They know that the total score for the schools is 375, so the expected result would be that each school has an average score of 75. The actual average scores from the schools are: $50, 93, 67, 78$, and 87. The district administrators want to determine if this is statistically significant. Or in simpler terms, should they be worried about the distribution of scores. The chi-squared measure here is

$$\chi^2 = \frac{(50 - 75)^2}{75} + \frac{(93 - 75)^2}{75} + \frac{(67 - 75)^2}{75} + \frac{(78 - 75)^2}{75} + \frac{(87 - 75)^2}{75} = 15.55$$
$$(3.24)$$

Examining a chi-squared significance table, it is found that this value is significant. With a degree of freedom of 4 and a significance level of 95%, the critical value is 9.488. Thus, the administrators observe that the variance between the schools' scores and the expected values cannot be associated with pure chance.

3.2.5   Regression and Correlation

Both *bivariate regression* and *correlation* can be used to evaluate the strength of a relationship between two variables. Regression is generally used to predict future values based on past values by fitting a set of points to a curve. Correlation, however, is used to examine the degree to which the values for two variables behave similarly.

Linear regression assumes that a linear relationship exists between the input data and the output data. The common formula for a linear relationship is used in this model:

$$y = c_0 + c_1 x_1 + \cdots + c_n x_n \qquad (3.25)$$

Here there are n input variables, which are called *predictors* or *regressors*; one output variable (the variable being predicted), which is called the *response*; and $n + 1$ constants, which are chosen during the modeling process to match the input examples (or sample). This is sometimes called *multiple linear regression* because there is more than one predictor. Example 3.5 is an example of the use of linear regression.

EXAMPLE 3.5

It is known that a state has a fixed sales tax, but it is not known what the amount happens to be. The problem is to derive the equation for the amount of sales tax given an input purchase amount. We can state the desired linear equation to be $y = c_0 + c_1 x_1$. So we really only need to have two samples of actual data to determine the values of c_0 and c_1. Suppose that we know $\langle 10, 0.5 \rangle$ and $\langle 25, 1.25 \rangle$ are actual purchase amount and tax amount pairs. Using these data points, we easily determine that $c_0 = 0$ and $c_1 = 0.05$. Thus, the general formula is $y = 0.05\, x_i$. This would be used to predict a value of y for any known x_i value.

Admittedly, Example 3.5 is an extremely simple problem. However, it illustrates how we all use the basic classification and/or prediction techniques frequently. Figure 3.3 illustrates the more general use of linear regression with one input value. Here we have a sample of data that we wish to model using a linear model. The line generated by the linear regression technique is shown in the figure. Note, however, that the actual data points usually do not fit the linear model exactly. Thus, this model is an estimate of what the actual input–output relationship is. We can use the generated linear model to predict an output value given an input value, but unlike that for Example 3.5, the prediction would be an estimate rather than the actual output value.

Two different data variables, X and Y, may behave very similarly. *Correlation* is the problem of determining how much alike the two variables actually are. One standard formula to measure linear correlation is the *correlation coefficient r*. Given two variables, X and Y, the correlation coefficient is a real value $r \in [-1, 1]$. A positive number indicates a positive correlation, whereas a negative number indicates a negative correlation. Here negative correlation indicates that one variable increases while the other decreases in value. The closer the value of r is to 0, the smaller the correlation. A perfect relationship exists with a value of 1 or -1, whereas no correlation exists with a value of 0. When looking at a scatter plot of the two variables, the closer the values are to a straight

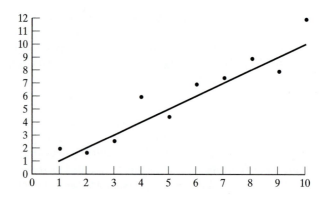

FIGURE 3.3: Simple linear regression.

line, the closer the r value is to 1 or -1. The value for r is defined as

$$r = \frac{\sum (x_i - \bar{X})(y_i - \bar{Y})}{\sqrt{\sum (x_i - \bar{X})^2 \sum (y_i - \bar{Y})^2}} \tag{3.26}$$

where $\bar{X}$ and $\bar{Y}$ are the means for X and Y, respectively. Suppose that $X = \langle 2, 4, 6, 8, 10 \rangle$. If $Y = X$, then $r = 1$. When $Y = \langle 1, 3, 5, 7, 9 \rangle$, $r = 1$. If $Y = \langle 9, 7, 5, 3, 1 \rangle$, $r = -1$.

When two data variables have a strong correlation, they are similar. Thus, the correlation coefficient can be used to define similarity for clustering or classification.

3.3 SIMILARITY MEASURES

The use of similarity measures is well known to anyone who has performed Internet searches using a search engine. In such a search, the set of all Web pages represents the whole database, and these are divided into two classes: those that answer your query and those that do not. Those that answer your query should be more like each other than those that do not answer your query. The similarity in this case is defined by the query you state, usually based on a keyword list. Thus, the retrieved pages are similar because they all contain (to some degree) the keyword list you have specified.

The idea of similarity measures can be abstracted and applied to more general classification problems. The difficulty lies in how the similarity measures are defined and applied to the items in the database. Since most similarity measures assume numeric (and often discrete) values, they may be difficult to use for more general data types. A mapping from the attribute domain to a subset of the integers may be used.

> **DEFINITION 3.2.** The **similarity** between two tuples t_i and t_j, $\text{sim}(t_i, t_j)$, in a database D is a mapping from $D \times D$ to the range $[0, 1]$. Thus, $\text{sim}(t_i, t_j) \in [0, 1]$.

The objective is to define the similarity mapping such that documents that are more alike have a higher similarity value. Thus, the following are desirable characteristics of a good similarity measure:

- $\forall t_i \in D, \text{sim}(t_i, t_i) = 1$

- $\forall t_i, t_j \in D, \text{sim}(t_i, t_j) = 0$ if t_i and t_j are not alike at all

- $\forall t_i, t_j, t_k \in D, \text{sim}(t_i, t_j) < \text{sim}(t_i, t_k)$ if t_i is more like t_k than it is like t_j

So how does one define such a similarity mapping? This, of course, is the difficult part. Often the concept of "alikeness" is itself not well defined. When the idea of similarity measure is used in classification where the classes are predefined, this problem is somewhat simpler than when it is used for clustering where the classes are not known in advance. Again, think of the IR example. Each IR query provides the class definition in the form of the IR query itself. So the classification problem then becomes one of determining similarity not among all tuples in the database but between each tuple and the query. This makes the problem an $O(n)$ problem rather than an $O(n^2)$ problem.

Here are some of the more common similarity measures used in traditional IR systems and more recently in Internet search engines:

- **Dice:** $\text{sim}(t_i, t_j) = \dfrac{2\sum_{h=1}^{k} t_{ih}t_{jh}}{\sum_{h=1}^{k} t_{ih}^2 + \sum_{h=1}^{k} t_{jh}^2}$

- **Jaccard:** $\text{sim}(t_i, t_j) = \dfrac{\sum_{h=1}^{k} t_{ih}t_{jh}}{\sum_{h=1}^{k} t_{ih}^2 + \sum_{h=1}^{k} t_{jh}^2 - \sum_{h=1}^{k} t_{ih}t_{jh}}$

- **Cosine:** $\text{sim}(t_i, t_j) = \dfrac{\sum_{h=1}^{k} t_{ih}t_{jh}}{\sqrt{\sum_{h=1}^{k} t_{ih}^2 \sum_{h=1}^{k} t_{jh}^2}}$

- **Overlap:** $\text{sim}(t_i, t_j) = \dfrac{\sum_{h=1}^{k} t_{ih}t_{jh}}{\min\left(\sum_{h=1}^{k} t_{ih}^2, \sum_{h=1}^{k} t_{jh}^2\right)}$

In these formulas it is assumed that similarity is being evaluated between two vectors $t_i = \langle t_{i1}, \ldots, t_{ik} \rangle$ and $t_j = \langle t_{j1}, \ldots, t_{jk} \rangle$, and vector entries usually are assumed to be nonnegative numeric values. They could, for example, be a count of the number of times an associated keyword appears in the document. If there is no overlap (i.e., one of the two vectors always has a 0 in one of the two terms), the resulting value is 0. If the two are identical, the resulting measure is 1. The overlap measure, however, does not satisfy this restriction. These formulas have their origin in measuring similarities between sets based on the intersection between the two sets. Dice's coefficient relates the overlap to the average size of the two sets together. Jaccard's coefficient is used to measure the overlap of two sets as related to the whole set caused by their union. The cosine coefficient relates the overlap to the geometric average of the two sets. The overlap metric determines the degree to which the two sets overlap.

   Distance or dissimilarity measures are often used instead of similarity measures. As implied, these measure how "unlike" items are. Traditional distance measures may be used in a two-dimensional space. These include

- **Euclidean:** $\text{dis}(t_i, t_j) = \sqrt{\sum_{h=1}^{k} (t_{ih} - t_{jh})^2}$

- **Manhattan:** $\text{dis}(t_i, t_j) = \sum_{h=1}^{k} |(t_{ih} - t_{jh})|$

To compensate for the different scales between different attribute values, the attribute values may be normalized to be in the range [0, 1]. If nominal values rather than numeric values are used, some approach to determining the difference is needed. One method is to assign a difference of 0 if the values are identical and a difference of 1 if they are different.

3.4   DECISION TREES

A decision tree is a predictive modeling technique used in classification, clustering, and prediction tasks. Decision trees use a "divide and conquer" technique to split the problem search space into subsets. It is based on the "Twenty Questions" game that children play, as illustrated by Example 3.6. Figure 3.4 graphically shows the steps in the game. This tree has as the root the first question asked. Each subsequent level in the tree consists of questions at that stage in the game. Nodes at the third level show questions asked

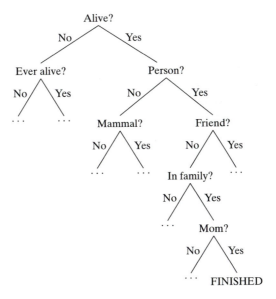

FIGURE 3.4: Decision tree for Example 3.6.

at the third level in the game. Leaf nodes represent a successful guess as to the object being predicted. This represents a correct prediction. Each question successively divides the search space much as a binary search does. As with a binary search, questions should be posed so that the remaining space is divided into two equal parts. Often young children tend to ask poor questions by being too specific, such as initially asking "Is it my Mother?" This is a poor approach because the search space is not divided into two equal parts.

EXAMPLE 3.6

Stephanie and Shannon are playing a game of "Twenty Questions." Shannon has in mind some object that Stephanie tries to guess with no more than 20 questions. Stephanie's first question is "Is this object alive?" Based on Shannon's answer, Stephanie then asks a second question. Her second question is based on the answer that Shannon provides to the first question. Suppose that Shannon says "yes" as her first answer. Stephanie's second question is "Is this a person?" When Shannon responds "yes," Stephanie asks "Is it a friend?" When Shannon says "no," Stephanie then asks "Is it someone in my family?" When Shannon responds "yes," Stephanie then begins asking the names of family members and can immediately narrow down the search space to identify the target individual. This game is illustrated in Figure 3.4.

DEFINITION 3.3. A **decision tree (DT)** is a tree where the root and each internal node is labeled with a question. The arcs emanating from each node represent each possible answer to the associated question. Each leaf node represents a prediction of a solution to the problem under consideration.

Definition 3.4. A **decision tree (DT) model**[2] is a computational model consisting of three parts:

1. A decision tree as defined in Definition 3.3.
2. An algorithm to create the tree.
3. An algorithm that applies the tree to data and solves the problem under consideration.

The building of the tree may be accomplished via an algorithm that examines data from a training sample or could be created by a domain expert. Most decision tree techniques differ in how the tree is created. We examine several decision tree technique in later chapters of the book. Algorithm 3.2 shows the basic steps in applying a tuple to the DT, step three in Definition 3.4. We assume here that the problem to be performed is one of prediction, so the last step is to make the prediction as dictated by the final leaf node in the tree. The complexity of the algorithm is straightforward to analyze. For each tuple in the database, we search the tree from the root down to a particular leaf. At each level, the maximum number of comparisons to make depends on the branching factor at that level. So the complexity depends on the product of the number of levels and the maximum branching factor.

Algorithm 3.2

```
Input:
    T       //Decision tree
    D       //Input database
Output:
    M       //Model prediction
DTProc algorithm:
            //Simplistic algorithm to illustrate prediction
              technique using DT
    for each t ∈ D do
      n = root node of T;
      while n not leaf node do
          Obtain answer to question on n applied to t;
          Identify arc from t, which contains correct answer;
          n = node at end of this arc;
      Make prediction for t based on labeling of n;
```

We use Example 3.7 to further illustrate the use of decision trees.

EXAMPLE 3.7

Suppose that students in a particular university are to be classified as short, tall, or medium based on their height. Assume that the database schema is {name, address, gender, height, age, year, major}. To construct a decision tree, we must identify the attributes that are important to the classification problem at hand. Suppose that height, age, and gender are

---

[2]Note that we have two separate definitions: one for the tree itself and one for the model. Although we differentiate between the two here, the more common approach is to use the term *decision tree* for either.

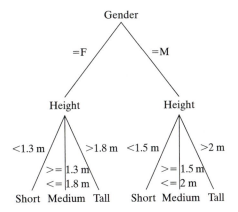

FIGURE 3.5: Decision tree for Example 3.7.

chosen. Certainly, a female who is 1.95 m in height is considered as tall, while a male of the same height may not be considered tall. Also, a child 10 years of age may be tall if he or she is only 1.5 m. Since this is a set of university students, we would expect most of them to be over 17 years of age. We thus decide to filter out those under this age and perform their classification separately. We may consider these students to be outliers because their ages (and more important their height classifications) are not typical of most university students. Thus, for classification we have only gender and height. Using these two attributes, a decision tree building algorithm will construct a tree using a sample of the database with known classification values. This training sample forms the basis of how the tree is constructed. One possible resulting tree after training is shown in Figure 3.5.

3.5 NEURAL NETWORKS

The first proposal to use an artificial neuron appeared in 1943, but computer usage of neural networks did not actually begin until the 1980s. *Neural networks (NN)*, often referred to as *artificial neural networks (ANN)* to distinguish them from biological neural networks, are modeled after the workings of the human brain. The NN is actually an information processing system that consists of a graph representing the processing system as well as various algorithms that access that graph. As with the human brain, the NN consists of many connected processing elements. The NN, then, is structured as a directed graph with many nodes (processing elements) and arcs (interconnections) between them. The nodes in the graph are like individual neurons, while the arcs are their interconnections. Each of these processing elements functions independently from the others and uses only local data (input and output to the node) to direct its processing. This feature facilitates the use of NNs in a distributed and/or parallel environment.

The NN approach, like decision trees, requires that a graphical structure be built to represent the model and then that the structure be applied to the data. The NN can be viewed as a directed graph with source (*input*), sink (*output*), and internal (*hidden*) nodes. The input nodes exist in a *input layer*, while the output nodes exist in an *output layer*. The hidden nodes exist over one or more *hidden layers*. To perform the data mining task, a tuple is input through the input nodes and the output node determines what the prediction is. Unlike decision trees, which have only one input node (the root of the tree), the NN has one input node for each attribute value to be examined to solve the data mining function. Unlike decision trees, after a tuple is processed, the NN may be changed to improve future performance. Although the structure of the graph does not change, the labeling of the edges may change.

In addition to solving complex problems, NNs can "learn" from prior applications. That is, if a poor solution to the problem is made, the network is modified to produce a better solution to this problem the next time. A major drawback to the use of NNs is the fact that they are difficult to explain to end users (unlike decision trees, which are easy to understand). Also, unlike decision trees, NNs usually work only with numeric data.

To better illustrate the process, we reexamine Example 3.7 and show a simple NN for this problem in Figure 3.6. We first must determine the basic structure of the graph. Since there are two important attributes, we assume that there are two input nodes. Since we are to classify into three classes, we use three output nodes. The number of hidden layers in the NN is not easy to determine. In most cases, one or two is enough. In this example, we assume that there is one hidden layer and thus a total of three layers in the general structure. We arbitrarily assume that there are two nodes in this hidden layer. Each node is labeled with a function that indicates its effect on the data coming into that node. At the input layer, functions f_1 and f_2 simply take the corresponding attribute value in and replicate it as output on each of the arcs coming out of the node. The functions at the hidden layer, f_3 and f_4, and those at the output layer, f_5, f_6, and f_7, perform more complicated functions, which are investigated later in this section. The arcs are all labeled with weights, where w_{ij} is the weight between nodes i and j. During processing, the functions at each node are applied to the input data to produce the output. For example, the output of node 3 is

$$f_3(w_{13}h + w_{23}g) \tag{3.27}$$

where h and g are the input height and gender values. Note that to determine the output of a node we must know: the values input on each arc, the weights on all input arcs, the technique used to combine the input values (a weighted sum is used here), and the function f_3 definition.

As with decision trees, we define a neural network in two parts: one for the data structure and one for the general approach used, including the data structure and the algorithms needed to use it.

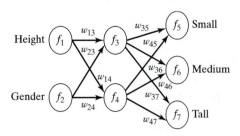

FIGURE 3.6: Neural network for Example 3.7.

DEFINITION 3.5. A **neural network (NN)** is a directed graph, $F = \langle V, A \rangle$ with vertices $V = \{1, 2, \ldots, n\}$ and arcs $A = \{\langle i, j \rangle \mid 1 \leq i, j \leq n\}$, with the following restrictions:

1. V is partitioned into a set of input nodes, V_I, hidden nodes, V_H, and output nodes, V_O.

2. The vertices are also partitioned into layers $\{1, \ldots, k\}$ with all input nodes in layer 1 and output nodes in layer k. All hidden nodes are in layers 2 to $k - 1$ which are called the **hidden layers**.

3. Any arc $\langle i, j \rangle$ must have node i in layer $h - 1$ and node j in layer h.

4. Arc $\langle i, j \rangle$ is labeled with a numeric value w_{ij}.

5. Node i is labeled with a function f_i.

Definition 3.5 is a very simplistic view of NNs. Although there are many more complicated types that do not fit this definition (as we will see later in the text), this defines the most common type of NN, and the one that is used most often throughout this text. More general NNs include some with arcs between any two nodes at any layers. Any approaches that use a more generalized view of a graph for NNs will be adequately defined before usage.

DEFINITION 3.6. A **neural network (NN) model** is a computational model consisting of three parts:

1. Neural network graph that defines the data structure of the neural network.

2. Learning algorithm that indicates how learning takes place.

3. Recall techniques that determine how information is obtained from the network. We discuss propagation in this text.

NNs have been used in pattern recognition, speech recognition and synthesis, medical applications (diagnosis, drug design), fault detection, problem diagnosis, robot control, and computer vision. In business, NNs have been used to "advise" booking of airline seats to increase profitability. As a matter of fact, NNs can be used to compute any function. Although NNs can solve problems that seem more elusive to other AI techniques, they have a long training time (time during which the learning takes place) and thus are not appropriate for real-time applications. NNs may contain many processing elements and thus can be used in massively parallel systems.

Artificial NNs can be classified based on the type of connectivity and learning. The basic type of connectivity discussed in this text is *feedforward*, where connections are only to layers later in the structure. Alternatively, a NN may be *feedback* where some links are back to earlier layers. Learning can be either supervised or unsupervised, as is discussed in section 4.5.2.

Figure 3.7 shows a sample node, i, in a neural network. Here there are k input arcs coming from nodes $1, 2, \ldots, k$. with weights of $w_{1i}, \ldots, w_{ki}$ and input values of $x_{1i}, \ldots, x_{ki}$. The values that flow on these arcs are shown on dashed arcs because they do not really exist as part of the graph itself. There is one output value y_i produced. During propagation this value is output on all output arcs of the node. The activation function,

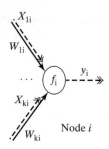

FIGURE 3.7: Neural network node.

f_i, is applied to the inputs, which are scaled by applying the corresponding weights. The weight in the NN may be determined in two ways. In simple cases where much is known about the problem, the weights may be predetermined by a domain expert. The more common approach is to have them determined via a learning process.

The structure of the NN may also be viewed from the perspective of matrices. Input and weight on the arcs into node i are

$$[x_{1i} \ldots x_{ki}]^{T}, [w_{1i} \ldots w_{ki}] \tag{3.28}$$

There is one output value from node i, y_i, which is propagated to all output arcs during the propagation process. Using summation to combine the inputs, then, the output of a node is

$$y_i = f_i \left(\sum_{j=1}^{k} w_{ji} \, x_{ji} \right) = f_i \left([w_{1i} \ldots w_{ki}] \begin{bmatrix} x_{1i} \\ \ldots \\ x_{ki} \end{bmatrix} \right) \tag{3.29}$$

Here f_i is the activation function. Because NNs are complicated, domain experts and data mining experts are often advised to assist in their use. This in turn complicates the process.

Overfitting occurs when the NN is trained to fit one set of data almost exactly. The error that occurs with the given training data is quite small; however, when new data are examined, the error is very large. In effect, the NN has "memorized" the training set and cannot generalize to more data. Larger and more complicated NNs can be trained to represent more complex functions. To avoid overfitting, smaller NNs are advisable. However, this is difficult to determine beforehand. Another approach that can be used to avoid overfitting is to stop the learning process early. Using a larger training set also helps.

3.5.1   Activation Functions

The output of each node i in the NN is based on the definition of a function f_i, *activation function*, associated with it. An activation function is sometimes called a *processing element function* or a *squashing function*. The function is applied to the set of inputs coming in on the input arcs. Figure 3.7 illustrates the process. There have been many proposals for activation functions, including threshold, sigmoid, symmetric sigmoid, and Gaussian.

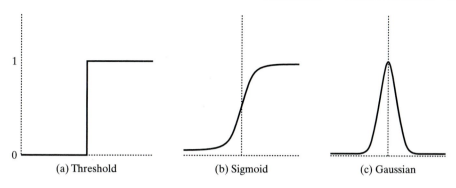

(a) Threshold   (b) Sigmoid   (c) Gaussian

FIGURE 3.8: Sample activation functions.

An activation function may also be called a *firing rule*, relating it back to the workings of the human brain. When the input to a neuron is large enough, it *fires*, sending an electrical signal out on its axon (output link). Likewise, in an artificial NN the output may be generated only if the input is above a certain level; thus, the idea of a firing rule. When dealing only with binary output, the output is either 0 or 1, depending on whether the neuron should fire. Some activation functions use -1 and 1 instead, while still others output a range of values. Based on these ideas, the input and output values are often considered to be either 0 or 1. The model used in this text is more general, allowing any numeric values for weights and input/output values. In addition, the functions associated with each node may be more complicated than a simple threshold function. Since many learning algorithms use the derivative of the activation function, in these cases the function should have a derivative that is easy to find.

An activation function, f_i, is applied to the input values $\{x_{1i}, \ldots, x_{ki}\}$ and weights $\{w_{1i}, \ldots, w_{ki}\}$. These inputs are usually combined in a sum of products form $S = (\sum_{h=1}^{k}(w_{hi}x_{hi}))$. If a bias input exists, this formula becomes $S = w_{0i} + (\sum_{h=1}^{k}(w_{hi}x_{hi}))$. The following are alternative definitions for activation functions, $f_i(S)$ at node i. Activation functions may be *unipolar*, with values in $[0, 1]$, or *bipolar*, with values in $[-1, 1]$. The functions are also shown in Figure 3.8.

- **Linear:** A linear activation function produces a linear output value based on the input. The following is a typical activation function

$$f_i(S) = cS \qquad (3.30)$$

  Here c is a constant positive value. With the linear function, the output value has no limits in terms of maximum or minimum values.

- **Threshold or step:** The output value is either a 1 or 0, depending on the sum of the products of the input values and their associated weights. As seen in Figure 3.8(a), values above a threshold, T, will be 1 or 0:

$$f_i(S) = \left\{ \begin{array}{ll} 1 & \text{if } S > T \\ 0 & \text{otherwise} \end{array} \right\} \qquad (3.31)$$

The binary output values may also be 1 or -1. Alternatively, the 1 value may be replaced by any constant. A variation of this "hard limit" threshold function is a linear threshold function. With the *linear threshold function*, also called a *ramp function* or a *piecewise linear function*, the value of the activation function increases gradually from the low value to the high value. One such function is

$$f_i(S) = \begin{cases} 1 & \text{if } S > T_2 \\ \dfrac{S - T_1}{T_2 - T_1} & \text{if } T_1 \le S \le T_2 \\ 0 & \text{if } S < T_1 \end{cases} \tag{3.32}$$

Here the linear increase is between T_1 and T_2. As with the regular threshold function, the value may be between -1 and 1 or 0 and 1.

- **Sigmoid:** As seen in Figure 3.8(b), this is an "S"-shaped curve with output values between -1 and 1 (or 0 and 1), and which is monotonically increasing. Although there are several types of sigmoid functions, they all have this characteristic "S" shape. A common one is the *logistic function*

$$f_i(S) = \frac{1}{(1 + e^{-cS})} \tag{3.33}$$

Here c is a constant positive value that changes the slope of the function. This function possesses a simple derivative: $\frac{\partial f_i}{\partial S} = f_i(1 - f_i)$.

- **Hyperbolic tangent:** A variation of the sigmoid function is the hyperbolic tangent function shown here

$$f_i(S) = \frac{(1 - e^{-S})}{(1 + e^{-cS})} \tag{3.34}$$

This function has an output centered at zero, which may help with learning.

- **Gaussian:** The Gaussian function, Figure 3.8(c), is a bell-shaped curve with output values in the range [0, 1]. A typical Gaussian function is

$$f_i(S) = e^{\frac{-S^2}{v}} \tag{3.35}$$

Here S is the mean and V is the predefined positive variance of the function.

These are only a representative subset of the possible set of activation functions that could be and have been used.

Nodes in NNs often have an extra input called a *bias*. This bias value of 1 is input on an arc with a weight of $-\theta$. The summation with bias input thus becomes

$$S_i = \sum_{j=1}^{k} w_{ji} x_{ji} - \theta \tag{3.36}$$

The effect of the bias input is to move the activation function on the X axis by a value of θ. Thus, a weight of $-\theta$ becomes a threshold of θ.

3.6   GENETIC ALGORITHMS

Genetic algorithms are examples of *evolutionary computing* methods and are optimization-type algorithms. Given a population of potential problem solutions (individuals), evolutionary computing expands this population with new and potentially better solutions. The basis for evolutionary computing algorithms is biological evolution, where over time evolution produces the best or "fittest" individuals. Chromosomes, which are DNA strings, provide the abstract model for a living organism. Subsections of the chromosomes, which are called *genes*, are used to define different traits of the individual. During reproduction, genes from the parents are combined to produce the genes for the child.

In data mining, genetic algorithms may be used for clustering, prediction, and even association rules. You can think of these techniques as finding the "fittest" models from a set of models to represent the data. In this approach a starting model is assumed and through many iterations, models are combined to create new models. The best of these, as defined by a fitness function, are then input into the next iteration. Algorithms differ in how the model is represented, how different individuals in the model are combined, and how the fitness function is used.

When using genetic algorithms to solve a problem, the first thing, and perhaps the most difficult task, that must be determined is how to model the problem as a set of individuals. In the real world, individuals may be identified by a complete encoding of the DNA structure. An individual typically is viewed as an array or tuple of values. Based on the recombination (crossover) algorithms, the values are usually numeric and may be binary strings. These individuals are like a DNA encoding in that the structure for each individual represents an encoding of the major features needed to model the problem. Each individual in the population is represented as a string of characters from the given alphabet.

> **DEFINITION 3.7.** Given an alphabet A, an **individual** or **chromosome** is a string $I = I_1, I_2, \ldots, I_n$ where $I_j \in A$. Each character in the string, I_j, is called a **gene**. The values that each character can have are called the **alleles**. A **population**, P, is a set of individuals.

Although individuals are often represented as bit strings, any encoding is possible. An array with nonbinary characters could be used, as could more complicated data structures including trees and arrays. The only real restriction is that the genetic operators (mutation, crossover) must be defined.

In genetic algorithms, reproduction is defined by precise algorithms that indicate how to combine the given set of individuals to produce new ones. These are called *crossover* algorithms. Given two individuals (*parents* from the population, the crossover technique generates new individuals (*offspring* or *children*) by switching subsequences of the strings. Figure 3.9 illustrates the process of crossover. The locations indicating the crossover points are shown in the figure with the vertical lines. In Figure 3.9(a) crossover is achieved by interchanging the last three bits of the two strings. In part (b) the center three bits are interchanged. Figure 3.9 shows single and multiple crossover points. There are many variations of the crossover approach, including determining crossover points randomly. A crossover probability is used to determine how many new offspring are created via crossover. In addition, the actual crossover point may vary within one algorithm.

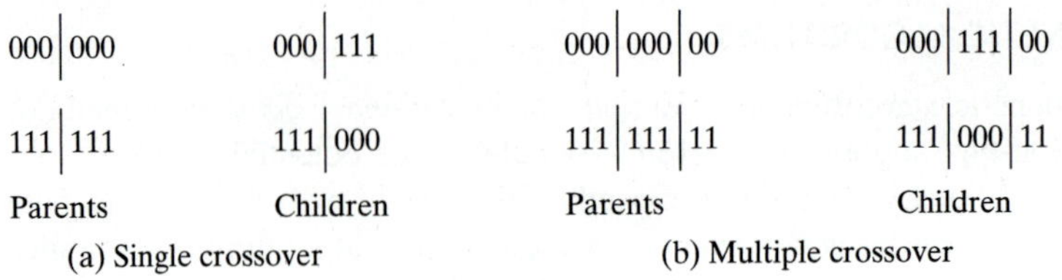

$$000 \mid 000 \qquad 000 \mid 111 \qquad 000 \mid 000 \mid 00 \qquad 000 \mid 111 \mid 00$$

$$111 \mid 111 \qquad 111 \mid 000 \qquad 111 \mid 111 \mid 11 \qquad 111 \mid 000 \mid 11$$

Parents Children Parents Children

(a) Single crossover (b) Multiple crossover

FIGURE 3.9: Crossover.

As in nature, however, mutations sometimes appear, and these also may be present in genetic algorithms. The mutation operation randomly changes characters in the off-spring. A very small probability of mutation is set to determine whether a character should change.

Since genetic algorithms attempt to model nature, only the strong survive. When new individuals are created, a choice must be made about which individuals will survive. This may be the new individuals, the old ones, or more likely a combination of the two. The third major component of genetic algorithms, then, is the part that determines the best (or fittest) individuals to survive.

One of the most important components of a genetic algorithm is determining how to select individuals. A fitness function, f, is used to determine the best individuals in a population. This is then used in the selection process to choose parents. Given an objective by which the population can be measured, the fitness function indicates how well the goodness objective is being met by an individual.

DEFINITION 3.8. Given a population, P, a **fitness function**, f, is a mapping $f : P \rightarrow \mathbf{R}$.

The simplest selection process is to select individuals based on their fitness:

$$p_{I_i} = \frac{f(I_i)}{\sum\limits_{I_j \in P} f(I_j)} \tag{3.37}$$

Here p_{I_i} is the probability of selecting individual I_i. This type of selection is called *roulette wheel selection*. One problem with this approach is that it is still possible to select individuals with a very low fitness value. In addition, when the distribution is quite skewed with a small number of extremely fit individuals, these individuals may be chosen repeatedly. In addition, as the search continues, the population becomes less diverse so that the selection process has little effect.

DEFINITION 3.9. A **genetic algorithm (GA)** is a computational model consisting of five parts:

1. Starting set of individuals, P.
2. Crossover technique.
3. Mutation algorithm.
4. Fitness function.

5. Algorithm that applies the crossover and mutation techniques to P iteratively using the fitness function to determine the best individuals in P to keep. The algorithm replaces a predefined number of individuals from the population with each iteration and terminates when some threshold is met.

Suppose that each solution to the problem to be solved is represented as one of these individuals. A complete search of all possible individuals would yield the best individual or solution to the problem using the predefined fitness function. Since the search space is quite large (perhaps infinite), what a genetic algorithm does is to prune from the search space individuals who will not solve the problem. In addition, it only creates new individuals who probably will be much different from those previously examined. Since genetic algorithms do not search the entire space, they may not yield the best result. However, they can provide approximate solutions to difficult problems.

ALGORITHM 3.3

```
Input:
    P       //Initial population
Output:
    P'      //Improved population
Genetic algorithm:
                //Algorithm to illustrate genetic algorithm
    repeat
        N =| P |;
        P' = Ø;
        repeat
            i₁, i₂ = select(P);
            o₁, o₂ = cross(i₁, i₂);
            o₁ = mutate(o₁);
            o₂ = mutate(o₂);
            P' = P' ∪ {o₁, o₂};
        until | P' |= N;
        P = P';
    until termination criteria satisfied;
```

Algorithm 3.3 outlines the steps performed by a genetic algorithm. Initially, a population of individuals, P, is created. Although different approaches can be used to perform this step, they typically are generated randomly. From this population, a new population, P', of the same size is created. The algorithm repeatedly selects individuals from whom to create new ones. These parents, i_1, i_2, are then used to produce two offspring, o_1, o_2, using a crossover process. Then mutants may be generated. The process continues until the new population satisfies the termination condition. We assume here that the entire population is replaced with each iteration. An alternative would be to replace the two individuals with the smallest fitness. Although this algorithm is quite general, it is representative of all genetic algorithms. There are many variations on this general theme.

Genetic algorithms have been used to solve most data mining problems, including classification, clustering, and generating association rules. Typical applications of genetic algorithms include scheduling, robotics, economics, biology, and pattern recognition.

The major advantage to the use of genetic algorithms is that they are easily parallelized. There are, however, many disadvantages to their use:

- Genetic algorithms are difficult to understand and to explain to end users.

- The abstraction of the problem and method to represent individuals is quite difficult.

- Determining the best fitness function is difficult.

- Determining how to do crossover and mutation is difficult.

3.7 EXERCISES

1. Given the following set of values $\{1, 3, 9, 15, 20\}$, determine the jackknife estimate for both the mean and standard deviation of the mean.

2. Redo Example 3.1 assuming that a coin is tossed six times with the following results: $\{0, 1, 0, 0, 1, 0\}$.

3. Complete Example 3.3 by determining the correct classification for each x_i.

4. Use linear regression with one predictor to determine the formula for the output given the following samples: $\langle 1, 3 \rangle$ and $\langle 2, 5 \rangle$. Then predict the output value with an input of 5.

5. Calculate the correlation coefficient r for the following:

   (a) X values: 1, 2, 3, 4, 5, 6, 7, 8, 9, 10
       Y values: 5, 7, 8, 9, 10, 12, 13, 15, 18, 20

   (b) X values: 1, 2, 3, 4, 5, 6, 7, 8, 9, 10
       Y values: 10, 18, 15, 13, 12, 10, 9, 8, 7, 5

   (c) X values: 3, 5, 2, 1, 10
       Y values: 10, 5, 8, 7, 2

6. Find the similarity between $\langle 0, 1, 0.5, 0.3, 1 \rangle$ and $\langle 1, 0, 0.5, 0, 0 \rangle$ using the Dice, Jaccard, and cosine similarity measures.

7. Given the decision tree in Figure 3.5, classify each of the following students: $\langle$Mary, 20, F, 2 m, Senior, Math$\rangle$, $\langle$Dave, 19, M, 1.7 m, Sophomore, Computer Science$\rangle$, and $\langle$Martha, 18, F, 1.2 m, Freshman, English$\rangle$.

8. Using the NN shown in Figure 3.6, classify the same students as those used in exercise 7. Assume that the input nodes use an identity function, the hidden nodes use a hyperbolic tangent activation function, the output layer uses a sigmoidal function, and a weighted sum is used to calculate input to each node in the hidden and output layers. You may assume any value for the constants in the activation functions. Assume that the trained weights are defined by the difference between the node numbers at either end of the arc. For example, the weight $w_{13} = 0.2$ and $w_{47} = 0.3$.

9. Given an initial population $\{\langle 101010 \rangle, \langle 001100 \rangle, \langle 010101 \rangle, \langle 000010 \rangle\}$, apply the genetic algorithm to find a better population. Suppose the fitness function is defined as the sum of the bit values for each individual and that mutation always occurs by negating the second bit. The termination condition is that the average fitness value for the entire population must be greater than 4. Also, an individual is chosen

for crossover only if its fitness is greater than 2. (Hint: You can use different crossover points.)

3.8 BIBLIOGRAPHIC NOTES

Data mining owes much of its development to previous work in machine learning, statistics, and databases [Man96]. The contribution of statistics to data mining can be traced back to the seminal work by Bayes in 1763. The EM algorithm dates back to [DLR77]. An examination of the impact statistics has had on the development of data mining techniques can be found in [IP96], [GMPS96], and [Mit99]. Many data mining techniques find their birth in the machine learning field. Excellent studies of the relationship between machine learning and data mining can be found in two recent books, [MBK99] and [WF00].

The first proposal for NNs was [MP43]. A special issue of *Computer* was devoted to examining NNs in March 1988. Excellent overviews of NNs can be found in [Hay99]. Several excellent texts on NNs exist, including [Kas96], [Has95], and [Sim96].

A complete discussion of similarity measures can be found in [SM83].

Genetic algorithms were first proposed in 1975 by John Holland [Hol75]. A great survey of genetic algorithms is available in [Gol89].

CORE TOPICS

PART TWO
CORE TOPICS

C H A P T E R 4

Classification

4.1 INTRODUCTION

Classification is perhaps the most familiar and most popular data mining technique. Examples of classification applications include image and pattern recognition, medical diagnosis, loan approval, detecting faults in industry applications, and classifying financial market trends. Estimation and prediction may be viewed as types of classification. When someone estimates your age or guesses the number of marbles in a jar, these are actually classification problems. Prediction can be thought of as classifying an attribute value into one of a set of possible classes. It is often viewed as forecasting a continuous value, while classification forecasts a discrete value. Example 1.1 in Chapter 1 illustrates the use of classification for credit card purchases. The use of decision trees and neural networks (NNs) to classify people according to their height was illustrated in Chapter 3. Before the use of current data mining techniques, classification was frequently performed by simply applying knowledge of the data. This is illustrated in Example 4.1.

EXAMPLE 4.1

Teachers classify students as A, B, C, D, or F based on their grades. By using simple boundaries (60, 70, 80, 90), the following classification is possible:

$$90 \leq \text{grade} \qquad \text{A}$$
$$80 \leq \text{grade} < 90 \qquad \text{B}$$
$$70 \leq \text{grade} < 80 \qquad \text{C}$$
$$60 \leq \text{grade} < 70 \qquad \text{D}$$
$$\text{grade} < 60 \qquad \text{F}$$

All approaches to performing classification assume some knowledge of the data. Often a training set is used to develop the specific parameters required by the technique. *Training data* consist of sample input data as well as the classification assignment for the data. Domain experts may also be used to assist in the process.

The classification problem is stated as shown in Definition 4.1:

> **DEFINITION 4.1.** Given a database $D = \{t_1, t_2, \ldots, t_n\}$ of tuples (items, records) and a set of classes $C = \{C_1, \ldots, C_m\}$, the **classification problem** is to define a mapping $f : D \rightarrow C$ where each t_i is assigned to one class. A **class**, C_j, contains precisely those tuples mapped to it; that is, $C_j = \{t_i \mid f(t_i) = C_j, 1 \le i \le n,$ and $t_i \in D\}$.

Our definition views classification as a mapping from the database to the set of classes. Note that the classes are predefined, are nonoverlapping, and partition the entire database. Each tuple in the database is assigned to exactly one class. The classes that exist for a classification problem are indeed *equivalence classes*. In actuality, the problem usually is implemented in two phases:

1. Create a specific model by evaluating the training data. This step has as input the training data (including defined classification for each tuple) and as output a definition of the model developed. The model created classifies the training data as accurately as possible.

2. Apply the model developed in step 1 by classifying tuples from the target database.

Although the second step actually does the classification (according to the definition in Definition 4.1), most research has been applied to step 1. Step 2 is often straightforward.

As discussed in [KLR$^+$98], there are three basic methods used to solve the classification problem:

- **Specifying boundaries.** Here classification is performed by dividing the input space of potential database tuples into regions where each region is associated with one class.

- **Using probability distributions.** For any given class, C_j, $P(t_i \mid C_j)$ is the PDF for the class evaluated at one point, t_i.[1] If a probability of occurrence for each class, $P(C_j)$ is known (perhaps determined by a domain expert), then $P(C_j)P(t_i \mid C_j)$ is used to estimate the probability that t_i is in class C_j.

- **Using posterior probabilities.** Given a data value t_i, we would like to determine the probability that t_i is in a class C_j. This is denoted by $P(C_j \mid t_i)$ and is called the *posterior probability*. One classification approach would be to determine the posterior probability for each class and then assign t_i to the class with the highest probability.

The naive divisions used in Example 4.1 as well as decision tree techniques are examples of the first modeling approach. Neural networks fall into the third category.

---

[1]In this discussion each tuple in the database is assumed to consist of a single value rather than a set of values.

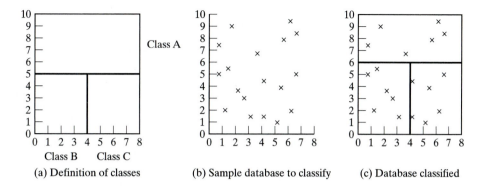

(a) Definition of classes   (b) Sample database to classify   (c) Database classified

FIGURE 4.1: Classification problem.

Suppose we are given that a database consists of tuples of the form $t = \langle x, y \rangle$ where $0 \leq x \leq 8$ and $0 \leq y \leq 10$. Figure 4.1 illustrates the classification problem. Figure 4.1(a) shows the predefined classes by dividing the reference space, Figure 4.1(b) provides sample input data, and Figure 4.1(c) shows the classification of the data based on the defined classes.

A major issue associated with classification is that of overfitting. If the classification strategy fits the training data exactly, it may not be applicable to a broader population of data. For example, suppose that the training data has erroneous or noisy data. Certainly in this case, fitting the data exactly is not desired.

In the following sections, various approaches to performing classification are examined. Table 4.1 contains data to be used throughout this chapter to illustrate the various techniques. This example assumes that the problem is to classify adults as short, medium, or tall. Table 4.1 lists height in meters. The last two columns of this table show two classifications that could be made, labeled Output1 and Output2, respectively. The Output1 classification uses the simple divisions shown below:

$$2 \text{ m} \leq \text{Height} \qquad \text{Tall}$$
$$1.7 \text{ m} < \text{Height} < 2 \text{ m} \quad \text{Medium}$$
$$\text{Height} \leq 1.7 \text{ m} \qquad \text{Short}$$

The Output2 results require a much more complicated set of divisions using both height and gender attributes.

In this chapter we examine classification algorithms based on the categorization as seen in Figure 4.2. Statistical algorithms are based directly on the use of statistical information. Distance-based algorithms use similarity or distance measures to perform the classification. Decision tree and NN approaches use these structures to perform the classification. Rule-based classification algorithms generate *if–then* rules to perform the classification.

4.1.1   Issues in Classification

Missing Data.   Missing data values cause problems during both the training phase and the classification process itself. Missing values in the training data must be handled

TABLE 4.1: Data for Height Classification

Name	Gender	Height	Output1	Output2
Kristina	F	1.6 m	Short	Medium
Jim	M	2 m	Tall	Medium
Maggie	F	1.9 m	Medium	Tall
Martha	F	1.88 m	Medium	Tall
Stephanie	F	1.7 m	Short	Medium
Bob	M	1.85 m	Medium	Medium
Kathy	F	1.6 m	Short	Medium
Dave	M	1.7 m	Short	Medium
Worth	M	2.2 m	Tall	Tall
Steven	M	2.1 m	Tall	Tall
Debbie	F	1.8 m	Medium	Medium
Todd	M	1.95 m	Medium	Medium
Kim	F	1.9 m	Medium	Tall
Amy	F	1.8 m	Medium	Medium
Wynette	F	1.75 m	Medium	Medium

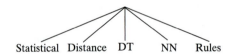

Statistical Distance DT NN Rules

FIGURE 4.2: Classification algorithm categorization.

and may produce an inaccurate result. Missing data in a tuple to be classified must be able to be handled by the resulting classification scheme. There are many approaches to handling missing data:

- Ignore the missing data.

- Assume a value for the missing data. This may be determined by using some method to predict what the value could be.

- Assume a special value for the missing data. This means that the value of missing data is taken to be a specific value all of its own.

Notice the similarity between missing data in the classification problem and that of *nulls* in traditional databases.

Measuring Performance. Table 4.1 shows two different classification results using two different classification tools. Determining which is best depends on the interpretation of the problem by users. The performance of classification algorithms is usually examined by evaluating the accuracy of the classification. However, since classification is often a fuzzy problem, the correct answer may depend on the user. Traditional algorithm evaluation approaches such as determining the space and time overhead can be used, but these approaches are usually secondary.

Classification accuracy is usually calculated by determining the percentage of tuples placed in the correct class. This ignores the fact that there also may be a cost associated with an incorrect assignment to the wrong class. This perhaps should also be determined.

We can examine the performance of classification much as is done with information retrieval systems. With only two classes, there are four possible outcomes with the classification, as is shown in Figure 4.3. The upper left and lower right quadrants [for both Figure 4.3(a) and (b)] represent correct actions. The remaining two quadrants are incorrect actions. The performance of a classification could be determined by associating costs with each of the quadrants. However, this would be difficult because the total number of costs needed is m^2, where m is the number of classes.

Given a specific class, C_j, and a database tuple, t_i, that tuple may or may not be assigned to that class while its actual membership may or may not be in that class. This again gives us the four quadrants shown in Figure 4.3(c), which can be described in the following ways:

- **True positive (TP):** t_i predicted to be in C_j and is actually in it.

- **False positive (FP):** t_i predicted to be in C_j but is not actually in it.

- **True negative (TN):** t_i not predicted to be in C_j and is not actually in it.

- **False negative (FN):** t_i not predicted to be in C_j but is actually in it.

An *OC (operating characteristic) curve* or *ROC (receiver operating characteristic) curve* or *ROC (relative operating characteristic) curve* shows the relationship between false positives and true positives. An OC curve was originally used in the communications area to examine false alarm rates. It has also been used in information retrieval to examine *fallout* (percentage of retrieved that are not relevant) versus recall (percentage of retrieved that are relevant). In the OC curve the horizontal axis has the percentage of false positives and the vertical axis has the percentage of true positives for a database sample. At the

RET REL	NOTRET REL	Assigned Class A in Class A	Assigned Class B in Class A	True positive	False negative
RET NOTREL	NOTRET NOTREL	Assigned Class A in Class B	Assigned Class B in Class B	False positive	True negative
(a) Information retrieval		(b) Classification into Class A		(c) Class prediction	

FIGURE 4.3: Comparing classification performance to information retrieval.

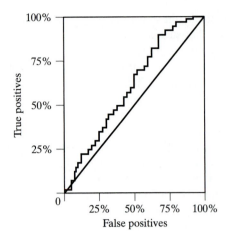

FIGURE 4.4: Operating characteristic curve.

TABLE 4.2: Confusion Matrix

Actual Membership	Assignment		
	Short	Medium	Tall
Short	0	4	0
Medium	0	5	3
Tall	0	1	2

beginning of evaluating a sample, there are none of either category, while at the end there are 100 percent of each. When evaluating the results for a specific sample, the curve looks like a jagged stair-step, as seen in Figure 4.4, as each new tuple is either a false positive or a true positive. A more smoothed version of the OC curve can also be obtained.

A confusion matrix illustrates the accuracy of the solution to a classification problem. Given m classes, a *confusion matrix* is an $m \times m$ matrix where entry $c_{i,j}$ indicates the number of tuples from D that were assigned to class C_j but where the correct class is C_i. Obviously, the best solutions will have only zero values outside the diagonal. Table 4.2 shows a confusion matrix for the height example in Table 4.1 where the Output1 assignment is assumed to be correct and the Output2 assignment is what is actually made.

4.2 STATISTICAL-BASED ALGORITHMS

4.2.1 Regression

Regression problems deal with estimation of an output value based on input values. When used for classification, the input values are values from the database D and the output values represent the classes. Regression can be used to solve classification problems, but it can also be used for other applications such as forecasting. Although not explicitly described in this text, regression can be performed using many different types of techniques, including NNs. In actuality, regression takes a set of data and fits the data to a formula.

Looking at Figure 3.3 in Chapter 3, we see that a simple *linear regression* problem can be thought of as estimating the formula for a straight line (in a two-dimensional space). This can be equated to partitioning the data into two classes. With the banking example, these would be to approve or reject a loan application. The straight line is the break-even point or the division between the two classes.

In Chapter 2, we briefly introduced linear regression using the formula

$$y = c_0 + c_1 x_1 + \cdots + c_n x_n \tag{4.1}$$

By determining the *regression coefficients* $c_0, c_1, \ldots, c_n$ the relationship between the output parameter, y, and the input parameters, $x_1, \ldots, x_n$ can be estimated. All high school algebra students are familiar with determining the formula for a straight line, $y = mx + b$, given two points in the xy plane. They are determining the regression coefficients m and b. Here the two points represent the training data.

Admittedly, Example 3.5 is an extremely simple problem. However, it illustrates how we all use the basic classification or prediction techniques frequently. Figure 4.5 illustrates the more general use of linear regression with one input value. Here there is a sample of data that we wish to model (shown by the scatter dots) using a linear model. The line generated by the linear regression technique is shown in the figure. Notice, however, that the actual data points do not fit the linear model exactly. Thus, this model is an estimate of what the actual input–output relationship is. We can use the generated linear model to predict an output value given an input value, but unlike that for Example 3.5, the prediction is an estimate rather than the actual output value. If we attempt to fit data that are not linear to a linear model, the results will be a poor model of the data, as illustrated by Figure 4.5.

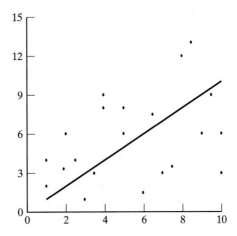

FIGURE 4.5: Example of poor fit for linear regression.

There are many reasons why the linear regression model may not be used to estimate output data. One is that the data do not fit a linear model. It is possible, however, that the data generally do actually represent a linear model, but the linear model generated is poor because noise or outliers exist in the data. *Noise* is erroneous data. *Outliers* are data values that are exceptions to the usual and expected data. Example 4.2 illustrates outliers. In these cases the observable data may actually be described by the following:

$$y = c_0 + c_1 x_1 + \cdots + c_n x_n + \epsilon \tag{4.2}$$

Here ϵ is a random error with a mean of 0. As with point estimation, we can estimate the accuracy of the fit of a linear regression model to the actual data using a mean squared error function.

EXAMPLE 4.2

Suppose that a graduate level abstract algebra class has 100 students. Kristina consistently outperforms the other students on exams. On the final exam, Kristina gets a grade of 99. The next highest grade is 75, with the range of grades being between 5 and 99. Kristina clearly is resented by the other students in the class because she does not perform at the same level they do. She "ruins the curve." If we were to try to fit a model to the grades, this one outlier grade would cause problems because any model that attempted to include it would then not accurately model the remaining data.

We illustrate the process using a simple linear regression formula and assuming k points in our training sample. We thus have the following k formulas:

$$y_i = c_0 + c_1 x_{1i} + \epsilon_i, i = 1, \ldots, k \tag{4.3}$$

With a simple linear regression, given an observable value (x_{1i}, y_i), ϵ_i is the error, and thus the squared error technique introduced in Chapter 2 can be used to indicate the error. To minimize the error, a *method of least squares* is used to minimize the least squared error. This approach finds coefficients c_0, c_1 so that the squared error is minimized for the set of observable values. The sum of the squares of the errors is

$$L = \sum_{i=1}^{k} \epsilon_i^2 = \sum_{i=1}^{k} (y_i - c_0 - c_1 x_{1i})^2 \tag{4.4}$$

Taking the partial derivatives (with respect to the coefficients) and setting equal to zero, we can obtain the *least squares estimates* for the coefficients, $\hat{c}_0$ and $\hat{c}_1$.

Regression can be used to perform classification using two different approaches:

1. **Division:** The data are divided into regions based on class.
2. **Prediction:** Formulas are generated to predict the output class value.

The first case views the data as plotted in an n-dimensional space without any explicit class values shown. Through regression, the space is divided into regions—one per class. With the second approach, a value for each class is included in the graph. Using regression, the formula for a line to predict class values is generated.

Example 4.3 illustrates the division process, while Example 4.4 illustrates the prediction process using the data from Table 4.1. For simplicity, we assume the training data include only data for short and medium people and that the classification is performed using the Output1 column values. If you extend this example to all three classes, you will see that it is a nontrivial task to use linear regression for classification. It also will become obvious that the result may be quite poor.

EXAMPLE 4.3

By looking at the data in the Output1 column from Table 4.1 and the basic understanding that the class to which a person is assigned is based only on the numeric value of his or her height, in this example we apply the linear regression concept to determine how to distinguish between the short and medium classes. Figure 4.6(a) shows the points under consideration. We thus have the linear regression formula of $y = c_0 + \epsilon$. This implies that we are actually going to be finding the value for c_0 that best partitions the height numeric values into those that are short and those that are medium. Looking at the data in Table 4.1, we see that only 12 of the 15 entries can be used to differentiate between short and medium persons. We thus obtain the following values for y_i in our training data: {1.6, 1.9, 1.88, 1.7, 1.85, 1.6, 1.7, 1.8, 1.95, 1.9, 1.8, 1.75}. We wish to minimize

$$L = \sum_{i=1}^{12} \epsilon_i^2 = \sum_{i=1}^{12} (y_i - c_0)^2$$

Taking the derivative with respect to c_0 and setting equal to zero we get

$$-2 \sum_{i=1}^{12} y_i + \sum_{i=1}^{12} 2c_0 = 0$$

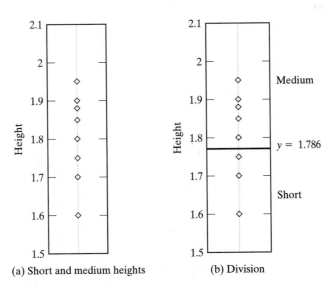

(a) Short and medium heights   (b) Division

FIGURE 4.6: Classification using division for Example 4.3.

Solving for c_0 we find that

$$c_0 = \frac{\sum_{i=1}^{12} y_i}{12} = 1.786$$

We thus have the division between short and medium persons as being determined by $y = 1.786$, as seen in Figure 4.6(b).

EXAMPLE 4.4

We now look at predicting the class using the short and medium data as input and looking at the Output1 classification. The data are the same as those in Example 4.3 except that we now look at the classes as indicated in the training data. Since regression assumes numeric data, we assume that the value for the short class is 0 and the value for the medium class is 1. Figure 4.7(a) shows the data for this example: $\{(1.6, 0), (1.9, 1), (1.88, 1), (1.7, 0), (1.85, 1), (1.6, 0), (1.7, 0), (1.8, 1), (1.95, 1), (1.9, 1), (1.8, 1), (1.75, 1)\}$. In this case we are using the regression formula with one variable:

$$y = c_0 + c_1 x_1 + \epsilon$$

We thus wish to minimize

$$L = \sum_{i=1}^{12} \epsilon_i^2 = \sum_{i=1}^{12} (y_i - c_0 - c_1 x_{1i})^2$$

Taking the partial derivative with respect to c_0 and setting equal to zero we get

$$\frac{\partial L}{\partial c_0} = -2 \sum_{i=1}^{12} y_i + \sum_{i=1}^{12} 2c_0 + \sum_{i=1}^{12} 2c_1 x_{1i} = 0$$

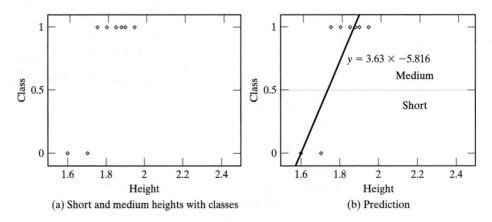

(a) Short and medium heights with classes

(b) Prediction

FIGURE 4.7: Classification using prediction for Example 4.4.

To simplify the notation, in the rest of the example we drop the range values for the summation because all are the same. Solving for c_0, we find that:

$$c_0 = \frac{\sum y_i - \sum c_1 x_{1i}}{12}$$

Now taking the partial of L with respect to c_1, substituting the value for c_0, and setting equal to zero we obtain

$$\frac{\partial L}{\partial c_1} = 2\sum (y_i - c_0 - c_1 x_{1i})(-x_{1i}) = 0$$

Solving for c_1, we finally have

$$c_1 = \frac{\sum (x_{1i} y_i) - \dfrac{\sum x_{1i} \sum y_i}{12}}{\sum (x_{1i}^2) - \dfrac{\left(\sum x_{1i}\right)^2}{12}}$$

We can now solve for c_0 and c_1. Using the data from the 12 points in the training data, we have $\sum x_{1i} = 21.43$, $\sum y_i = 8$, $\sum (x_{1i} y_i) = 14.83$, and $\sum (x_{1i}^2) = 38.42$. Thus, we get $c_1 = 3.63$ and $c_0 = -5.816$. The prediction for the class value is thus

$$y = -5.816 + 3.63 x_1$$

This line is plotted in Figure 4.7(b).

In Example 4.4 a line that predicts the class value is generated. This was done for two classes, but it also could have been done for all three classes. Unlike the division approach where class membership is obvious based on the region within which a point occurs, with prediction the class to which a point belongs is less obvious. Here we predict a class value. In Figure 4.7(b) the class value is predicted based on the height value alone. Since the prediction line is continuous, however, the class membership is not always obvious. For example, if the prediction for a value is 0.4, what would its class be? We can determine the class by splitting the line. So a height is in the short class if its prediction value is less than 0.5 and it is in the medium class if its value is greater than 0.5. In Example 4.4 the value of x_1 where $y = 0.5$ is 1.74. Thus, this is really the division between the short class and the medium class.

If the predictors in the linear regression function are modified by some function (square, square root, etc.), then the model looks like

$$y = c_0 + f_1(x_1) + \cdots + f_n(x_n) \tag{4.5}$$

where f_i is the function being used to transform the predictor. In this case the regression is called *nonlinear regression*. Linear regression techniques, while easy to understand, are not applicable to most complex data mining applications. They do not work well with nonnumeric data. They also make the assumption that the relationship between the input value and the output value is linear, which of course may not be the case.

Linear regression is not always appropriate because the data may not fit a straight line, but also because the straight line values can be greater than 1 and less than 0. Thus, they certainly cannot be used as the probability of occurrence of the target class. Another commonly used regression technique is called *logistic regression*. Instead of fitting the data to a straight line, logistic regression uses a logistic curve such as is illustrated in Figure 4.8. The formula for a univariate logistic curve is

$$p = \frac{e^{(c_0 + c_1 x_1)}}{1 + e^{(c_0 + c_1 x_1)}} \tag{4.6}$$

The logistic curve gives a value between 0 and 1 so it can be interpreted as the probability of class membership. As with linear regression, it can be used when classification into two classes is desired. To perform the regression, the logarithmic function can be applied to obtain the logistic function

$$\log_e \left(\frac{p}{1 - p} \right) = c_0 + c_1 x_1 \tag{4.7}$$

Here p is the probability of being in the class and $1 - p$ is the probability that it is not. However, the process chooses values for c_0 and c_1 that maximize the probability of observing the given values.

4.2.2 Bayesian Classification

Assuming that the contribution by all attributes are independent and that each contributes equally to the classification problem, a simple classification scheme called *naive Bayes* classification has been proposed that is based on Bayes rule of conditional probability as stated in Definition 3.1. This approach was briefly outlined in Chapter 3. By analyzing

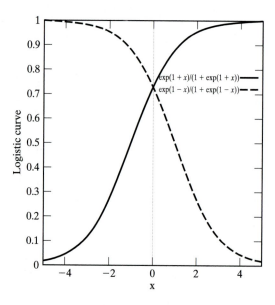

FIGURE 4.8: Logistic curve.

the contribution of each "independent" attribute, a conditional probability is determined. A classification is made by combining the impact that the different attributes have on the prediction to be made. The approach is called "naive" because it assumes the independence between the various attribute values. Given a data value x_i the probability that a related tuple, t_i, is in class C_j is described by $P(C_j \mid x_i)$. Training data can be used to determine $P(x_i)$, $P(x_i \mid C_j)$, and $P(C_j)$. From these values, Bayes theorem allows us to estimate the posterior probability $P(C_j \mid x_i)$ and then $P(C_j \mid t_i)$.

Given a training set, the naive Bayes algorithm first estimates the prior probability $P(C_j)$ for each class by counting how often each class occurs in the training data. For each attribute, x_i, the number of occurrences of each attribute value x_i can be counted to determine $P(x_i)$. Similarly, the probability $P(x_i \mid C_j)$ can be estimated by counting how often each value occurs in the class in the training data. Note that we are looking at attribute values here. A tuple in the training data may have many different attributes, each with many values. This must be done for all attributes and all values of attributes. We then use these derived probabilities when a new tuple must be classified. This is why naive Bayes classification can be viewed as both a descriptive and a predictive type of algorithm. The probabilities are descriptive and are then used to predict the class membership for a target tuple.

When classifying a target tuple, the conditional and prior probabilities generated from the training set are used to make the prediction. This is done by combining the effects of the different attribute values from the tuple. Suppose that tuple t_i has p independent attribute values $\{x_{i1}, x_{i2}, \ldots, x_{ip}\}$ From the descriptive phase, we know $P(x_{ik} \mid C_j)$, for each class C_j and attribute x_{ik}. We then estimate $P(t_i \mid C_j)$ by

$$P(t_i \mid C_j) = \prod_{k=1}^{p} P(x_{ik} \mid C_j) \tag{4.8}$$

At this point in the algorithm, we then have the needed prior probabilities $P(C_j)$ for each class and the conditional probability $P(t_i \mid C_j)$. To calculate $P(t_i)$, we can estimate the likelihood that t_i is in each class. This can be done by finding the likelihood that this tuple is in each class and then adding all these values. The probability that t_i is in a class is the product of the conditional probabilities for each attribute value. The posterior probability $P(C_j \mid t_i)$ is then found for each class. The class with the highest probability is the one chosen for the tuple. Example 4.5 illustrates the use of naive Bayes classification.

EXAMPLE 4.5

Using the Output1 classification results for Table 4.1, there are four tuples classified as short, eight as medium, and three as tall. To facilitate classification, we divide the height attribute into six ranges:

$$(0, 1.6], (1.6, 1.7], (1.7, 1.8], (1.8, 1.9], (1.9, 2.0], (2.0, \infty)$$

Table 4.3 shows the counts and subsequent probabilities associated with the attributes. With these training data, we estimate the prior probabilities:

$P(\text{short}) = 4/15 = 0.267$, $P(\text{medium}) = 8/15 = 0.533$, and $P(\text{tall}) = 3/15 = 0.2$

TABLE 4.3: Probabilities Associated with Attributes

Attribute	Value	Count			Probabilities		
		Short	Medium	Tall	Short	Medium	Tall
Gender	M	1	2	3	1/4	2/8	3/3
	F	3	6	0	3/4	6/8	0/3
Height	(0, 1.6]	2	0	0	2/4	0	0
	(1.6, 1.7]	2	0	0	2/4	0	0
	(1.7, 1.8]	0	3	0	0	3/8	0
	(1.8, 1.9]	0	4	0	0	4/8	0
	(1.9, 2]	0	1	1	0	1/8	1/3
	(2, ∞)	0	0	2	0	0	2/3

We use these values to classify a new tuple. For example, suppose we wish to classify $t = \langle$Adam $, M, 1.95$ m$\rangle$. By using these values and the associated probabilities of gender and height, we obtain the following estimates:

$$
\begin{aligned}
P(t \mid \text{short}) &= 1/4 \times 0 = 0 \\
P(t \mid \text{medium}) &= 2/8 \times 1/8 = 0.031 \\
P(t \mid \text{tall}) &= 3/3 \times 1/3 = 0.333
\end{aligned}
$$

Combining these, we get

$$
\begin{aligned}
\text{Likelihood of being short} &= 0 \times 0.267 = 0 & (4.9) \\
\text{Likelihood of being medium} &= 0.031 \times 0.533 = 0.0166 & (4.10) \\
\text{Likelihood of being tall} &= 0.33 \times 0.2 = 0.066 & (4.11)
\end{aligned}
$$

We estimate $P(t)$ by summing up these individual likelihood values since t will be either short or medium or tall:

$$
P(t) = 0 + 0.0166 + 0.066 = 0.0826 \tag{4.12}
$$

Finally, we obtain the actual probabilities of each event:

$$
\begin{aligned}
P(\text{short} \mid t) &= \frac{0 \times 0.0267}{0.0826} = 0 & (4.13) \\
P(\text{medium} \mid t) &= \frac{0.031 \times 0.533}{0.0826} = 0.2 & (4.14) \\
P(\text{tall} \mid t) &= \frac{0.333 \times 0.2}{0.0826} = 0.799 & (4.15)
\end{aligned}
$$

Therefore, based on these probabilities, we classify the new tuple as tall because it has the highest probability.

The naive Bayes approach has several advantages. First, it is easy to use. Second, unlike other classification approaches, only one scan of the training data is required. The naive Bayes approach can easily handle missing values by simply omitting that probability when calculating the likelihoods of membership in each class. In cases where there are simple relationships, the technique often does yield good results.

Although the naive Bayes approach is straightforward to use, it does not always yield satisfactory results. First, the attributes usually are not independent. We could use a subset of the attributes by ignoring any that are dependent on others. The technique does not handle continuous data. Dividing the continuous values into ranges could be used to solve this problem, but the division of the domain into ranges is not an easy task, and how this is done can certainly impact the results.

4.3 DISTANCE-BASED ALGORITHMS

Each item that is mapped to the same class may be thought of as more similar to the other items in that class than it is to the items found in other classes. Therefore, similarity (or distance) measures may be used to identify the "alikeness" of different items in the database. The concept of similarity measure was introduced in Chapter 2 with respect to IR retrieval. Certainly, the concept is well known to anyone who has performed Internet searches using a search engine. In these cases, the set of Web pages represents the whole database and these are divided into two classes: those that answer your query and those that do not. Those that answer your query should be more alike than those that do not answer your query. The similarity in this case is defined by the query you state, usually a keyword list. Thus, the retrieved pages are similar because they all contain (to some degree) the keyword list you have specified.

The idea of similarity measures can be abstracted and applied to more general classification problems. The difficulty lies in how the similarity measures are defined and applied to the items in the database. Since most similarity measures assume numeric (and often discrete) values, they might be difficult to use for more general or abstract data types. A mapping from the attribute domain to a subset of the integers may be used.

Using a similarity measure for classification where the classes are predefined is somewhat simpler than using a similarity measure for clustering where the classes are not known in advance. Again, think of the IR example. Each IR query provides the class definition in the form of the IR query itself. So the classification problem then becomes one of determining similarity not among all tuples in the database but between each tuple and the query. This makes the problem an $O(n)$ problem rather than an $O(n^2)$ problem.

4.3.1 Simple Approach

Using the IR approach, if we have a representative of each class, we can perform classification by assigning each tuple to the class to which it is most similar. We assume here that each tuple, t_i, in the database is defined as a vector $\langle t_{i1}, t_{i2}, \ldots, t_{ik} \rangle$ of numeric values. Likewise, we assume that each class C_j is defined by a tuple $\langle C_{j1}, C_{j2}, \ldots, C_{jk} \rangle$ of numeric values. The classification problem is then restated in Definition 4.2.

DEFINITION 4.2. Given a database $D = \{t_1, t_2, \ldots, t_n\}$ of tuples where each tuple $t_i = \langle t_{i1}, t_{i2}, \ldots, t_{ik} \rangle$ contains numeric values and a set of classes $C = \{C_1, \ldots, C_m\}$ where each class $C_j = \langle C_{j1}, C_{j2}, \ldots, C_{jk} \rangle$ has numeric values, the classification problem is to assign each t_i to the class C_j such that $\text{sim}(t_i, C_j) \geq \text{sim}(t_i, C_l) \forall C_l \in C$ where $C_l \neq C_j$.

To calculate these similarity measures, the representative vector for each class must be determined. Referring to the three classes in Figure 4.1(a), we can determine a representative for each class by calculating the center of each region. Thus class A is represented by $\langle 4, 7.5 \rangle$, class B by $\langle 2, 2.5 \rangle$, and class C by $\langle 6, 2.5 \rangle$. A simple classification technique, then, would be to place each item in the class where it is most similar (closest) to the center of that class. The representative for the class may be found in other ways. For example, in pattern recognition problems, a predefined pattern can be used to represent each class. Once a similarity measure is defined, each item to be classified will be compared to each predefined pattern. The item will be placed in the class with the largest similarity value. Algorithm 4.1 illustrates a straightforward distance-based approach assuming that each class, c_i, is represented by its center or centroid. In the algorithm we use c_i to be the center for its class. Since each tuple must be compared to the center for a class and there are a fixed (usually small) number of classes, the complexity to classify one tuple is $O(n)$.

ALGORITHM 4.1

Input:
```
    c₁,...,cₘ      //Centers for each class
    t       //Input tuple to classify
```
Output:
```
    c       //Class to which t is assigned
```
Simple distance-based algorithm
```
dist = ∞;
for i := 1 to m do
    if dis(cⱼ, t) < dist, then
        c = i;
        dist = dist(cⱼ, t);
```

Figure 4.9 illustrates the use of this approach to perform classification using the data found in Figure 4.1. The three large dark circles are the class representatives for the three classes. The dashed lines show the distance from each item to the closest center.

4.3.2 *K* Nearest Neighbors

One common classification scheme based on the use of distance measures is that of the *K nearest neighbors (KNN)*. The KNN technique assumes that the entire training set includes not only the data in the set but also the desired classification for each item. In effect, the training data become the model. When a classification is to be made for a new item, its distance to each item in the training set must be determined. Only the *K* closest entries in the training set are considered further. The new item is then placed in the class that contains the most items from this set of *K* closest items. Figure 4.10 illustrates

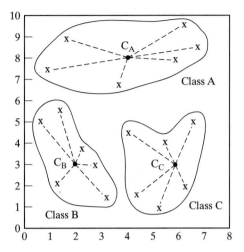

FIGURE 4.9: Classification using simple distance algorithm.

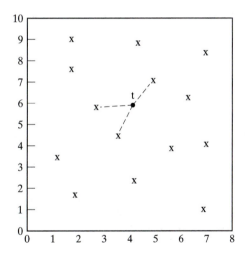

FIGURE 4.10: Classification using KNN.

the process used by KNN. Here the points in the training set are shown and $K = 3$. The three closest items in the training set are shown; t will be placed in the class to which most of these are members.

Algorithm 4.2 outlines the use of the KNN algorithm. We use T to represent the training data. Since each tuple to be classified must be compared to each element in the training data, if there are q elements in the training set, this is $O(q)$. Given n elements to be classified, this becomes an $O(nq)$ problem. Given that the training data are of a constant size (although perhaps quite large), this can then be viewed as an $O(n)$ problem.

ALGORITHM 4.2

Input:
    T //Training data
    K //Number of neighbors
    t //Input tuple to classify
Output:
    c //Class to which t is assigned
KNN algorithm:
        //Algorithm to classify tuple using KNN
    $N = \emptyset$;
            //Find set of neighbors, N, for t
    for each $d \in T$ **do**
       if $|N| \le K$, **then**
          $N = N \cup \{d\}$;
       else
          if $\exists\ u \in N$ such that $\text{sim}(t, u) \le \text{sim}(t, d)$, **then**
             begin
                $N = N - \{u\}$;
                $N = N \cup \{d\}$;
             end
             //Find class for classification
    $c = $ class to which the most $u \in N$ are classified;

Example 4.6 illustrates this technique using the sample data from Table 4.1. The KNN technique is extremely sensitive to the value of K. A rule of thumb is that $K \le \sqrt{\text{number of training items}}$ [KLR$^+$98]. For this example, that value is 3.46. Commercial algorithms often use a default value of 10.

EXAMPLE 4.6

Using the sample data from Table 4.1 and the Output1 classification as the training set output value, we classify the tuple $\langle$Pat, F, 1.6$\rangle$. Only the height is used for distance calculation so that both the Euclidean and Manhattan distance measures yield the same results; that is, the distance is simply the absolute value of the difference between the values. Suppose that $K = 5$ is given. We then have that the K nearest neighbors to the input tuple are $\{\langle$Kristina, F, 1.6$\rangle$, $\langle$Kathy, F, 1.6$\rangle$, $\langle$Stephanie, F, 1.7$\rangle$, $\langle$Dave, M, 1.7$\rangle$, $\langle$Wynette, F, 1.75$\rangle\}$. Of these five items, four are classified as short and one as medium. Thus, the KNN will classify Pat as short.

4.4 DECISION TREE–BASED ALGORITHMS

The decision tree approach is most useful in classification problems. With this technique, a tree is constructed to model the classification process. Once the tree is built, it is applied to each tuple in the database and results in a classification for that tuple. There are two basic steps in the technique: building the tree and applying the tree to the database. Most research has focused on how to build effective trees as the application process is straightforward.

The decision tree approach to classification is to divide the search space into rectangular regions. A tuple is classified based on the region into which it falls. A definition for a decision tree used in classification is contained in Definition 4.3. There are alternative definitions; for example, in a binary DT the nodes could be labeled with the predicates themselves and each arc would be labeled with yes or no (like in the "Twenty Questions" game).

DEFINITION 4.3. Given a database $D = \{t_1, \ldots, t_n\}$ where $t_i = \langle t_{i1}, \ldots, t_{ih} \rangle$ and the database schema contains the following attributes $\{A_1, A_2, \ldots, A_h\}$. Also given is a set of classes $C = \{C_1, \ldots, C_m\}$. A **decision tree (DT)** or **classification tree** is a tree associated with D that has the following properties:

- Each internal node is labeled with an attribute, A_i.

- Each arc is labeled with a predicate that can be applied to the attribute associated with the parent.

- Each leaf node is labeled with a class, C_j.

Solving the classification problem using decision trees is a two-step process:

1. **Decision tree induction:** Construct a DT using training data.
2. For each $t_i \in D$, apply the DT to determine its class.

Based on our definition of the classification problem, Definition 4.1, the constructed DT represents the logic needed to perform the mapping. Thus, it implicitly defines the mapping. Using the DT shown in Figure 3.5 from Chapter 3, the classification of the sample data found in Table 4.1 is that shown in the column labeled Output2. A different DT could yield a different classification. Since the application of a given tuple to a DT is relatively straightforward, we do not consider the second part of the problem further. Instead, we focus on algorithms to construct decision trees. Several algorithms are surveyed in the following subsections.

There are many advantages to the use of DTs for classification. DTs certainly are easy to use and efficient. Rules can be generated that are easy to interpret and understand. They scale well for large databases because the tree size is independent of the database size. Each tuple in the database must be filtered through the tree. This takes time proportional to the height of the tree, which is fixed. Trees can be constructed for data with many attributes.

Disadvantages also exist for DT algorithms. First, they do not easily handle continuous data. These attribute domains must be divided into categories to be handled. The approach used is that the domain space is divided into rectangular regions [such as is seen in Figure 4.1(a)]. Not all classification problems are of this type. The division shown by the simple loan classification problem in Figure 2.4(a) in Chapter 2 cannot be handled by DTs. Handling missing data is difficult because correct branches in the tree could not be taken. Since the DT is constructed from the training data, overfitting may occur. This can be overcome via tree pruning. Finally, correlations among attributes in the database are ignored by the DT process.

ALGORITHM 4.3

```
Input:
    D      //Training data
Output:
    T      //Decision tree
DTBuild algorithm:
        //Simplistic algorithm to illustrate naive approach
            to building DT
    T = ∅;
    Determine best splitting criterion;
    T = Create root node node and label with splitting attribute;
    T = Add arc to root node for each split predicate and label;
    for each arc do
        D = Database created by applying splitting predicate to D;
        if stopping point reached for this path, then
            T' = Create leaf node and label with appropriate class;
        else
            T' = DTBuild(D);
        T = Add T' to arc;
```

There have been many decision tree algorithms. We illustrate the tree-building phase in the simplistic DTBuild Algorithm 4.3. Attributes in the database schema that will be used to label nodes in the tree and around which the divisions will take place are called the *splitting attributes*. The predicates by which the arcs in the tree are labeled are called the *splitting predicates*. In the decision trees shown in Figure 4.11, the splitting attributes are {gender, height}. The splitting predicates for gender are {= female, = male}, while those for height include {<1.3 m, >1.8 m, <1.5 m, >2 m}. The splitting predicates for height differ based on whether the tuple is for a male or a female. This recursive algorithm builds the tree in a top-down fashion by examining the training data. Using the initial training data, the "best" splitting attribute is chosen first. Algorithms differ in how they determine the "best attribute" and its "best predicates" to use for splitting. Once this has been determined, the node and its arcs are created and added to the created tree. The algorithm continues recursively by adding new subtrees to each branching arc. The algorithm terminates when some "stopping criteria" is reached. Again, each algorithm determines when to stop the tree differently. One simple approach would be to stop when the tuples in the reduced training set all belong to the same class. This class is then used to label the leaf node created.

Note that the major factors in the performance of the DT building algorithm are the size of the training set and how the best splitting attribute is chosen. The following issues are faced by most DT algorithms:

- **Choosing splitting attributes:** Which attributes to use for splitting attributes impacts the performance applying the built DT. Some attributes are better than others. In the data shown in Table 4.1, the name attribute definitely should not be used and the gender may or may not be used. The choice of attribute involves not only an examination of the data in the training set but also the informed input of domain experts.

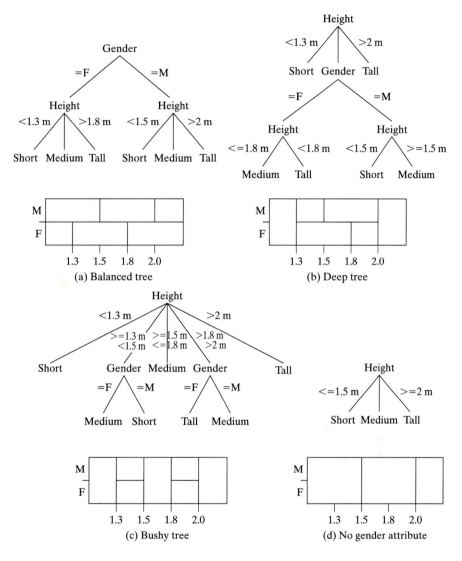

FIGURE 4.11: Comparing decision trees.

- **Ordering of splitting attributes:** The order in which the attributes are chosen is also important. In Figure 4.11(a) the gender attribute is chosen first. Alternatively, the height attribute could be chosen first. As seen in Figure 4.11(b), in this case the height attribute must be examined a second time, requiring unnecessary comparisons.

- **Splits:** Associated with the ordering of the attributes is the number of splits to take. With some attributes, the domain is small, so the number of splits is obvious based on the domain (as with the gender attribute). However, if the domain is continuous or has a large number of values, the number of splits to use is not easily determined.

- **Tree structure:** To improve the performance of applying the tree for classification, a balanced tree with the fewest levels is desirable. However, in this case, more complicated comparisons with multiway branching [see Figure 4.11(c)] may be needed. Some algorithms build only binary trees.

- **Stopping criteria:** The creation of the tree definitely stops when the training data are perfectly classified. There may be situations when stopping earlier would be desirable to prevent the creation of larger trees. This is a trade-off between accuracy of classification and performance. In addition, stopping earlier may be performed to prevent overfitting. It is even conceivable that more levels than needed would be created in a tree if it is known that there are data distributions not represented in the training data.

- **Training data:** The structure of the DT created depends on the training data. If the training data set is too small, then the generated tree might not be specific enough to work properly with the more general data. If the training data set is too large, then the created tree may overfit.

- **Pruning:** Once a tree is constructed, some modifications to the tree might be needed to improve the performance of the tree during the classification phase. The pruning phase might remove redundant comparisons or remove subtrees to achieve better performance.

To illustrate some of these design decisions, Figure 4.11 shows four different decision trees that can be used to classify persons according to height. The first tree is a duplicate of that from Chapter 3. The first three trees of this figure all perform the same classification. However, they all perform it differently. Underneath each tree is a table showing the logical divisions used by the associated tree for classification. A nice feature of Figure 4.11(a) is that it is balanced. The tree is of the same depth for any path from root to leaf. Figures 4.11(b) and (c), however, are not balanced. In addition, the height of the tree in (b) is greater than that of any of the others, implying a slightly worse behavior when used for classification. However, all of these factors impact the time required to do the actual classification. These may not be crucial performance issues unless the database is extremely large. In that case a balanced shorter tree would be desirable. The tree shown in Figure 4.11(d) does not represent the same classification logic as the others.

The training data and the tree induction algorithm determine the tree shape. Thus, the best-shaped tree that performs perfectly on the training set is desirable. Some algorithms create only binary trees. Binary trees are easily created, but they tend to be deeper. The performance results when applying these types of trees for classification may be worse because more comparisons usually are needed. However, since these comparisons are simpler than those that require multiway branches, the ultimate performance may be comparable.

The DT building algorithms may initially build the tree and then prune it for more effective classification. With pruning techniques, portions of the tree may be removed or combined to reduce the overall size of the tree. Portions of the tree relating to classification using an unimportant attribute may be removed. This sort of change with a node close to the root could ripple down to create major changes in the lower parts of the tree. For example, with the data in Figure 4.1, if a tree were constructed by looking at values of the name attribute, all nodes labeled with that attribute would be removed. Lower-level nodes would move up or be combined in some way. The approach to doing this could become quite complicated. In the case of overfitting, lower-level subtrees may be removed completely. Pruning may be performed while the tree is being created, thus preventing a tree from becoming too large. A second approach prunes the tree after it is built.

The time and space complexity of DT algorithms depends on the size of the training data, q; the number of attributes, h; and the shape of the resulting tree. In the worst case, the DT that is built may be quite deep and not bushy. As the tree is built, for each of these nodes, each attribute will be examined to determine if it is the best. This gives a time complexity to build the tree of $O(h\,q\log q)$. The time to classify a database of size n is based on the height of the tree. Assuming a height of $O(\log q)$, this is then $O(n\log q)$.

In the following subsections we examine several popular DT approaches.

4.4.1   ID3

The ID3 technique to building a decision tree is based on information theory and attempts to minimize the expected number of comparisons. The basic idea of the induction algorithm is to ask questions whose answers provide the most information. This is similar to the intuitive approach taken by adults when playing the "Twenty Questions" game. The first question an adult might ask could be "Is the thing alive?" while a child might ask "Is it my Daddy?" The first question divides the search space into two large search domains, while the second performs little division of the space. The basic strategy used by ID3 is to choose splitting attributes with the highest information gain first. The amount of information associated with an attribute value is related to the probability of occurrence. Looking at the "Twenty Questions" example, the child's question divides the search space into two sets. One set (Daddy) has an infinitesimal probability associated with it and the other set is almost certain, while the question the adult makes divides the search space into two subsets with almost equal probability of occurring.

The concept used to quantify information is called entropy. Entropy is used to measure the amount of uncertainty or surprise or randomness in a set of data. Certainly, when all data in a set belong to a single class, there is no uncertainty. In this case the entropy is zero. The objective of decision tree classification is to iteratively partition the given data set into subsets where all elements in each final subset belong to the same class. In Figure 4.12(a, b, and c) will help to explain the concept. Figure 4.12(a) shows $\log(1/p)$ as the probability p ranges from 0 to 1. This intuitively shows the amount of surprise based on the probability. When $p = 1$, there is no surprise. This means that if an event has a probability of 1 and you are told that the event occurred, you would not be surprised. As $p \to 0$, the surprise increases. When we deal with a divide and conquer approach such as that used with decision trees, the division results in multiple probabilities whose sum is 1. In the "Twenty Questions" game, the $P(\text{Daddy}) < P(\neg\text{Daddy})$ and $P(\text{Daddy}) + P(\neg\text{Daddy}) = 1$. To measure the information associated with this division, we must be able to combine the information associated with both events. That is, we must be able to calculate the average information associated with the division. This can be performed by adding the two values together and taking into account the probability that each occurs. Figure 4.12(b) shows the function $p\log(1/p)$,

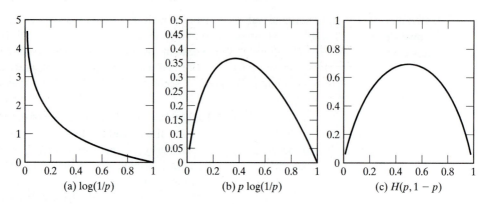

FIGURE 4.12: Entropy.

which is the expected information based on probability of an event. To determine the expected information associated with two events, we add the individual values together. This function $p \log(1/p) + (1 - p) \log(1/(1 - p))$ is plotted in Figure 4.12(c). Note that the maximum occurs when the two probabilities are equal. This supports our intuitive idea that the more sophisticated questions posed by the adult are better than those posed by the child.

The formal definition of entropy is shown in Definition 4.4. The value for entropy is between 0 and 1 and reaches a maximum when the probabilities are all the same.

DEFINITION 4.4. Given probabilities $p_1, p_2, \ldots, p_s$ where $\sum_{i=1}^{s} p_i = 1$, **entropy** is defined as

$$H(p_1, p_2, \ldots, p_s) = \sum_{i=1}^{s} (p_i \log(1/p_i)) \tag{4.16}$$

Given a database state, D, $H(D)$ finds the amount of order (or lack thereof) in that state. When that state is split into s new states $S = \{D_1, D_2, \ldots, D_s\}$, we can again look at the entropy of those states. Each step in ID3 chooses the state that orders splitting the most. A database state is completely ordered if all tuples in it are in the same class. ID3 chooses the splitting attribute with the highest gain in information, where gain is defined as the difference between how much information is needed to make a correct classification before the split versus how much information is needed after the split. Certainly, the split should reduce the information needed by the largest amount. This is calculated by determining the differences between the entropies of the original dataset and the weighted sum of the entropies from each of the subdivided datasets. The entropies of the split datasets are weighted by the fraction of the dataset being placed in that division. The ID3 algorithm calculates the *gain* of a particular split by the following formula:

$$\text{Gain}(D, S) = H(D) - \sum_{i=1}^{s} P(D_i) H(D_i) \tag{4.17}$$

Example 4.7 and associated Figure 4.13 illustrate this process using the height example. In this example, six divisions of the possible ranges of heights are used. This

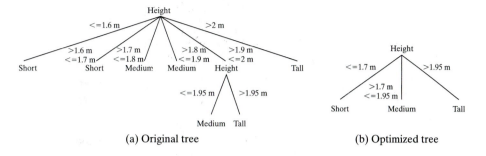

(a) Original tree (b) Optimized tree

FIGURE 4.13: Classification problem.

division into ranges is needed when the domain of an attribute is continuous or (as in this case) consists of many possible values. While the choice of these divisions is somewhat arbitrary, a domain expert should be able to perform the task.

EXAMPLE 4.7

The beginning state of the training data in Table 4.1 (with the Output1 classification) is that $(4/15)$ are short, $(8/15)$ are medium, and $(3/15)$ are tall. Thus, the entropy of the starting set is

$$4/15 \, \log(15/4) + 8/15 \, \log(15/8) + 3/15 \, \log(15/3) = 0.4384$$

Choosing the gender as the splitting attribute, there are nine tuples that are F and six that are M. The entropy of the subset that are F is

$$3/9 \, \log(9/3) + 6/9 \, \log(9/6) = 0.2764 \tag{4.18}$$

whereas that for the M subset is

$$1/6 \, \log(6/1) + 2/6 \, \log(6/2) + 3/6 \, \log(6/3) = 0.4392 \tag{4.19}$$

The ID3 algorithm must determine what the gain in information is by using this split. To do this, we calculate the weighted sum of these last two entropies to get

$$((9/15) \, 0.2764) + ((6/15) \, 0.4392) = 0.34152 \tag{4.20}$$

The gain in entropy by using the gender attribute is thus

$$0.4384 - 0.34152 = 0.09688 \tag{4.21}$$

Looking at the height attribute, we have two tuples that are 1.6, two are 1.7, one is 1.75, two are 1.8, one is 1.85, one is 1.88, two are 1.9, one is 1.95, one is 2, one is 2.1, and one is 2.2. Determining the split values for height is not easy. Even though the training dataset has these 11 values, we know that there will be many more. Just as with continuous data, we divide into ranges:

$$(0, 1.6], (1.6, 1.7], (1.7, 1.8], (1.8, 1.9], (1.9, 2.0], (2.0, \infty)$$

There are 2 tuples in the first division with entropy $(2/2(0) + 0 + 0) = 0$, 2 in $(1.6, 1.7]$ with entropy $(2/2(0) + 0 + 0) = 0$, 3 in $(1.7, 1.8]$ with entropy $(0 + 3/3(0) + 0) = 0$, 4 in $(1.8, 1.9]$ with entropy $(0 + 4/4(0) + 0) = 0$, 2 in $(1.9, 2.0]$ with entropy $(0 + 1/2(0.301) + 1/2(0.301)) = 0.301$, and two in the last with entropy $(0 + 0 + 2/2(0)) = 0$. All of these states are completely ordered and thus an entropy of 0 except for the $(1.9, 2.0]$ state. The gain in entropy by using the height attribute is thus

$$0.4384 - 2/15(0.301) = 0.3983 \tag{4.22}$$

Thus, this has the greater gain, and we choose this over gender as the first splitting attribute. Within this division there are two males, one medium and one tall. This has occurred because this grouping was too large. A further subdivision on height is needed, and this generates the DT seen in Figure 4.13(a).

Figure 4.13(a) illustrates a problem in that the tree has multiple splits with identical results. In addition, there is a subdivision of range $(1.9, 2.0]$. Figure 4.13(b) shows an optimized version of the tree.

4.4.2 C4.5 and C5.0

The decision tree algorithm C4.5 improves ID3 in the following ways:

- **Missing data:** When the decision tree is built, missing data are simply ignored. That is, the gain ratio is calculated by looking only at the other records that have a value for that attribute. To classify a record with a missing attribute value, the value for that item can be predicted based on what is known about the attribute values for the other records.

- **Continuous data:** The basic idea is to divide the data into ranges based on the attribute values for that item that are found in the training sample.

- **Pruning:** There are two primary pruning strategies proposed in C4.5:

  - With *subtree replacement*, a subtree is replaced by a leaf node if this replacement results in an error rate close to that of the original tree. Subtree replacement works from the bottom of the tree up to the root.

  - Another pruning strategy, called *subtree raising*, replaces a subtree by its most used subtree. Here a subtree is raised from its current location to a node higher up in the tree. Again, we must determine the increase in error rate for this replacement.

- **Rules:** C4.5 allows classification via either decision trees or rules generated from them. In addition, some techniques to simplify complex rules are proposed. One approach is to replace the left-hand side of a rule by a simpler version if all records in the training set are treated identically. An "otherwise" type of rule can be used to indicate what should be done if no other rules apply.

- **Splitting:** The ID3 approach favors attributes with many divisions and thus may lead to overfitting. In the extreme, an attribute that has a unique value for each tuple in the training set would be the best because there would be only one tuple (and thus one class) for each division. An improvement can be made by taking into account the cardinality of each division. This approach uses the GainRatio as opposed to Gain. The GainRatio is defined as

$$\text{GainRatio}(D, S) = \frac{\text{Gain}(D, S)}{H\left(\dfrac{\mid D_1 \mid}{\mid D \mid}, \dots, \dfrac{\mid D_s \mid}{\mid D \mid}\right)} \tag{4.23}$$

For splitting purposes, C4.5 uses the largest GainRatio that ensures a larger than average information gain. This is to compensate for the fact that the GainRatio value is skewed toward splits where the size of one subset is close to that of the starting one. Example 4.8 shows the calculation of GainRatio for the first split in Example 4.7.

EXAMPLE 4.8

To calculate the GainRatio for the gender split, we first find the entropy associated with the split ignoring classes

$$H\left(\frac{9}{15}, \frac{6}{15}\right) = \frac{9}{15}\log\left(\frac{15}{9}\right) + \frac{6}{15}\log\left(\frac{15}{6}\right) = 0.292 \tag{4.24}$$

This gives the GainRatio value for the gender attribute as

$$\frac{0.09688}{0.292} = 0.332 \tag{4.25}$$

The entropy for the split on height (ignoring classes) is

$$H\left(\frac{2}{15}, \frac{2}{15}, \frac{3}{15}, \frac{4}{15}, \frac{2}{15}\right) \tag{4.26}$$

C5.0 (called See 5 on Windows) is a commercial version of C4.5 now widely used in many data mining packages such as Clementine and RuleQuest. It is targeted toward use with large datasets. The DT induction is close to that of C4.5, but the rule generation is different. Unlike C4.5, the precise algorithms used for C5.0 have not been divulged. C5.0 does include improvements to generate rules. Results show that C5.0 improves on memory usage by about 90 percent, runs between 5.7 and 240 times faster than C4.5, and produces more accurate rules [Res01].

One major improvement to the accuracy of C5.0 is based on boosting. *Boosting* is an approach to combining different classifiers. While boosting normally increases the time that it takes to run a specific classifier, it does improve the accuracy. The error rate has been shown to be less than half of that found with C4.5 on some datasets [Res01]. Boosting does not always help when the training data contains a lot of noise. Boosting works by creating multiple training sets from one training set. Each item in the training set is assigned a weight. The weight indicates the importance of this item to the classification. A classifier is constructed for each combination of weights used. Thus, multiple classifiers are actually constructed. When C5.0 performs a classification, each classifier is assigned a vote, voting is performed, and the target tuple is assigned to the class with the most number of votes.

4.4.3 CART

Classification and regression trees (CART) is a technique that generates a binary decision tree. As with ID3, entropy is used as a measure to choose the best splitting attribute and criterion. Unlike ID3, however, where a child is created for each subcategory, only two children are created. The splitting is performed around what is determined to be the best split point. At each step, an exhaustive search is used to determine the best split, where "best" is defined by

$$\Phi(s/t) = 2P_L P_R \sum_{j=1}^{m} \mid P(C_j \mid t_L) - P(C_j \mid t_R) \mid \qquad (4.27)$$

This formula is evaluated at the current node, t, and for each possible splitting attribute and criterion, s. Here L and R are used to indicate the left and right subtrees of the current node in the tree. P_L, P_R are the probability that a tuple in the training set will be on the left or right side of the tree. This is defined as $\frac{|\text{tuples in subtree}|}{|\text{tuples in training set}|}$. We assume that the right branch is taken on equality. $P(C_j \mid t_L)$ or $P(C_j \mid t_R)$ is the probability that a tuple is in this class, C_j, and in the left or right subtree. This is defined as the $\frac{|\text{tuples of class } j \text{ in subtree}|}{|\text{tuples at the target node}|}$. At each step, only one criterion is chosen as the best over all possible criteria. Example 4.9 shows its use with the height example with Output1 results.

EXAMPLE 4.9

The first step is to determine the split attribute and criterion for the first split. We again assume that there are six subranges to consider with the height attribute. Using these ranges, we have the potential split values of 1.6, 1.7, 1.8, 1.9, 2.0. We thus have a choice of six split points, which yield the following goodness measures:

$$\Phi(\text{Gender}) = 2(6/15)(9/15)(2/15 + 4/15 + 3/15) = 0.224 \qquad (4.28)$$
$$\Phi(1.6) = 0 \qquad (4.29)$$
$$\Phi(1.7) = 2(2/15)(13/15)(0 + 8/15 + 3/15) = 0.169 \qquad (4.30)$$
$$\Phi(1.8) = 2(5/15)(10/15)(4/15 + 6/15 + 3/15) = 0.385 \qquad (4.31)$$
$$\Phi(1.9) = 2(9/15)(6/15)(4/15 + 2/15 + 3/15) = 0.256 \qquad (4.32)$$
$$\Phi(2.0) = 2(12/15)(3/15)(4/15 + 8/15 + 3/15) = 0.32 \qquad (4.33)$$

The largest of these is the split at 1.8. The remainder of this example is left as an exercise.

Since gender is really unordered, we assume $M < F$.

As illustrated with the gender attribute, CART forces that an ordering of the attributes be used. CART handles missing data by simply ignoring that record in calculating the goodness of a split on that attribute. The tree stops growing when no split will improve the performance. Note that even though it is the best for the training data, it may not be the best for all possible data to be added in the future. The CART algorithm also contains a pruning strategy, which we will not discuss here but which can be found in [KLR$^+$98].

4.4.4 Scalable DT Techniques

We briefly examine some DT techniques that address creation of DTs for large datasets.

The SPRINT (*Scalable PaRallelizable INduction of decision Trees*) algorithm addresses the scalability issue by ensuring that the CART technique can be applied regardless of availability of main memory. In addition, it can be easily parallelized. With SPRINT, a gini index is used to find the best split. Here *gini* for a database D is defined as

$$\text{gini}(D) = 1 - \sum p_j^2 \tag{4.34}$$

where p_j is the frequency of class C_j in D. The goodness of a split of D into subsets D_1 and D_2 is defined by

$$\text{gini}_{\text{split}}(D) = \frac{n_1}{n}(\text{gini}(D_1)) + \frac{n_2}{n}(\text{gini}(D_2)) \tag{4.35}$$

The split with the best gini value is chosen. Unlike the earlier approaches, SPRINT does not need to sort the data by goodness value at each node during the DT induction process. With continuous data, the split point is chosen to be the midpoint of every pair of consecutive values from the training set.

By maintaining aggregate metadata concerning database attributes, the *RainForest* approach allows a choice of split attribute without needing a training set. For each node of a DT, a table called the *attribute-value class (AVC) label group* is used. The table summarizes for an attribute the count of entries per class or attribute value grouping. Thus, the AVC table summarizes the information needed to determine splitting attributes. The size of the table is not proportional to the size of the database or training set, but rather to the product of the number of classes, unique attribute values, and potential splitting attributes. This reduction in size (for large training sets) facilitates the scaling of DT induction algorithms to extremely large training sets. During the tree-building phase, the training data are scanned, the AVC is built, and the best splitting attribute is chosen. The algorithm continues by splitting the training data and constructing the AVC for the next node.

4.5 NEURAL NETWORK–BASED ALGORITHMS

With neural networks (NNs), just as with decision trees, a model representing how to classify any given database tuple is constructed. The activation functions typically are sigmoidal. When a tuple must be classified, certain attribute values from that tuple are input into the directed graph at the corresponding source nodes. There often is one sink node for each class. The output value that is generated indicates the probability that the corresponding input tuple belongs to that class. The tuple will then be assigned to the class with the highest probability of membership. The learning process modifies the labeling of the arcs to better classify tuples. Given a starting structure and value for all the labels in the graph, as each tuple in the training set is sent through the network, the projected classification made by the graph can be compared with the actual classification. Based on the accuracy of the prediction, various labelings in the graph can change. This learning process continues with all the training data or until the classification accuracy is adequate.

Solving a classification problem using NNs involves several steps:

1. Determine the number of output nodes as well as what attributes should be used as input. The number of hidden layers (between the source and the sink nodes) also must be decided. This step is performed by a domain expert.

2. Determine weights (labels) and functions to be used for the graph.

3. For each tuple in the training set, propagate it through the network and evaluate the output prediction to the actual result. If the prediction is accurate, adjust labels to ensure that this prediction has a higher output weight the next time. If the prediction is not correct, adjust the weights to provide a lower output value for this class.

4. For each tuple $t_i \in D$, propagate t_i through the network and make the appropriate classification.

There are many issues to be examined:

- **Attributes (number of source nodes):** This is the same issue as determining which attributes to use as splitting attributes.

- **Number of hidden layers:** In the simplest case, there is only one hidden layer.

- **Number of hidden nodes:** Choosing the best number of hidden nodes per hidden layer is one of the most difficult problems when using NNs. There have been many empirical and theoretical studies attempting to answer this question. The answer depends on the structure of the NN, types of activation functions, training algorithm, and problem being solved. If too few hidden nodes are used, the target function may not be learned (underfitting). If too many nodes are used, overfitting may occur. Rules of thumb are often given that are based on the size of the training set.

- **Training data:** As with DTs, with too much training data the NN may suffer from overfitting, while too little and it may not be able to classify accurately enough.

- **Number of sinks:** Although it is usually assumed that the number of output nodes is the same as the number of classes, this is not always the case. For example, with two classes there could only be one output node, with the resulting value being the probability of being in the associated class. Subtracting this value from one would give the probability of being in the second class.

- **Interconnections:** In the simplest case, each node is connected to all nodes in the next level.

- **Weights:** The weight assigned to an arc indicates the relative weight between those two nodes. Initial weights are usually assumed to be small positive numbers and are assigned randomly.

- **Activation functions:** Many different types of activation functions can be used.

- **Learning technique:** The technique for adjusting the weights is called the learning technique. Although many approaches can be used, the most common approach is some form of backpropagation, which is discussed in a subsequent subsection.

- **Stop:** The learning may stop when all the training tuples have propagated through the network or may be based on time or error rate.

There are many advantages to the use of NNs for classification:

- NNs are more robust than DTs because of the weights.

- The NN improves its performance by learning. This may continue even after the training set has been applied.

- The use of NNs can be parallelized for better performance.

- There is a low error rate and thus a high degree of accuracy once the appropriate training has been performed.

- NNs are more robust than DTs in noisy environments.

Conversely, NNs have many disadvantages:

- NNs are difficult to understand. Nontechnical users may have difficulty understanding how NNs work. While it is easy to explain decision trees, NNs are much more difficult to understand.

- Generating rules from NNs is not straightforward.

- Input attribute values must be numeric.

- Testing

- Verification

- As with DTs, overfitting may result.

- The learning phase may fail to converge.

- NNs may be quite expensive to use.

4.5.1 Propagation

The normal approach used for processing is called *propagation*. Given a tuple of values input to the NN, $X = \langle x_1, \ldots, x_h \rangle$, one value is input at each node in the input layer. Then the summation and activation functions are applied at each node, with an output value created for each output arc from that node. These values are in turn sent to the subsequent nodes. This process continues until a tuple of output values, $Y = \langle y_1, \ldots, y_m \rangle$, is produced from the nodes in the output layer. The process of propagation is shown in Algorithm 4.4 using a neural network with one hidden layer. Here a hyperbolic tangent activation function is used for the nodes in the hidden layer, while a sigmoid function is used for nodes in the output layer. We assume that the constant c in the activation function has been provided. We also use k to be the number of edges coming into a node.

ALGORITHM 4.4

```
Input:
    N                      //neural network
    X = ⟨x₁,...,xₕ⟩         //Input tuple consisting of values for
                              input attributes only
Output:
    Y = ⟨y₁,...,yₘ⟩         //Tuple consisting of output values from NN
Propagation algorithm:
            //Algorithm illustrates propagation of a tuple
                through a NN
    for each node i in the input layer do
        Output xᵢ on each output arc from i;
    for each hidden layer do
        for each node i do
```
$$S_i = \left(\sum_{j=1}^{k}(w_{ji}x_{ji})\right);$$
```
        for each output arc from i do
```
$$\text{Output } \frac{(1-e^{-S_i})}{(1+e^{-cS_i})};$$
```
    for each node i in the output layer do
```
$$S_i = \left(\sum_{j=1}^{k}(w_{ji}x_{ji})\right);$$
$$\text{Output } y_i = \frac{1}{(1+e^{-c\,S_i})};$$

A simple application of propagation is shown in Example 4.10 for the height data. Here the classification performed is the same as that seen with the decision tree in Figure 4.11(d).

EXAMPLE 4.10

Figure 4.14 shows a very simple NN used to classify university students as short, medium, or tall. There are two input nodes, one for the gender data and one for the height data. There are three output nodes, each associated with one class and using a simple threshold activation function. Activation function f_3 is associated with the short class, f_4 is associated with the medium class, and f_5 is associated with the tall class. In this case, the weights of each arc from the height node is 1. The weights on the gender arcs is 0. This implies that in this case the gender values are ignored. The plots for the graphs of the three activation functions are shown.

4.5.2 NN Supervised Learning

The NN starting state is modified based on feedback of its performance with the data in the training set. This type of learning is referred to as *supervised* because it is known a priori what the desired output should be. *Unsupervised* learning can also be performed if the output is not known. With unsupervised approaches, no external teacher set is used. A training set may be provided, but no labeling of the desired outcome is included. In this case, similarities and differences between different tuples in the training set are uncovered. In this chapter, we examine supervised learning. We briefly explore unsupervised learning in Chapter 5.

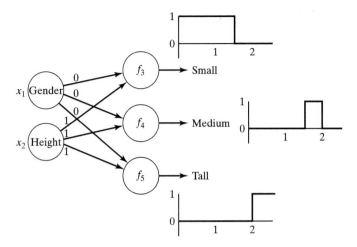

FIGURE 4.14: Example propagation for tall data.

Supervised learning in an NN is the process of adjusting the arc weights based on its performance with a tuple from the training set. The behavior of the training data is known a priori and thus can be used to fine-tune the network for better behavior in future similar situations. Thus, the training set can be used as a "teacher" during the training process. The output from the network is compared to this known desired behavior. Algorithm 4.5 outlines the steps required. One potential problem with supervised learning is that the error may not be continually reduced. It would, of course, be hoped that each iteration in the learning process reduces the error so that it is ultimately below an acceptable level. However, this is not always the case. This may be due to the error calculation technique or to the approach used for modifying the weights. This is actually the general problem of NNs. They do not guarantee convergence or optimality.

ALGORITHM 4.5

```
Input:
    N      //Starting neural network
    X      //Input tuple from training set
    D      //Output tuple desired
Output:
    N      //Improved neural network
SupLearn algorithm:
            //Simplistic algorithm to illustrate approach
               to NN learning
    Propagate X through N producing output Y;
    Calculate error by comparing D to Y;
    Update weights on arcs in N to reduce error;
```

Notice that this algorithm must be associated with a means to calculate the error as well as some technique to adjust the weights. Many techniques have been proposed to calculate the error. Assuming that the output from node i is y_i but should be d_i, the error produced from a node in any layer can be found by

$$| y_i - d_i |$$ (4.36)

The *mean squared error (MSE)* is found by

$$\frac{(y_i - d_i)^2}{2}$$ (4.37)

This MSE can then be used to find a total error over all nodes in the network or over only the output nodes. In the following discussion, the assumption is made that only the final output of the NN is known for a tuple in the training data. Thus, the *total MSE* error over all *m* output nodes in the NN is

$$\sum_{i=1}^{m} \frac{(y_i - d_i)^2}{m}$$ (4.38)

This formula could be expanded over all tuples in the training set to see the total error over all of them. Thus, an error can be calculated for a specific test tuple or for the total set of all entries.

The Hebb and delta rules are approaches to change the weight on an input arc to a node based on the knowledge that the output value from that node is incorrect. With both techniques, a *learning rule* is used to modify the input weights. Suppose for a given node, j, the input weights are represented as a tuple $\langle w_{1j}, \ldots, w_{kj} \rangle$, while the input and output values are $\langle x_{1j}, \ldots, x_{kj} \rangle$ and y_j, respectively. The objective of a learning technique is to change the weights based on the output obtained for a specific input tuple. The change in weights using the *Hebb rule* is represented by the following rule

$$\Delta w_{ij} = c x_{ij} y_j$$ (4.39)

Here c is a constant often called the *learning rate*. A rule of thumb is that $c = \frac{1}{|\text{\# entries in training set}|}$.

A variation of this approach, called the *delta rule*, examines not only the output value y_j but also the desired value d_j for output. In this case the change in weight is found by the rule

$$\Delta w_{ij} = c x_{ij} (d_j - y_j)$$ (4.40)

The nice feature of the delta rule is that it minimizes the error $d_j - y_j$ at each node.

Backpropagation is a learning technique that adjusts weights in the NN by propagating weight changes backward from the sink to the source nodes. Backpropagation is the most well known form of learning because it is easy to understand and generally applicable. Backpropagation can be thought of as a generalized delta rule approach.

Figure 4.15 shows the structure and use of one node, j, in a neural network graph. The basic node structure is shown in part (a). Here the representative input arc has a weight of $w_{?j}$, where ? is used to show that the input to node j is coming from another node shown here as ?. Of course, there probably are multiple input arcs to a node. The output weight is similarly labeled $w_{j?}$. During *propagation*, data values input at the input layer flow through the network, with final values coming out of the network at the output layer. The propagation technique is shown in part (b) Figure 4.15.

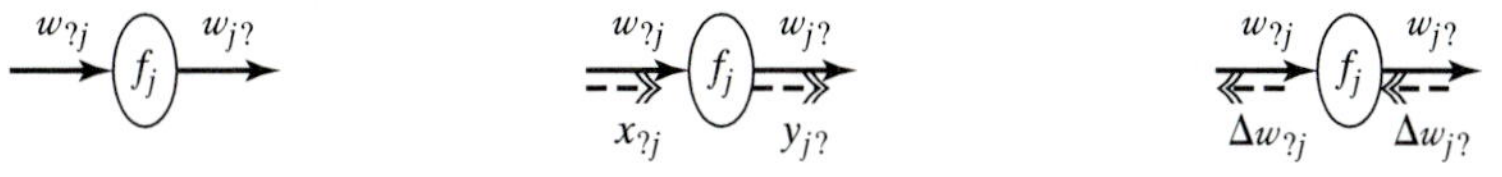

(a) Node j in NN   (b) Propagation at Node j   (c) Back-propagation at Node j

FIGURE 4.15: Neural network usage.

Here the smaller dashed arrow underneath the regular graph arc shows the input value $x_{?j}$ flowing into node j. The activation function f_j is applied to all the input values and weights, with output values resulting. There is an associated input function that is applied to the input values and weights before applying the activation function. This input function is typically a weighted sum of the input values. Here $y_{j?}$ shows the output value flowing (propagating) to the next node from node j. Thus, propagation occurs by applying the activation function at each node, which then places the output value on the arc to be sent as input to the next nodes. In most cases, the activation function produces only one output value that is propagated to the set of connected nodes. The NN can be used for classification and/or learning. During the classification process, only propagation occurs. However, when learning is used after the output of the classification occurs, a comparison to the known classification is used to determine how to change the weights in the graph. In the simplest types of learning, learning progresses from the output layer backward to the input layer. Weights are changed based on the changes that were made in weights in subsequent arcs. This backward learning process is called backpropagation and is illustrated in Figure 4.15(c). Weight $w_{j?}$ is modified to become $w_{j?} + \triangle w_{j?}$. A learning rule is applied to this $\triangle w_{j?}$ to determine the change at the next higher level $\triangle w_{?j}$.

ALGORITHM 4.6

Input:
    N //Starting neural network
    $X = \langle x_1, \ldots, x_h \rangle$ //Input tuple from training set
    $D = \langle d_1, \ldots, d_m \rangle$ //Output tuple desired
Output:
N //Improved neural network
Backpropagation algorithm:
                        //Illustrate backpropagation
    Propagation(N, X);
    $E = 1/2 \sum_{i=1}^{m} (d_i - y_i)^2$;
    Gradient(N, E);

A simple version of the backpropagation algorithm is shown in Algorithm 4.6. The MSE is used to calculate the error. Each tuple in the training set is input to this algorithm. The last step of the algorithm uses *gradient descent* as the technique to modify the weights in the graph. The basic idea of gradient descent is to find the set of weights that minimizes the MSE. $\frac{\partial E}{\partial w_{ji}}$ gives the slope (or gradient) of the error function for one weight. We thus wish to find the weight where this slope is zero. Figure 4.16 and Algorithm 4.7 illustrate the concept. The stated algorithm assumes only one hidden layer. More hidden layers would be handled in the same manner with the error propagated backward.

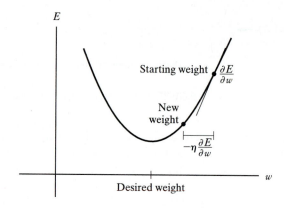

FIGURE 4.16: Gradient descent.

ALGORITHM 4.7

Input:
    N //Starting neural network
    E //Error found from back algorithm
Output:
    N //Improved neural network
Gradient algorithm:
        //Illustrates incremental gradient descent
    for each node i in output layer **do**
      for each node j input to i **do**
        $\Delta w_{ji} = \eta(d_i - y_i)y_j(1 - y_i)y_i;$
        $w_{ji} = w_{ji} + \Delta w_{ji};$
    layer = previous layer;
    for each node j in this layer **do**
      for each node k input to j **do**
        $\Delta w_{kj} = \eta y_k \frac{1-(y_j)^2}{2} \sum_m (d_m - y_m)w_{jm}y_m(1 - y_m);$
        $w_{kj} = w_{kj} + \Delta w_{kj};$

This algorithm changes weights by working backward from the output layer to the input layer. There are two basic versions of this algorithm. With the *batch* or *offline* approach, the weights are changed once after all tuples in the training set are applied and a total MSE is found. With the *incremental* or *online* approach, the weights are changed after each tuple in the training set is applied. The incremental technique is usually preferred because it requires less space and may actually examine more potential solutions (weights), thus leading to a better solution. In this equation, η is referred to as the *learning parameter*. It typically is found in the range $(0, 1)$, although it may be larger. This value determines how fast the algorithm learns.

Applying a learning rule back through multiple layers in the network may be difficult. Doing this for the hidden layers is not as easy as doing it with the output layer. Overall, however, we are trying to minimize the error at the output nodes, not at each node in the network. Thus, the approach that is used is to propagate the output errors backward through the network.

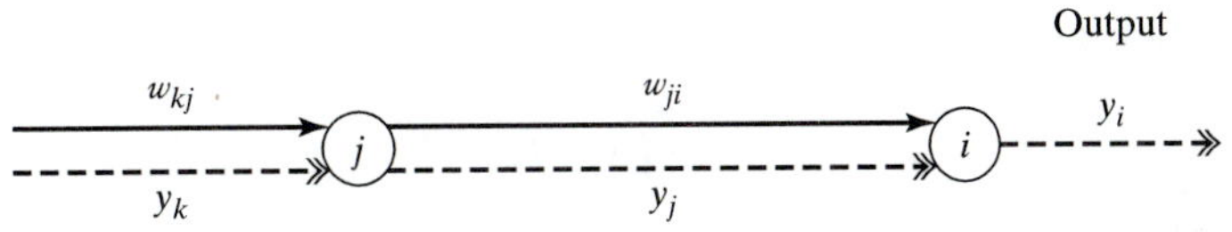

Output

FIGURE 4.17: Nodes for gradient descent.

Figure 4.17 shows the structure we use to discuss the gradient descent algorithm. Here node i is at the output layer and node j is at the hidden layer just before it; y_i is the output of i and y_j is the output of j.

The learning function in the gradient descent technique is based on using the following value for delta at the output layer:

$$\Delta w_{ji} = -\eta \frac{\partial E}{\partial w_{ji}} = -\eta \frac{\partial E}{\partial y_i} \frac{\partial y_i}{\partial S_i} \frac{\partial S_i}{\partial w_{ji}} \tag{4.41}$$

Here the weight w_{ji} is that at one arc coming into i from j. Assuming a sigmoidal activation function in the output layer, for the output layer we have

$$\frac{\partial y_i}{\partial S_i} = \frac{\partial}{\partial S_i}\left(\frac{1}{(1+e^{-S_i})}\right) = \left(1 - \left(\frac{1}{1+e^{-S_i}}\right)\right)\left(\frac{1}{1+e^{-S_i}}\right) = (1-y_i)y_i \tag{4.42}$$

Also,

$$\frac{\partial S_i}{\partial w_{ji}} = y_j \tag{4.43}$$

For nodes in the output layer, the third partial is

$$\frac{\partial E}{\partial y_i} = \frac{\partial}{\partial y_i}\left(\frac{1}{2}\sum_m (d_m - y_m)^2\right) = -(d_i - y_i) \tag{4.44}$$

We thus have the formula in Algorithm 4.7:

$$\Delta w_{ji} = \eta(d_i - y_i)y_j\left(1 - \frac{1}{1+e^{-S_i}}\right)\frac{1}{1+e^{-S_i}} = \eta(d_i - y_i)y_j(1-y_i)y_i \tag{4.45}$$

For a node j in the hidden layer, calculating the change in the weight for arcs coming into it is more difficult. Using Figure 4.17, we derive this change as

$$\Delta w_{kj} = -\eta \frac{\partial E}{\partial w_{kj}} \tag{4.46}$$

where

$$\frac{\partial E}{\partial w_{kj}} = \sum_m \frac{\partial E}{\partial y_m} \frac{\partial y_m}{\partial S_m} \frac{\partial S_m}{\partial y_j} \frac{\partial y_j}{\partial S_j} \frac{\partial S_j}{\partial w_{kj}} \tag{4.47}$$

Here the variable m ranges over all output nodes with arcs from j. We then derive

$$\frac{\partial E}{\partial y_m} = -(d_m - y_m) \tag{4.48}$$

$$\frac{\partial y_m}{\partial S_m} = (1 - y_m)y_m \tag{4.49}$$

$$\frac{\partial S_m}{\partial y_j} = w_{jm} \tag{4.50}$$

For hidden layers, where a hyperbolic tangent activation function is assumed, we have

$$\frac{\partial y_j}{\partial S_j} = \frac{\partial}{\partial S_j}\left(\frac{(1-e^{-S_j})}{(1+e^{-S_j})}\right) = \frac{\left(1+\left(\frac{1-e^{-S_j}}{1+e^{-S_j}}\right)\right)\left(1-\left(\frac{1-e^{-S_j}}{1+e^{-S_j}}\right)\right)}{2} = \frac{1-y_j^2}{2}$$

(4.51)

Also,

$$\frac{\partial S_j}{\partial w_{kj}} = y_k$$

(4.52)

This gives us the formula in Algorithm 4.7:

$$\Delta w_{kj} = \eta \, y_k \frac{1-(y_j)^2}{2}\sum_m (d_m - y_m)w_{jm}y_m(1-y_m)$$

(4.53)

Another common formula for the change in weight is

$$\Delta w_{ji}(t+1) = -\eta\frac{\partial E}{\partial w_{ji}} + \alpha\Delta w_{ji}(t)$$

(4.54)

Here the change in weight at time $t+1$ is based not only on the same partial derivative as earlier, but also on the last change in weight. Here α is called the *momentum* and is used to prevent oscillation problems that may occur without it.

4.5.3 Radial Basis Function Networks

A *radial function* or a *radial basis function (RBF)* is a class of functions whose value decreases (or increases) with the distance from a central point. The Gaussian activation function shown in Equation 3.35 is an RBF with a central point of 0. An RBF has a Gaussian shape, and an *RBF network* is typically an NN with three layers. The input layer is used to simply input the data. A Gaussian activation function is used at the hidden layer, while a linear activation function is used at the output layer. The objective is to have the hidden nodes learn to respond only to a subset of the input, namely, that where the Gaussian function is centered. This is usually accomplished via supervised learning. When RBF functions are used as the activation functions on the hidden layer, the nodes can be sensitive to a subset of the input values. Figure 4.18 shows the basic structure of an RBF unit with one output node.

4.5.4 Perceptrons

The simplest NN is called a *perceptron*. A perceptron is a single neuron with multiple inputs and one output. The original perceptron proposed the use of a step activation function, but it is more common to see another type of function such as a sigmoidal function. A simple perceptron can be used to classify into two classes. Using a unipolar activation function, an output of 1 would be used to classify into one class, while an output of 0 would be used to pass in the other class. Example 4.11 illustrates this.

EXAMPLE 4.11

Figure 4.19(a) shows a perceptron with two inputs and a bias input. The three weights are $3, 2$, and -6, respectively. The activation function f_4 is thus applied to the value

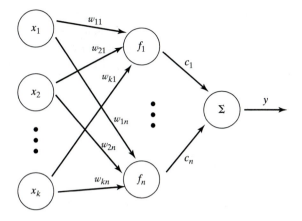

FIGURE 4.18: Radial basis function network.

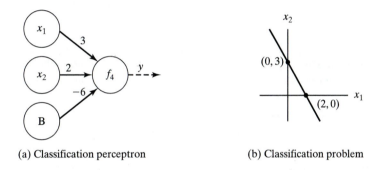

(a) Classification perceptron   (b) Classification problem

FIGURE 4.19: Perceptron classification example.

$S = 3x_1 + 2x_2 - 6$. Using a simple unipolar step activation function, we get

$$f_4 = \left\{ \begin{array}{ll} 1 & \text{if } S > 0 \\ 0 & \text{otherwise} \end{array} \right\} \tag{4.55}$$

An alternative way to view this classification problem is shown in Figure 4.19(b). Here x_1 is shown on the horizontal axis and x_2 is shown on the vertical axis. The area of the plane to the right of the line $x_2 = 3 - 3/2x_1$ represents one class and the rest of the plane represents the other class.

The simple feedforward NN that was introduced in Chapter 3 is actually called a *multilayer perceptron (MLP)*. An MLP is a network of perceptrons. Figure 3.6 showed an MLP used for classifying the height example given in Table 4.1. The neurons are placed in layers with outputs always flowing toward the output layer. If only one layer exists, it is called a perceptron. If multiple layers exist, it is an MLP.

In the 1950s a Russian mathematician, Andrey Kolmogorov, proved that an MLP needs no more than two hidden layers. *Kolmogorov's theorem* states that a mapping between two sets of numbers can be performed using an NN with only one hidden layer. In this case, the NN is to have one input node for each attribute input, and given n input attributes the hidden layer should have $(2n + 1)$ nodes, each with input from each of the input nodes. The output layer has one node for each desired output value.

4.6 RULE-BASED ALGORITHMS

One straightforward way to perform classification is to generate *if–then* rules that cover all cases. For example, we could have the following rules to determine classification of grades:

$$\text{If } 90 \leq \text{grade, then class} \ = \ A$$
$$\text{If } 80 \leq \text{grade and grade} < 90, \text{ then class} \ = \ B$$
$$\text{If } 70 \leq \text{grade and grade} < 80, \text{then class} \ = \ C$$
$$\text{If } 60 \leq \text{grade and grade} < 70, \text{then class} \ = \ D$$
$$\text{If grade} < 60, \text{then class} \ = \ F$$

A *classification rule*, $r = \langle a, c \rangle$, consists of the *if* or *antecedent*, a, part and the *then* or *consequent* portion, c. The antecedent contains a predicate that can be evaluated as true or false against each tuple in the database (and obviously in the training data). These rules relate directly to the corresponding DT that could be created. A DT can always be used to generate rules, but they are not equivalent. There are differences between rules and trees:

- The tree has an implied order in which the splitting is performed. Rules have no order.

- A tree is created based on looking at all classes. When generating rules, only one class must be examined at a time.

There are algorithms that generate rules from trees as well as algorithms that generate rules without first creating DTs.

4.6.1 Generating Rules from a DT

The process to generate a rule from a DT is straightforward and is outlined in Algorithm 4.8. This algorithm will generate a rule for each leaf node in the decision tree. All rules with the same consequent could be combined together by ORing the antecedents of the simpler rules.

ALGORITHM 4.8

```
Input:
    T       //Decision tree
Output:
    R       //Rules
```

```
Gen algorithm:
        //Illustrate simple approach to generating
          classification rules from a DT
    R = Ø
    for each path from root to a leaf in T do
        a = True
        for each non-leaf node do
            a = a∧ (label of node combined with label of incident
                 outgoing arc)
        c = label of leaf node
        R = R ∪ r = ⟨a, c⟩
```

Using this algorithm, the following rules are generated for the DT in Figure 4.13(a):

$$\{\langle(\text{Height} \leq 1.6 \text{ m}), \text{ Short}\rangle$$

$$\langle((\text{Height} > 1.6 \text{ m}) \wedge (\text{Height} \leq 1.7 \text{ m})), \text{Short}\rangle$$

$$\langle((\text{Height} > 1.7 \text{ m}) \wedge (\text{Height} \leq 1.8 \text{ m})), \text{Medium}\rangle$$

$$\langle((\text{Height} > 1.8 \text{ m}) \wedge (\text{Height} \leq 1.9 \text{ m})), \text{Medium}\rangle$$

$$\langle((\text{Height} > 1.9 \text{ m}) \wedge (\text{Height} \leq 2 \text{ m}) \wedge (\text{Height} \leq 1.95 \text{ m})), \text{Medium}\rangle$$

$$\langle((\text{Height} > 1.9 \text{ m}) \wedge (\text{Height} \leq 2 \text{ m}) \wedge (\text{Height} > 1.95 \text{ m})), \text{Tall}\rangle$$

$$\langle(\text{Height} > 2 \text{ m}), \text{Tall}\rangle\}$$

An optimized version of these rules is then:

$$\{\langle(\text{Height} \leq 1.7 \text{ m}), \text{Short}\rangle$$

$$\langle((\text{Height} > 1.7 \text{ m}) \wedge (\text{Height} \leq 1.95 \text{ m})), \text{Medium}\rangle$$

$$\langle(\text{Height} > 1.95 \text{ m}), \text{Tall}\rangle\}$$

4.6.2   Generating Rules from a Neural Net

To increase the understanding of an NN, classification rules may be derived from it. While the source NN may still be used for classification, the derived rules can be used to verify or interpret the network. The problem is that the rules do not explicitly exist. They are buried in the structure of the graph itself. In addition, if learning is still occurring, the rules themselves are dynamic. The rules generated tend both to be more concise and to have a lower error rate than rules used with DTs. The basic idea of the RX algorithm is to cluster output values with the associated hidden nodes and input. A major problem with rule extraction is the potential size that these rules should be. For example, if you have a node with n inputs each having 5 values, there are 5^n different input combinations to this one node alone. These patterns would all have to be accounted for when constructing rules. To overcome this problem and that of having continuous ranges of output values from nodes, the output values for both the hidden and output layers are first discretized. This is accomplished by clustering the values and dividing continuous values into disjoint ranges. The rule extraction algorithm, RX, shown in Algorithm 4.9 is derived from [LSL95].

ALGORITHM 4.9

```
Input:
    D       //Training data
    N       //Initial neural network
Output:
    R       //Derived rules
RX algorithm:
        //Rule extraction algorithm to extract rules from NN
    cluster output node activation values;
    cluster hidden node activation values;
    generate rules that describe the output values in terms of
      the hidden activation values;
    generate rules that describe hidden output values in
      terms of inputs;
    combine the two sets of rules.
```

4.6.3 Generating Rules Without a DT or NN

These techniques are sometimes called *covering* algorithms because they attempt to generate rules exactly cover a specific class [WF00]. Tree algorithms work in a top-down divide and conquer approach, but this need not be the case for covering algorithms. They generate the best rule possible by optimizing the desired classification probability. Usually the "best" attribute–value pair is chosen, as opposed to the best attribute with the tree-based algorithms. Suppose that we wished to generate a rule to classify persons as tall. The basic format for the rule is then

$$\text{If ? then class} = \text{tall}$$

The objective for the covering algorithms is to replace the "?" in this statement with predicates that can be used to obtain the "best" probability of being tall.

One simple approach is called 1R because it generates a simple set of rules that are equivalent to a DT with only one level. The basic idea is to choose the best attribute to perform the classification based on the training data. "Best" is defined here by counting the number of errors. In Table 4.4 this approach is illustrated using the height example,

TABLE 4.4: 1R Classification

Option	Attribute	Rules	Errors	Total Errors
1	Gender	F $\rightarrow$ Medium	3/9	6/15
		M $\rightarrow$ Tall	3/6	
2	Height	(0, 1.6] $\rightarrow$ Short	0/2	1/15
		(1.6, 1.7] $\rightarrow$ Short	0/2	
		(1.7, 1.8] $\rightarrow$ Medium	0/3	
		(1.8, 1.9] $\rightarrow$ Medium	0/4	
		(1.9, 2.0] $\rightarrow$ Medium	1/2	
		(2.0, ∞) $\rightarrow$ Tall	0/2	

Output1. If we only use the gender attribute, there are a total of 6/15 errors, whereas if we use the height attribute, there are only 1/15. Thus, the height would be chosen and the six rules stated in the table would be used. As with ID3, 1R tends to choose attributes with a large number of values leading to overfitting. 1R can handle missing data by adding an additional attribute value for the value of *missing*. Algorithm 4.10, which is adapted from [WF00], shows the outline for this algorithm.

ALGORITHM 4.10

```
Input:
    D        //Training data
    R        //Attributes to consider for rules
    C        //Classes
Output:
    R        //Rules
1R algorithm:
        //1R algorithm generates rules based on one attribute
    R = ∅;
    for each A ∈ R do
        RA = ∅;
        for each possible value, v, of A do
            //v may be a range rather than a specific value
            for each Cj ∈ C find count(Cj);
                // Here count is the number of occurrences of this
                    class for this attribute
            let Cm be the class with the largest count;
            RA = RA ∪ ((A = v) → (class = Cm));
        ERRA = number of tuples incorrectly classified by RA;
    R = RA where ERRA is minimum;
```

Another approach to generating rules without first having a DT is called *PRISM*. PRISM generates rules for each class by looking at the training data and adding rules that completely describe all tuples in that class. Its accuracy is 100 percent. Example 4.12 illustrates the use of PRISM. Algorithm 4.11, which is adapted from [WF00], shows the process. Note that the algorithm refers to attribute–value pairs. Note that the values will include an operator so that in Example 4.12 the first attribute–value pair chosen is with attribute height and value 72.0. As with earlier classification techniques, this must be modified to handle continuous attributes. In the example, we have again used the ranges of height values used in earlier examples.

EXAMPLE 4.12

Using the data in Table 4.1 and the Output1 classification, the following shows the basic probability of putting a tuple in the tall class based on the given attribute–value pair:

$$
\begin{array}{rl}
\text{Gender} = F & 0/9 \\
\text{Gender} = M & 3/6 \\
\text{Height} <= 1.6 & 0/2 \\
1.6 < \text{Height} <= 1.7 & 0/2
\end{array}
$$

$$1.7 < \text{Height} <= 1.8 \qquad 0/3$$
$$1.8 < \text{Height} <= 1.9 \qquad 0/4$$
$$1.9 < \text{Height} <= 2.0 \qquad 1/2$$
$$2.0 < \text{Height} \qquad 2/2$$

Based on this analysis, we would generate the rule

If $2.0 < \text{height}$, then class $= $ tall

Since all tuples that satisfy this predicate are tall, we do not add any additional predicates to this rule. We now need to generate additional rules for the tall class. We thus look at the remaining 13 tuples in the training set and recalculate the accuracy of the corresponding predicates:

$$\text{Gender} = F \qquad 0/9$$
$$\text{Gender} = M \qquad 1/4$$
$$\text{Height} <= 1.6 \qquad 0/2$$
$$1.6 < \text{Height} <= 1.7 \qquad 0/2$$
$$1.7 < \text{Height} <= 1.8 \qquad 0/3$$
$$1.8 < \text{Height} <= 1.9 \qquad 0/4$$
$$1.9 < \text{Height} <= 2.0 \qquad 1/2$$

Based on the analysis, we see that the last height range is the most accurate and thus generate the rule:

If $2.0 < \text{height}$, then class $= $ tall

However, only one of the tuples that satisfies this is actually tall, so we need to add another predicate to it. We then look only at the other predicates affecting these two tuples. We now see a problem in that both of these are males. The problem is actually caused by our "arbitrary" range divisions. We now divide the range into two subranges:

$$1.9 < \text{Height} <= 1.95 \qquad 0/1$$
$$1.95 < \text{Height} <= 2.0 \qquad 1/1$$

We thus add this second predicate to the rule to obtain

If $2.0 < \text{height}$ and $1.95 < \text{height} <= 2.0$, then class $= $ tall

or

If $1.95 < \text{height}$, then class $= $ tall

This problem does not exist if we look at tuples individually using the attribute–value pairs. However, in that case we would not generate the needed ranges for classifying the actual data. At this point, we have classified all tall tuples. The algorithm would then proceed by classifying the short and medium classes. This is left as an exercise.

ALGORITHM 4.11

```
Input:
    D       //Training data
    C       //Classes
Output:
    R       //Rules
PRISM algorithm:
            //PRISM algorithm generates rules based on best
                attribute-value pairs
    R = ∅;
    for each Cⱼ ∈ C do
        repeat
            T = D; //All instances of class Cⱼ will be systematically
                    removed from T
            p = true; //Create new rule with empty left-hand side
            r = (If p then Cⱼ);
            repeat
                for each attribute A value v pair found in T do
                    calculate ( |(tuples∈T with A=v)∧p∧(∈Cⱼ)| / |(tuples ∈T with A=v)∧p| );
                    find A = v that maximizes this value;
                    p = p ∧ (A = v);
                    T = {tuples in T that satisfy A = v};
            until all tuples in T belong to Cⱼ;
            D = D − T;
            R = R ∪ r;
        until there are no tuples in D that belong to Cⱼ;
```

4.7 COMBINING TECHNIQUES

Given a classification problem, no one classification technique always yields the best results. Therefore, there have been some proposals that look at combining techniques. While discussing C5.0, we briefly introduced one technique for combining classifiers called boosting. Two basic techniques can be used to accomplish this:

- A *synthesis* of approaches takes multiple techniques and blends them into a new approach. An example of this would be using a prediction technique, such as linear regression, to predict a future value for an attribute that is then used as input to a classification NN. In this way the NN is used to predict a future classification value.

- Multiple *independent* approaches can be applied to a classification problem, each yielding its own class prediction. The results of these individual techniques can then be combined in some manner. This approach has been referred to as *combination of multiple classifiers (CMC)*.

One approach to combine independent classifiers assumes that there are n independent classifiers and that each generates the posterior probability $P_k(C_j \mid t_i)$ for each class. The values are combined with a weighted linear combination

$$\sum_{k=1}^{n} w_k P_k(C_j \mid t_i) \qquad (4.56)$$

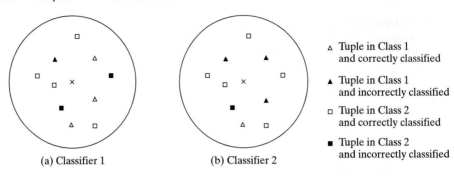

(a) Classifier 1   (b) Classifier 2

△ Tuple in Class 1 and correctly classified

▲ Tuple in Class 1 and incorrectly classified

□ Tuple in Class 2 and correctly classified

■ Tuple in Class 2 and incorrectly classified

FIGURE 4.20: Combination of multiple classifiers.

Here the weights, w_k, can be assigned by a user or learned based on the past accuracy of each classifier. Another technique is to choose the classifier that has the best accuracy in a database sample. This is referred to as a *dynamic classifier selection (DCS)*. Example 4.13, which is modified from [LJ98], illustrates the use of DCS. Another variation is simple voting: assign the tuple to the class to which a majority of the classifiers have assigned it. This may have to be modified slightly in case there are many classes and no majority is found.

EXAMPLE 4.13

Two classifiers exist to classify tuples into two classes. A target tuple, X, needs to be classified. Using a nearest neighbor approach, the 10 tuples closest to X are identified. Figure 4.20 shows the 10 tuples closest to X. In Figure 4.20(a) the results for the first classifier are shown, while in Figure 4.20(b) those for the second classifier are shown. The tuples designated with triangles should be in class 1, while those shown as squares should be in class 2. Any shapes that are darkened indicate an incorrect classification by that classifier. To combine the classifiers using DCS, look at the general accuracy of each classifier. With classifier 1, 7 tuples in the neighborhood of X are correctly classified, while with the second classifier, only 6 are correctly classified. Thus, X will be classified according to how it is classified with the first classifier.

Recently, a new CMC technique, *adaptive classifier combination (ACC)*, has been proposed [LJ98]. Given a tuple to classify, the neighborhood around it is first determined, then the tuples in that neighborhood are classified by each classifier, and finally the accuracy for each class is measured. By examining the accuracy across all classifiers for each class, the tuple is placed in the class that has the highest local accuracy. In effect, the class chosen is that to which most of its neighbors are accurately classified independent of classifier. Example 4.14 illustrates the use of ACC.

EXAMPLE 4.14

Using the same data as in Example 4.13, the ACC technique examines how accurate all classifiers are for each class. With the tuples in class 1, classifier 1 accurately classifies 3 tuples, while classifier 2 accurately classifies only 1 tuple. A measure of the accuracy for both classifiers with respect to class 1 is then: $3/4 + 1/4$. When looking at class 2, the measure is: $4/6 + 5/6$. Thus, X is placed in class 2.

4.8 SUMMARY

No one classification technique is always superior to the others in terms of classification accuracy. However, there are advantages and disadvantages to the use of each. The regression approaches force the data to fit a predefined model. If a linear model is chosen, then the data are fit into that model even though it might not be linear. It requires that linear data be used. The KNN technique requires only that the data be such that distances can be calculated. This can then be applied even to nonnumeric data. Outliers are handled by looking only at the K nearest neighbors. Bayesian classification assumes that the data attributes are independent with discrete values. Thus, although it is easy to use and understand, results may not be satisfactory. Decision tree techniques are easy to understand, but they may lead to overfitting. To avoid this, pruning techniques may be needed. ID3 is applicable only to categorical data. Improvements on it, C4.5 and C5, allow the use of continuous data and improved techniques for splitting. CART creates binary trees and thus may result in very deep trees.

When looking at the approaches based on complexity analysis, we see that they are all very efficient. This is due to the fact that once the model is created, applying it for classification is relatively straightforward. The statistical techniques, regression and naive Bayes, require constant time to classify a tuple once the models are built. The distance-based approaches, simple and KNN, are also constant but require that each tuple be compared either to a representative for each class or to all items in the training set. Assuming there are q of these, the KNN then requires $O(q)$ time per tuple. DT classification techniques, ID3, C4.5, and CART require a number of comparisons that are (in the worst case) equal to the longest path from a root to a leaf node. Thus, they require $O(\log q)$ time per tuple. Since q is a constant, we can view these as being performed in constant time as well. The NN approaches again require that a tuple be propagated through the graph. Since the size of the graph is constant, this can be viewed as being performed in constant time. Thus, all algorithms are $O(n)$ to classify the n items in the database.

4.9 EXERCISES

1. Explain the differences between the definition of the classification problem found in Definition 4.1 and an alternative one with the mapping from C to D.
2. Using the data in Table 4.1, draw OC curves assuming that the Output2 column is the correct classification and Output1 is what is seen. You will need to draw three curves, one for each class.
3. Using the data in Table 4.1, construct a confusion matrix assuming Output is the correct assignment and Output1 is what is actually made.
4. Apply the method of least squares technique to determine the division between medium and tall persons using the training data in Table 4.1 and the classification shown in the Output1 column (see Example 4.3). You may use either the division technique or the prediction technique.

5. Apply the method of least squares technique to determine the division between medium and tall persons using the training data in Table 4.1 and the classification shown in the Output2 column. This uses both the height data and the gender data to do the classification. Use the division technique.

6. Redo Exercise 5 using the prediction technique.

7. Use KNN to classify ⟨Jim, M, 2.0⟩ with $K = 5$ using the height data and assuming that Output2 is correct.

8. Explain the difference between $P(t_i \mid C_j)$ and $P(C_j \mid t_i)$.

9. Redo Example 4.5 using Output2 data.

10. Determine the expected number of comparisons for each tree shown in Figure 4.11.

11. Generate a DT for the height example in Table 4.1 using the ID3 algorithm and the training classifications shown in the Output2 column of that table.

12. Repeat Exercise 11 using the GainRatio instead of the Gain.

13. Construct the confusion matrix for the results of Exercises 11 and 12.

14. Using 1R, generate rules for the height example using the Output2 column in Table 4.1.

15. Complete Example 4.9 by generating the DT for the height example (using the Output1 classification) using the CART algorithm.

16. Suppose that the output for Mary in Exercise 8 in Chapter 3 should have been 0 for small, 0 for medium, and 1 for tall. Use the gradient descent algorithm to modify the weights in the NN.

17. Complete Example 4.12 by generating rules for the short and medium classes.

18. (**Implementation**) Various classification algorithms can be found online. Obtain code for both CART and C4.5. Apply these programs to the height example in Table 4.1 using the training classifications shown in the Output2 column. Compare these results to those found in Exercises 11 and 12.

19. Generate rules from each of the trees found in Exercise 18.

20. (**Implementation/research**) Various datasets that have been used for classification benchmarks can be found online. Obtain a real-life classification dataset and generate decision trees using the programs you found in Exercise 18. Compare these two trees. Which is better? Why?

21. (**Research**) Compare at least three different guideline that have been proposed for determining the optimal number of hidden nodes in an NN.

4.10 BIBLIOGRAPHIC NOTES

Classification is perhaps the oldest data mining technique. Plant and animal classification dates back to the 1700s or earlier. A historical investigation of classification and clustering can be found in one of the first clustering texts [Har75]. There are many classification texts, including [BFOS98]. A recent study has compared 33 different classification algorithms.[2]

---

[2]Tjen-Sien Lim, Wei-Yin Loh, and Yu-Shan-Shih, "A Comparison of Prediction Accuracy, Complexity, and Training Time of Thirty-three Old and New Classification Algorithms," *Machine Learning*, vol. 40, 2000, pp. 203–229.

There are detailed discussions of linear regression for classification in [HTF01]. It was reported that the accuracy for multiclass problems was very poor. A better linear approach is to use *linear discriminant analysis (LDA)*, which is also discussed in that book.

Chi squared automatic interaction detection (CHAID) was one of the earliest decision tree algorithms, proposed by Hartigan in 1975 [Har75]. CHAID uses the chi squared statistic to determine splitting. It can use only categorical values. The chi squared test is used to prevent the tree from growing too big. A modified version of CHAID was proposed in 1980 by Kass; it reduces the overall time, but does not guarantee the best result. Kass proposes that pairs of categories (for the predictor variable) be merged if there is no statistically significant difference between them. The resulting set of categories defines the split [Kas80]. With *exhaustive CHAID*, which was proposed in 1991, the split point is determined by merging pairs of categories until only one pair remains [BdVS91]. The predictor with the best overall prediction is then chosen for the split.

ID3 was first proposed in the mid 1970s by Quinlan [Qui86]. A thorough investigation of C4.5 can be found in the seminal text on the subject [Qui93].

CART was developed by Breimen in 1984 [BFOS84]. In 1997, another binary decision tree technique was proposed [LS97]. *QUEST (quick unbiased efficient statistical tree)* addresses the problems in CART that it tends to select variables with many values, which creates a bias in the model. QUEST handles variable selection and split point differently. Also, unlike CART, QUEST does not perform an exhaustive search, so it is more efficient. The approach used by QUEST is to determine the association between each predictor variable and target variable. The variable with the largest association is chosen. The split point (for that variable) is then determined.

Many different techniques have been proposed to prune decision trees. A survey by Breslow and Aha in 1997[3] looked at techniques to simplify trees. These included techniques to control the tree site (pruning), modify the test space, change the way the searching of the test space was conducted, reduce the size of the input data set (e.g., feature selection), and use alternative data structures. Pruning approaches include pre-pruning algorithms that affect the size of the tree as it is created.[4] Post-pruning algorithms change the tree after it is created.[5]

Pattern recognition is a type of classification used in many diverse applications, including medical diagnosis, assembly line parts inspection, speech recognition, printed character recognition, military target recognition, robot navigation, and fingerprint analysis. While these applications can use the general strategies outlined in this chapter, there has been much work in the development of algorithms specifically targeted to individual applications. The interested reader is referred to some of the many texts available on pattern recognition, including [Bis95], [DHS00], [Fuk90], [GJJ96], and [TK98].

---

[3]L. Breslow and D.W. Aha, "Comparing Tree-Simplification Procedures," *Proceedings of the Sixth International Workshop on Artificial Intelligence and Statistics*, 1997, pp. 67–74.

[4]Floriana Esposito, Donato Malerba, and Giovanni Semeraro, "A Comparative Analysis of Methods for Pruning Decision Trees, "*IEEE Transactions on Pattern Analysis and Machine Intelligence*, vol. 19, no. 5, May 1997, pp. 476–491.

[5]Tapio Elomaa and Matti Kaariainen, "An Analysis of Reduced Error Pruning," *Journal of Intelligence Research*, vol. 15, 2001, pp. 163–187.

Classification of large datasets has been proposed to be handled in several ways. Sampling has been proposed in [Cat91]. Partitioning the data and creating classifiers for each was proposed in [CS93]. Parallelization of classification algorithms has been examined [Fif92]. The SLIQ approach addresses scalability by a presorting step instead of sorting at each node, which some decision tree techniques require [MAR96]. The second improvement with SLIQ is that the tree is grown in a breadth-first fashion as opposed to a depth-first manner. In [SAM96], the authors not only propose SPRINT, but also design and compare several parallel implementations of SPRINT and SLIQ. Rainforest was proposed in 1998 [GRG98].

Although an RBF network could conceivably be of any shape, a seminal paper by Broomhead and Lowe proposed the structure discussed in this chapter [BL88]. An excellent and complete introduction to RBF networks is found in [Orr96]. The idea of the perceptron was proposed by Rosenblatt in [Ros58]. The MLP *is due to* Rumelhart and McClelland[RM86]. Discussions of choice for number of hidden layers in an MLP can be found in [Bis95] and [Hay99]. Kolmogorov's famous theorem is reported in [Kol57].

The 1R algorithm was studied in [Hol93] and [WF00]. PRISM was proposed in [Cen87]. Extracting rules from neural networks has been investigated since the early 1990s [Liu95], [TS93], [LSL95], and [LSL96].

C H A P T E R 5

Clustering

5.1 INTRODUCTION

Clustering is similar to classification in that data are grouped. However, unlike classification, the groups are not predefined. Instead, the grouping is accomplished by finding similarities between data according to characteristics found in the actual data. The groups are called *clusters*. Some authors view clustering as a special type of classification. In this text, however, we follow a more conventional view in that the two are different. Many definitions for clusters have been proposed:

- Set of like elements. Elements from different clusters are not alike.

- The distance between points in a cluster is less than the distance between a point in the cluster and any point outside it.

A term similar to clustering is *database segmentation*, where like tuples (records) in a database are grouped together. This is done to partition or segment the database into components that then give the user a more general view of the data. In this text, we do not differentiate between segmentation and clustering. A simple example of clustering is found in Example 5.1. This example illustrates the fact that determining how to do the clustering is not straightforward.

EXAMPLE 5.1

An international online catalog company wishes to group its customers based on common features. Company management does not have any predefined labels for these groups. Based on the outcome of the grouping, they will target marketing and advertising campaigns to the different groups. The information they have about the customers includes

TABLE 5.1: Sample Data for Example 5.1

Income	Age	Children	Marital Status	Education
$25,000	35	3	Single	High school
$15,000	25	1	Married	High school
$20,000	40	0	Single	High school
$30,000	20	0	Divorced	High school
$20,000	25	3	Divorced	College
$70,000	60	0	Married	College
$90,000	30	0	Married	Graduate school
$200,000	45	5	Married	Graduate school
$100,000	50	2	Divorced	College

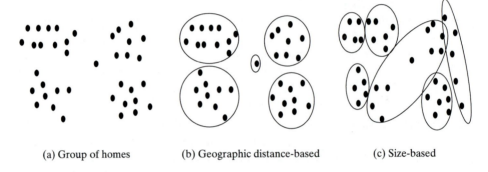

(a) Group of homes   (b) Geographic distance-based   (c) Size-based

FIGURE 5.1: Different clustering attributes.

income, age, number of children, marital status, and education. Table 5 shows some tuples from this database for customers in the United States. Depending on the type of advertising, not all attributes are important. For example, suppose the advertising is for a special sale on children's clothes. We could target the advertising only to the persons with children. One possible clustering is that shown by the divisions of the table. The first group of people have young children and a high school degree, while the second group is similar but have no children. The third group has both children and a college degree. The last two groups have higher incomes and at least a college degree. The very last group has children. Different clusterings would have been found by examining age or marital status.

As illustrated in Figure 5.1, a given set of data may be clustered on different attributes. Here a group of homes in a geographic area is shown. The first type of clustering is based on the location of the home. Homes that are geographically close to each other are clustered together. In the second clustering, homes are grouped based on the size of the house.

Clustering has been used in many application domains, including biology, medicine, anthropology, marketing, and economics. Clustering applications include plant and animal classification, disease classification, image processing, pattern recognition, and document retrieval. One of the first domains in which clustering was used was biological taxonomy. Recent uses include examining Web log data to detect usage patterns.

When clustering is applied to a real-world database, many interesting problems occur:

- Outlier handling is difficult. Here the elements do not naturally fall into any cluster. They can be viewed as solitary clusters. However, if a clustering algorithm attempts to find larger clusters, these outliers will be forced to be placed in some cluster. This process may result in the creation of poor clusters by combining two existing clusters and leaving the outlier in its own cluster.

- Dynamic data in the database implies that cluster membership may change over time.

- Interpreting the semantic meaning of each cluster may be difficult. With classification, the labeling of the classes is known ahead of time. However, with clustering, this may not be the case. Thus, when the clustering process finishes creating a set of clusters, the exact meaning of each cluster may not be obvious. Here is where a domain expert is needed to assign a label or interpretation for each cluster.

- There is no one correct answer to a clustering problem. In fact, many answers may be found. The exact number of clusters required is not easy to determine. Again, a domain expert may be required. For example, suppose we have a set of data about plants that have been collected during a field trip. Without any prior knowledge of plant classification, if we attempt to divide this set of data into similar groupings, it would not be clear how many groups should be created.

- Another related issue is what data should be used for clustering. Unlike learning during a classification process, where there is some a priori knowledge concerning what the attributes of each classification should be, in clustering we have no supervised learning to aid the process. Indeed, clustering can be viewed as similar to unsupervised learning.

We can then summarize some basic features of clustering (as opposed to classification):

- The (best) number of clusters is not known.

- There may not be any a priori knowledge concerning the clusters.

- Cluster results are dynamic.

The clustering problem is stated as shown in Definition 5.1. Here we assume that the number of clusters to be created is an input value, k. The actual content (and interpretation) of each cluster, K_j, $1 \leq j \leq k$, is determined as a result of the function definition. Without loss of generality, we will view that the result of solving a clustering problem is that a set of clusters is created: $K = \{K_1, K_2, \ldots, K_k\}$.

> **DEFINITION 5.1.** Given a database $D = \{t_1, t_2, \ldots, t_n\}$ of tuples and an integer value k, the **clustering problem** is to define a mapping $f : D \rightarrow \{1, \ldots, k\}$ where each t_i is assigned to one cluster K_j, $1 \leq j \leq k$. A **cluster**, K_j, contains precisely those tuples mapped to it; that is, $K_j = \{t_i \mid f(t_i) = K_j, 1 \leq i \leq n, \text{ and } t_i \in D\}$.

A classification of the different types of clustering algorithms is shown in Figure 5.2. Clustering algorithms themselves may be viewed as hierarchical or partitional. With

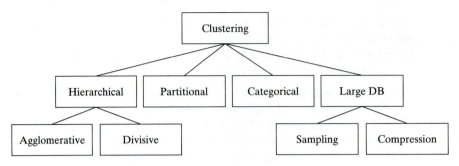

FIGURE 5.2: Classification of clustering algorithms.

hierarchical clustering, a nested set of clusters is created. Each level in the hierarchy has a separate set of clusters. At the lowest level, each item is in its own unique cluster. At the highest level, all items belong to the same cluster. With hierarchical clustering, the desired number of clusters is not input. With *partitional* clustering, the algorithm creates only one set of clusters. These approaches use the desired number of clusters to drive how the final set is created. Traditional clustering algorithms tend to be targeted to small numeric databases that fit into memory. There are, however, more recent clustering algorithms that look at categorical data and are targeted to larger, perhaps dynamic, databases. Algorithms targeted to larger databases may adapt to memory constraints by either sampling the database or using data structures, which can be compressed or pruned to fit into memory regardless of the size of the database. Clustering algorithms may also differ based on whether they produce overlapping or nonoverlapping clusters. Even though we consider only nonoverlapping clusters, it is possible to place an item in multiple clusters. In turn, nonoverlapping clusters can be viewed as extrinsic or intrinsic. *Extrinsic* techniques use labeling of the items to assist in the classification process. These algorithms are the traditional classification supervised learning algorithms in which a special input training set is used. *Intrinsic* algorithms do not use any a priori category labels, but depend only on the adjacency matrix containing the distance between objects. All algorithms we examine in this chapter fall into the intrinsic class.

The types of clustering algorithms can be furthered classified based on the implementation technique used. Hierarchical algorithms can be categorized as agglomerative or divisive. "*Agglomerative*" implies that the clusters are created in a bottom-up fashion, while *divisive* algorithms work in a top-down fashion. Although both hierarchical and partitional algorithms could be described using the agglomerative vs. divisive label, it typically is more associated with hierarchical algorithms. Another descriptive tag indicates whether each individual element is handled one by one, *serial* (sometimes called *incremental*), or whether all items are examined together, *simultaneous*. If a specific tuple is viewed as having attribute values for all attributes in the schema, then clustering algorithms could differ as to how the attribute values are examined. As is usually done with decision tree classification techniques, some algorithms examine attribute values one at a time, *monothetic*. *Polythetic* algorithms consider all attribute values at one time. Finally, clustering algorithms can be labeled based on the mathematical formulation given to the algorithm: graph theoretic or matrix algebra. In this chapter we generally use the graph approach and describe the input to the clustering algorithm as an adjacency matrix labeled with distance measures.

We discuss many clustering algorithms in the following sections. This is only a representative subset of the many algorithms that have been proposed in the literature. Before looking at these algorithms, we first examine possible similarity measures and examine the impact of outliers.

5.2 SIMILARITY AND DISTANCE MEASURES

There are many desirable properties for the clusters created by a solution to a specific clustering problem. The most important one is that a tuple within one cluster is more like tuples within that cluster than it is similar to tuples outside it. As with classification, then, we assume the definition of a similarity measure, $\text{sim}(t_i, t_l)$, defined between any two tuples, $t_i, t_l \in D$. This provides a more strict and alternative clustering definition, as found in Definition 5.2. Unless otherwise stated, we use the first definition rather than the second. Keep in mind that the similarity relationship stated within the second definition is a desirable, although not always obtainable, property.

> **DEFINITION 5.2.** Given a database $D = \{t_1, t_2, \ldots, t_n\}$ of tuples, a similarity measure, $\text{sim}(t_i, t_l)$, defined between any two tuples, $t_i, t_l \in D$, and an integer value k, the **clustering problem** is to define a mapping $f : D \rightarrow \{1, \ldots, k\}$ where each t_i is assigned to one cluster K_j, $1 \leq j \leq k$. Given a cluster, K_j, $\forall t_{jl}, t_{jm} \in K_j$ and $t_i \notin K_j$, $\text{sim}(t_{jl}, t_{jm}) > \text{sim}(t_{jl}, t_i)$.

A distance measure, $\text{dis}(t_i, t_j)$, as opposed to similarity, is often used in clustering. The clustering problem then has the desirable property that given a cluster, K_j, $\forall t_{jl}$, $t_{jm} \in K_j$ and $t_i \notin K_j$, $\text{dis}(t_{jl}, t_{jm}) \leq \text{dis}(t_{jl}, t_i)$.

Some clustering algorithms look only at numeric data, usually assuming metric data points. *Metric* attributes satisfy the triangular inequality. The clusters can then be described by using several characteristic values. Given a cluster, K_m of N points $\{t_{m1}, t_{m2}, \ldots, t_{mN}\}$, we make the following definitions [ZRL96]:

$$\text{centroid} \;=\; C_m = \frac{\sum\limits_{i=1}^{N}(t_{mi})}{N} \tag{5.1}$$

$$\text{radius} \;=\; R_m = \sqrt{\frac{\sum\limits_{i=1}^{N}(t_{mi} - C_m)^2}{N}} \tag{5.2}$$

$$\text{diameter} \;=\; D_m = \sqrt{\frac{\sum\limits_{i=1}^{N}\sum\limits_{j=1}^{N}(t_{mi} - t_{mj})^2}{(N)(N - 1)}} \tag{5.3}$$

Here the centroid is the "middle" of the cluster; it need not be an actual point in the cluster. Some clustering algorithms alternatively assume that the cluster is represented by one centrally located object in the cluster called a *medoid*. The radius is the square root of the average mean squared distance from any point in the cluster to the centroid, and the diameter is the square root of the average mean squared distance between all pairs of points in the cluster. We use the notation M_m to indicate the medoid for cluster K_m.

Many clustering algorithms require that the distance between clusters (rather than elements) be determined. This is not an easy task given that there are many interpretations for distance between clusters. Given clusters K_i and K_j, there are several standard alternatives to calculate the distance between clusters. A representative list is:

- **Single link:** Smallest distance between an element in one cluster and an element in the other. We thus have $dis(K_i, K_j) = min(dis(t_{il}, t_{jm})) \forall t_{il} \in K_i \notin K_j$ and $\forall t_{jm} \in K_j \notin K_i$.

- **Complete link:** Largest distance between an element in one cluster and an element in the other. We thus have $dis(K_i, K_j) = max(dis(t_{il}, t_{jm})) \forall t_{il} \in K_i \notin K_j$ and $\forall t_{jm} \in K_j \notin K_i$.

- **Average:** Average distance between an element in one cluster and an element in the other. We thus have $dis(K_i, K_j) = mean(dis(t_{il}, t_{jm})) \forall t_{il} \in K_i \notin K_j$ and $\forall t_{jm} \in K_j \notin K_i$.

- **Centroid:** If clusters have a representative centroid, then the centroid distance is defined as the distance between the centroids. We thus have $dis(K_i, K_j) = dis(C_i, C_j)$, where C_i is the centroid for K_i and similarly for C_j.

- **Medoid:** Using a medoid to represent each cluster, the distance between the clusters can be defined by the distance between the medoids: $dis(K_i, K_j) = dis(M_i, M_j)$.

5.3 OUTLIERS

As mentioned earlier, *outliers* are sample points with values much different from those of the remaining set of data. Outliers may represent errors in the data (perhaps a malfunctioning sensor recorded an incorrect data value) or could be correct data values that are simply much different from the remaining data. A person who is 2.5 meters tall is much taller than most people. In analyzing the height of individuals, this value probably would be viewed as an outlier.

Some clustering techniques do not perform well with the presence of outliers. This problem is illustrated in Figure 5.3. Here if three clusters are found (solid line), the outlier will occur in a cluster by itself. However, if two clusters are found (dashed line), the two (obviously) different sets of data will be placed in one cluster because they are closer together than the outlier. This problem is complicated by the fact that many clustering algorithms actually have as input the number of desired clusters to be found.

Clustering algorithms may actually find and remove outliers to ensure that they perform better. However, care must be taken in actually removing outliers. For example, suppose that the data mining problem is to predict flooding. Extremely high water level values occur very infrequently, and when compared with the normal water level values may seem to be outliers. However, removing these values may not allow the data mining algorithms to work effectively because there would be no data that showed that floods ever actually occurred.

Outlier detection, or *outlier mining*, is the process of identifying outliers in a set of data. Clustering, or other data mining, algorithms may then choose to remove or treat these values differently. Some outlier detection techniques are based on statistical techniques. These usually assume that the set of data follows a known distribution and that outliers can be detected by well-known tests such as *discordancy tests*. However, these

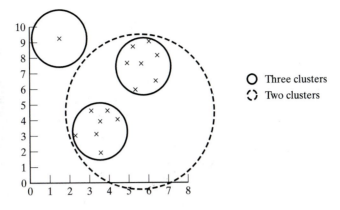

FIGURE 5.3: Outlier clustering problem.

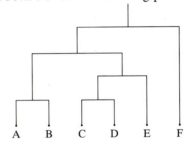

FIGURE 5.4: Dendrogram for Example 5.2.

tests are not very realistic for real-world data because real-world data values may not follow well-defined data distributions. Also, most of these tests assume a single attribute value, and many attributes are involved in real-world datasets. Alternative detection techniques may be based on distance measures.

5.4 HIERARCHICAL ALGORITHMS

As mentioned earlier, hierarchical clustering algorithms actually creates sets of clusters. Example 5.2 illustrates the concept. Hierarchical algorithms differ in how the sets are created. A tree data structure, called a *dendrogram*, can be used to illustrate the hierarchical clustering technique and the sets of different clusters. The root in a dendrogram tree contains one cluster where all elements are together. The leaves in the dendrogram each consist of a single element cluster. Internal nodes in the dendrogram represent new clusters formed by merging the clusters that appear as its children in the tree. Each level in the tree is associated with the distance measure that was used to merge the clusters. All clusters created at a particular level were combined because the children clusters had a distance between them less than the distance value associated with this level in the tree. A dendrogram for Example 5.2 is seen in Figure 5.4.

EXAMPLE 5.2

Figure 5.5 shows six elements, {A, B, C, D, E, F}, to be clustered. Parts (a) to (e) of the figure show five different sets of clusters. In part (a) each cluster is viewed to consist of

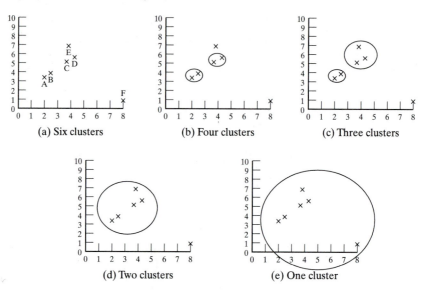

FIGURE 5.5: Five levels of clustering for Example 5.2.

a single element. Part (b) illustrates four clusters. Here there are two sets of two-element clusters. These clusters are formed at this level because these two elements are closer to each other than any of the other elements. Part (c) shows a new cluster formed by adding a close element to one of the two-element clusters. In part (d) the two-element and three-element clusters are merged to give a five-element cluster. This is done because these two clusters are closer to each other than to the remote element cluster, {F}. At the last stage, part (e), all six elements are merged.

The space complexity for hierarchical algorithms is $O(n^2)$ because this is the space required for the adjacency matrix. The space required for the dendrogram is $O(kn)$, which is much less than $O(n^2)$. The time complexity for hierarchical algorithms is $O(kn^2)$ because there is one iteration for each level in the dendrogram. Depending on the specific algorithm, however, this could actually be $O(maxd \; n^2)$ where *maxd* is the maximum distance between points. Different algorithms may actually merge the closest clusters from the next lowest level or simply create new clusters at each level with progressively larger distances.

Hierarchical techniques are well suited for many clustering applications that naturally exhibit a nesting relationship between clusters. For example, in biology, plant and animal taxonomies could easily be viewed as a hierarchy of clusters.

5.4.1   Agglomerative Algorithms

Agglomerative algorithms start with each individual item in its own cluster and iteratively merge clusters until all items belong in one cluster. Different agglomerative algorithms differ in how the clusters are merged at each level. Algorithm 5.1 illustrates the typical agglomerative clustering algorithm. It assumes that a set of elements and distances between them is given as input. We use an $n \times n$ vertex adjacency matrix, A, as input.

Here the adjacency matrix, A, contains a distance value rather than a simple boolean value: $A[i, j] = \text{dis}(t_i, t_j)$. The output of the algorithm is a dendrogram, DE, which we represent as a set of ordered triples $\langle d, k, K \rangle$ where d is the threshold distance, k is the number of clusters, and K is the set of clusters. The dendrogram in Figure 5.7(a) would be represented by the following:

$$\{\langle 0, 5, \{\{A\}, \{B\}, \{C\}, \{D\}, \{E\}\}\rangle, \langle 1, 3, \{\{A, B\}, \{C, D\}, \{E\}\}\rangle$$
$$\langle 2, 2, \{\{A, B, C, D\}, \{E\}\}\rangle, \langle 3, 1, \{\{A, B, C, D, E\}\}\rangle\}$$

Outputting the dendrogram produces a set of clusters rather than just one clustering. The user can determine which of the clusters (based on distance threshold) he or she wishes to use.

ALGORITHM 5.1

```
Input:
    D = {t₁, t₂, ..., tₙ}    //Set of elements
    A        //Adjacency matrix showing distance between elements
Output:
    DE    // Dendrogram represented as a set of ordered triples
Agglomerative algorithm:
    d = 0;
    k = n;
    K = {{t₁}, ..., {tₙ}};
    DE = {⟨d, k, K⟩};  // Initially dendrogram contains each element
                          in its own cluster.
    repeat
        oldk = k;
        d = d + 1;
        A_d = Vertex adjacency matrix for graph with threshold
             distance of d;
        ⟨k, K⟩ = NewClusters(A_d, D);
        if oldk ≠ k then
            DE = DE ∪ ⟨d, k, K⟩; // New set of clusters added to dendrogram.
        until k = 1
```

This algorithm uses a procedure called *NewClusters* to determine how to create the next level of clusters from the previous level. This is where the different types of agglomerative algorithms differ. It is possible that only two clusters from the prior level are merged or that multiple clusters are merged. Algorithms also differ in terms of which clusters are merged when there are several clusters with identical distances. In addition, the technique used to determine the distance between clusters may vary. *Single link*, *complete link*, and *average link* techniques are perhaps the most well known agglomerative techniques based on well-known graph theory concepts.

All agglomerative approaches experience excessive time and space constraints. The space required for the adjacency matrix is $O(n^2)$ where there are n items to cluster. Because of the iterative nature of the algorithm, the matrix (or a subset of it) must be accessed multiple times. The simplistic algorithm provided in Algorithm 5.1 performs at most *maxd* examinations of this matrix, where *maxd* is the largest distance between any two points. In addition, the complexity of the *NewClusters* procedure could be expensive. This is a potentially severe problem in large databases. Another issue with the agglomerative approach is that it is not incremental. Thus, when new elements are added or old ones are removed or changed, the entire algorithm must be rerun. More recent incremental variations, as discussed later in this text, address this problem.

Single Link Technique. The single link technique is based on the idea of finding maximal connected components in a graph. A *connected component* is a graph in which there exists a path between any two vertices. With the single link approach, two clusters are merged if there is at least one edge that connects the two clusters; that is, if the minimum distance between any two points is less than or equal to the threshold distance being considered. For this reason, it is often called the *nearest neighbor* clustering technique. Example 5.3 illustrates this process.

EXAMPLE 5.3

Table 5.2 contains five sample data items with the distance between the elements indicated in the table entries. When viewed as a graph problem, Figure 5.6(a) shows the general graph with all edges labeled with the respective distances. To understand the idea behind the hierarchical approach, we show several graph variations in Figures 5.6(b), (c), (d), and (e). Figure 5.6(b) shows only those edges with a distance of 1 or less. There are only two edges. The first level of single link clustering then will combine the connected clusters (single elements from the first phase), giving three clusters: {A,B}, {C,D}, and {E}. During the next level of clustering, we look at edges with a length of 2 or less. The graph representing this threshold distance is shown in Figure 5.6(c). Note that we now have an edge (actually three) between the two clusters {A,B} and {C,D}. Thus, at this level of the single link clustering algorithm, we merge these two clusters to obtain a total of two clusters: {A,B,C,D} and {E}. The graph that is created with a threshold distance of 3 is shown in Figure 5.6(d). Here the graph is connected, so the two clusters from the last level are merged into one large cluster that contains all elements. The dendrogram for this single link example is shown in Figure 5.7(a). The labeling on the right-hand side shows the threshold distance used to merge the clusters at each level.

The single link algorithm is obtained by replacing the *NewClusters* procedure in the agglomerative algorithm with a procedure to find connected components of a graph. We assume that this connected components procedure has as input a graph (actually represented by a vertex adjacency matrix and set of vertices) and as outputs a set of

TABLE 5.2: Sample Data for Example 5.3

Item	A	B	C	D	E
A	0	1	2	2	3
B	1	0	2	4	3
C	2	2	0	1	5
D	2	4	1	0	3
E	3	3	5	3	0

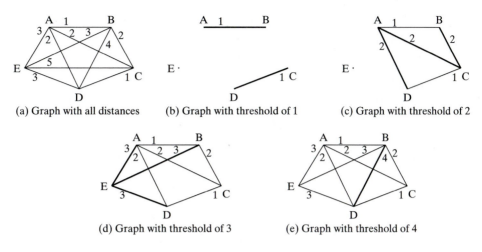

FIGURE 5.6: Graphs for Example 5.3.

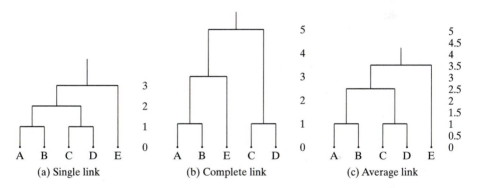

FIGURE 5.7: Dendrograms for Example 5.3.

connected components defined by a number (indicating the number of components) and an array containing the membership of each component. Note that this is exactly what the last two entries in the ordered triple are used for by the dendrogram data structure.

The single link approach is quite simple, but it suffers from several problems. This algorithm is not very efficient because the connected components procedure, which is an $O(n^2)$ space and time algorithm, is called at each iteration. A more efficient algorithm could be developed by looking at which clusters from an earlier level can be merged at each step. Another problem is that the clustering creates clusters with long chains.

An alternative view to merging clusters in the single link approach is that two clusters are merged at a stage where the threshold distance is d if the minimum distance between any vertex in one cluster and any vertex in the other cluster is at most d.

There have been other variations of the single link algorithm. One variation, based on the use of a *minimum spanning tree (MST)*, is shown in Algorithm 5.2. Here we assume that a procedure, *MST*, produces a minimum spanning tree given an adjacency matrix as input. The clusters are merged in increasing order of the distance found in the MST. In the algorithm we show that once two clusters are merged, the distance between them in the tree becomes ∞. Alternatively, we could have replaced the two nodes and edge with one node.

ALGORITHM 5.2

Input:
　　$D = \{t_1, t_2, \ldots, t_n\}$ //Set of elements
　　A //Adjacency matrix showing distance between elements
Output:
　　DE // Dendrogram represented as a set of ordered triples
MST single link algorithm:
　　$d = 0$
　　$k = n$
　　$K = \{\{t_1\}, \ldots, \{t_n\}\}$
　　$DE = \langle d, k, K \rangle$; // Initially dendrogram contains each element in
　　　　its own cluster.
　　$M = MST(A)$;
　　repeat
　　　　$\text{old}k = k$;
　　　　$K_i, K_j = $ two clusters closest together in MST;
　　　　$K = K - \{K_i\} - \{K_j\} \cup \{K_i \cup K_j\}$;
　　　　$k = \text{old}k - 1$;
　　　　$d = \text{dis}(K_i, K_j)$;
　　　　$DE = DE \cup \langle d, k, K \rangle$; // New set of clusters added to dendrogram.
　　　　$\text{dis}(K_i, K_j) = \infty$
　　until $k = 1$

　　We illustrate this algorithm using the data in Example 5.3. Figure 5.8 shows one MST for the example. The algorithm will merge A and B and then C and D (or the reverse). These two clusters will then be merged at a threshold of 2. Finally, E will be merged at a threshold of 3. Note that we get exactly the same dendrogram as in Figure 5.7(a).

　　The time complexity of this algorithm is $O(n^2)$ because the procedure to create the minimum spanning tree is $O(n^2)$ and it dominates the time of the algorithm. Once it is created having $n - 1$ edges, the *repeat* loop will be repeated only $n - 1$ times.

　　The single linkage approach is infamous for its chain effect; that is, two clusters are merged if only two of their points are close to each other. There may be points in the respective clusters to be merged that are far apart, but this has no impact on the algorithm. Thus, resulting clusters may have points that are not related to each other at all, but simply happen to be near (perhaps via a transitive relationship) points that are close to each other.

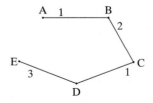

FIGURE 5.8: MST for Example 5.3.

Complete Link Algorithm.   Although the complete link algorithm is similar to the single link algorithm, it looks for cliques rather than connected components. A *clique* is a maximal graph in which there is an edge between any two vertices. Here a procedure is used to find the maximum distance between any clusters so that two clusters are merged if the maximum distance is less than or equal to the distance threshold. In this algorithm, we assume the existence of a procedure, clique, which finds all cliques in a graph. As with the single link algorithm, this is expensive because it is an $O(n^2)$ algorithm.

Clusters found with the complete link method tend to be more compact than those found using the single link technique. Using the data found in Example 5.3, Figure 5.7(b) shows the dendrogram created. A variation of the complete link algorithm is called the *farthest neighbor algorithm*. Here the closest clusters are merged where the distance is the smallest measured by looking at the maximum distance between any two points.

Average Link.   The average link technique merges two clusters if the average distance between any two points in the two target clusters is below the distance threshold. The algorithm used here is slightly different from that found in single and complete link algorithms because we must examine the complete graph (not just the threshold graph) at each stage. Thus, we restate this algorithm in Algorithm 5.3.

ALGORITHM 5.3

```
Input:
    D = {t₁, t₂, ..., tₙ}    //Set of elements
    A        //Adjacency matrix showing distance between elements
Output:
    DE      // Dendrogram represented as a set of ordered triples
Average link algorithm:
    d = 0;
    k = n;
    K = {{t₁}, ..., {tₙ}};
    DE = ⟨d, k, K⟩; // Initially dendrogram contains each element
                    in its own cluster.
    repeat
        oldk = k;
        d = d + 0.5;
        for each pair of Kᵢ, Kⱼ ∈ K do
            ave = average distance between all tᵢ ∈ Kᵢ and tⱼ ∈ Kⱼ;
            if ave ≤ d, then
                K = K − {Kᵢ} − {Kⱼ} ∪ {Kᵢ ∪ Kⱼ};
                k = oldk − 1;
                DE = DE ∪ ⟨d, k, K⟩; // New set of clusters added
                                        to dendrogram.
    until k = 1
```

Note that in this algorithm we increment d by 0.5 rather than by 1. This is a rather arbitrary decision based on understanding of the data. Certainly, we could have used an increment of 1, but we would have had a dendrogram different from that seen in Figure 5.7(c).

5.4.2 Divisive Clustering

With divisive clustering, all items are initially placed in one cluster and clusters are repeatedly split in two until all items are in their own cluster. The idea is to split up clusters where some elements are not sufficiently close to other elements.

One simple example of a divisive algorithm is based on the MST version of the single link algorithm. Here, however, we cut out edges from the MST from the largest to the smallest. Looking at Figure 5.8, we would start with a cluster containing all items: $\{A, B, C, D, E\}$. Looking at the MST, we see that the largest edge is between D and E. Cutting this out of the MST, we then split the one cluster into two: $\{E\}$ and $\{A, B, C, D\}$. Next we remove the edge between B and C. This splits the one large cluster into two: $\{A, B\}$ and $\{C, D\}$. These will then be split at the next step. The order depends on how a specific implementation would treat identical values. Looking at the dendrogram in Figure 5.7(a), we see that we have created the same set of clusters as with the agglomerative approach, but in reverse order.

5.5 PARTITIONAL ALGORITHMS

Nonhierarchical or partitional clustering creates the clusters in one step as opposed to several steps. Only one set of clusters is created, although several different sets of clusters may be created internally within the various algorithms. Since only one set of clusters is output, the user must input the desired number, k, of clusters. In addition, some metric or criterion function is used to determine the goodness of any proposed solution. This measure of quality could be the average distance between clusters or some other metric. The solution with the best value for the criterion function is the clustering solution used. One common measure is a squared error metric, which measures the squared distance from each point to the centroid for the associated cluster:

$$\sum_{m=1}^{k} \sum_{t_{mi} \in K_m} \text{dis}(C_m, t_{mi})^2 \tag{5.4}$$

A problem with partitional algorithms is that they suffer from a combinatorial explosion due to the number of possible solutions. Clearly, searching all possible clustering alternatives usually would not be feasible. For example, given a measurement criteria, a naive approach could look at all possible sets of k clusters. There are $S(n, k)$ possible combinations to examine. Here

$$S(n, k) = \frac{1}{k!} \sum_{i=1}^{k} (-1)^{k-i} \binom{k}{i} (i)^n \tag{5.5}$$

There are 11,259,666,000 different ways to cluster 19 items into 4 clusters. Thus, most algorithms look only at a small subset of all the clusters using some strategy to identify sensible clusters. Because of the plethora of partitional algorithms, we will look at only a representative few. We have chosen some of the most well known algorithms as well as some others that have appeared recently in the literature.

5.5.1 Minimum Spanning Tree

Since we have agglomerative and divisive algorithms based on the use of an MST, we also present a partitional MST algorithm. This is a very simplistic approach, but it illustrates how partitional algorithms work. The algorithm is shown in Algorithm 5.4. Since the clustering problem is to define a mapping, the output of this algorithm shows the clusters as a set of ordered pairs $\langle t_i, j \rangle$ where $f(t_i) = K_j$.

ALGORITHM 5.4

```
Input:
    D = {t₁, t₂, ..., tₙ}   //Set of elements
    A        //Adjacency matrix showing distance between elements
    k        //Number of desired clusters
Output:
    f        //Mapping represented as a set of ordered pairs
Partitional MST algorithm:
    M = MST(A)
    identify inconsistent edges in M;
    remove k - 1 inconsistent edges;
    create output representation;
```

The problem is how to define "inconsistent." It could be defined as in the earlier division MST algorithm based on distance. This would remove the largest $k-1$ edges from the starting completely connected graph and yield the same results as this corresponding level in the dendrogram. Zahn proposes more reasonable inconsistent measures based on the weight (distance) of an edge as compared to those close to it. For example, an inconsistent edge would be one whose weight is much larger than the average of the adjacent edges.

The time complexity of this algorithm is again dominated by the *MST* procedure, which is $O(n^2)$. At most, $k - 1$ edges will be removed, so the last three steps of the algorithm, assuming each step takes a constant time, is only $O(k - 1)$. Although determining the inconsistent edges in M may be quite complicated, it will not require a time greater than the number of edges in M. When looking at edges adjacent to one edge, there are at most $k - 2$ of these edges. In this case, then, the last three steps are $O(k^2)$, and the total algorithm is still $O(n^2)$.

5.5.2 Squared Error Clustering Algorithm

The *squared error* clustering algorithm minimizes the squared error. The *squared error for a cluster* is the sum of the squared Euclidean distances between each element in the cluster and the cluster centroid, C_k. Given a cluster K_i, let the set of items mapped to that cluster be $\{t_{i1}, t_{i2}, \ldots, t_{im}\}$. The squared error is defined as

$$se_{K_i} = \sum_{j=1}^{m} \|t_{ij} - C_k\|^2 \tag{5.6}$$

Given a set of clusters $K = \{K_1, K_2, \ldots, K_k\}$, the *squared error* for K is defined as

$$se_K = \sum_{j=1}^{k} se_{K_j} \tag{5.7}$$

In actuality, there are many different examples of squared error clustering algorithms. They all follow the basic algorithm structure shown in Algorithm 5.5.

ALGORITHM 5.5

```
Input:
   D = {t₁, t₂,..., tₙ}    //Set of elements
   k        //Number of desired clusters
Output:
   K        //Set of clusters
```
Squared error algorithm:
```
   assign each item tᵢ to a cluster;
   calculate center for each cluster;
   repeat
      assign each item tᵢ to the cluster which has the closest center;
      calculate new center for each cluster;
      calculate squared error;
   until the difference between successive squared errors
      is below a threshold;
```

For each iteration in the squared error algorithm, each tuple is assigned to the cluster with the closest center. Since there are k clusters and n items, this is an $O(kn)$ operation. Assuming t iterations, this becomes an $O(tkn)$ algorithm. The amount of space may be only $O(n)$ because an adjacency matrix is not needed, as the distance between all items is not used.

5.5.3 *K*-Means Clustering

K-means is an iterative clustering algorithm in which items are moved among sets of clusters until the desired set is reached. As such, it may be viewed as a type of squared error algorithm, although the convergence criteria need not be defined based on the squared error. A high degree of similarity among elements in clusters is obtained, while a high degree of dissimilarity among elements in different clusters is achieved simultaneously. The *cluster mean* of $K_i = \{t_{i1}, t_{i2}, \ldots, t_{im}\}$ is defined as

$$m_i = \frac{1}{m} \sum_{j=1}^{m} t_{ij} \tag{5.8}$$

This definition assumes that each tuple has only one numeric value as opposed to a tuple with many attribute values. The K-means algorithm requires that some definition of cluster mean exists, but it does not have to be this particular one. Here the mean is defined identically to our earlier definition of centroid. This algorithm assumes that the desired number of clusters, k, is an input parameter. Algorithm 5.6 shows the K-means algorithm. Note that the initial values for the means are arbitrarily assigned. These could be assigned randomly or perhaps could use the values from the first k input items themselves. The convergence criteria could be based on the squared error, but they need not be. For example, the algorithm could stop when no (or a very small) number of tuples are assigned to different clusters. Other termination techniques have simply looked at a fixed number of iterations. A maximum number of iterations may be included to ensure stopping even without convergence.

ALGORITHM 5.6

```
Input:
   D = {t₁, t₂,..., tₙ}    //Set of elements
```

```
    k       //Number of desired clusters
Output:
    K       //Set of clusters
K-means algorithm:
    assign initial values for means m₁, m₂, ..., mₖ;
    repeat
        assign each item tᵢ to the cluster which has the closest mean;
        calculate new mean for each cluster;
    until convergence criteria is met;
```

The K-means algorithm is illustrated in Example 5.4.

EXAMPLE 5.4

Suppose that we are given the following items to cluster:

$$\{2, 4, 10, 12, 3, 20, 30, 11, 25\} \tag{5.9}$$

and suppose that $k = 2$. We initially assign the means to the first two values: $m_1 = 2$ and $m_2 = 4$. Using Euclidean distance, we find that initially $K_1 = \{2, 3\}$ and $K_2 = \{4, 10, 12, 20, 30, 11, 25\}$. The value 3 is equally close to both means, so we arbitrarily choose K_1. Any desired assignment could be used in the case of ties. We then recalculate the means to get $m_1 = 2.5$ and $m_2 = 16$. We again make assignments to clusters to get $K_1 = \{2, 3, 4\}$ and $K_2 = \{10, 12, 20, 30, 11, 25\}$. Continuing in this fashion, we obtain the following:

m_1	m_2	K_1	K_2
3	18	$\{2, 3, 4, 10\}$	$\{12, 20, 30, 11, 25\}$
4.75	19.6	$\{2, 3, 4, 10, 11, 12\}$	$\{20, 30, 25\}$
7	25	$\{2, 3, 4, 10, 11, 12\}$	$\{20, 30, 25\}$

Note that the clusters in the last two steps are identical. This will yield identical means, and thus the means have converged. Our answer is thus $K_1 = \{2, 3, 4, 10, 11, 12\}$ and $K_2 = \{20, 30, 25\}$.

The time complexity of K-means is $O(tkn)$ where t is the number of iterations. K-means finds a local optimum and may actually miss the global optimum. K-means does not work on categorical data because the mean must be defined on the attribute type. Only convex-shaped clusters are found. It also does not handle outliers well. One variation of K-means, *K-modes*, does handle categorical data. Instead of using means, it uses modes. A typical value for k is 2 to 10.

Although the K-means algorithm often produces good results, it is not time-efficient and does not scale well. By saving distance information from one iteration to the next, the actual number of distance calculations that must be made can be reduced.

Some K-means variations examine ways to improve the chances of finding the global optimum. This often involves careful selection of the initial clusters and means. Another variation is to allow clusters to be split and merged. The variance within a cluster is examined, and if it is too large, a cluster is split. Similarly, if the distance between two cluster centroids is less than a predefined threshold, they will be combined.

5.5.4   Nearest Neighbor Algorithm

An algorithm similar to the single link technique is called the *nearest neighbor algorithm*. With this serial algorithm, items are iteratively merged into the existing clusters that are closest. In this algorithm a threshold, t, is used to determine if items will be added to existing clusters or if a new cluster is created.

ALGORITHM 5.7

```
Input:
    D = {t₁, t₂, ..., tₙ}    //Set of elements
    A       //Adjacency matrix showing distance between elements
Output:
    K       //Set of clusters
Nearest neighbor algorithm:
    K₁ = {t₁};
    K = {K₁};
    k = 1;
    for i = 2 to n do
        find the tₘ in some cluster Kₘ in K such that dis(tᵢ, tₘ) is
            the smallest;
        if dis(tᵢ, tₘ), ≤ t then
            Kₘ = Kₘ ∪ tᵢ
        else
            k = k + 1;
            Kₖ = {tᵢ};
```

Example 5.5 shows the application of the nearest neighbor algorithm to the data shown in Table 5.2 assuming a threshold of 2. Notice that the results are the same as those seen in Figure 5.7(a) at the level of 2.

EXAMPLE 5.5

Initially, A is placed in a cluster by itself, so we have $K_1 = \{A\}$. We then look at B to decide if it should be added to K_1 or be placed in a new cluster. Since $dis(A, B) = 1$, which is less than the threshold of 2, we place B in K_1 to get $K_1 = \{A, B\}$. When looking at C, we see that its distance to both A and B is 2, so we add it to the cluster to get $K_1 = \{A, B, C\}$. The $dis(D, C) = 1 < 2$, so we get $K_1 = \{A, B, C, D\}$. Finally, looking at E, we see that the closest item in K_1 has a distance of 3, which is greater than 2, so we place it in its own cluster: $K_2 = \{E\}$.

The complexity of the nearest neighbor algorithm actually depends on the number of items. For each loop, each item must be compared to each item already in a cluster. Obviously, this is n in the worst case. Thus, the time complexity is $O(n^2)$. Since we do need to examine the distances between items often, we assume that the space requirement is also $O(n^2)$.

5.5.5   PAM Algorithm

The *PAM (partitioning around medoids)* algorithm, also called the *K-medoids* algorithm, represents a cluster by a medoid. Using a medoid is an approach that handles outliers well. The PAM algorithm is shown in Algorithm 5.8. Initially, a random set of k items is taken to be the set of medoids. Then at each step, all items from the input dataset that are not currently medoids are examined one by one to see if they should be medoids. That is, the algorithm determines whether there is an item that should replace one of the existing medoids. By looking at all pairs of medoid, non-medoid objects, the algorithm chooses the pair that improves the overall quality of the clustering the best and exchanges them. Quality here is measured by the sum of all distances from a non-medoid object to the medoid for the cluster it is in. An item is assigned to the cluster represented by the medoid to which it is closest (minimum distance). We assume that K_i is the cluster represented by medoid t_i. Suppose t_i is a current medoid and we wish to determine whether it should be exchanged with a non-medoid t_h. We wish to do this swap only if the overall impact to the cost (sum of the distances to cluster medoids) represents an improvement.

Following the lead in [NH94], we use C_{jih} to be the cost change for an item t_j associated with swapping medoid t_i with non-medoid t_h. The cost is the change to the sum of all distances from items to their cluster medoids. There are four cases that must be examined when calculating this cost:

1. $t_j \in K_i$, but $\exists$ another medoid t_m where $\text{dis}(t_j, t_m) \leq \text{dis}(t_j, t_h)$;
2. $t_j \in K_i$, but $\text{dis}(t_j, t_h) \leq \text{dis}(t_j, t_m) \forall$ other medoids t_m;
3. $t_j \in K_m, \notin K_i$, and $\text{dis}(t_j, t_m) \leq \text{dis}(t_j, t_h)$; and
4. $t_j \in K_m, \notin K_i$, but $\text{dis}(t_j, t_h) \leq \text{dis}(t_j, t_m)$.

We leave it as an exercise to determine the cost of each of these cases. The total impact to quality by a medoid change TC_{ih} then is given by

$$TC_{ih} = \sum_{j=1}^{n} C_{jih} \tag{5.10}$$

ALGORITHM 5.8

```
Input:
    D = {t₁, t₂, ..., tₙ}    //Set of elements
    A        //Adjacency matrix showing distance between elements
    k        //Number of desired clusters
Output:
    K        //Set of clusters
PAM algorithm:
    arbitrarily select k medoids from D;
    repeat
        for each tₕ not a medoid do
            for each medoid tᵢ do
                calculate TCᵢₕ;
        find i, h where TCᵢₕ is the smallest;
        if TCᵢₕ < 0, then
            replace medoid tᵢ with tₕ;
    until TCᵢₕ ≥ 0;
    for each tᵢ ∈ D do
        assign tᵢ to Kⱼ, where dis(tᵢ, tⱼ) is the smallest over all medoids;
```

Example 5.6 shows the application of the PAM algorithm to the data shown in Table 5.2 assuming a threshold of 2.

EXAMPLE 5.6

Suppose that the two medoids that are initially chosen are A and B. Based on the distances shown in Table 5.2 and randomly placing items when distances are identical to the two medoids, we obtain the clusters $\{A, C, D\}$ and $\{B, E\}$ The three non-medoids, $\{C, D, E\}$, are then examined to see which (if any) should be used to replace A or B. We thus have six costs to determine: $TC_{AC}, TC_{AD}, TC_{AE}, TC_{BC}, TC_{BD},$ and TC_{BE}. Here we use the name of the item instead of a numeric subscript value. We obtain the following:

$$TC_{AC} = C_{AAC} + C_{BAC} + C_{CAC} + C_{DAC} + C_{EAC} = 1 + 0 - 2 - 1 + 0 = -2 \quad (5.11)$$

Here A is no longer a medoid, and since it is closer to B, it will be placed in the cluster with B as medoid, and thus its cost is $C_{AAC} = 1$. The cost for B is 0 because it stays a cluster medoid. C is now a medoid, so it has a negative cost based on its distance to the old medoid; that is, $C_{CAB} = -2$. D is closer to C than it was to A by a distance of 1, so its cost is $C_{DAC} = -1$. Finally, E stays in the same cluster with the same distance, so its cost change is 0. Thus, we have that the overall cost is a reduction of 2. Figure 5.9 illustrates the calculation of these six costs. Looking at these, we see that the minimum cost is 2 and that there are several ways to reduce this cost. Arbitrarily choosing the first swap, we get C and B as the new medoids with the clusters being $\{C, D\}$ and $\{B, A, E\}$. This concludes the first iteration of PAM. At the next iteration, we examine changing medoids again and pick the choice that best reduces the cost. The iterations stop when no changes will reduce the cost. We leave the rest of this problem to the reader as an exercise.

PAM does not scale well to large datasets because of its computational complexity. For each iteration, we have $k(n-k)$ pairs of objects i, h for which a cost, TC_{ih}, should be determined. Calculating the cost during each iteration requires that the cost be calculated for all other non-medoids t_j. There are $n - k$ of these. Thus, the total complexity per iteration is $n(n - k)^2$. The total number of iterations can be quite large, so PAM is not an alternative for large databases. However, there are some clustering algorithms based on PAM that are targeted to large datasets.

CLARA (Clustering LARge Applications) improves on the time complexity of PAM by using samples of the dataset. The basic idea is that it applies PAM to a sample of the underlying database and then uses the medoids found as the medoids for the complete clustering. Each item from the complete database is then assigned to the cluster with the medoid to which it is closest. To improve the CLARA accuracy, several samples can be drawn with PAM applied to each. The sample chosen as the final clustering is the one that performs the best. Because of the sampling, CLARA is more efficient than PAM for large databases. However, it may not be as effective, depending on the sample size. Five samples of size $40 + 2k$ seem to give good results [KR90].

CLARANS (clustering large applications based upon randomized search) improves on CLARA by using multiple different samples. In addition to the normal input to PAM,

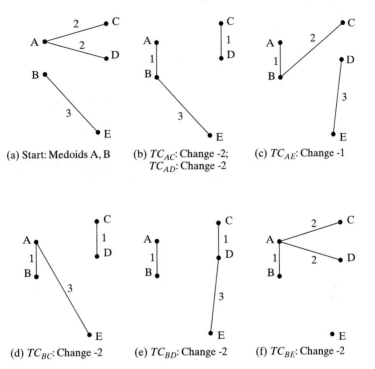

FIGURE 5.9: Cost calculations for Example 5.6.

CLARANS requires two additional parameters: *maxneighbor* and *numlocal*. *Maxneighbor* is the number of neighbors of a node to which any specific node can be compared. As *maxneighbor* increases, CLARANS looks more and more like PAM because all nodes will be examined. *Numlocal* indicates the number of samples to be taken. Since a new clustering is performed on each sample, this also indicates the number of clusterings to be made. Performance studies indicate that *numlocal* $= 2$ and *maxneighbor* $= \max((0.0125 \times k(n - k)), 250)$ are good choices [NH94]. CLARANS is shown to be more efficient than either PAM or CLARA for any size dataset. CLARANS assumes that all data are in main memory. This certainly is not a valid assumption for large databases.

5.5.6 Bond Energy Algorithm

The *bond energy algorithm (BEA)* was developed and has been used in the database design area to determine how to group data and how to physically place data on a disk. It can be used to cluster attributes based on usage and then perform logical or physical design accordingly. With BEA, the *affinity* (bond) between database attributes is based on common usage. This bond is used by the clustering algorithm as a similarity measure. The actual measure counts the number of times the two attributes are used together in a given time. To find this, all common queries must be identified.

The idea is that attributes that are used together form a cluster and should be stored together. In a distributed database, each resulting cluster is called a *vertical fragment* and

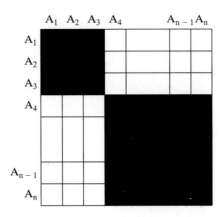

FIGURE 5.10: Clustered affinity matrix for BEA (modified from [ÖV99]).

may be stored at different sites from other fragments. The basic steps of this clustering algorithm are:

1. Create an attribute affinity matrix in which each entry indicates the affinity between the two associate attributes. The entries in the similarity matrix are based on the frequency of common usage of attribute pairs.

2. The BEA then converts this similarity matrix to a BOND matrix in which the entries represent a type of nearest neighbor bonding based on probability of co-access. The BEA algorithm rearranges rows or columns so that similar attributes appear close together in the matrix.

3. Finally, the designer draws boxes around regions in the matrix with high similarity.

The resulting matrix, modified from [ÖV99], is illustrated in Figure 5.10 The two shaded boxes represent the attributes that have been grouped together into two clusters.

Two attributes A_i and A_j have a high affinity if they are frequently used together in database applications. At the heart of the BEA algorithm is the global affinity measure. Suppose that a database schema consists of n attributes $\{A_1, A_2, \ldots, A_n\}$. The global affinity measure, AM, is defined as

$$AM = \sum_{i=1}^{n}(\text{bond}(A_i, A_{i-1}) + \text{bond}(A_i, A_{i+1})) \qquad (5.12)$$

5.5.7 Clustering with Genetic Algorithms

There have been clustering techniques based on the use of genetic algorithms. To determine how to perform clustering with genetic algorithms, we first must determine how to represent each cluster. One simple approach would be to use a bit-map representation for each possible cluster. So, given a database with four items, $\{A, B, C, D\}$, we would represent one solution to creating two clusters as 1001 and 0110. This represents the two clusters $\{A, D\}$ and $\{B, C\}$.

Algorithm 5.9 shows one possible iterative refinement technique for clustering that uses a genetic algorithm. The approach is similar to that in the squared error approach in that an initial random solution is given and successive changes to this converge on a local optimum. A new solution is generated from the previous solution using crossover and mutation operations. Our algorithm shows only crossover. The use of crossover to create a new solution from a previous solution is shown in Example 5.7. The new "solution" must be created in such a way that it represents a valid k clustering. A fitness function must be used and may be defined based on an inverse of the squared error. Because of the manner in which crossover works, genetic clustering algorithms perform a global search rather than a local search of potential solutions.

ALGORITHM 5.9

```
Input:
    D = {t₁, t₂, ..., tₙ}    //Set of elements
    k       //Number of desired clusters
Output:
    K       //Set of clusters
GA clustering algorithm:
    randomly create an initial solution;
    repeat
        use crossover to create a new solution;
    until termination criteria is met;
```

EXAMPLE 5.7

Suppose a database contains the following eight items $\{A, B, C, D, E, F, G, H\}$, which are to be placed into three clusters. We could initially place the items into the three clusters $\{A, C, E\}$, $\{B, F\}$, and $\{D, G, H\}$, which are represented by 10101000, 01000100, and 00010011, respectively. Suppose we choose the first and third individuals as parents and do a simple crossover at point 4. This yields the new solution: 00011000, 01000100, and 10100011.

5.5.8 Clustering with Neural Networks

Neural networks (NNs) that use unsupervised learning attempt to find features in the data that characterize the desired output. They look for clusters of like data. These types of NNs are often called *self-organizing neural networks*. There are two basic types of unsupervised learning: noncompetitive and competitive.

With the *noncompetitive* or *Hebbian* learning, the weight between two nodes is changed to be proportional to both output values. That is

$$\Delta w_{ji} = \eta y_j y_i \tag{5.13}$$

With *competitive* learning, nodes are allowed to compete and the winner takes all. This approach usually assumes a two-layer NN in which all nodes from one layer are connected to all nodes in the other layer. As training occurs, nodes in the output layer become associated with certain tuples in the input dataset. Thus, this provides a grouping of these tuples together into a cluster. Imagine every input tuple having each attribute value input to a specific input node in the NN. The number of input nodes is the same as the number of attributes. We can thus associate each weight to each output node with one of the attributes from the input tuple. When a tuple is input to the NN, all output nodes produce an output value. The node with the weights more similar to the input tuple is declared the winner. Its weights are then adjusted. This process continues with each tuple input from the training set. With a large and varied enough training set, over time each output node should become associated with a set of tuples. The input weights to the node are then close to an average of the tuples in this cluster.

Self-Organizing Feature Maps.   A *self-organizing feature map (SOFM)* or *self-organizing map (SOM)* is an NN approach that uses competitive unsupervised learning. Learning is based on the concept that the behavior of a node should impact only those nodes and arcs near it. Weights are initially assigned randomly and adjusted during the learning process to produce better results. During this learning process, hidden features or patterns in the data are uncovered and the weights are adjusted accordingly. SOFMs were developed by observing how neurons work in the brain and in ANNs. That is [BS97]:

- The firing of neurons impact the firing of other neurons that are near it.

- Neurons that are far apart seem to inhibit each other.

- Neurons seem to have specific nonoverlapping tasks.

The term *self-organizing* indicates the ability of these NNs to organize the nodes into clusters based on the similarity between them. Those nodes that are closer together are more similar than those that are far apart. This hints at how the actual clustering is performed. Over time, nodes in the output layer become matched to input nodes, and patterns of nodes in the output layer emerge.

Perhaps the most common example of a SOFM is the *Kohonen self-organizing map,* which is used extensively in commercial data mining products to perform clustering. There is one input layer and one special layer, which produces output values that compete. In effect, multiple outputs are created and the best one is chosen. This extra layer is not technically either a hidden layer or an output layer, so we refer to it here as the *competitive layer.* Nodes in this layer are viewed as a two-dimensional grid of nodes as seen in Figure 5.11. Each input node is connected to each node in this grid. Propagation occurs by sending the input value for each input node to each node in the competitive layer. As with regular NNs, each arc has an associated weight and each node in the competitive layer has an activation function. Thus, each node in the competitive layer produces an output value, and the node with the best output wins the competition and is determined to be the output for that input. An attractive feature of Kohonen nets is that the data can be fed into the multiple competitive nodes in parallel. Training occurs by adjusting weights so that the best output is even better the next time this input is used. "Best" is determined by computing a distance measure.

A common approach is to initialize the weights on the input arcs to the competitive layer with normalized values. The similarity between output nodes and input vectors is then determined by the dot product of the two vectors. Given an input tuple $X = \langle x_1, \ldots, x_h \rangle$ and weights on arcs input to a competitive node i as $w_{1i}, \ldots, w_{hi}$, the

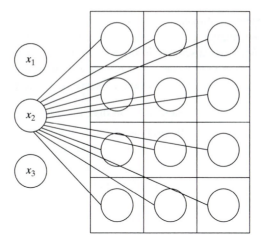

FIGURE 5.11: Kohonen network.

similarity between X and i can be calculated by

$$\text{sim}(X, i) = \sum_{j=1}^{h} x_j \, w_{ji} \tag{5.14}$$

The competitive node most similar to the input node wins the competitive. Based on this, the weights coming into i as well as those for the nodes immediately surrounding it in the matrix are increased. This is the learning phase. Given a node i, we use the notation N_i to represent the union of i and the nodes near it in the matrix. Thus, the learning process uses

$$\Delta w_{kj} = \left\{ \begin{array}{ll} c(x_k - w_{kj}) & \text{if } j \in N_i \\ 0 & \text{otherwise} \end{array} \right\} \tag{5.15}$$

In this formula, c indicates the learning rate and may actually vary based on the node rather than being a constant. The basic idea of SOM learning is that after each input tuple in the training set, the winner and its neighbors have their weights changed to be closer to that of the tuple. Over time, a pattern on the output nodes emerges, which is close to that of the training data. At the beginning of the training process, the neighborhood of a node may be defined to be large. However, the neighborhood may decrease during the processing.

5.6   CLUSTERING LARGE DATABASES

The clustering algorithms presented in the preceding sections are some of the classic clustering techniques. When clustering is used with dynamic databases, these algorithms may not be appropriate. First, they all assume that [because most are $O(n^2)$] sufficient main memory exists to hold the data to be clustered and the data structures needed to support them. With large databases containing thousands of items (or more), these assumptions are not realistic. In addition, performing I/Os continuously through the multiple iterations of an algorithm is too expensive. Because of these main memory restrictions, the algorithms do not scale up to large databases. Another issue is that some assume that the data are present all at once. These techniques are not appropriate for dynamic databases. Clustering techniques should be able to adapt as the database changes.

The algorithms discussed in the following subsections each examine an issue associated with performing clustering in a database environment. It has been argued that to perform effectively on large databases, a clustering algorithm should [BFR98]:

1. require no more (preferably less) than one scan of the database.
2. have the ability to provide status and "best" answer so far during the algorithm execution. This is sometimes referred to as the ability to be *online*.
3. be suspendable, stoppable, and resumable.
4. be able to update the results incrementally as data are added or removed from the database.
5. work with limited main memory.
6. be capable of performing different techniques for scanning the database. This may include sampling.
7. process each tuple only once.

Recent research at Microsoft has examined how to efficiently perform the clustering algorithms with large databases [BFR98]. The basic idea of this scaling approach is as follows:

1. Read a subset of the database into main memory.
2. Apply clustering technique to data in memory.
3. Combine results with those from prior samples.
4. The in-memory data are then divided into three different types: those items that will always be needed even when the next sample is brought in, those that can be discarded with appropriate updates to data being kept in order to answer the problem, and those that will be saved in a compressed format. Based on the type, each data item is then kept, deleted, or compressed in memory.
5. If termination criteria are not met, then repeat from step 1.

This approach has been applied to the K-means algorithm and has been shown to be effective.

5.6.1   BIRCH

BIRCH (balanced iterative reducing and clustering using hierarchies) is designed for clustering a large amount of metric data. It assumes that there may be a limited amount of main memory and achieves a linear I/O time requiring only one database scan. It is incremental and hierarchical, and it uses an outlier handling technique. Here points that are found in sparsely populated areas are removed. The basic idea of the algorithm is that a tree is built that captures needed information to perform clustering. The clustering is then performed on the tree itself, where labelings of nodes in the tree contain the needed information to calculate distance values. A major characteristic of the BIRCH algorithm is the use of the *clustering feature*, which is a triple that contains information about a cluster (see Definition 5.3). The clustering feature provides a summary of the information about one cluster. By this definition it is clear that BIRCH applies only to numeric data.

This algorithm uses a tree called a *CF tree* as defined in Definition 5.4. The size of the tree is determined by a threshold value, T, associated with each leaf node. This is the maximum diameter allowed for any leaf. Here *diameter* is the average of the pairwise distance between all points in the cluster. Each internal node corresponds to a cluster that is composed of the subclusters represented by its children.

DEFINITION 5.3. A **clustering feature (CF)** is a triple $(N, \vec{LS}, SS)$, where the number of the points in the cluster is N, $\vec{LS}$ is the sum of the points in the cluster, and SS is the sum of the squares of the points in the cluster.

DEFINITION 5.4. A **CF tree** is a balanced tree with a branching factor (maximum number of children a node may have) B. Each internal node contains a CF triple for each of its children. Each leaf node also represents a cluster and contains a CF entry for each subcluster in it. A subcluster in a leaf node must have a diameter no greater than a given threshold value T.

Unlike a dendrogram, a CF tree is searched in a top-down fashion. Each node in the CF tree contains clustering feature information about its subclusters. As points are added to the clustering problem, the CF tree is built. A point is inserted into the cluster (represented by a leaf node) to which it is closest. If the diameter for the leaf node is greater than T, then a splitting and balancing of the tree is performed (similar to that used in a B-tree). The algorithm adapts to main memory size by changing the threshold value. A larger threshold, T, yields a smaller CF tree. This process can be performed without rereading the data. The clustering feature data provides enough information to perform this condensation. The complexity of the algorithm is $O(n)$.

ALGORITHM 5.10

Input:
```
    D = {t₁, t₂, ..., tₙ}    //Set of elements
    T       // Threshold for CF tree construction
```
Output:
```
    K       //Set of clusters
```
BIRCH clustering algorithm:
```
    for each tᵢ ∈ D do
        determine correct leaf node for tᵢ insertion;
        if threshold condition is not violated, then
            add tᵢ to cluster and update CF triples;
        else
            if room to insert tᵢ, then
                insert tᵢ as single cluster and update CF triples;
            else
                split leaf node and redistribute CF features;
```

Algorithm 5.10 outlines the steps performed in BIRCH. Not shown in this algorithm are the parameters needed for the CF tree construction, such as its branching factor, the page block size, and memory size. Based on size, each node has room for a fixed number, B, of clusters (i.e., CF triples). The first step creates the CF tree in memory. The threshold value can be modified if necessary to ensure that the tree fits into the available memory space. Insertion into the CF tree requires scanning the tree from the root down, choosing the node closest to the new point at each level. The distance here is calculated by looking at the distance between the new point and the centroid of the cluster. This can be easily calculated with most distance measures (e.g., Euclidean or Manhattan) using the CF triple. When the new item is inserted, the CF triple is appropriately updated, as is each triple on the path from the root down to the leaf. It is then added to the closest leaf node found by adjusting the CF value for that node. When an item is inserted into a cluster at the leaf node of the tree, the cluster must satisfy the threshold value. If it does, then the CF entry for that cluster is modified. If it does not, then that item is added to that node as a single-item cluster.

Node splits occur if no space exists in a given node. This is based on the size of the physical page because each node size is determined by the page size. An attractive feature of the CF values is that they are additive; that is, if two clusters are merged, the resulting CF is the addition of the CF values for the starting clusters. Once the tree is built, the leaf nodes of the CF tree represent the current clusters.

In reality, this algorithm, Algorithm 5.10, is only the first of several steps proposed for the use of BIRCH with large databases. The complete outline of steps is:

1. Create initial CF tree using a modified version of Algorithm 5.10. This in effect "loads" the database into memory. If there is insufficient memory to construct the CF tree with a given threshold, the threshold value is increased and a new smaller CF tree is constructed. This can be done by inserting the leaf nodes of the previous tree into the new small tree.

2. The clustering represented by the CF tree may not be natural because each entry has a limited size. In addition, the input order can negatively impact the results. These problems can be overcome by another global clustering approach applied to the leaf nodes in the CF tree. Here each leaf node is treated as a single point for clustering. Although the original work proposes a centroid-based agglomerative hierarchical clustering algorithm to cluster the subclusters, other clustering algorithms could be used.

3. The last phase (which is optional) reclusters all points by placing them in the cluster that has the closest centroid. Outliers, points that are too far from any centroid, can be removed during this phase.

BIRCH is linear in both space and I/O time. The choice of threshold value is imperative to an efficient execution of the algorithm. Otherwise, the tree may have to be rebuilt many times to ensure that it can be memory-resident. This gives the worst-case time complexity of $O(n^2)$.

5.6.2 DBSCAN

The approach used by *DBSCAN (density-based spatial clustering of applications with noise)* is to create clusters with a minimum size and density. Density is defined as a minimum number of points within a certain distance of each other. This handles the outlier problem by ensuring that an outlier (or a small set of outliers) will not create a cluster. One input parameter, *MinPts*, indicates the minimum number of points in any cluster. In addition, for each point in a cluster there must be another point in the cluster whose distance from it is less than a threshold input value, *Eps*. The *Eps-neighborhood* or *neighborhood* of a point is the set of points within a distance of *Eps*. The desired number of clusters, k, is not input but rather is determined by the algorithm itself.

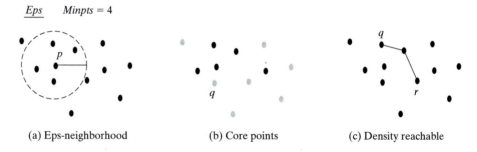

(a) Eps-neighborhood   (b) Core points   (c) Density reachable

FIGURE 5.12: DBSCAN example.

DBSCAN uses a new concept of density. We first must look at some definitions from [EKSX96]. Definition 5.5 defines *directly density-reachable*. The first part of the definition ensures that the second point is "close enough" to the first point. The second portion of the definition ensures that there are enough *core points* close enough to each other. These core points form the main portion of a cluster in that they are all close to each other. A directly density-reachable point must be close to one of these core points, but it need not be a core point itself. In that case, it is called a *border point*. A point is said to be *density-reachable* from another point if there is a chain from one to the other that contains only points that are directly density-reachable from the previous point. This guarantees that any cluster will have a core set of points very close to a large number of other points (core points) and then some other points (border points) that are sufficiently close to at least one core point.

DEFINITION 5.5. Given values *Eps* and *MinPts*, a point p is **directly density-reachable** from q if

- $\text{dis}(p, q) \leq Eps$

  and

- $| \{r \mid \text{dis}(r, q) \leq Eps\} | \geq \text{MinPts}$

Figure 5.12 illustrates the concepts used by DBSCAN. This figure shows 12 points. The assumed *Eps* value is illustrated by the straight line. In part (a) it is shown that there are 4 points within the neighborhood of point p. As is seen, p is a core point because it has 4 (*MinPts* value) points within its neighborhood. Part (b) shows the 5 core points in the figure. Note that of the 4 points that are in the neighborhood of p, only 3 are themselves core points. These 4 points are said to be directly density-reachable from p. Point q is not a core point and is thus called a border point. We have partitioned the points into a core set of points that are all close to each other; then border points, which are close to at least one of the core points; and finally the remaining points, which are not close to any core point. Part (C) shows that even though point r is not a core point, it is density-reachable from q.

Algorithm 5.11 outlines the DBSCAN algorithm. Because of the restrictions on what constitutes a cluster when the algorithm finishes, there will be points not assigned to a cluster. These are defined as noise.

ALGORITHM 5.11

```
Input:
    D = {t₁, t₂, ..., tₙ}    //Set of elements
    MinPts        // Number of points in cluster
    Eps    // Maximum distance for density measure
Output:
    K = {K₁, K₂, ..., Kₖ}        //Set of clusters
DBSCAN algorithm:
    k = 0;    // Initially there are no clusters.
    for i = 1 to n do
        if tᵢ is not in a cluster, then
            X = {tⱼ | tⱼ is density-reachable from tᵢ};
            if X is a valid cluster, then
                k = k + 1;
                Kₖ = X;
```

The expected time complexity of DBSCAN is $O(n \lg n)$. It is possible that a border point could belong to two clusters. The stated algorithm will place this point in whichever cluster is generated first. DBSCAN was compared with CLARANS and found to be more efficient by a factor of 250 to 1900 [EKSX96]. In addition, it successfully found all clusters and noise from the test dataset, whereas CLARANS did not.

5.6.3 CURE Algorithm

One objective for the *CURE (Clustering Using REpresentatives)* clustering algorithm is to handle outliers well. It has both a hierarchical component and a partitioning component. First, a constant number of points, c, are chosen from each cluster. These well-scattered points are then shrunk toward the cluster's centroid by applying a shrinkage factor, α. When α is 1, all points are shrunk to just one—the centroid. These points represent the cluster better than a single point (such as a medoid or centroid) could. With multiple representative points, clusters of unusual shapes (not just a sphere) can be better represented. CURE then uses a hierarchical clustering algorithm. At each step in the agglomerative algorithm, clusters with the closest pair of representative points are chosen to be merged. The distance between them is defined as the minimum distance between any pair of points in the representative sets from the two clusters.

The basic approach used by CURE is shown in Figure 5.13. The first step shows a sample of the data. A set of clusters with its representative points exists at each step in the processing. In Figure 5.13(b) there are three clusters, each with two representative points. The representative points are shown as darkened circles. As discussed in the following paragraphs, these representative points are chosen to be far from each other as well as from the mean of the cluster. In part (c), two of the clusters are merged and two new representative points are chosen. Finally, in part (d), these points are shrunk toward the mean of the cluster. Notice that if one representative centroid had been chosen for the clusters, the smaller cluster would have been merged with the bottom cluster instead of with the top cluster.

CURE handles limited main memory by obtaining a random sample to find the initial clusters. The random sample is partitioned, and each partition is then partially clustered. These resulting clusters are then completely clustered in a second pass. The

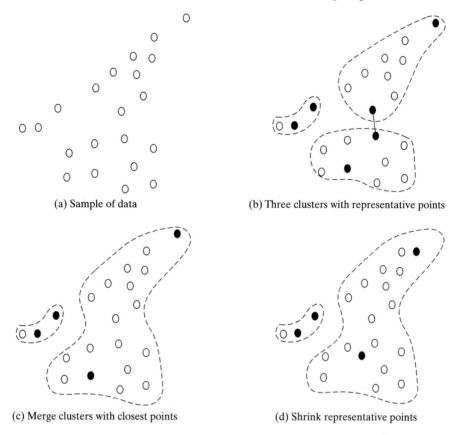

(a) Sample of data   (b) Three clusters with representative points

(c) Merge clusters with closest points   (d) Shrink representative points

FIGURE 5.13: CURE example.

sampling and partitioning are done solely to ensure that the data (regardless of database size) can fit into available main memory. When the clustering of the sample is complete, the labeling of data on disk is performed. A data item is assigned to the cluster with the closest representative points. The basic steps of CURE for large databases are:

1. Obtain a sample of the database.
2. Partition the sample into p partitions of size $\frac{n}{p}$. This is done to speed up the algorithm because clustering is first performed on each partition.
3. Partially cluster the points in each partition using the hierarchical algorithm (see Algorithm 5.12). This provides a first guess at what the clusters should be. The number of clusters is $\frac{n}{pq}$ for some constant q.
4. Remove outliers. Outliers are eliminated by the use of two different techniques. The first technique eliminates clusters that grow very slowly. When the number of clusters is below a threshold, those clusters with only one or two items are deleted. It is possible that close outliers are part of the sample and would not be identified by the first outlier elimination technique. The second technique removes very small clusters toward the end of the clustering phase.

5. Completely cluster all data in the sample using Algorithm 5.12. Here, to ensure processing in main memory, the input includes only the cluster representatives from the clusters found for each partition during the partial clustering step (3).

6. Cluster the entire database on disk using c points to represent each cluster. An item in the database is placed in the cluster that has the closest representative point to it. These sets of representative points are small enough to fit into main memory, so each of the n points must be compared to ck representative points.

The time complexity of CURE is $O(n^2 \lg n)$, while space is $O(n)$. This is worst-case behavior. The improvements proposed for main memory processing certainly improve on this time complexity because the entire clustering algorithm is performed against only the sample. When clustering is performed on the complete database, a time complexity of only $O(n)$ is required. A heap and k-D tree data structure are used to ensure this performance. One entry in the heap exists for each cluster. Each cluster has not only its representative points, but also the cluster that is closest to it. Entries in the heap are stored in increasing order of the distances between clusters. We assume that each entry u in the heap contains the set of representative points, $u.rep$; the mean of the points in the cluster, $u.mean$; and the cluster closest to it, $u.closest$. We use the heap operations: *heapify* to create the heap, *min* to extract the minimum entry in the heap, *insert* to add a new entry, and *delete* to delete an entry. A *merge* procedure is used to merge two clusters. It determines the new representative points for the new cluster. The basic idea of this process is to first find the point that is farthest from the mean. Subsequent points are then chosen based on being the farthest from those points that were previously chosen. A predefined number of points is picked. A *k-D tree* is a balanced binary tree that can be thought of as a generalization of a binary search tree. It is used to index data of k dimensions where the ith level of the tree indexes the ith dimension. In CURE, a k-D tree is used to assist in the merging of clusters. It stores the representative points for each cluster. Initially, there is only one representative point for each cluster, the sole item in it. Operations performed on the tree are: *delete* to delete an entry form the tree, *insert* to insert an entry into it, and *build* to initially create it. The hierarchical clustering algorithm itself, which is from [GRS98], is shown in Algorithm 5.12. We do not include here either the sampling algorithms or the merging algorithm.

ALGORITHM 5.12

```
Input:
    D = {t₁, t₂,..., tₙ}   //Set of elements
    k       // Desired number of clusters
Output:
    Q       //Heap containing one entry for each cluster
CURE algorithm:
    T = build(D);
    Q = heapify(D); // Initially build heap with one entry per item;
    repeat
        u = min(Q);
        delete(Q, u.close);
        w = merge(u, v);
        delete(T, u);
        delete(T, v);
```

```
    insert(T, w);
  for each x ∈ Q do
      x.close = find closest cluster to x;
      if x is closest to w, then
          w.close = x;
      insert(Q, w);
  until number of nodes in Q is k;
```

Performance experiments compared CURE to BIRCH and the MST approach [GRS98]. The quality of the clusters found by CURE is better. While the value of the shrinking factor α does impact results, with a value between 0.2 and 0.7, the correct clusters are still found. When the number of representative points per cluster is greater than five, the correct clusters are still always found. A random sample size of about 2.5% and the number of partitions is greater than one or two times k seem to work well. The results with large datasets indicate that CURE scales well and outperforms BIRCH.

5.7 CLUSTERING WITH CATEGORICAL ATTRIBUTES

Traditional algorithms do not always work with categorical data. Example 5.8 illustrates some problems that exist when clustering categorical data. This example uses a hierarchical-based centroid algorithm to illustrate the problems. The problem illustrated here is that the centroid tends to weaken the relationship between the associated cluster and other clusters. The problems worsens as more and more clusters are merged. The number of attributes appearing in the mean increases, while the individual values actually decreases. This makes the centroid representations very similar and makes distinguishing between clusters difficult.

EXAMPLE 5.8

Consider an information retrieval system where documents may contain keywords {book, water, sun, sand, swim, read}. Suppose there are four documents, where the first contains the word {book}, the second contains {water, sun, sand, swim}, the third contains {water, sun, swim, read}, and the fourth contains {read, sand}. We can represent the four books using the following boolean points: (1, 0, 0, 0, 0, 0), (0, 1, 1, 1, 1, 0), (0, 1, 1, 0, 1, 1), (0, 0, 0, 1, 0, 1). We can use the Euclidean distance to develop the following adjacency matrix of distances:

	1	2	3	4
1	0	2.24	2.24	1.73
2	2.24	0	1.41	2
3	2.24	1.41	0	2
4	1.73	2	2	0

The distance between points 2 and 3 is the smallest (1.41), and thus they are merged. When they are merged, we get a cluster containing {(0, 1, 1, 1, 1, 0), (0, 1, 1, 0, 1, 1)} with a centroid of (0, 1, 1, 0.5, 1, 0.5). At this point we have a distance from this new cluster centroid to the original points 1 and 4 being 2.24 and 1.73, respectively, while the distance between original points 1 and 4 is 1.73. Thus, we could next merge these points even though they have no keywords in common. So with $k = 2$ we have the following clusters: $\{\{1, 4\}, \{2, 3\}\}$.

The *ROCK (RObust Clustering using linKs)* clustering algorithm is targeted to both boolean data and categorical data. A novel approach to identifying similarity is based on the number of links between items. A pair of items are said to be *neighbors* if their similarity exceeds some threshold. This need not be defined based on a precise metric, but rather a more intuitive approach using domain experts could be used. The number of *links* between two items is defined as the number of common neighbors they have. The objective of the clustering algorithm is to group together points that have more links. The algorithm is a hierarchical agglomerative algorithm using the number of links as the similarity measure rather than a measure based on distance.

Instead of using a Euclidean distance, a different distance, such as the Jaccard coefficient, has been proposed. One proposed similarity measure based on the Jaccard coefficient is defined as

$$\text{sim}(t_i, t_j) = \frac{|\,t_i \cap t_j\,|}{|\,t_i \cup t_j\,|} \qquad (5.16)$$

If the tuples are viewed to be sets of items purchased (i.e., market basket data), then we look at the number of items they have in common divided by the total number in both. The denominator is used to normalize the value to be between 0 and 1.

The number of links between a pair of points can be viewed as the number of unique paths of length 2 between them. The authors argue that the use of links rather than similarity (distance) measures provides a more global approach because the similarity between points is impacted by other points as well. Example 5.9 illustrates the use of links by the ROCK algorithm using the data from Example 5.8 using the Jaccard coefficient. Note that different threshold values for neighbors could be used to get different results. Also note that a hierarchical approach could be used with different threshold values for each level in the dendrogram.

EXAMPLE 5.9

Using the data from Example 5.8, we have the following table of similarities (as opposed to the distances given in the example):

	1	2	3	4
1	1	0	0	0
2	0	1	0.6	0.2
3	0	0.6	1	0.2
4	0	0.2	0.2	1

Suppose we say that the threshold for a neighbor is 0.6, then we have the following are the neighbors: $\{(2, 3), (2, 4), (3, 4)\}$. Note that in the following we add to these that a point is a neighbor of itself so that we have the additional neighbors: $\{(1, 1), (2, 2), (3, 3), (4, 4)\}$. The following table shows the number of links (common neighbors between points) assuming that the threshold for a neighbor is 0.6:

	1	2	3	4
1	1	0	0	0
2	0	3	3	3
3	0	3	3	3
4	0	3	3	3

In this case, then, we have the following clusters: $\{\{1\}, \{2, 3, 4\}\}$. Comparing this to the set of clustering found with a traditional Euclidean distance, we see that a "better" set of clusters has been created.

The ROCK algorithm is divided into three general parts:

1. Obtaining a random sample of the data.
2. Performing clustering on the data using the link agglomerative approach. A goodness measure is used to determine which pair of points is merged at each step.
3. Using these clusters the remaining data on disk are assigned to them.

The goodness measure used to merge clusters is:

$$g(K_i, K_j) = \frac{\text{link}(K_i, K_j)}{(n_i + n_j)^{1+2f(\Theta)} - n_i^{1+2f(\Theta)} - n_j^{1+2f(\Theta)}}. \tag{5.17}$$

Here $\text{link}(K_i, K_j)$ is the number of links between the two clusters. Also, n_i and n_j are the number of points in each cluster. The denominator is used to normalize the number of links because larger clusters would be expected to have more links simply because they are larger. $n_i^{1+2f(\Theta)}$ is an estimate for the number of links between pairs of points in K_i when the threshold used for the similarity measure is Θ. The function $f(\Theta)$ depends on the data, but it is found to satisfy the property that each item in K_i has approximately $n_i^{f(\Theta)}$ neighbors in the cluster. Obviously, if all points in the cluster are connected, $f(\Theta) = 1$. Then n_i^3 is the number of links between points in K_i.

The first step in the algorithm converts the adjacency matrix into a boolean matrix where an entry is 1 if the two corresponding points are neighbors. As the adjacency matrix is of size n^2, this is an $O(n^2)$ step. The next step converts this into a matrix indicating the links. This can be found by calculating $S \times S$, which can be done in $O(n^{2.37})$ [GRS99]. The hierarchical clustering portion of the algorithm then starts by placing each point in the sample in a separate cluster. It then successively merges clusters until k clusters are found. To facilitate this processing, both local and global heaps are used. A local heap, q, is created to represent each cluster. Here q contains every cluster that has a nonzero link to the cluster that corresponds to this cluster. Initially, a cluster is created for each point, t_i. The heap for t_i, $q[t_i]$, contains every cluster that has a nonzero link to $\{t_i\}$ The global heap contains information about each cluster. All information in the heap is ordered based on the goodness measure, which is shown in Equation 5.17.

5.8 COMPARISON

The different clustering algorithms discussed in this chapter are compared in Table 5.3. Here we include a classification of the type of algorithm, space and time complexity, and general notes concerning applicability.

TABLE 5.3: Comparison of Clustering Algorithms

Algorithm	Type	Space	Time	Notes
Single link	Hierarchical	$O(n^2)$	$O(kn^2)$	Not incremental
Average link	Hierarchical	$O(n^2)$	$O(kn^2)$	Not incremental
Complete link	Hierarchical	$O(n^2)$	$O(kn^2)$	Not incremental
MST	Hierarchical/ partitional	$O(n^2)$	$O(n^2)$	Not incremental
Squared error	Partitional	$O(n)$	$O(tkn)$	Iterative
K-means	Partitional	$O(n)$	$O(tkn)$	Iterative; No categorical
Nearest neighbor	Partitional	$O(n^2)$	$O(n^2)$	Iterative
PAM	Partitional	$O(n^2)$	$O(tk(n-k)^2)$	Iterative; Adapted agglomerative; Outliers
BIRCH	Partitional	$O(n)$	$O(n)$ (no rebuild)	CF-tree; Incremental; Outliers
CURE	Mixed	$O(n)$	$O(n)$	Heap; k-D tree; Incremental; Outliers; Sampling
ROCK	Agglomerative	$O(n^2)$	$O(n^2 lgn)$	Sampling; Categorical; Links
DBSCAN	Mixed	$O(n^2)$	$O(n^2)$	Sampling; Outliers

The single link, complete link, and average link techniques are all hierarchical techniques with $O(n^2)$ time and space complexity. While we discussed the agglomerative versions of these are also divisive versions, which create the clusters in a top-down manner. They all assume the data are present and thus are not incremental. There are several clustering algorithms based on the construction of an MST. There are both hierarchical and partitional versions. Their complexity is identical to that for the other hierarchical techniques, and since they depend on the construction of the MST, they are not incremental. Both K-means and the squared error techniques are iterative, requiring $O(tkn)$ time. The nearest neighbor is not iterative, but the number of clusters is not predetermined. Thus, the worst-case complexity can be $O(n^2)$. BIRCH appears to be quite efficient, but remember that the CF-tree may need to be rebuilt. The time complexity in the table assumes that the tree is not rebuilt. CURE is an improvement on these by using sampling and partitioning to handle scalability well and uses multiple points rather than just one point to represent each cluster. Using multiple points allows the approach to detect nonspherical clusters. With sampling, CURE obtains an $O(n)$ time complexity. However, CURE does not handle categorical data well. This also allows it to be more resistant to the negative impact of outliers. K-means and PAM work by iteratively reassigning items to clusters, which may not find a global optimal assignment. The results of the K-means algorithm is quite sensitive to the presence of outliers. Through the use of the CF-tree, Birch is both dynamic and scalable. However, it detects only spherical type clusters. DBSCAN is a density-based approach. The time complexity of DBSCAN can be improved to $O(n lgn)$ with appropriate spatial indices. We have not included the genetic algorithms in this table because their performance totally depends on the technique chosen to represent individuals, how crossover is done, and the termination condition used.

5.9   EXERCISES

1. A major problem with the single link algorithm is that clusters consisting of long chains may be created. Describe and illustrate this concept.

2. Show the dendrogram created by the single, complete, and average link clustering algorithms using the following adjacency matrix:

Item	A	B	C	D
A	0	1	4	5
B	1	0	2	6
C	4	2	0	3
D	5	6	3	0

3. Construct a graph showing all edges for the data in Exercise 2. Find an MST for this graph. Is the MST single link hierarchical clustering the same as that found using the traditional single link algorithm?

4. Convert Algorithm 5.1 to a generic divisive algorithm. What technique would be used to split clusters in the single link and complete link versions?

5. Trace the results of applying the squared error Algorithm 5.5 to the data from Example 5.4 into two clusters. Indicate the convergence threshold you have used.

6. Use the K-means algorithm to cluster the data in Example 5.4 into three clusters.

7. Trace the use of the nearest neighbor algorithm on the data of Exercise 2 assuming a threshold of 3.

8. Determine the cost C_{jih} for each of the four cases given for the PAM algorithm.

9. Finish the application of PAM in Example 5.6.

10. (**Research**) Perform a survey of recently proposed clustering algorithms. Identify where they fit in the classification tree in Figure 5.2. Describe their approach and performance.

5.10   BIBLIOGRAPHIC NOTES

There are many excellent books examining the concept of clustering. In [JD88], a thorough treatment of clustering algorithms, including application domains, and statement of algorithms, is provided. This work also looks at a different classification of clustering techniques. Other clustering and prediction books include [Har75], [JS71], [SS73], [TB70], and [WI98].

A survey article of clustering with a complete list of references was published in 1999 [JMF99]. It covers more clustering techniques than are found in this chapter. Included are fuzzy clustering, evolutionary techniques, and a comparison of the two. An excellent discussion of applications is also included. Fuzzy clustering associates a membership function with every item and every cluster. Imagine that each cluster is represented as a vector of membership values, one for each element. Other clustering surveys have been published in [NH94] and [HKT01].

Clustering tutorials have been presented at SIGMOD 1999 [HK99] and PAKDD-02.[1]

The agglomerative clustering methods are among the oldest techniques. Proposals include SLINK [Sib73] for single linkage and CLINK [Def77] for complete linkage. An excellent study of these algorithms can be found in [KR90]. The AGNES and DIANA techniques are some of the earliest methods. *AGNES (AGglomerative NESting)* is agglomerative, while *DIANA (DIvisia ANAlysis)* is divisive. Both are known not to scale well. Articles on single link clustering date back to 1951 [FLP$^+$51]. The EM algorithm has frequently been used to perform interative clustering [DLR77]. There have been many variations of the K-means clustering algorithm. The earliest reference is to a version by Forgy in 1965 [For65], [McQ67]. Another approach for partitional clustering is to allow splitting and merging of clusters. Here merging is performed based on the distance between the centroids of two clusters. A cluster is split if its variance is above a certain threshold. One proposed algorithm performing this is called ISODATA [BH65]. CURE, predominantly a hierarchical technique, was first proposed in [GRS98]. Finding connected components in a graph is a well-known graph technique that is described in any graph theory or data structures text such as [Har72].

The MST partitional algorithm was originally proposed by Zahn [Zha71].

A recent work has looked at extending the definition of clustering to be more applicable to categorical data. *CAtegorical ClusTering Using Summaries (CACTUS)* generalizes the traditional definition of clustering and distance. To perform the clustering, it uses summary information obtained from the actual data. The summary information fits into main memory and can be easily constructed. The definition of similarity between tuples is given by looking at the support of two attribute values within the database D. Given two categorical attribute A_i, A_j with domains D_i, D_j, respectively, the *support* of the attribute pair (a_i, a_j) is defined as:

$$\sigma_D(a_i, a_j) = |\ \{t \in D : t.A_i = a_i \wedge t.A_j = a_j\}\ | \qquad (5.18)$$

The similarity of attributes used for clustering is based on the support [GGR99b].

Several techniques have been proposed to scale up clustering algorithms to work effectively on large databases. Sampling and data compressions are perhaps the most common techniques. With sampling, the algorithm is applied to a large enough sample to ideally produce a good clustering result. Both BIRCH and CACTUS employ compression techniques. A more recent data compression approach, data bubbles, has been applied to hierarchical clustering [BKKS01]. A *data bubble* is a compressed data item that represents a larger set of items in the database. Given a set of items, a data bubble consists of (a representative item, cardinality of set, radius of set, estimated average k nearest neighbor distances in the set). Another compression technique for hierarchical clustering, which actually compresses the dendrogram, has recently been proposed [XD01b].

A recent article has proposed outlier detection algorithms that scale well to large datasets and can be used to model the previous statistical tests [KN98].

---

[1]Osmar Zaiane and Andrew Foss, "Data Clustering Analysis, from Simple Groupings to Scalable Clustering with Constraints," Tutorial at Sixth Pacific-Asia Conference on Knowledge Discovery and Data Mining, May 6, 2002.

Discussion of the bond energy algorithm and its use can be found in [WTMSW72], [ÖV99], and [TF82]. It can be used to cluster attributes based on use and then perform logical or physical clustering.

DBSCAN was first proposed in [EKSX96]. Other density-based algorithms include DENCLUE [HK98] and OPTICS [].

ROCK was proposed by Guha in [GRS99].

There have been many approaches targeted to clustering of large databases, including BIRCH [ZRL96], CLARANS [NH94], CURE [GRS98], DBSCAN [EKSX96], and ROCK [GRS99]. Specifics concerning CF tree maintenance can be found in the literature [ZRL96]. A discussion of the use of R*-trees in DBSCAN can be found in [EKSX96]. It is possible that a border point could belong to two clusters. A recent algorithm, *CHAMELEON*, is a hierarchical clustering algorithm that bases merging of clusters on both closeness and their interconnection [KHK99]. When dealing with large databases, the requirement to fix the number of clusters dynamically can be a major problem. Recent research into *online* (or *iterative*) clustering algorithms has been performed. "Online" implies that the algorithm can be performed dynamically as the data are generated, and thus it works well for dynamic databases. In addition, some work has examined how to adapt, thus allowing the user to change the number of clusters dynamically. These *adaptive* algorithms avoid having to completely recluster the database if the users' needs change. One recent online approach represents the clusters by profiles (such as cluster mean and size). These profiles are shown to the user, and the user has the ability to change the parameters (number of clusters) at any time during processing. One recent clustering approach is both online and adaptive, OAK (online adaptive clustering) [XD01b]. OAK can also handle outliers effectively by adjusting a viewing parameter, which gives the user a broader view of the clustering, so that he or she can choose his or her desired clusters.

NNs have been used to solve the clustering problem [JMF99]. Kohonen's self-organizing maps are introduced in [Koh82]. One of the earliest algorithms was the leader clustering algorithm proposed by Hartigan [Har75]. Its time complexity is only $O(kn)$ and its space is only $O(k)$. A common NN applied is a competitive one such as an SOFM where the learning is nonsupervised [JMF99].

References to clustering algorithms based on genetic algorithms include [JB91] and [BRE91].

CHAPTER 6

Association Rules

6.1 INTRODUCTION

The purchasing of one product when another product is purchased represents an association rule. Association rules are frequently used by retail stores to assist in marketing, advertising, floor placement, and inventory control. Although they have direct applicability to retail businesses, they have been used for other purposes as well, including predicting faults in telecommunication networks. Association rules are used to show the relationships between data items. These uncovered relationships are not inherent in the data, as with functional dependencies, and they do not represent any sort of causality or correlation. Instead, association rules detect common usage of items. Example 6.1 illustrates this.

EXAMPLE 6.1

A grocery store chain keeps a record of weekly transactions where each transaction represents the items bought during one cash register transaction. The executives of the chain receive a summarized report of the transactions indicating what types of items have sold at what quantity. In addition, they periodically request information about what items are commonly purchased together. They find that 100% of the time that PeanutButter is purchased, so is Bread. In addition, 33.3% of the time PeanutButter is purchased, Jelly is also purchased. However, PeanutButter exists in only about 50% of the overall transactions.

A database in which an association rule is to be found is viewed as a set of tuples, where each tuple contains a set of items. For example, a tuple could be {PeanutButter, Bread, Jelly}, which consists of the three items: peanut butter, bread, and jelly. Keeping grocery story cash register transactions in mind, each item represents an item purchased, while each tuple is the list of items purchased at one time. In the simplest cases, we are not interested in quantity or cost, so these may be removed from the records before processing. Table 6.1 is used throughout this chapter to illustrate different algorithms. Here there are five transactions and five items: {Beer, Bread, Jelly, Milk, PeanutButter}. Throughout this chapter we list items in alphabetical order within a transaction. Although this is not required, algorithms often assume that this sorting is done in a preprocessing step.

The *support* of an item (or set of items) is the percentage of transactions in which that item (or items) occurs. Table 6.2 shows the support for all subsets of items from our total set. As seen, there is an exponential growth in the sets of items. In this case we could have 31 sets of items from the original set of five items (ignoring the empty set). This explosive growth in potential sets of items is an issue that most association

TABLE 6.1: Sample Data to Illustrate Association Rules

Transaction	Items
t_1	Bread, Jelly, PeanutButter
t_2	Bread, PeanutButter
t_3	Bread, Milk, PeanutButter
t_4	Beer, Bread
t_5	Beer, Milk

TABLE 6.2: Support of All Sets of Items Found in Table 6.1

Set	Support	Set	Support
Beer	40	Beer, Bread, Milk	0
Bread	80	Beer, Bread, PeanutButter	0
Jelly	20	Beer, Jelly, Milk	0
Milk	40	Beer, Jelly, PeanutButter	0
PeanutButter	60	Beer, Milk, PeanutButter	0
Beer, Bread	20	Bread, Jelly, Milk	0
Beer, Jelly	0	Bread, Jelly, PeanutButter	20
Beer, Milk	20	Bread, Milk, PeanutButter	20
Beer, PeanutButter	0	Jelly, Milk, PeanutButter	0
Bread, Jelly	20	Beer, Bread, Jelly, Milk	0
Bread, Milk	20	Beer, Bread, Jelly, PeanutButter	0
Bread, PeanutButter	60	Beer, Bread, Milk, PeanutButter	0
Jelly, Milk	0	Beer, Jelly, Milk, PeanutButter	0
Jelly, PeanutButter	20	Bread, Jelly, Milk, PeanutButter	0
Milk, PeanutButter	20	Beer, Bread, Jelly, Milk, PeanutButter	0
Beer, Bread, Jelly	0		

rule algorithms must contend with, as the conventional approach to generating association rules is in actuality counting the occurrence of sets of items in the transaction database.

Note that we are dealing with categorical data. Given a target domain, the underlying set of items usually is known, so that an encoding of the transactions could be performed before processing. As we will see, however, association rules can be applied to data domains other than categorical.

> **DEFINITION 6.1.** Given a set of *items* $I = \{I_1, I_2, \ldots, I_m\}$ and a database of transactions $D = \{t_1, t_2, \ldots, t_n\}$ where $t_i = \{I_{i1}, I_{i2}, \ldots, I_{ik}\}$ and $I_{ij} \in I$, an **association rule** is an implication of the form $X \Rightarrow Y$ where $X, Y \subset I$ are sets of items called *itemsets* and $X \cap Y = \emptyset$.

> **DEFINITION 6.2.** The **support (s)** for an association rule $X \Rightarrow Y$ is the percentage of transactions in the database that contain $X \cup Y$.

> **DEFINITION 6.3.** The **confidence or strength** (α) for an association rule $X \Rightarrow Y$ is the ratio of the number of transactions that contain $X \cup Y$ to the number of transactions that contain X.

A formal definition, from [AIS93], is found in Definition 6.1. We generally are not interested in all implications but only those that are important. Here importance usually is measured by two features called *support* and *confidence* as defined in Definitions 6.2 and 6.3. Table 6.3 shows the support and confidence for several association rules, including those from Example 6.1.

The selection of association rules is based on these two values as described in the definition of the association rule problem in Definition 6.4. Confidence measures the strength of the rule, whereas support measures how often it should occur in the database. Typically, large confidence values and a smaller support are used. For example, look at Bread $\Rightarrow$ PeanutButter in Table 6.3. With $\alpha = 75\%$, this indicates that this rule holds 75% of the time that it could. That is, 3/4 times that Bread occurs, so does PeanutButter. This is a stronger rule than Jelly $\Rightarrow$ Milk because there are no times Milk is purchased when Jelly is bought. An advertising executive probably would not want to base an advertising campaign on the fact that when a person buys Jelly he also buys Milk. Lower values for support may be allowed as support indicates the percentage of time the rule occurs throughout the database. For example, with Jelly $\Rightarrow$ PeanutButter, the confidence is 100% but the support is only 20%. It may be the case that this association

TABLE 6.3: Support and Confidence for Some Association Rules

$X \Rightarrow Y$	s	α
Bread $\Rightarrow$ PeanutButter	60%	75%
PeanutButter $\Rightarrow$ Bread	60%	100%
Beer $\Rightarrow$ Bread	20%	50%
PeanutButter $\Rightarrow$ Jelly	20%	33.3%
Jelly $\Rightarrow$ PeanutButter	20%	100%
Jelly $\Rightarrow$ Milk	0%	0%

rule exists only in 20% of the transactions, but when the *antecedent* Jelly occurs, the *consequent* always occurs. Here an advertising strategy targeted to people who purchase Jelly would be appropriate.

The discussion so far has centered around the use of association rules in the *market basket* area. Example 6.2 illustrates a use for association rules in another domain: telecommunications. This example, although quite simplified from the similar real-world problem, illustrates the importance of association rules in other domains and the fact that support need not always be high.

EXAMPLE 6.2

A telephone company must ensure that a high percentage of all phone calls are made within a certain period of time. Since each phone call must be routed through many switches, it is imperative that each switch work correctly. The failure of any switch could result in a call not being completed or being completed in an unacceptably long period of time. In this environment, a potential data mining problem would be to predict a failure of a node. Then, when the node is predicted to fail, measures can be taken by the phone company to route all calls around the node and replace the switch. To this end, the company keeps a history of calls through a switch. Each call history indicates the success or failure of the switch, associated timing, and error indication. The history contains results of the last and prior traffic through the switch. A transaction of the type ⟨success, failure⟩ indicates that the most recent call could not be handled successfully, while the call before that was handled fine. Another transaction ⟨ERR1, failure⟩ indicates that the previous call was handled but an error occurred, ERR1. This error could be something like excessive time. The data mining problem can then be stated as finding association rules of the type $X \Rightarrow$ Failure. If these types of rules occur with a high confidence, we could predict failure and immediately take the node off-line. Even though the support might be low because the X condition does not frequently occur, most often when it occurs, the node fails with the next traffic.

DEFINITION 6.4. Given a set of *items* $I = \{I_1, I_2, \ldots, I_m\}$ and a database of transactions $D = \{t_1, t_2, \ldots, t_n\}$ where $t_i = \{I_{i1}, I_{i2}, \ldots, I_{ik}\}$ and $I_{ij} \in I$, the **association rule problem** is to identify all association rules $X \Rightarrow Y$ with a minimum support and confidence. These values (s, α) are given as input to the problem.

The efficiency of association rule algorithms usually is discussed with respect to the number of scans of the database that are required and the maximum number of itemsets that must be counted.

6.2   LARGE ITEMSETS

The most common approach to finding association rules is to break up the problem into two parts:

1. Find large itemsets as defined in Definition 6.5.
2. Generate rules from frequent itemsets.

An *itemset* is any subset of the set of all items, I.

DEFINITION 6.5. A **large (frequent) itemset** is an itemset whose number of occurrences is above a threshold, s. We use the notation L to indicate the complete set of large itemsets and l to indicate a specific large itemset.

Once the large itemsets have been found, we know that any interesting association rule, $X \Rightarrow Y$, must have $X \cup Y$ in this set of frequent itemsets. Note that the subset of any large itemset is also large. Because of the large number of notations used in association rule algorithms, we summarize them in Table 6.4. When a specific term has a subscript, this indicates the size of the set being considered. For example, l_k is a large itemset of size k. Some algorithms divide the set of transactions into partitions. In this case, we use p to indicate the number of partitions and a superscript to indicate which partition. For example, D^i is the ith partition of D.

Finding large itemsets generally is quite easy but very costly. The naive approach would be to count all itemsets that appear in any transaction. Given a set of items of size m, there are 2^m subsets. Since we are not interested in the empty set, the potential number of large itemsets is then $2^m - 1$. Because of the explosive growth of this number, the challenge of solving the association rule problem is often viewed as how to efficiently determine all large itemsets. (When $m = 5$, there are potentially 31 itemsets. When $m = 30$, this becomes 1073741823.) Most association rule algorithms are based on smart ways to reduce the number of itemsets to be counted. These potentially large itemsets are called *candidates*, and the set of all counted (potentially large) itemsets is the *candidate itemset (c)*. One performance measure used for association rule algorithms is the size of C. Another problem to be solved by association rule algorithms is what data structure is to be used during the counting process. As we will see, several have been proposed. A trie or hash tree are common.

When all large itemsets are found, generating the association rules is straightforward. Algorithm 6.1, which is modified from [AS94], outlines this technique. In this algorithm we use a function *support*, which returns the support for the input itemset.

TABLE 6.4: Association Rule Notation

Term	Description
D	Database of transactions
t_i	Transaction in D
s	Support
α	Confidence
X, Y	Itemsets
$X \Rightarrow Y$	Association rule
L	Set of large itemsets
l	Large itemset in L
C	Set of candidate itemsets
p	Number of partitions

ALGORITHM 6.1

Input:

D	//Database of transactions
I	//Items
L	//Large itemsets
s	//Support
α	//Confidence

Output:

R	//Association Rules satisfying s and α

ARGen algorithm:

$R = \emptyset$;

for each $l \in L$ **do**

   for each $x \subset l$ such that $x \neq \emptyset$ **do**

      if $\frac{support(l)}{support(x)} \geq \alpha$ **then**

         $R = R \cup \{x \Rightarrow (l - x)\}$;

To illustrate this algorithm, again refer to the data in Table 6.1 with associated supports shown in Table 6.2. Suppose that the input support and confidence are $s = 30\%$ and $\alpha = 50\%$, respectively. Using this value of s, we obtain the following set of large itemsets:

$$L = \{\{Beer\}, \{Bread\}, \{Milk\}, \{PeanutButter\}\{Bread, PeanutButter\}\}.$$

We now look at what association rules are generated from the last large itemset. Here $l = \{Bread, PeanutButter\}$. There are two nonempty subsets of l: {Bread} and {PeanutButter}. With the first one we see:

$$\frac{support(\{Bread, PeanutButter\})}{support(\{Bread\})} = \frac{60}{80} = 0.75$$

This means that the confidence of the association rule Bread $\Rightarrow$ PeanutButter is 75%, just as is seen in Table 6.3. Since this is above α, it is a valid association rule and is added to R. Likewise with the second large itemset

$$\frac{support(\{Bread, PeanutButter\})}{support(\{PeanutButter\})} = \frac{60}{60} = 1$$

This means that the confidence of the association rule PeanutButter $\Rightarrow$ Bread is 100%, and this is a valid association rule.

    All of the algorithms discussed in subsequent sections look primarily at ways to efficiently discover large itemsets.

6.3 BASIC ALGORITHMS

6.3.1 Apriori Algorithm

The Apriori algorithm is the most well known association rule algorithm and is used in most commercial products. It uses the following property, which we call the *large itemset property*:

        Any subset of a large itemset must be large.

The large itemsets are also said to be *downward closed* because if an itemset satisfies the minimum support requirements, so do all of its subsets. Looking at the contrapositive of this, if we know that an itemset is small, we need not generate any supersets of it as candidates because they also must be small. We use the lattice shown in Figure 6.1(a) to illustrate the concept of this important property. In this case there are four items $\{A, B, C, D\}$. The lines in the lattice represent the subset relationship, so the large itemset property says that any set in a path above an itemset must be large if the original itemset is large. In Figure 6.1 (b) the nonempty subsets of ACD[1] are seen as $\{AC, AD, CD, A, C, D\}$. If ACD is large, so is each of these subsets. If any one of these subsets is small, then so is ACD.

The basic idea of the Apriori algorithm is to generate candidate itemsets of a particular size and then scan the database to count these to see if they are large. During scan i, candidates of size i, C_i are counted. Only those candidates that are large are used to generate candidates for the next pass. That is L_i are used to generate C_{i+1}. An itemset is considered as a candidate only if all its subsets also are large. To generate candidates of size $i+1$, joins are made of large itemsets found in the previous pass. Table 6.5 shows the process using the data found in Table 6.1 with $s = 30\%$ and $\alpha = 50\%$. There are no candidates of size three because there is only one large itemset of size two.

An algorithm called Apriori-Gen is used to generate the candidate itemsets for each pass after the first. All singleton itemsets are used as candidates in the first pass. Here the set of large itemsets of the previous pass, L_{i-1}, is joined with itself to determine the candidates. Individual itemsets must have all but one item in common in order to be combined. Example 6.3 further illustrates the concept. After the first scan, every large itemset is combined with every other large itemset.

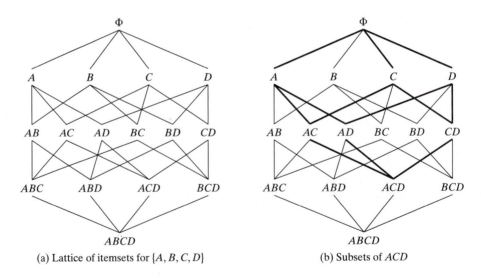

(a) Lattice of itemsets for $\{A, B, C, D\}$ (b) Subsets of ACD

FIGURE 6.1: Downward closure.

---

[1] Following the usual convention with association rule discussions, we simply list the items in the set rather than using the traditional set notation. So here we use ACD to mean $\{A, C, D\}$.

TABLE 6.5: Using Apriori with Transactions in Table 6.1

Pass	Candidates	Large Itemsets
1	{Beer}, {Bread}, {Jelly}, {Milk}, {PeanutButter}	{Beer}, {Bread}, {Milk}, {PeanutButter}
2	{Beer, Bread}, {Beer, Milk}, {Beer, PeanutButter}, {Bread, Milk}, {Bread, PeanutButter}, {Milk, PeanutButter}	{Bread, PeanutButter}

TABLE 6.6: Sample Clothing Transactions

Transaction	Items	Transaction	Items
t_1	Blouse	t_{11}	TShirt
t_2	Shoes, Skirt, TShirt	t_{12}	Blouse, Jeans, Shoes, Skirt, TShirt
t_3	Jeans, TShirt	t_{13}	Jeans, Shoes, Shorts, TShirt
t_4	Jeans, Shoes, TShirt	t_{14}	Shoes, Skirt, TShirt
t_5	Jeans, Shorts	t_{15}	Jeans, TShirt
t_6	Shoes, TShirt	t_{16}	Skirt, TShirt
t_7	Jeans, Skirt	t_{17}	Blouse, Jeans, Skirt
t_8	Jeans, Shoes, Shorts, TShirt	t_{18}	Jeans, Shoes, Shorts, TShirt
t_9	Jeans	t_{19}	Jeans
t_{10}	Jeans, Shoes, TShirt	t_{20}	Jeans, Shoes, Shorts, TShirt

EXAMPLE 6.3

A woman's clothing store has 10 cash register transactions during one day, as shown in Table 6.6. When Apriori is applied to the data, during scan one, we have six candidate itemsets, as seen in Table 6.7. Of these, 5 candidates are large. When Apriori-Gen is applied to these 5 candidates, we combine every one with all the other 5. Thus, we get a total of $4 + 3 + 2 + 1 = 10$ candidates during scan two. Of these, 7 candidates are large. When we apply Apriori-Gen at this level, we join any set with another set that has one item in common. Thus, {Jeans, Shoes} is joined with {Jeans, Shorts} but not with {Shorts, TShirt}. {Jeans, Shoes} will be joined with any other itemset containing either Jeans or Shoes. When it is joined, the new item is added to it. There are four large itemsets after scan four. When we go to join these we must match on two of the three attributes. For example {Jeans, Shoes, Shorts} After scan four, there is only one large itemset. So we obtain no new itemsets of size five to count in the next pass. joins with {Jeans, Shoes, TShirt} to yield new candidate {Jeans, Shoes, Shorts, TShirt}.

The Apriori-Gen algorithm is shown in Algorithm 6.2. Apriori-Gen is guaranteed to generate a superset of the large itemsets of size i, $C_i \supset L_i$, when input L_{i-1}. A

TABLE 6.7: Apriori-Gen Example

Scan	Candidates	Large Itemsets
1	{Blouse}, {Jeans}, {Shoes}, {Shorts}, {Skirt}, {TShirt}	{Jeans}, {Shoes}, {Shorts} {Skirt}, {Tshirt}
2	{Jeans, Shoes}, {Jeans, Shorts}, {Jeans, Skirt}, {Jeans, TShirt}, {Shoes, Shorts}, {Shoes, Skirt}, {Shoes, TShirt}, {Shorts, Skirt}, {Shorts, TShirt}, {Skirt, TShirt}	{Jeans, Shoes}, {Jeans, Shorts}, {Jeans, TShirt}, {Shoes, Shorts}, {Shoes, TShirt}, {Shorts, TShirt}, {Skirt, TShirt}
3	{Jeans, Shoes, Shorts}, {Jeans, Shoes, TShirt}, {Jeans, Shorts, TShirt}, {Jeans, Skirt, TShirt}, {Shoes, Shorts, TShirt}, {Shoes, Skirt, TShirt}, {Shorts, Skirt, TShirt}	{Jeans, Shoes, Shorts}, {Jeans, Shoes, TShirt}, {Jeans, Shorts, TShirt}, {Shoes, Shorts, TShirt}
4	{Jeans, Shoes, Shorts, TShirt}	{Jeans, Shoes, Shorts, TShirt}
5	$\emptyset$	$\emptyset$

pruning step, not shown, could be added at the end of this algorithm to prune away any candidates that have subsets of size $i - 1$ that are not large.

ALGORITHM 6.2

Input:
  L_{i-1} //Large itemsets of size $i - 1$
Output:
  C_i //Candidates of size i
Apriori-gen algorithm:
  $C_i = \emptyset$;
  for each $I \in L_{i-1}$ **do**
    for each $J \neq I \in L_{i-1}$ **do**
      if $i - 2$ of the elements in I and J are equal **then**
        $C_k = C_k \cup \{I \cup J\}$;

Given the large itemset property and Apriori-Gen, the Apriori algorithm itself (see Algorithm 6.3) is rather straightforward. In this algorithm we use c_i to be the count for item $I_i \in I$.

ALGORITHM 6.3

Input:
  I //Itemsets
  D //Database of transactions
  s //Support
Output:
  L //Large itemsets
Apriori algorithm:
  $k = 0$; //k is used as the scan number.
  $L = \emptyset$;

```
C₁ = I;        //Initial candidates are set to be the items.
repeat
    k = k+1;
    Lₖ = ∅;
    for each Iᵢ ∈ Cₖ do
        cᵢ = 0;    // Initial counts for each itemset are 0.
    for each tⱼ ∈ D do
        for each Iᵢ ∈ Cₖ do
            if Iᵢ ∈ tⱼ then
                cᵢ = cᵢ + 1;
    for each Iᵢ ∈ Cₖ do
        if cᵢ ≥ (s× |D|) do
            Lₖ = Lₖ ∪ Iᵢ;
    L = L ∪ Lₖ;
    Cₖ₊₁ = Apriori-Gen(Lₖ)
until Cₖ₊₁ = ∅;
```

The Apriori algorithm assumes that the database is memory-resident. The maximum number of database scans is one more than the cardinality of the largest large itemset. This potentially large number of database scans is a weakness of the Apriori approach.

6.3.2   Sampling Algorithm

To facilitate efficient counting of itemsets with large databases, sampling of the database may be used. The original sampling algorithm reduces the number of database scans to one in the best case and two in the worst case. The database sample is drawn such that it can be memory-resident. Then any algorithm, such as Apriori, is used to find the large itemsets for the sample. These are viewed as *potentially large* (*PL*) itemsets and used as candidates to be counted using the entire database. Additional candidates are determined by applying the *negative border* function, BD^-, against the large itemsets from the sample. The entire set of candidates is then $C = BD^-(PL) \cup PL$. The negative border function is a generalization of the Apriori-Gen algorithm. It is defined as the minimal set of itemsets that are not in *PL*, but whose subsets are all in *PL*. Example 6.4 illustrates the idea.

EXAMPLE 6.4

Suppose the set of items is $\{A, B, C, D\}$. The set of large itemsets found to exist in a sample of the database is $PL = \{A, C, D, CD\}$. The first scan of the entire database, then, generates the set of candidates as follows: $C = BD^-(PL) \cup PL = \{B, AC, AD\} \cup \{A, C, D, CD\}$. Here we add AC because both A and C are in *PL*. Likewise we add AD. We could not have added ACD because neither AC nor AD is in *PL*. When looking at the lattice (Figure 6.2), we add only sets where all subsets are already in *PL*. Note that we add B because all its subsets are vacuously in *PL*.

Algorithm 6.4 shows the sampling algorithm. Here the Apriori algorithm is shown to find the large itemsets in the sample, but any large itemset algorithm could be used. Any algorithm to obtain a sample of the database could be used as well. The set of large

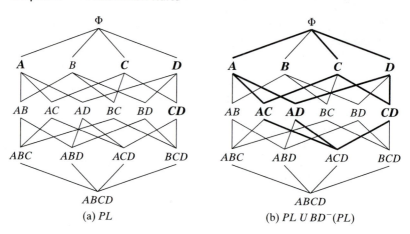

FIGURE 6.2: Negative border.

itemsets is used as a set of candidates during a scan of the entire database. If an itemset is large in the sample, it is viewed to be potentially large in the entire database. Thus, the set of large itemsets from the sample is called *PL*. In an attempt to obtain all the large itemsets during the first scan, however, *PL* is expanded by its negative border. So the total set of candidates is viewed to be $C = PL \cup BD^-(PL)$.

During the first scan of the database, all candidates in C are counted. If all candidates that are large are in *PL* [none in $BD^-(PL)$], then all large itemsets are found. If, however, some large itemsets are in the negative border, a second scan is needed. Think of $BD^-(PL)$ as a buffer area on the border of large itemsets. The set of all itemsets is divided into four areas: those that are known to be large, those that are known to be small, those that are on the negative border of those known to be large, and the others. The negative border is a buffer zone between those known to be large and the others. It represents the smallest possible set of itemsets that could potentially be large. Because of the large itemset property, we know that if there are no large itemsets in this area, then there can be none in the rest of the set.

During the second scan, additional candidates are generated and counted. This is done to ensure that all large itemsets are found. Here *ML*, the missing large itemsets, are those in *L* that are not in *PL*. Since there are some large itemsets in *ML*, there may be some in the rest of the set of itemsets. To find all the remaining large itemsets in the second scan, the sampling algorithm repeatedly applies the negative border function until the set of possible candidates does not grow further. While this creates a potentially large set of candidates (with many not large), it does guarantee that only one more database scan is required.

ALGORITHM 6.4

```
Input:
    I       //Itemsets
    D       //Database of transactions
    s       //Support
Output:
    L       //Large itemsets
```

Sampling algorithm:

```
    Ds = Sample drawn from D;
    PL = Apriori(I, Ds, smalls);
    C = PL ∪ BD⁻(PL);
    L = ∅;
    for each Iᵢ ∈ C do
        cᵢ = 0;          // Initial counts for each itemset are 0;
    for each tⱼ ∈ D do              // First scan count.
        for each Iᵢ ∈ C do
            if Iᵢ ∈ tⱼ, then
                cᵢ = cᵢ + 1;
    for each Iᵢ ∈ C do
        if cᵢ ≥ (s× |D|) do
            L = L ∪ Iᵢ;
    ML = {x | x ∈ BD⁻(PL) ∧ x ∈ L};              //Missing large itemsets.
    if ML ≠ ∅, then
        C = L;        // Set candidates to be the large itemsets.
        repeat
            C = C ∪ BD⁻(C);          // Expand candidate sets
                                       using negative border.
        until no new itemsets are added to C;
        for each Iᵢ ∈ C do
            cᵢ = 0;                // Initial counts for each itemset are 0.
        for each tⱼ ∈ D do                // Second scan count.
            for each Iᵢ ∈ C do
                if Iᵢ ∈ tⱼ, then
                    cᵢ = cᵢ + 1;
        if cᵢ ≥ (s× |D|) do
            L = L ∪ Iᵢ;
```

The algorithm shows that the application of the Apriori algorithm to the sample is performed using a support called *smalls*. Here *smalls* can be any support values less than *s*. The idea is that by reducing the support when finding large itemsets in the sample, more of the true large itemsets from the complete database will be discovered. We illustrate the use of the sampling algorithm on the grocery store data in Example 6.5.

EXAMPLE 6.5

We use the sampling algorithm to find all large itemsets in the grocery data where $s = 20\%$. Suppose that the sample database is determined to be the first two transactions:

$$D_S = \{t_1 = \{Bread, Jelly, PeanutButter\}, t_2 = \{Bread, PeanutButter\}\}$$

If we reduce *s* to be smalls = 10%, then for an itemset to be large in the sample it must occur in at least 0.1×2 transactions. So it must occur in one of the two transactions. When we apply *Apriori* to D_S we get:

$$PL = \{\{Bread\}, \{Jelly\}, \{PeanutButter\}, \{Bread, Jelly\}, \{Bread, PeanutButter\},$$
$$\{Jelly, PeanutButter\}, \{Bread, Jelly, PeanutButter\}\}$$

When we apply the negative border, we get

$$BD^-(PL) = \{\{Beer\}, \{Milk\}\}$$

We thus use the following set of candidates to count during the first database scan:

$$PL = \{\{Bread\}, \{Jelly\}, \{PeanutButter\}, \{Bread, Jelly\}, \{Bread, PeanutButter\},$$
$$\{Jelly, PeanutButter\}, \{Bread, Jelly, PeanutButter\}, \{Beer\}, \{Milk\}\}$$

Remember that during this scan we use $s = 20\%$ and apply it against all five transactions in the entire database. For an itemset to be large, then, we must have an itemset in $20\% \times 5$ or at least one transaction. We then find that both $\{Beer\}$ and $\{Milk\}$ are large. Thus, $ML = \{\{Beer\}, \{Milk\}\}$. Following the algorithm, we first set $C = L$, which in this case is also PL. Applying the negative border, we get

$$C = BD^-(C) = \{\{Beer, Bread\}, \{Beer, Jelly\}, \{Beer, Milk\}, \{Beer, PeanutButter\},$$
$$\{Bread, Milk\}, \{Jelly, Milk\}, \{Milk, PeanutButter\}, \{Jelly, Milk\}\}$$

Since this has uncovered new itemsets, we again apply it and this time find all itemsets of size three. A last application then finds all itemsets of size four, and we scan the database using all remaining itemsets not already known to be large.

Example 6.5 illustrates a potential problem with the use of the sampling algorithm; that is, a very large set of candidates may be used during the second scan. This is required to ensure that all large itemsets are found during the second scan. However, the set of candidates generated by successive applications of the negative border function will not always generate the entire set of itemsets. This happened in Example 6.5 because we found that all itemsets in PL were large and all itemsets in $BD^-(PL)$ also were large. If instead of using a support of 20%, we had used one of 40%, the results would be different, as shown in Example 6.6.

EXAMPLE 6.6

Suppose that smalls and D_S are as were used in Example 6.5. We thus find that PL and $BD^-(PL)$ are the same. During the first scan of the entire database, we identify large itemsets only if they have a support of at least 40%. Looking at Table 6.2, we see that from the initial scan we obtain the following large itemsets:

$$L = \{\{Bread\}, \{PeanutButter\}, \{Bread, PeanutButter\}, \{Beer\}, \{Milk\}\}$$

Here $ML = \{\{Beer\}, \{Milk\}\}$, so we need a second scan. When we first apply the negative border we get

$$C = BD^-(C) = \{\{Beer, Bread\}, \{Beer, Milk\}, \{Beer, PeanutButter\},$$
$$\{Bread, Milk\}, \{Milk, PeanutButter\}\}$$

Note that this is smaller than what we found with Example 6.5. Since Jelly is missing, we will not generate the entire set of itemsets during repeated application of BD^-. The second application yields

$$C = BD^-(C) \quad = \quad \{\{\text{Beer, Bread, Milk}\}, \{\text{Beer, Bread, PeanutButter}\},$$
$$\{\text{Beer, Milk, PeanutButter}\}, \{\text{Bread, Milk, PeanutButter}\}\}$$

The final application obtains

$$C = BD^-(C) = \{\{\text{Beer, Bread, Milk, PeanutButter}\}\}$$

6.3.3 Partitioning

Various approaches to generating large itemsets have been proposed based on a partitioning of the set of transactions. In this case, D is divided into p partitions $D^1, D^2, \ldots, D^p$. Partitioning may improve the performance of finding large itemsets in several ways:

- By taking advantage of the large itemset property, we know that a large itemset must be large in at least one of the partitions. This idea can help to design algorithms more efficiently than those based on looking at the entire database.

- Partitioning algorithms may be able to adapt better to limited main memory. Each partition can be created such that it fits into main memory. In addition, it would be expected that the number of itemsets to be counted per partition would be smaller than those needed for the entire database.

- By using partitioning, parallel and/or distributed algorithms can be easily created, where each partition could be handled by a separate machine.

- Incremental generation of association rules may be easier to perform by treating the current state of the database as one partition and treating the new entries as a second partition.

The basic partition algorithm reduces the number of database scans to two and divides the database into partitions such that each can be placed into main memory. When it scans the database, it brings that partition of the database into main memory and counts the items in that partition alone. During the first database scan, the algorithm finds all large itemsets in each partition. Although any algorithm could be used for this purpose, the original proposal assumes that some level-wise approach, such as Apriori, is used. Here L^i represents the large itemsets from partition D^i. During the second scan, only those itemsets that are large in at least one partition are used as candidates and counted to determine if they are large across the entire database. Algorithm 6.5 shows this basic partition algorithm.

D^1	t_1	Bread, Jelly, PeanutButter
	t_2	Bread, PeanutButter
D^2	t_3	Bread, Milk, PeanutButter
	t_4	Beer, Bread
	t_5	Beer, Milk

$L^1 = \{\{Bread\}, \{Jelly\}, \{PeanutButter\}, \{Bread, Jelly\}, \{Bread, PeanutButter\},$
$\{Jelly, PeanutButter\}, \{Bread, Jelly, PeanutButter\}\}$

$L^2 = \{\{Beer\}, \{Bread\}, \{Milk\}, \{PeanutButter\}, \{Beer, Bread\}, \{Beer, Milk\},$
$\{Bread, Milk\}, \{Bread, PeanutButter\}, \{Milk, PeanutButter\},$
$\{Bread, Milk, PeanutButter\}\}$

FIGURE 6.3: Partitioning example.

ALGORITHM 6.5

Input:
```
    I        //Itemsets
    D = {D¹, D², ..., Dᵖ}         //Database of transactions divided
                                     into partitions
    s        //Support
```
Output:
```
    L        //Large itemsets
```
Partition algorithm:
```
    C = ∅;
    for i = 1 to p do   //Find large itemsets in each partition.
        Lⁱ = Apriori(I, Dⁱ, s);
        C = C ∪ Lⁱ;
    L = ∅;
    for each Iᵢ ∈ C do
        cᵢ = 0;          //Initial counts for each itemset are 0.
    for each tⱼ ∈ D do //    Count candidates during second scan.
        for each Iᵢ ∈ C do
            if Iᵢ ∈ tⱼ, then
                cᵢ = cᵢ + 1;
    for each Iᵢ ∈ C do
        if cᵢ ≥ (s× | D |) do
            L = L ∪ Iᵢ;
```

Figure 6.3 illustrates the use of the partition algorithm using the market basket data. Here the database is partitioned into two parts, the first containing two transactions and the second with three transactions. Using a support of 10%, the resulting large itemsets L^1 and L^2 are shown. If the items are uniformly distributed across the partitions, then a large fraction of the itemsets will be large. However, if the data are not uniform, there may be a large percentage of false candidates.

6.4 PARALLEL AND DISTRIBUTED ALGORITHMS

Most parallel or distributed association rule algorithms strive to parallelize either the data, known as *data parallelism*, or the candidates, referred to as *task parallelism*. With task parallelism, the candidates are partitioned and counted separately at each processor. Obviously, the partition algorithm would be easy to parallelize using the task parallelism approach. Other dimensions in differentiating different parallel association rule algorithms are the load-balancing approach used and the architecture. The data parallelism algorithms have reduced communication cost over the task, because only the initial candidates (the set of items) and the local counts at each iteration must be distributed. With task parallelism, not only the candidates but also the local set of transactions must be broadcast to all other sites. However, the data parallelism algorithms require that memory at each processor be large enough to store all candidates at each scan (otherwise the performance will degrade considerably because I/O is required for both the database and the candidate set). The task parallelism approaches can avoid this because only the subset of the candidates that are assigned to a processor during each scan must fit into memory. Since not all partitions of the candidates must be the same size, the task parallel algorithms can adapt to the amount of memory at each site. The only restriction is that the total size of all candidates be small enough to fit into the total size of memory in all processors combined. Note that there are some variations of the basic algorithms discussed in this section that address these memory issues. Performance studies have shown that the data parallelism tasks scale linearly with the number of processors and the database size. Because of the reduced memory requirements, however, the task parallelism may work where data parallelism may not work.

6.4.1 Data Parallelism

One data parallelism algorithm is the *count distribution algorithm (CDA)*. The database is divided into p partitions, one for each processor. Each processor counts the candidates for its data and then broadcasts its counts to all other processors. Each processor then determines the global counts. These then are used to determine the large itemsets and to generate the candidates for the next scan. The algorithm is shown in Algorithm 6.6.

ALGORITHM 6.6

```
Input:
    I       //Itemsets
    P¹, P², ..., Pᵖ;        //Processors
    D = D¹, D², ..., Dᵖ;         //Database divided into partitions
    s       //Support
Output:
    L       //Large itemsets
Count distribution algorithm:
    perform in parallel at each processor Pˡ; //Count in parallel.
        k = 0;          //k is used as the scan number.
        L = ∅;
        C₁ = I;         //Initial candidates are set to be the items.
        repeat
            k = k + 1;
            Lₖ = ∅;
            for each Iᵢ ∈ Cₖ do
                cˡᵢ = 0;                //Initial counts for each itemset are 0.
            for each tⱼ ∈ Dˡ do
                for each Iᵢ ∈ Cₖ do
                    if Iᵢ ∈ tⱼ then
                        cˡᵢ = cˡᵢ + 1;
            broadcast cˡᵢ to all other processors;
            for each Iᵢ ∈ Cₖ do       //Determine global counts.
                cᵢ = ∑ᵖₗ₌₁ cˡᵢ;
            for each Iᵢ ∈ Cₖ do
                if cᵢ ≥ (s × | D¹ ∪ D² ∪ ··· ∪ Dᵖ |) do
                    Lₖ = Lₖ ∪ Iᵢ;
            L = L ∪ Lₖ;
            Cₖ₊₁ = Apriori-Gen(Lₖ)
        until Cₖ₊₁ = ∅;
```

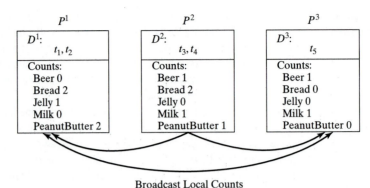

FIGURE 6.4: Data parallelism using CDA (modified from [DXGH00]).

Figure 6.4, which is modified from [DXGH00], illustrates the approach used by the CDA algorithm using the grocery store data. Here there are three processors. The first two transactions are counted at P^1, the next two at P^2, and the last one at P^3. When the local counts are obtained, they are then broadcast to the other sites so that global counts can be generated.

6.4.2 Task Parallelism

The *data distribution algorithm (DDA)* demonstrates task parallelism. Here the candidates as well as the database are partitioned among the processors. Each processor in parallel counts the candidates given to it using its local database partition. Following our convention, we use C_k^l to indicate the candidates of size k examined at processor P^l. Also, L_k^l are the local large k-itemsets at processor l. Then each processor broadcasts its database partition to all other processors. Each processor then uses this to obtain a global count for its data and broadcasts this count to all other processors. Each processor then can determine globally large itemsets and generate the next candidates. These candidates then are divided among the processors for the next scan. Algorithm 6.7 shows this approach. Here we show that the candidates are actually sent to each processor. However, some prearranged technique could be used locally by each processor to determine its own candidates. This algorithm suffers from high message traffic whose impact can be reduced by overlapping communication and processing.

ALGORITHM 6.7

```
Input:
    I        //Itemsets
    P¹, P², ..., Pᵖ;           //Processors
    D = D¹, D², ..., Dᵖ;              //Database divided into partitions
    s       //Support
Output:
    L       //Large itemsets
Data distribution algorithm:
    C₁ = I;
```

```
for each 1 ≤ l ≤ p do          //Distribute size 1 candidates
                                   to each processor.
     determine C₁ˡ and distribute to Pˡ;
perform in parallel at each processor Pˡ//Count in parallel.
     k = 0;          //k is used as the scan number.
     L = ∅;
     repeat
         k = k + 1;
         Lₖˡ = ∅;
         for each Iᵢ ∈ Cₖˡ do
             cᵢˡ = 0;                //Initial counts for each itemset are 0.
         for each tⱼ ∈ Dˡ do
             for each Iᵢ ∈ Cₖˡ do
                 if Iᵢ ∈ tⱼ, then
                     cᵢˡ = cᵢˡ + 1;               //Determine local counts.
         broadcast Dˡ to all other processors;
         for every other processor m ≠ l do
             for each tⱼ ∈ Dᵐ do
                 for each Iᵢ ∈ Cₖˡ do
                     if Iᵢ ∈ tⱼ, then
                         cᵢˡ = cᵢˡ + 1;          //Determine
                                                    global counts.
         if cᵢ ≥ (s × | D¹ ∪ D² ∪ ⋯ ∪ Dᵖ |) do
             Lₖˡ = Lₖˡ ∪ Iᵢ;
         broadcast Lₖˡ to all other processors;
         Lₖ = Lₖ¹ ∪ Lₖ² ∪ ⋯ ∪ Lₖᵖ;                //Global large
                                                    k-itemsets.
         Cₖ₊₁ = Apriori-gen(Lₖ)
         Cₖ₊₁ˡ ⊂ Cₖ₊₁;                           //Determine next set of
                                                    local candidates.
     until Cₖ₊₁ˡ = ∅ ;
```

Figure 6.5, which is modified from [DXGH00], illustrates the approach used by the DDA algorithm using the grocery store data. Here there are three processors. P^1 is counting Beer and Bread, P^2 is counting Jelly and Milk, and P^3 is counting PeanutButter. The first two transactions initially are counted at P^1, the next two at P^2, and the last one at P^3. When the local counts are obtained, the database partitions are then broadcast to the other sites so that each site can obtain a global count.

6.5 COMPARING APPROACHES

Although we have covered only the major association rule algorithms that have been proposed, there have been many such algorithms (see Bibliography). Algorithms can be classified along the following dimensions [DXGH00]:

- **Target:** The algorithms we have examined generate all rules that satisfy a given support and confidence level. Alternatives to these types of algorithms are those that generate some subset of the algorithms based on the constraints given.

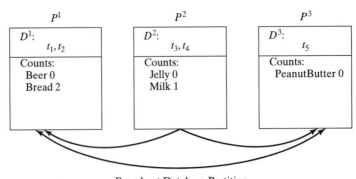

FIGURE 6.5: Task parallelism using DDA (modified from [DXGH00]).

- **Type:** Algorithms may generate regular association rules or more advanced association rules such as those introduced in section 6.7 and Chapters 8 and 9.

- **Data type:** We have examined rules generated for data in categorical databases. Rules may also be derived for other types of data such as plain text. This concept is further investigated in Section 6.7 and in Chapter 7 when we look at Web usage mining.

- **Data source:** Our investigation has been limited to the use of association rules for market basket data. This assumes that data are present in a transaction. The absence of data may also be important.

- **Technique:** The most common strategy to generate association rules is that of finding large itemsets. Other techniques may also be used.

- **Itemset strategy:** Itemsets may be counted in different ways. The most naive approach is to generate all itemsets and count them. As this is usually too space-intensive, the bottom-up approach used by Apriori, which takes advantage of the large itemset property, is the most common approach. A top-down technique could also be used.

- **Transaction strategy:** To count the itemsets, the transactions in the database must be scanned. All transactions could be counted, only a sample may be counted, or the transactions could be divided into partitions.

- **Itemset data structure:** The most common data structure used to store the candidate itemsets and their counts is a hash tree. Hash trees provide an effective technique to store, access, and count itemsets. They are efficient to search, insert, and delete itemsets. A *hash tree* is a multiway search tree where the branch to be taken at each level in the tree is determined by applying a hash function as opposed to comparing key values to branching points in the node. A leaf node in the hash tree contains the candidates that hash to it, stored in sorted order. Each internal node actually contains a hash table with links to children nodes. Figure 6.6 shows one possible hash tree for candidate itemsets of size 3, which were shown

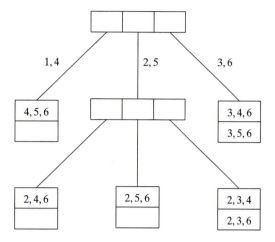

FIGURE 6.6: Hash tree for C_3 shown in Table 6.7.

in Table 6.7. For simplicity we have replaced each item with its numeric value in order: Blouse is 1, Jeans is 2, and so on. Here items $1, 4$ hash to the first entry; $2, 5$ hash to the second entry; and $3, 6$ hash to the third entry.

- **Transaction data structure:** Transactions may be viewed as in a flat file or as a TID list, which can be viewed as an inverted file. The items usually are encoded (as seen in the hash tree example), and the use of bit maps has also been proposed.

- **Optimization:** These techniques look at how to improve on the performance of an algorithm given data distribution (skewness) or amount of main memory.

- **Architecture:** Sequential, parallel, and distributed algorithms have been proposed.

- **Parallelism strategy:** Both data parallelism and task parallelism have been used.

Table 6.8 (derived from [DXGH00]) provides a high-level comparison of the association rule algorithms we have covered in this chapter. When m is the number of items, the maximum number of scans is $m + 1$ for the level-wise algorithms. This applies to the parallel algorithms because they are based on Apriori. Both sampling algorithms and

TABLE 6.8: Comparison of Association Rule Algorithms (modified from [DXGH00])

Partitioning	Scans	Data Structure	Parallelism
Apriori	$m + 1$	hash tree	none
Sampling	2	not specified	none
Partitioning	2	hash table	none
CDA	$m + 1$	hash tree	data
DDA	$m + 1$	hash tree	task

partitioning algorithms require at most two complete scans of the transaction database. However, remember that the sampling algorithm must access the database to read the sample into memory and then many scans of it into memory may be required. Similarly, for the partitioning algorithm, each partition must be read into memory and may be scanned there multiple times.

6.6 INCREMENTAL RULES

All algorithms discussed so far assume a static database. However, in reality we cannot assume this. With these prior algorithms, generating association rules for a new database state requires a complete rerun of the algorithm. Several approaches have been proposed to address the issue of how to maintain the association rules as the underlying database changes. Most of the proposed approaches have addressed the issue of how to modify the association rules as inserts are performed on the database. These *incremental updating* approaches concentrate on determining the large itemsets for $D \cup db$ where D is a database state and db are updates to it and where the large itemsets for D, L are known.

One incremental approach, *fast update (FUP)*, is based on the Apriori algorithm. Each iteration, k, scans both db and D with candidates generated from the prior iteration, $k - 1$, based on the large itemsets at that scan. In addition, we use as part of the candidate set for scan k to be L_k found in D. The difference is that the number of candidates examined at each iteration is reduced through pruning of the candidates. Although other pruning techniques are used, primary pruning is based on the fact that we already know L from D. Remember that according to the large itemset property, an itemset must be large in at least one of these partitions of the new database. For each scan k of db, L_k plus the counts for each itemset in L_k are used as input. When the count for each item in L_k is found in db, we automatically know whether it will be large in the entire database without scanning D. We need not even count any items in L_k during the scan of db if they have a subset that is not large in the entire database.

6.7 ADVANCED ASSOCIATION RULE TECHNIQUES

In this section we investigate several techniques that have been proposed to generate association rules that are more complex than the basic rules.

6.7.1 Generalized Association Rules

Using a concept hierarchy that shows the set relationship between different items, generalized association rules allow rules at different levels. Example 6.7 illustrates the use of these generalized rules using the concept hierarchy in Figure 6.7. Association rules could be generated for any and all levels in the hierarchy. A *generalized association rule*, $X \Rightarrow Y$, is defined like a regular association rule with the restriction that no item in Y may be above any item in X. When generating generalized association rules, all possible rules are generated using one or more given hierarchies. Several algorithms have been proposed to generate generalized rules. The simplest would be to expand each transaction by adding (for each item in it) all items above it in any hierarchy.

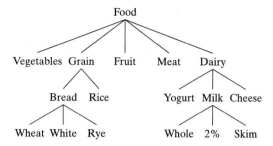

FIGURE 6.7: Concept hierarchy.

EXAMPLE 6.7

Figure 6.7 shows a partial concept hierarchy for food. This hierarchy shows that Wheat Bread is a type of Bread, which is a type of grain. An association rule of the form Bread $\Rightarrow$ PeanutButter has a lower support and threshold than one of the form Grain $\Rightarrow$ PeanutButter. There obviously are more transactions containing any type of grain than transactions containing Bread. Likewise, Wheat Bread $\Rightarrow$ Peanutbutter has a lower threshold and support than Bread $\Rightarrow$ PeanutButter.

6.7.2 Multiple-Level Association Rules

A variation of generalized rules are *multiple-level association rules*. With multiple-level rules, itemsets may occur from any level in the hierarchy. Using a variation of the Apriori algorithm, the concept hierarchy is traversed in a top-down manner and large itemsets are generated. When large itemsets are found at level i, large itemsets are generated for level $i + 1$. Large k-itemsets at one level in the concept hierarchy are used as candidates to generate large k-itemsets for children at the next level.

Modification to the basic association rule ideas may be changed. We expect that there is more support for itemsets occurring at higher levels in the concept hierarchy. Thus, the minimum support required for association rules may vary based on level in the hierarchy. We would expect that the frequency of itemsets at higher levels is much greater than the frequency of itemsets at lower levels. Thus, for the reduced minimum support concept, the following rules apply:

- The minimum support for all nodes in the hierarchy at the same level is identical.

- If α_i is the minimum support for level i in the hierarchy and α_{i-1} is the minimum support for level $i - 1$, then $\alpha_{i-1} > \alpha_i$.

6.7.3 Quantitative Association Rules

The association rule algorithms discussed so far assume that the data are categorical. A *quantitative association rule* is one that involves categorical and quantitative data. An example of a quantitative rule is:

A customer buys wine for between $30 and $50 a bottle $\Rightarrow$ she also buys caviar

This differs from a traditional association rule such as:

A customer buys wine $\Rightarrow$ she also buys caviar.

The cost quantity has been divided into an interval (much as was done when we looked at handling numeric data in clustering and classification). In these cases, the items are not simple literals. For example, instead of having the items {Bread, Jelly}, we might have the items {(Bread:[0 . . . 1]), (Bread:(1 . . . 2]), (Bread:(2 . . . ∞)), (Jelly:[0 . . . 1.5]), (Jelly:(1.5 . . . 3]), (Jelly:(3 . . . ∞))}.

The basic approach to finding quantitative association rules is found in Algorithm 6.8. Here we show the Apriori algorithm being used to generate the large itemsets, but any such algorithm could be used.

ALGORITHM 6.8

```
Input:
    I       //Itemsets
    p¹, p², ..., pᵖ;        //Processors
    D = D¹, D², ..., Dᵖ;            //Database divided into partitions
    s       //Support
Output:
    L       //Large itemsets
Quantitative association rule algorithm:
    for each Iⱼ ∈ I do    //Partition items.
        if Iⱼ is to be partitioned, then
            determine number of partitions;
            map attribute values into new partitions creating new items;
            replace Iⱼ in I with the new items Iⱼ₁, ..., Iⱼₘ;
    Apriori(I, D, s);
```

Because we have divided what was one item into several items, the minimum support and confidence used for quantitative rules may need to be lowered. The minimum support problem obviously is worse with a large number of intervals. Thus, an alternative solution would be to combine adjacent intervals when calculating support. Similarly, when there are a small number of intervals, the confidence threshold may need to be lowered. For example, look at $X \Rightarrow Y$. Suppose there are only two intervals for X. Then the count for those transactions containing X will be quite high when compared to those containing Y (if this is a more typical item with many intervals).

6.7.4 Using Multiple Minimum Supports

When looking at large databases with many types of data, using one minimum support value can be a problem. Different items behave differently. It certainly is easier to obtain a given support threshold with an attribute that has only two values than it is with an attribute that has hundreds of values. It might be more meaningful to find a rule of the form

$$\text{SkimMilk} \implies \text{WheatBread}$$

with a support of 3% than it is to find

$$\text{Milk} \implies \text{Bread}$$

with a support of 6%. Thus, having only one support value for all association rules may not work well. Some useful rules could be missed. This is particularly of interest when looking at generalized association rules, but it may arise in other situations as well. Think of generating association rules from a non–market basket database. As was seen with quantitative rules, we may partition attribute values into ranges. Partitions that have a small number of values obviously will produce lower supports than those with a large number of values. If a larger support is used, we might miss out on generating meaningful association rules.

This problem is called the *rare item problem*. If the minimum support is too high, then rules involving items that rarely occur will not be generated. If it is set too low, then too many rules may be generated, many of which (particularly for the frequently occurring items) are not important. Different approaches have been proposed to handle this. One approach is to partition the data based on support and generate association rules for each partition separately. Alternatively, we could group rare items together and generate association rules for these groupings. A more recent approach to handling this problem is to combine clustering and association rules. First we cluster the data together based on some clustering criteria, and then we generate rules for each cluster separately. This is a generalization of the partitioning of the data solution.

One approach, *MISapriori*, allows a different support threshold to be indicated for each item. Here *MIS* stands for *minimum item support*. The minimum support for a rule is the minimum of all the minimum supports for each item in the rule. An interesting problem occurs when multiple minimum supports are used. The minimum support requirement for an itemset may be met even though it is not met for some of its subsets. This seems to violate the large itemset property. Example 6.8, which is adapted from [LHM99], illustrates this. A variation of the downward closure property, called the *sorted downward closure* property, is satisfied and used for the MISapriori algorithm. First the items are sorted in ascending MIS value. Then the candidate generation at scan 2 looks only at adding to a large item any item following it (larger than or equal to MIS value) in the sorted order.

EXAMPLE 6.8

Suppose we have three items, $\{A, B, C\}$, with minimum supports $MIS(A) = 20\%$, $MIS(B) = 3\%$, and $MIS(C) = 4\%$. Because the support for A is so large, it may be small, while both AB and AC may be large because the required support for $AB = \min(MIS(A), MIS(B)) = 3\%$ and $AC = \min(MIS(A), MIS(C)) = 4\%$.

6.7.5 Correlation Rules

A *correlation rule* is defined as a set of itemsets that are correlated. The motivation for developing these correlation rules is that negative correlations may be useful.

Example 6.9, which is modified from [BMS77], illustrates this concept. In this example, even though the probability of purchasing two items together seems high, it is much higher if each item is purchased without the other item. Correlation satisfies upward closure in the itemset lattice. Thus, if a set is correlated, so is every superset of it.

EXAMPLE 6.9

Suppose there are two items, $\{A, B\}$ where $A \Rightarrow B$ has a support of 15% and a confidence of 60%. Because these values are high, a typical association rule algorithm probably would deduce this to be a valuable rule. However, if the probability to purchase item B is 70%, then we see that the probability of purchasing B has actually gone down, presumably because A was purchased. Thus, there appears to be a negative correlation between buying A and buying B. The correlation can be expressed as

$$\text{correlation}(A \Longrightarrow B) = \frac{P(A, B)}{P(A)\ P(B)} \qquad (6.1)$$

which in this case is: $\frac{0.15}{0.25 \times 0.7} = 0.857$. Because this correlation value is lower than 1, it indicates a negative correlation between A and B.

6.8 MEASURING THE QUALITY OF RULES

Support and confidence are the normal methods used to measure the quality of an association rule:

$$s(A \Longrightarrow B) = P(A, B) \qquad (6.2)$$

and

$$\alpha(A \Longrightarrow B) = P(B \mid A) \qquad (6.3)$$

However, there are some problems associated with these metrics. For example, confidence totally ignores $P(B)$. A rule may have a high support and confidence but may be an obvious rule. For example, if someone purchases potato chips, there may be a high likelihood that he or she would also buy a cola. This rule is not really of interest because it is not surprising. Various concepts such as surprise and interest have been used to evaluate the quality or usefulness of rules. We briefly examine some of these in this section.

With correlation rules, we saw that correlation may be used to measure the relationship between items in a rule. This may also be expressed as the *lift* or *interest*

$$\text{interest}(A \Longrightarrow B) = \frac{P(A, B)}{P(A)\ P(B)} \qquad (6.4)$$

This measure takes into account both $P(A)$ and $P(B)$. A problem with this measure is that it is symmetric. Thus, there is no difference between the value for interest($A \Rightarrow B$) and the value for interest($B \Rightarrow A$).

As with lift, *conviction* takes into account both $P(A)$ and $P(B)$. From logic we know that implication $A \to B \equiv \neg(A \wedge \neg B)$. A measure of the independence of the negation of implication, then, is $\frac{P(A, \neg B)}{P(A)\ P(\neg B)}$. To take into account the negation, the conviction measure inverts this ratio. The formula for *conviction* is [BMS77]

$$\text{conviction}(A \Longrightarrow B) = \frac{P(A)\ P(\neg B)}{P(A, \neg B)} \tag{6.5}$$

Conviction has a value of 1 if A and B are not related. Rules that always hold have a value of ∞.

The usefulness of discovered association rules may be tied to the amount of surprise associated with the rules or how they deviate from previously known rules. Here *surprise* is a measure of the changes of correlations between items over time. For example, if you are aware that beer and pretzels are often purchased together, it would be a surprise if this relationship actually lowered significantly. Thus, this rule beer $\Rightarrow$ pretzel would be of interest even if the confidence decreased.

Another technique to measure the significance of rules by using the chi squared test for independence has been proposed. This significance test was proposed for use with correlation rules. Unlike the support or confidence measurement, the chi squared significance test takes into account both the presence and the absence of items in sets. Here it is used to measure how much an itemset (potential correlation rule) count differs from the expected. The chi squared test is well understood because it has been used in the statistics community for quite a while. Unlike support and confidence, where arbitrary values must be chosen to determine which rules are of interest, the chi squared values are well understood with existing tables that show the critical values to be used to determine relationships between items.

The chi squared statistic can be calculated in the following manner. Suppose the set of items is $I = \{I_1, I_2, \ldots, I_m\}$. Because we are interested in both the occurrence and the nonoccurrence of an item, a transaction t_j can be viewed as

$$t_j \in \{I_1, \bar{I}_1\} \times \{I_2, \bar{I}_2\} \times \cdots \times \{I_m, \bar{I}_m\} \tag{6.6}$$

Given any possible itemset X, it also is viewed as a subset of the Cartesian product. The chi squared statistic is then calculated for X as

$$\chi^2 = \sum_{X \in I} \frac{(O(X) - E[X])^2}{E[X]} \tag{6.7}$$

Here $O(X)$ is the count of the number of transactions that contain the items in X. For one item I_i, the expected value is $E[I_i] = O(I_i)$, the count of the number of transactions that contain I_i. $E[\bar{I}_i] = n - O(I_i)$. The expected value $E[X]$ is calculated assuming independence and is thus defined as

$$E[X] = n \times \prod_{i=1}^{m} \frac{E[I_i]}{n} \tag{6.8}$$

Here n is the number of transactions.

Table 6.9, which is called a *contingency table*, shows the distribution of the data in Example 6.9 assuming that the sample has 100 items in it. From this we find

TABLE 6.9: Contingency Table for Example 6.9

	B	$\bar{B}$	Total
A	15	10	25
$\bar{A}$	55	20	75
Total	70	30	100

$E[AB] = 17.5$, $E[A\bar{B}] = 7.5$, $E[\bar{A}B] = 52.5$, and $E[\bar{A}\bar{B}] = 22.5$. Using these values, we calculate χ^2 for this example as

$$\chi^2 = \sum_{X \in I} \frac{(O(X) - E[X])^2}{E[X]} = \frac{(15 - 17.5)^2}{17.5} + \frac{(10 - 7.5)^2}{7.5} + \frac{(55 - 52.5)^2}{52.5}$$

$$+ \frac{(20 - 22.5)^2}{22.5} = 1.587 \tag{6.9}$$

If all values were independent, then the chi squared statistic should be 0. A chi squared table (found in most statistics books) can be examined to interpret this value. Examining a table of critical values for the chi squared statistic, we see that a chi squared value less than 3.84 indicates that we should not reject the independent assumption. This is done with 95% confidence. Thus, even though there appears to be a negative correlation between A and B, it is not statistically significant.

6.9 EXERCISES

1. Trace the results of using the Apriori algorithm on the grocery store example with $s = 20\%$ and $\alpha = 40\%$. Be sure to show the candidate and large itemsets for each database scan. Also indicate the association rules that will be generated.

2. Prove that all potentially large itemsets are found by the repeated application of BD^- as is used in the sampling algorithm.

3. Trace the results of using the sampling algorithm on the clothing store example with $s = 20\%$ and $\alpha = 40\%$. Be sure to show the use of the negative border function as well as the candidates and large itemsets for each database scan.

4. Trace the results of using the partition algorithm on the grocery store example with $s = 20\%$ and $\alpha = 40\%$. For the grocery store example, use two partitions of size 2 and 3, respectively. You need not show all the steps involved in finding the large itemsets for each partition. Simply show the resulting large itemsets found for each partition.

5. Trace the results of using the count distribution algorithm on the clothing data with $s = 20\%$. Assume that there are three processors with partitions created from the beginning of the database of size 7, 7, and 6, respectively.

6. Trace the results of using the data distribution algorithm on the clothing data with $s = 20\%$. Assume that there are three processors with partitions created

from the beginning of the database of size 7, 7, and 6, respectively. Assume that candidates are distributed at each scan by dividing the total set into subsets of equal size.

7. Calculate the lift and conviction for the rules shown in Table 6.3. Compare these to the shown support and confidence.

8. Perform a survey of recent research examining techniques to generate rules incrementally.

6.10 BIBLIOGRAPHIC NOTES

The development of association rules can be traced to one paper in 1993 [AIS93]. Agrawal proposed the AIS algorithm before *Apriori* [AIS93]. However, this algorithm and another, SETM [HS95], do not take advantage of the large itemset property and thus generate too many candidate sets. The a priori algorithm is still the major technique used by commercial products to detect large itemsets. It was proposed by 1994 in [AS94]. Another algorithm proposed about the same time, OCD, uses sampling [MTV94]. It produces fewer candidates than AIS.

There have been many proposed algorithms that improve on Apriori. Apriori-TID does not use the database to count support [AS94]. Instead, it uses a special encoding fo the candidates from the previous pass. Apriori has better performance in early passes of the database while Apriori-*TID* has better performance in later. A combination of the two, Apriori-Hybrid, has been proposed [Sri96]. The dynamic itemset counting (DIC) algorithm divides the database into intervals (like the partitions in the partition algorithm) [BMUT77]. The scan of first interval counts the 1-itemsets. Then candidates of size 1 are generated. The scan of the second interval, then, counts the 1-itemsets as well as those 2-itemsets. In this manner itemsets are counted earlier. However, more memory space may be required. The partition algorithm was first studied in 1995 by Savasere [SON95], while the sampling algorithm is attributed to Toivonen in 1996 [Toi96]. The problem of uneven distribution of data in the partition algorithm was addressed in [LD98], where a set of algorithms were proposed that better prune away false candidates before the second scan.

The CDA and DDA algorithms were both proposed in [AS96]. Other data parallel algorithms include PDM [PCY95], DMA [CHN+96], and CCPD [ZOPL96]. Additional task parallel algorithms include IDD [HKK97], HPA [SK96], and PAR [ZPOL97]. A hybrid approach, hybrid distribution (HD), which combines the advantages of each technique has a speed-up close to the data parallelism approach [HKK97]. For a discussion of other parallel algorithms, see either [DXGH00] or [Zak99].

Many additional algorithms have been proposed. CARMA (continuous association rule mining algorithm) [Hid99] proposes a technique that is dynamic in that it allows the user to change the support and confidence while the algorithm is running. Some recent work has examined the use of an AI type search algorithm called *OPUS* [Web00]. OPUS prunes out portions of the search tree based on the desired rule characteristics. However, many scans of the database are required and, thus it assumes that the database is memory-resident.

An approach to determining if an item should be partitioned when generating quantitative rules has been proposed [SA96a]. Variations of quantitative rules include *profile association rules* where the left side of the rule represents some profile information about a customer while the right side of the rule contains the purchase information [ASY98]. Another variation on quantitative rules is a *ratio rule* [KLKF98]. These rules indicate the ratio between the quantitative values of individual items. When fuzzy regions are used instead of discrete partitions, we obtain *fuzzy association rules* [KFW98]. Recent research has examined association rules for multimedia data [ZHLH98].

After the initial work in [CHNW96], much additional work has examined association rules in an incremental environment. Several improvements on the original FUP have been proposed [CNT96] [CLK97]. Another technique aims at reducing the number of additional scans of the original database [TBAR97].

Generalized association rules were studied in [SA95]. Multiple-level association rules were proposed in [HF95]. Quantitative association rules were studied in [Sri96]. Algorithm 6.8 does not show how to determine whether an item should be partitioned. One technique proposed to do this is a metric called partial completeness [SA96a]. The rare item problem was investigated [Man98]. The MISapriori approach was subsequently proposed in [LHM99]. Correlation rules were first examined in [BMS77]. Many of the additional measures for rules were investigated in [BMS77].

A survey of association rules has recently appeared [DXGH00]. A survey of parallel and distribution association rule algorithms has also been published [Zak99]. One recent textbook is devoted to the study of association rules and sequential patterns [Ada00]. A recent tutorial [HLP01] has examined association rules and sequential patterns.

PART THREE

ADVANCED TOPICS

CHAPTER 7

Web Mining

7.1 INTRODUCTION
7.2 WEB CONTENT MINING
7.3 WEB STRUCTURE MINING
7.4 WEB USAGE MINING
7.5 EXERCISES
7.6 BIBLIOGRAPHIC NOTES

7.1 INTRODUCTION

Determining the size of the World Wide Web is extremely difficult. It 1999 it was estimated to contain over 350 million pages with growth at the rate of about 1 million pages a day [CvdBD99]. Google recently announced that it indexes 3 billion Web documents [Goo01]. The Web can be viewed as the the largest database available and presents a challenging task for effective design and access. Here we use the term *database* quite loosely because, of course, there is no real structure or schema to the Web. Thus, data mining applied to the Web has the potential to be quite beneficial. *Web mining* is mining of data related to the World Wide Web. This may be the data actually present in Web pages or data related to Web activity. Web data can be classified into the following classes [SCDT00]:

- Content of actual Web pages.

- Intrapage structure includes the HTML or XML code for the page.

- Interpage structure is the actual linkage structure between Web pages.

- Usage data that describe how Web pages are accessed by visitors.

- User profiles include demographic and registration information obtained about users. This could also include information found in cookies.

Web mining tasks can be divided into several classes. Figure 7.1 shows one taxonomy of Web mining activities [Zaï99]. Web content mining examines the content of Web pages as well as results of Web searching. The content includes text as well as graphics data. Web content mining is further divided into Web page content mining and search results mining. The first is traditional searching of Web pages via content, while

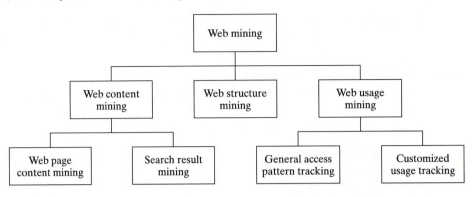

FIGURE 7.1: Web mining taxonomy (modified from [Zaï99]).

the second is a further search of pages found from a previous search. Thus, some mining activities have been built on top of traditional search engines, using their result as the data to be mined. With Web structure mining, information is obtained from the actual organization of pages on the Web. Content mining is similar to the work performed by basic IR techniques, but it usually goes farther than simply employing keyword searching. For example, clustering may be applied to Web pages to identify similar pages. The intrapage structure includes links within the page as well as the code (HTML, XML) for the page. Web usage mining looks at logs of Web access. General access pattern tracking is a type of usage mining that looks at a history of Web pages visited. This usage may be general or may be targeted to specific usage or users. Besides identifying what the traffic patterns look like, usage mining also involves the mining of these sequential patterns. For example, patterns can be clustered based on their similarity. This in turn can be used to cluster users into groups based on similar access behavior.

There are many applications for Web mining. One application is targeted advertising. *Targeting* is any technique that is used to direct business marketing or advertising to the most beneficial subset of the total population. The objective is to maximize the results of the advertising; that is, send it to all (and only) the set of potential customers who will buy. In this manner, the cost of sending an advertisement to someone who will not purchase that product can be avoided. Targeting attempts to send advertisements to people who have not been to a Web site to entice them to visit it. Thus, a targeted ad is found on a different Web site. All of the data mining techniques we have seen so far could be used to target advertising to a subset of the audience. In this manner, advertising costs can be reduced while either not impacting results or improving results. On the Web, targeting can be used to display advertising at Web sites visited by persons that fit into a business' target demographic area. By examining the Web log data to see what source sites access a Web site, information about the visitors can be obtained. This in turn can be used to sell advertising space to those companies that would benefit the most.

Although the different Web mining activities may be described separately, they are intrinsically related. A Webmaster usually wants to create the best set of pages to accomplish the desired objective for the pages (advertising, marketing, information dissemination, etc.). The effectiveness of a set of Web pages depends not only on the content and organization of individual Web pages, but also on the structure of the pages and their ease of use. Although there are many issues that impact the effectiveness of

Web sites (user interface, effective use of graphics, response time, etc.), in this chapter we cover only techniques that involve data mining.

7.2 WEB CONTENT MINING

Web content mining can be thought of as extending the work performed by basic search engines. There are many different techniques that can be used to search the Internet. Only a few of these techniques are discussed here. Most search engines are keyword-based. Web content mining goes beyond this basic IR technology. It can improve on traditional search engines through such techniques as concept hierarchies and synonyms, user profiles, and analyzing the links between pages. Traditional search engines must have crawlers to search the Web and gather information, indexing techniques to store the information, and query processing support to provide fast and accurate information to users. Data mining techniques can be used to help search engines provide the efficiency, effectiveness, and scalability needed.

One taxonomy of Web mining divided Web content mining into agent-based and database approaches [CMS97]. Agent-based approaches have software systems (agents) that perform the content mining. In the simplest case, search engines belong to this class, as do intelligent search agents, information filtering, and personalized Web agents. Intelligent search agents go beyond the simple search engines and use other techniques besides keyword searching to accomplish a search. For example, they may use user profiles or knowledge concerning specified domains. Information filtering utilizes IR techniques, knowledge of the link structures, and other approaches to retrieve and categorize documents. Personalized Web agents use information about user preferences to direct their search. The database approaches view the Web data as belonging to a database. There have been approaches that view the Web as a multilevel database, and there have been many query languages that target the Web.

Basic content mining is a type of text mining. As seen in Figure 7.2, a modified version of [Zaï99, Figure 2.1], text mining functions can be viewed in a hierarchy with the simplest functions at the top and the more complex functions at the bottom. Much research is currently under way that investigates the use of natural language processing techniques in text mining to uncover hidden semantics, such as question and answer systems. More

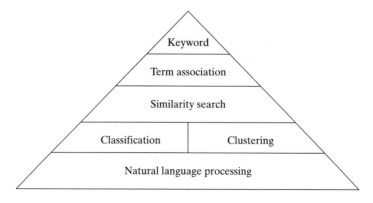

FIGURE 7.2: Text mining hierarchy (modified version of [Zaï99, Figure 2.1]).

traditional mining operations involve keyword searching, similarity measures, clustering, and classification.

Many Web content mining activities have centered around techniques to summarize the information found. In the simplest case, inverted file indices are created on keywords. Simple *search engines* retrieve relevant documents usually using a keyword-based retrieval technique similar to those found in traditional IR systems. While these do not perform data mining activities, their functionality could be extended to include more mining-type activities.

One problem associated with retrieval of data from Web documents is that they are not structured as in traditional databases. There is no schema or division into attributes. Traditionally, Web pages are defined using *hypertext markup language (HTML)*. Web pages created using HTML are only semistructured, thus making querying more difficult than with well-formed databases containing schemas and attributes with defined domains. HTML ultimately will be replaced by *extensible markup language (XML)*, which will provide structured documents and facilitate easier mining.

7.2.1   Crawlers

A *robot* (or *spider* or *crawler*) is a program that traverses the hypertext structure in the Web. The page (or set of pages) that the crawler starts with are referred to as the *seed URLs*. By starting at one page, all links from it are recorded and saved in a queue. These new pages are in turn searched and their links are saved. As these robots search the Web, they may collect information about each page, such as extract keywords and store in indices for users of the associated search engine. A crawler may visit a certain number of pages and then stop, build an index, and replace the existing index. This type of crawler is referred to as a *periodic crawler* because it is activated periodically. Crawlers are used to facilitate the creation of indices used by search engines. They allow the indices to be kept relatively up-to-date with little human intervention. Recent research has examined how to use an *incremental crawler*. Traditional crawlers usually replace the entire index or a section thereof. An incremental crawler selectively searches the Web and only updates the index incrementally as opposed to replacing it.

Because of the tremendous size of the Web, it has also been proposed that a *focused crawler* be used. A focused crawler visits pages related to topics of interest. This concept is illustrated in Figure 7.3. Figure 7.3(a) illustrates what happens with regular crawling, while Figure 7.3(b) illustrates focused crawling. The shaded boxes represent pages that are visited. With focused crawling, if it is determined that a page is not relevant or its links should not be followed, then the entire set of possible pages underneath it are pruned and not visited. With thousands of focused crawlers, more of the Web can be covered than with traditional crawlers. This facilitates better scalability as the Web grows. The focused crawler architecture consists of three primary components [CvdBD99]:

- A major piece of the architecture is a hypertext classifier that associates a relevance score for each document with respect to the crawl topic. In addition, the classifier determines a resource rating that estimates how beneficial it would be for the crawler to follow the links out of that page.

- A distiller determines which pages contain links to many relevant pages. These are called *hub pages*. These are thus highly important pages to be visited. These hub

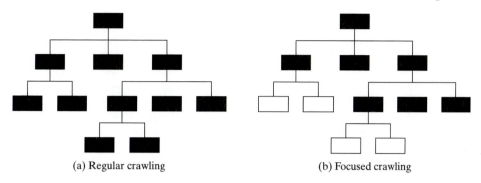

(a) Regular crawling   (b) Focused crawling

FIGURE 7.3: Focused crawling.

pages may not contain relevant information, but they would be quite important to facilitate continuing the search.

- The crawler performs the actual crawling on the Web. The pages it visits are determined via a priority-based structure governed by the priority associated with pages by the classifier and the distiller.

A performance objective for the focused crawler is a high precision rate or *harvest rate*.

To use the focused crawler, the user first identifies some sample documents that are of interest. While the user browses on the Web, he identifies the documents that are of interest. These are then classified based on a hierarchical classification tree, and nodes in the tree are marked as *good*, thus indicating that this node in the tree has associated with it document(s) that are of interest. These documents are then used as the seed documents to begin the focused crawling. During the crawling phase, as relevant documents are found it is determined whether it is worthwhile to follow the links out of these documents. Each document is classified into a leaf node of the taxonomy tree. One proposed approach, *hard focus*, follows links if there is an ancestor of this node that has been marked as good. Another technique, *soft focus*, identifies the probability that a page, d, is relevant as

$$R(d) = \sum_{good(c)} P(c \mid d) \tag{7.1}$$

Here c is a node in the tree (thus a page) and $good(c)$ is the indication that it has been labeled to be of interest. The priority of visiting a page not yet visited is the maximum of the relevance of pages that have been visited and point to it.

The hierarchical classification approach uses a hierarchical taxonomy and a naive Bayes classifier. A hierarchical classifier allows the classification to include information contained in the document as well as other documents near it (in the linkage structure). The objective is to classify a document d to the leaf node c in the hierarchy with the highest posterior probability $P(c \mid d)$. Based on statistics of a training set, each node c in the taxonomy has a probability. The probability that a document can be generated by the root topic, node c_1, obviously is 1. Following the argument found in [CDAR98], suppose $c_1, \ldots, c_k = c$ be the path from the root node to the leaf c. We thus know

$$P(c_i \mid d) = P(c_{i-1} \mid d) P(c_i \mid c_{i-1}, d) \qquad (7.2)$$

Using Bayes rule, we have

$$P(c_i \mid c_{i-1}, d) = \frac{P(c_i \mid c_{i-1}) P(d \mid c_i)}{\displaystyle\sum_{s \text{ is a sibling of } c_i} P(d \mid s)} \qquad (7.3)$$

$P(d \mid c_i)$ can be found using the Bernoulli model, in which a document is seen as a bag of words with no order [CvdBD99].

More recent work on focused crawling has proposed the use of context graphs. The *context focused crawler (CFC)* performs crawling in two steps. In the first phase, context graphs and classifiers are constructed using a set of seed documents as a training set. In the second phase, crawling is performed using the classifiers to guide it. In addition, the context graphs are updated as the crawl takes place. This is a major difference from the focused crawler, where the classifier is static after the learning phase. The CFC approach is designed to overcome problems associated with previous crawlers:

- There may be some pages that are not relevant but that have links to relevant pages. The links out of these documents should be followed.

- Relevant pages may actually have links into an existing relevant page, but no links into them from relevant pages. However, crawling can really only follow the links out of a page. It would be nice to identify pages that point to the current page. A type of *backward crawling* to determine these pages would be beneficial.

The CFC approach uses a *context graph*, which is a rooted graph in which the root represents a seed document and nodes at each level represent pages that have links to a node at the next higher level. Figure 7.4 contains three levels. The number of levels in a context graph is dictated by the user. A node in the graph with a path of length n to the seed document node represents a document that has links indirectly to the seed document through a path of length n. The number of back links followed is designated as input to the algorithm. Here n is called the *depth* of the context graph. The context graphs created for all seed documents are merged to create a *merged context graph*. The

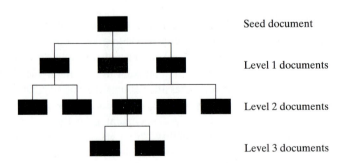

FIGURE 7.4: Context graph.

context graph is used to gather information about topics that are related to the topic being explored.

Backward crawling finds pages that are not pointed to by relevant documents but are themselves relevant. These types of pages may be new and may not yet have been discovered and linked to from other pages. Although backward links do not really exist in the Web, a backward crawl can be performed relatively easily because most search engines already maintain information about the back links. This type of information is similar to that often used by commercial citation servers, which find documents that cite a given document. The value of the *Science Citation Index* in performing traditional literature searches is well known. The use of backlinks on the Web can provide similar benefits.

CFC performs classification using a term frequency–inverse document frequency (TF–IDF) technique. The vocabulary used is formed from the documents in the seed set and is shown in the merged context graph. Each document is represented by a TF–IDF vector representation and is assigned to a particular level in the merged context graph.

7.2.2 Harvest System

The *Harvest* system is based on the use of caching, indexing, and crawling. Harvest is actually a set of tools that facilitate gathering of information from diverse sources. The Harvest design is centered around the use of gatherers and brokers. A *gatherer* obtains information for indexing from an Internet service provider, while a *broker* provides the index and query interface. The relationship between brokers and gatherers can vary. Brokers may interface directly with gatherers or may go through other brokers to get to the gatherers. Indices in Harvest are topic-specific, as are brokers. This is used to avoid the scalability problems found without this approach.

Harvest gatherers use the Essence system to assist in collecting data. Although not designed explicitly for use on the Web, *Essence* has been shown to be a valid technique for retrieving Web documents [HS93]. Essence classifies documents by creating a semantic index. *Semantic indexing* generates different types of information for different types of files and then creates indices on this information. This process may first classify files based on type and then summarize the files typically based on keywords. Essence uses the file extensions to help classify file types.

7.2.3 Virtual Web View

One proposed approach to handling the large amounts of somewhat unstructured data on the Web is to create a *multiple layered database (MLDB)* on top of the data in the Web (or a portion thereof). This database is massive and distributed. Each layer of this database is more generalized than the layer beneath it. Unlike the lowest level (the Web), the upper levels are structured and can be accessed (and mined) by an SQL-like query language. The MLDB provides an abstracted and condensed view of a portion of the Web. A view of the MLDB, which is called a *Virtual Web View (VWV)*, can be constructed.

The indexing approach used by MLDB does not require the use of spiders. The technique used is to have the Web servers (masters, administrators) themselves send their indices (or changes to indices) to the site(s) where indexing is being performed. This process is triggered when changes to the sites are made. Each layer of the index is smaller than that beneath it and to which it points. To assist in the creation of the first layer of the MLDB, both extraction and translation tools are proposed. Translation tools are used to convert Web documents to XML, while extraction tools extract the desired information from the Web pages and insert it into the first layer of the MLDB. Web documents that use XML and follow a standard format would not need any tools to create the layers. It is proposed that any translation functions be performed directly by the local administrators. The layer-1 data can be viewed as a massive distributed database.

The higher levels of the database become less distributed and more summarized as they move up the hierarchy. *Generalization* tools are proposed, and concept hierarchies are used to assist in the generalization process for constructing the higher levels of the MLDB. These hierarchies can be created using the *WordNet Semantic Network*. WordNet is a database of the English language. Nouns, adjectives, verbs, and adverbs are listed, divided into groups of synonyms, and linked together using both lexical and semantic relationships.

A Web data mining query language, WebML is proposed to provide data mining operations on the MLDB. WebML is an extension of DMQL. Documents are accessed using data mining operations and lists of keywords. A major feature of WebML are four primitive operations based on the use of concept hierarchies for the keywords [Zai99]:

1. COVERS: One concept covers another if it is higher (ancestor) in the hierarchy. This coverage is extended to include synonyms as well.
2. COVERED BY: This is the reverse of COVERS in that it reverses to descendents.
3. LIKE: The concept is a synonym.
4. CLOSE TO: One concept is close to another if it is a sibling in the hierarchy. Again, this is extended to include synonyms.

The following example illustrates WebML. The query finds all documents at the level of "www.engr.smu.edu" that have a keyword that covers the keyword cat:

```
SELECT *
FROM document in ''www.engr.smu.edu''
WHERE ONE OF keywords COVERS ''cat''
```

WebML allows queries to be stated such that the WHERE clause indicates selection based on the links found in the page, keywords for the page, and information about the domain where the document is found. Because WebML is an extension of DMQL, data mining functions such as classification, summarization, association rules, clustering, and prediction are included.

7.2.4 Personalization

Another example of Web content mining is in the area of *personalization*. With personalization, Web access or the contents of a Web page are modified to better fit the desires of the user. This may involve actually creating Web pages that are unique per user or using the desires of a user to determine what Web documents to retrieve.

With personalization, advertisements to be sent to a potential customer are chosen based on specific knowledge concerning that customer. Unlike targeting, personalization may be performed on the target Web page. The goal here is to entice a current customer to purchase something he or she may not have thought about purchasing. Perhaps the simplest example of personalization is the use of a visitor's name when he or she visits a page. Personalization is almost the opposite of targeting. With targeting, businesses display advertisements at other sites visited by their users. With personalization, when a particular person visits a Web site, the advertising can be designed specifically for that person. MSNBC, for example, allows personalization by asking the user to enter his or her zip code and favorite stock symbols [msn00]. Personalization includes such techniques as use of cookies, use of databases, and more complex data mining and machine learning strategies [BDH+95]. Example 7.1 illustrates a more complex use of personalization. Personalization may be performed in many ways—some are not data mining. For example, a Web site may require that a visitor log on and provide information. This not only facilitates storage of personalization information (by ID), but also avoids a common problem of user identification with any type of Web mining. Mining activities related to personalization require examining Web log data to uncover patterns of access behavior by use. This may actually fall into the category of Web usage mining.

EXAMPLE 7.1

Wynette Holder often does online shopping through XYZ.com. Every time she visits their site, she must first log on using an ID. This ID is used to track what she purchases as well as what pages she visits. Mining of the sales and Web usage data is performed by XYZ to develop a very detailed user profile for Wynette. This profile in turn is used to personalize the advertising they display. For example, Wynette loves chocolate. This is evidenced by the volume of chocolate she has purchased (and eaten) during the past year. When Wynette logs in, she goes directly to pages containing the clothes she is interested in buying. While looking at the pages, XYZ shows a banner ad about some special sale on Swiss milk chocolate. Wynette cannot resist. She immediately follows the link to this page and adds the chocolate to her shopping cart. She then returns to the page with the clothes she wants.

Personalization can be viewed as a type of clustering, classification, or even prediction. Through classification, the desires of a user are determined based on those for the class. With clustering, the desires are determined based on those users to which he or she is determined to be similar. Finally, prediction is used to predict what the user really wants to see. There are three basic types of Web page personalization [MCS00]:

- Manual techniques perform personalization through user registration preferences or via the use of rules that are used to classify individuals based on profiles or demographics.

- *Collaborative filtering* accomplishes personalization by recommending information (pages) that have previously been given high ratings from similar users.

- Content-based filtering retrieves pages based on similarity between them and user profiles.

One of the earliest uses of personalization was with My Yahoo! [MPR00]. With My Yahoo! a user himself personalizes what the screen looks like [Yah00]. He can provide preferences in such areas as weather, news, stock quotes, movies, and sports. Once the preferences are set up, each time the user logs in, his page is displayed. The personalization is accomplished by the user explicitly indicating what he wishes to see. Some observations about the use of personalization with My Yahoo! are [MPR00]:

- A few users will create very sophisticated pages by utilizing the customization provided.

- Most users do not seem to understand what personalization means and use only use the default page.

- Any personalization system should be able to support both types of users.

This personalization is not automatic, but more sophisticated approaches to personalization actually use data mining techniques to determine the user preferences. An automated personalization technique predicts future needs based on past needs or the needs of similar users.

News Dude uses the *interestingness* of a document to determine if a user is interested in it [BP99]. Here interestingness is based on the similarity between the document and that of what the user wishes. Similarity is measured by the co-occurrence of words in the documents and a user profile created for the user. The target application for News Dude is news stories. News Dude actually prunes out stories that are too close to stories the user has already seen. These are determined to be redundant articles. News Dude uses a two-level scheme to determine interestingness. One level is based on recent articles the user has read, while the second level is a more long-term profile of general interests. Thus, a short-term profile is created that summarizes recent articles read, and a long-term profile is created to summarize the general interests. A document is found to be interesting if it is sufficiently close to either. It was shown that the use of this two-level approach works better than either profile by itself [MPR00].

Another approach to automatic personalization is that used by *Firefly*. Firefly is based on the concept that humans often base decisions on what they hear from others. If someone likes a TV show, a friend of that person may also like the program. User profiles are created by users indicating their preferences. Prediction of a user's desires are then made based on what similar users like. This can be viewed as a type of clustering. This approach to Web mining is referred to as *collaborative filtering*. The initial application of Firefly has been to predict music that a user would like. Note that there is no examination of the actual content of Web documents, simply a prediction based on what similar users like. (One might argue whether this is really a content based Web mining approach.)

Another collaborative approach is called *Web Watcher*. Web Watcher prioritizes links found on a page based on a user profile and the results of other users with similar profiles who have visited this page [JFM97]. A user is required to indicate the intent of the browsing session. This profile is then matched to the links the user follows.

7.3 WEB STRUCTURE MINING

Web structure mining can be viewed as creating a model of the Web organization or a portion thereof. This can be used to classify Web pages or to create similarity measures between documents. We have already seen some structure mining ideas presented in the content mining section. These approaches used structure to improve on the effectiveness of search engines and crawlers.

7.3.1 PageRank

The *PageRank* technique was designed to both increase the effectiveness of search engines and improve their efficiency [PBMW98]. PageRank is used to measure the importance of a page and to prioritize pages returned from a traditional search engine using keyword searching. The effectiveness of this measure has been demonstrated by the success of Google [Goo00]. (The name *Google* comes from the word *googol*, which is 10^{100}.) The PageRank value for a page is calculated based on the number of pages that point to it. This is actually a measure based on the number of *backlinks* to a page. A backlink is a link pointing to a page rather than pointing out from a page. The measure is not simply a count of the number of backlinks because a weighting is used to provide more importance to backlinks coming from important pages. Given a page p, we use B_p to be the set of pages that point to p, and F_p to be the set of links out of p. The PageRank of a page p is defined as [PBMW98]

$$\text{PR}(p) = c \sum_{q \in B_p} \frac{\text{PR}(q)}{N_q} \tag{7.4}$$

Here $N_q = | F_q |$. The constant c is a value between 0 and 1 and is used for normalization.

A problem, called *rank sink*, that exists with this PageRank calculation is that when a cyclic reference occurs (page A points to page B and page B points to page A), the PR value for these pages increases. This problem is solved by adding an additional term to the formula:

$$\text{PR}'(p) = c \sum_{q \in B_p} \frac{\text{PR}(q)}{N_q} + c E(v) \tag{7.5}$$

where c is maximized. Here $E(v)$ is a vector that adds an artificial link. This simulates a random surfer who periodically decides to stop following links and jumps to a new page. $E(v)$ adds links of small probabilities between every pair of nodes.

The PageRank technique is different from other approaches that look at links. It does not count all links the same. The values are normalized by the number of links in the page.

7.3.2 Clever

One recent system developed at IBM, *Clever*, is aimed at finding both authoritative pages and hubs [CDK+99]. The authors define an *authority* as the "best source" for the requested information [CDK+99]. In addition, a *hub* is a page that contains links to authoritative pages. The Clever system identifies authoritative pages and hub pages by creating weights. A search can be viewed as having a goal of finding the best hubs and authorities.

Because of the distributed and unsupervised development of sites, a user has no way of knowing whether the information contained within a Web page is accurate. Currently, there is nothing to prevent someone from producing a page that contains not only errors, but also blatant lies. In addition, some pages might be of a higher quality than others. These pages are often referred to as being the most *authoritative*. Note that this is different from relevant. A page may be extremely relevant, but if it contains factual errors, users certainly do not want to retrieve it. The issue of authority usually does not surface in traditional IR.

Hyperlink-induced topic search (HITS) finds hubs and authoritative pages [Kle99a]. The HITS technique contains two components:

- Based on a given set of keywords (found in a query), a set of relevant pages (perhaps in the thousands) is found.

- Hub and authority measures are associated with these pages. Pages with the highest values are returned.

The HITS algorithm is outlined in Algorithm 7.1. A search engine, SE, is used to find a small set, *root set (R)*, of pages, P, which satisfy the given query, q. This set is then expanded into a larger set, *base set (B)*, by adding pages linked either to or from R. This is used to induce a subgraph of the Web. This graph is the one that is actually examined to find the hubs and authorities. In the algorithm, we use the notation $G(B, L)$ to indicate that the graph (subgraph) G is composed of vertices (pages in this case) B and directed edges or arcs (links) L. The weight used to find authorities, x_p, and the weight used to find hubs, y_p, are then calculated on G. Because pages at the same site often point to each other, we should not really use the structure of the links between these pages to help find hubs and authorities. The algorithm therefore removes these links from the graph. Hubs should point to many good authorities, and authorities should be pointed to by many hubs. This observation is the basis for the weight calculations shown in the algorithm. An implementation of the weight calculations using an adjacency matrix is found in the literature [Kle99a]. The approach is basically to iteratively recalculate the weights until they converge. The weights are normalized so that the sum of the squares of each is 1. Normally, the number of hubs and authorities found is each between 5 and 10.

ALGORITHM 7.1

```
Input:
    W           //WWW viewed as a directed graph
    q           //Query
    s           //Support
Output:
    A           //Set of authority pages
    H           //Set of hub pages
HITS algorithm
    R = SE(W, q)
    B = R ∪ {pages linked to from R} ∪ {pages that link to pages in R};
    G(B, L) =  Subgraph of W induced by B;
    G(B, L¹) =  Delete links in G within same site;
    x_p = Σ_q where ⟨q,p⟩∈L¹ Y_q;     // Find authority weights;
    Y_p = Σ_q where ⟨p,q⟩∈L¹ x_q;     // Find hub weights;
    A = {p | p has one of the highest x_p};
    H = {p | p has one of the highest y_p};
```

7.4 WEB USAGE MINING

Web usage mining performs mining on Web usage data, or Web logs. A *Web log* is a listing of page reference data. Sometimes it is referred to as *clickstream* data because each entry corresponds to a mouse click. These logs can be examined from either a client perspective or a server perspective. When evaluated from a server perspective, mining uncovers information about the sites where the service resides. It can be used to improve the design of the sites. By evaluating a client's sequence of clicks, information about a user (or group of users) is detected. This could be used to perform prefetching and caching of pages. Example 7.2 from [XD01a] illustrates Web usage mining.

EXAMPLE 7.2

The webmaster at ABC Corp. learns that a high percentage of users have the following pattern of reference to pages: ⟨A, B, A, C⟩. This means that a user accesses page A, then page B, then back to page A, and finally to page C. Based on this observation, he determines that a link is needed directly to page C from page B. He then adds this link.

Web usage mining can be used for many different purposes. By looking at the sequence of pages a user accesses, a profile about that user could be developed, thus aiding in personalization. With site mining, the overall quality and effectiveness of the pages at the site can be evaluated. One taxonomy of Web usage mining applications has included [SCDT00]:

- Personalization for a user can be achieved by keeping track of previously accessed pages. These pages can be used to identify the typical browsing behavior of a user and subsequently to predict desired pages.

- By determining frequent access behavior for users, needed links can be identified to improve the overall performance of future accesses.

- Information concerning frequently accessed pages can be used for caching.

- In addition to modifications to the linkage structure, identifying common access behaviors can be used to improve the actual design of Web pages and to make other modifications to the site. For example, suppose that visitors to an e-commerce site can be identified as customers or noncustomers. The behavior of customers can be compared with that for those who do not purchase anything. This can be used to identify changes to the overall design. It may be determined that many visitors never get past a particular page. That target page can be improved in an attempt to turn these visitors into customers.

- Web usage patterns can be used to gather business intelligence to improve sales and advertisement.

- Gathering statistics concerning how users actually access Web pages may or may not be viewed as part of mining.

Web usage mining actually consists of three separate types of activities [SCDT00]:

- Preprocessing activities center around reformatting the Web log data before processing.

- Pattern discovery activities form the major portion of the mining activities because these activities look to find hidden patterns within the log data.

- Pattern analysis is the process of looking at and interpreting the results of the discovery activities.

There are many issues associated with using the Web log for mining purposes:

- Identification of the exact user is not possible from the log alone.

- With a Web client cache, the exact sequence of pages a user actually visits is difficult to uncover from the server site. Pages that are rereferenced may be found in the cache.

- There are many security, privacy, and legal issues yet to be solved. For example, is the set of pages a person visits actually private information? Should a Web browser actually divulge information to other companies about the habits of its users? After all, this information could be valuable to potential advertisers.

7.4.1 Preprocessing

The Web usage log probably is not in a format that is usable by mining applications. As with any data to be used in a mining application, the data may need to be reformatted and cleansed. There are, in addition, some issues specifically related to the use of Web logs. Steps that are part of the preprocessing phase include cleansing, user identification, session identification, path completion, and formatting [CMS99].

> **DEFINITION 7.1.** Let P be a set of literals, called *pages* or *clicks*, and U be a set of users. A **log** is a set of triples $\{\langle u_1, p_1, t_1 \rangle, \ldots, \langle u_n, p_n, t_n \rangle\}$ where $u_i \in U$, $p_i \in P$, and t_i is a timestamp.

Standard log data consist of the following: source site, destination site, and timestamp, as shown in Definition 7.1. The source and destination sites could be listed as a URL or an IP address. The definition assumes that the source site is identified by a user ID and the destination site is identified by a page ID. Additional data such as Web browser information also may be included. Before processing the log, the data may be changed in several ways. For security or privacy reasons, the page addresses may be changed into unique (but nonidentifying) page identifications (such as alphabetic characters). This conversion also will save storage space. In addition, the data may be cleansed by removing any irrelevant information. As an example, the log entries with figures (gif, jpg, etc.) can be removed.

Data from the log may be grouped together to provide more information. All pages visited from one source could be grouped by a server to better understand the patterns of page references from each user (source site). Similarly, patterns from groups of sites may be discovered. References to the same site may be identified and examined to better understand who visits this page.

A common technique is for a server site to divide the log records into sessions. As shown in Definition 7.2 from [XD01a], a *session* is a set of page references from one source site during one logical period. Historically, a session would be identified by a user logging into a computer, performing work, and then logging off. The login and logoff represent the logical start and end of the session. With Web log data, this is harder to determine. Several approaches can be used to identify these logical periods:

- Combine all records from the same source site that occur within a time period.

- Add records to a session if they are from the same source site and the time between two consecutive timestamps is less than a certain threshold value.

NCR uses an approach based on the second concept. Any inactive period of 30 minutes or more ends a session [SP00]. Empirical results have shown that 25.5 minutes is appropriate [CP95].

> **DEFINITION 7.2.** Let L be a log. A **session** S is an ordered list of pages accessed by a user, i.e., $S = \langle \langle p_1, t_1 \rangle, \langle p_2, t_2 \rangle, \ldots, \langle p_n, t_n \rangle \rangle$, where there is a user $u_i \in U$ such that $\{ \langle u_i, p_1, t_1 \rangle, \langle u_i, p_2, t_2 \rangle, \ldots, \langle u_i, p_n, t_n \rangle \} \subseteq L$. Here $t_i \leq t_j$ iff $i \leq j$. Since only the ordering of the accesses is our main interest, the access time is often omitted. Thus, we write a session S as $\langle p_1, p_2, \ldots, p_n \rangle$.

Associated with each session is a unique identifier, which is called a session ID. The length of a session S is the number of pages in it, which is denoted as len(S). Let database D be a set of such sessions, and the total length of D be len(D) = $\sum_{S \in D}$ len(S).

There are many problems associated with the preprocessing activities, and most of these problems center around the correct identification of the actual user. User identification is complicated by the use of proxy servers, client side caching, and corporate firewalls. Tracking who is actually visiting a site (and where they come from) is difficult. Even though a visit to a Web page will include a source URL or IP address that indicates the source of the request, this may not always be accurate in determining the source location of the visitor. Users who access the Internet through an *Internet service provider (ISP)* will all have the source location of that provider. It is not unique to the individual. In addition, the same user may use different ISPs. Also, there will be many users accessing the Web at the same time from one machine. Cookies can be used to assist in identifying a single user regardless of machine used to access the Web. A *cookie* is a file that is used to maintain client–server information between accesses that the client makes to the server. The cookie file is stored at the client side and sent to the server with each access.

Identifying the actual sequence of pages accessed by a user is complicated by the use of client side caching. In this case, actual pages accessed will be missing from the server side log. Techniques can be used to complete the log by predicting missing pages. *Path completion* is an attempt to add page accesses that do not exist in the log but that actually occurred. Some missing pages can be easily added. For example, if a user visits page A and then page C, but there is no link from A to C, then at least one page in this path is missing. Algorithms are used both to infer missing pages and to generate an approximate timestamp.

7.4.2 Data Structures

Several unique data structures have been proposed to keep track of patterns identified during the Web usage mining process. A basic data structure that is one possible alternative is called a *trie*. A trie is a rooted tree, where each path from the root to a leaf represents a sequence. Tries are used to store strings for pattern-matching applications. Each character in the string is stored on the edge to the node. Common prefixes of strings are shared. A problem in using tries for many long strings is the space required. This is

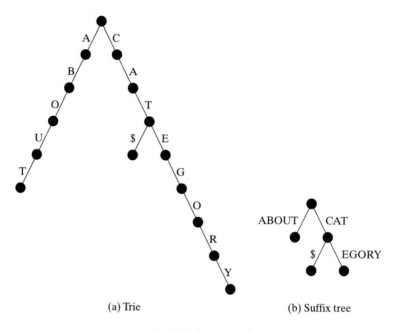

(a) Trie (b) Suffix tree

FIGURE 7.5: Sample tries.

illustrated in Figure 7.5(a), which shows a standard trie for the three strings {ABOUT, CAT, CATEGORY}. Note that there are many nodes with a degree of one. This is a waste of space that is solved by compressing nodes together when they have degrees of one. Figure 7.5(b) shows a compressed version of this trie. Here a path consisting of nodes with single children is compressed to one edge. Note in both trees the extra edge labeled "$." This symbol (or any symbol that is not in the alphabet and is used to construct the strings) is added to ensure that a string that is actually a prefix of another (CAT is a prefix of CATEGORY) terminates in a leaf node.

The compressed trie is called a *suffix tree*. A suffix tree has the following characteristics:

- Each internal node except the root has at least two children.

- Each edge represents a nonempty subsequence.

- The subsequences represented by sibling edges begin with different symbols.

With the help of a suffix tree, it is efficient not only to find any subsequence in a sequence, but also to find the common subsequences among multiple sequences. A suffix tree can also be constructed from a sequence in time and space linear in the length of the sequence. When given one session of page references, many different patterns may be found. The exact number of patterns depends on the exact definition of the pattern to be found (discussed in subsection 7.4.3). Example 7.3 illustrates this idea.

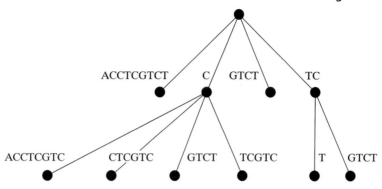

FIGURE 7.6: Sample suffix tree.

EXAMPLE 7.3

Suppose that one session has been identified to be $\langle C, A, C, C, T, C, G, T, C, T \rangle$. Many different patterns exist in this session. As a matter of fact, we could identify patterns starting at the first character, or the second, or any other. The suffix tree created for this session is shown in Figure 7.6. This tree does not contain the special "$" edges.

A slight variation on this suffix tree that is used to build a suffix tree for multiple sessions is called a *generalized suffix tree (GST)*.

7.4.3 Pattern Discovery

The most common data mining technique used on clickstream data is that of uncovering traversal patterns. A traversal pattern is a set of pages visited by a user in a session. Other types of patterns may be uncovered by Web usage mining. For example, association rules can look at pages accessed together in one session independent of ordering. Similar traversal patterns may be clustered together to provide a clustering of the users. This is different from clustering of pages, which tends to identify similar pages, not users.

Several different types of traversal patterns have been examined. These patterns differ in how the patterns are defined. The differences between the different types of patterns can be described by the following features:

- Duplicate page references (backward traversals and refreshes/reloads) may or may not be allowed.

- A pattern may be composed only of contiguous page references, or alternatively of any pages referenced in the same session.

- The pattern of references may or may not be maximal in the session. A frequent pattern is maximal if it has no subpattern that is also frequent.

Patterns found using different combinations of these three properties may be used to discover different features and thus may be used for different purposes. Knowledge of contiguous page references frequently made can be useful to predict future references

TABLE 7.1: Comparison of Different Types of Traversal Patterns (from [XD01a])

	Ordering	Duplicates	Consecutive	Maximal	Support
Association rules	N	N	N	N	$\frac{\text{freq}(X)}{\text{\# transactions}}$
Episodes	Y^1	N	N	N	$\frac{\text{freq}(X)}{\text{\# time windows}}$
Sequential patterns	Y	N	N	Y	$\frac{\text{freq}(X)}{\text{\# customers}}$
Forward sequences	Y	N	Y	Y	$\frac{\text{freq}(X)}{\text{\# forward sequences}}$
Maximal frequent sequences	Y	Y	Y	Y	$\frac{\text{freq}(X)}{\text{\# clicks}}$

[1] Serial episodes are ordered, parallel episodes are not, and general episodes are partially ordered.

and thus for prefetching and caching purposes. Knowledge of backward traversals often followed can be used to improve the design of a set of Web pages by adding new links to shorten future traversals. The maximal property is used primarily to reduce the number of meaningful patterns discovered. The use of such performance improvements as user side caching may actually alter the sequences visited by a user and impact any mining of the Web log data at the server side.

The different types of traversal patterns that have been studied and how they view these three features are shown in Table 7.1 (from [XD01a]). Example 7.4 illustrates a set of sessions to be used throughout this section. The sessions are listed in order, and all timestamps have been removed.

EXAMPLE 7.4

The XYZ Corporation maintains a set of five Web pages: $\{A, B, C, D, E\}$. The following sessions (listed in timestamp order) have been created: $D = \{S_1 = \{U_1, \langle A, B, C \rangle\}, S_2 = \{U_2, \langle A, C \rangle\}, S_3 = \{U_1, \langle B, C, E \rangle\}, S_4 = \{U_3, \langle A, C, D, C, E \rangle\}\}$. Here we have added to each session the user ID. Suppose the support threshold is 30%.

Association Rules. *Association rules* can be used to find what pages are accessed together. Here we are really finding large itemsets. A page is regarded as an item, and a session is regarded as a transaction with both duplicates and ordering ignored. The support is defined to be the number of occurrences of the itemset divided by the number of transactions or sessions. The application of the Apriori algorithm to the data in Example 7.2 is shown in Example 7.5.

EXAMPLE 7.5

Since there are four transactions and the support is 30%, an itemset must occur in at least two sessions. During the first scan, we find that $L_1 = \{\{A\}, \{B\}, \{C\}, \{E\}\}$, so $C_2 = \{\{A, B\}, \{A, C\}, \{A, E\}, \{B, C\}, \{B, E\}, \{C, E\}\}$. Counting these is scan two, we find $L_2 = \{\{A, C\}, \{B, C\}, \{C, E\}\}$ and then generate $C_3 = \{\{A, B, C\}, \{A, C, E\}, \{B, C, E\}\}$. Counting, we find that none of these are large. The large itemsets are then

$$L = \{\{A\}, \{B\}, \{C\}, \{E\}, \{A, C\}, \{B, C\}, \{C, E\}\}$$

Sequential Patterns.   Although initially proposed for use with market basket data, *sequential patterns* have also been applied to Web access logs. A sequential pattern (as applied to Web usage mining) is defined as an ordered set of pages that satisfies a given support and is maximal (i.e., it has no subsequence that is also frequent). Support is defined not as the percentage of sessions with the pattern, but rather the percentage of customers who have the pattern. Since a user may have many sessions, it is possible that a sequential pattern could span sessions. It also need not be contiguously accessed pages. A *k-sequence* is a sequence of length k (i.e., is it has k pages in it).

Algorithm 7.2 outlines the steps needed to find sequential patterns. After the sort step to put the data in the correct order, the remaining steps are somewhat similar to those of the Apriori algorithm. The sort step creates the actual customer sequences, which are the complete reference sequences from one user (across transactions). During the first scan it finds all large 1-itemsets. Obviously, a frequent 1-itemset is the same as a frequent 1-sequence. In subsequent scans, candidates are generated from the large itemsets of the previous scans and then are counted. In counting the candidates, however, the modified definition of support must be used. In the algorithm we show that AprioriAll is used to perform this step.

ALGORITHM 7.2

```
Input:
    D = {S₁, S₂, ..., Sₖ}          //Database of sessions
    s           //Support.
Output: Sequential patterns
Sequential patterns algorithm:
    D = sort D on user-ID and time of first page reference
          in each session;
    find L₁ in D;
    L = AprioriAll (D, s, L₁);
    find maximal reference sequences from L;
```

Generating sequential patterns for Example 7.5 is shown in Example 7.6. Here C_i represents the candidate i-sequences and L_i are the large i-sequences.

EXAMPLE 7.6

In this example, user U_1 actually has two transactions (sessions). To find his sequential patterns, we must think of his sequence as the actual concatenation of those pages in

S_1 and S_3. Also, since support is measured not by transactions but by users, a sequence is large if it is contained in at least one customer's sequence. After the sort step, we have that $D = \langle S_1 = \{U_1, \langle A, B, C\rangle\}, S_3 = \{U_1, \langle B, C, E\rangle\}, S_2 = \{U_2, \langle A, C\rangle\}, S_4 = \{U_3, \langle A, C, D, C, E\rangle\}$. We find $L_1\{\{A\}, \{B\}, \{C\}, \{D\}, \{E\}\}$ since each page is referenced by at least one customer. The following table outlines the steps taken by AprioriAll:

There are variations of this algorithm and several techniques used to improve the performance. The set of customer sequences is reformatted after L_1 is found. Each transaction is replaced with one that consists only of pages from L_1. Candidates may be pruned before counting by removing any candidates that have subsequences that are not large. Variations on AprioriAll are proposed to avoid generating so many candidates. In effect, these improvements are used only to avoid generating sequences that are not maximal.

$$C_1 = \{\langle A\rangle, \langle B\rangle, \langle C\rangle, \langle D\rangle, \langle E\rangle\}$$
$$L_1 = \{\langle A\rangle, \langle B\rangle, \langle C\rangle, \langle D\rangle, \langle E\rangle\}$$

$$C_2 = \{\langle A, B\rangle, \langle A, C\rangle, \langle A, D\rangle, \langle A, E\rangle, \langle B, A\rangle, \langle B, C\rangle, \langle B, D\rangle,$$
$$\langle B, E\rangle, \langle C, A\rangle, \langle C, B\rangle, \langle C, D\rangle, \langle C, E\rangle, \langle D, A\rangle, \langle D, B\rangle,$$
$$\langle D, C\rangle, \langle D, E\rangle, \langle E, A\rangle, \langle E, B\rangle, \langle E, C\rangle, \langle E, D\rangle\}$$
$$L_2 = \{\langle A, B\rangle, \langle A, C\rangle, \langle A, D\rangle, \langle A, E\rangle, \langle B, C\rangle,$$
$$\langle B, E\rangle, \langle C, B\rangle, \langle C, D\rangle, \langle C, E\rangle, \langle D, C\rangle, \langle D, E\rangle\}$$

$$C_3 = \{\langle A, B, C\rangle, \langle A, B, D\rangle, \langle A, B, E\rangle, \langle A, C, B\rangle, \langle A, C, D\rangle, \langle A, C, E\rangle,$$
$$\langle A, D, B\rangle, \langle A, D, C\rangle, \langle A, D, E\rangle, \langle A, E, B\rangle, \langle A, E, C\rangle, \langle A, E, D\rangle,$$
$$\langle B, C, E\rangle, \langle B, E, C\rangle, \langle C, B, D\rangle, \langle C, B, E\rangle, \langle C, D, B\rangle, \langle C, D, E\rangle,$$
$$\langle C, E, B\rangle, \langle C, E, D\rangle, \langle D, C, B\rangle, \langle D, C, E\rangle, \langle D, E, C\rangle\}$$
$$L_3 = \{\langle A, B, C\rangle, \langle A, B, E\rangle, \langle A, C, B\rangle, \langle A, C, D\rangle, \langle A, C, E\rangle, \langle A, D, C\rangle,$$
$$\langle A, D, E\rangle, \langle B, C, E\rangle, \langle C, B, E\rangle, \langle C, D, E\rangle, \langle D, C, E\rangle\}$$

$$C_4 = \{\langle A, B, C, E\rangle, \langle A, B, E, C\rangle, \langle A, C, B, D\rangle, \langle A, C, B, E\rangle,$$
$$\langle A, C, D, B\rangle, \langle A, C, D, E\rangle, \langle A, C, E, B\rangle, \langle A, C, E, D\rangle,$$
$$\langle A, D, C, E\rangle, \langle A, D, E, C\rangle\}$$
$$L_4 = \{\langle A, B, C, E\rangle, \langle A, C, B, E\rangle, \langle A, C, D, E\rangle, \langle A, D, C, E\rangle\}$$

$$C_5 = \emptyset$$

The *WAP-tree (web access pattern)* has been proposed to facilitate efficient counting. This tree is used to store the sequences and their counts. Once the tree is built, the original database of patterns is not needed. Each node in the tree is associated with an event (a page found at a particular time by a user). The node is labeled with the event and a count that is associated with the pattern prefix that ends at that event. Only individual frequent events are added to the tree.

Frequent Episodes.   *Episodes*, which originally were proposed for telecommunication alarm analysis, can also be applied to Web logs. All pages (corresponding to events) are ordered by their access time, and the users usually need not be identified (i.e., no sessions). By definition, an episode is a partially ordered set of pages [MTV95]. In addition, the individual page accesses must occur within a particular time frame. A *serial episode* is an episode in which the events are totally ordered. Note that they need not be contiguous, however. A *parallel episode* is a set of events where there need not be any particular ordering. They still do need to satisfy the time constraint, however. Finally, a *general episode* is one where the events satisfy some partial order. Note that even though these seem similar to the idea of sequential patterns and association rules, the added constraint of a time window does make an episode different from either of these. The original definition has no concept of user, but, of course, the idea of an episode could be applied to events by one user or across users. In addition, episodes need not be maximal.

Example 7.7 illustrates the concept of episodes applied to the data in Example 7.4. Here we keep the original ordering of the events.

EXAMPLE 7.7

The XYZ Corporation maintains a set of five Web pages $\{A, B, C, D, E\}$. Assume that the data in Example 7.2 have the following sequence (independent of user): $\langle A, B, C, A, C, B, C, A, C, D, C, E \rangle$. To find episodes, we must know the time window, so the following sequence shows each event with an integer timestamp: $\langle (A, 1), (B, 2), (C, 2), (A, 7), (C, 10), (B, 10), (C, 12), (A, 12), (C, 13), (D, 14), (C, 14), (E, 20) \rangle$. Suppose that we wish to find general episodes where the support threshold is 30% and the time window is 3. This means that only events that occur within a time window of 3 are valid. We assume that the time window is the difference between the last event and the first event in the episode. To illustrate episodes, Figure 7.7 illustrates the ordering of events as shown in a *DAG (directed acyclic graph)* where arcs are used to represent temporal ordering. The arcs are labeled with the time between successive events. Starting at the first event and looking at the maximum window size of 3, we see that we have two serial episodes: AC and AB. B and C occur as parallel episodes. Starting at the event looking at time 12, we have the following serial episodes: ACD, ACC, CCC, CCD, AC, CC, CC, CD. We have two parallel episodes: A and C, and C and D. There also is a general episode that can be seen as the subgraph from time 12 to time 14. When taking the frequency into account, an episode must occur a certain number of times in all windows.

Maximal Frequent Forward Sequences.   One approach to mining log traversal patterns is to remove any backward traversals [CPY98]. Each raw session is transformed into *forward reference* (i.e., removes the backward traversals and reloads/refreshes), from which the traversal patterns are then mined using improved level-wise algorithms. For

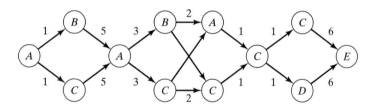

FIGURE 7.7: DAG for episodes.

example, for the session $\langle A, B, A, C \rangle$ in Example 7.2, the resulting forward sequences are $\langle A, B \rangle$ and $\langle A, C \rangle$. Looking at Example 7.8 and the sequence $\langle A, B, C, A, C, B, C, A, C, D, E \rangle$, we find the following maximal forward references:

$$\langle A, B, C \rangle, \langle A, C \rangle, \langle A, C, D \rangle, \langle A, C, E \rangle$$

As observed by the authors, the "real" access patterns made to get to the really used pages would not include these backward references. They assume that the backward reference is included only because of the structure of the pages, not because they really want to do this. The resulting set of forward references are called *maximal forward references*. They are called maximal because they are not subsequences of other forward references. The set of important reference patterns are those that occur with frequency above a desired threshold. In actuality, we are interested in finding consecutive subsequences within the forward references. A *large reference sequence* is a reference sequence (consecutive subsequence of a maximal forward reference) that appears more than a minimum number of times. The minimum number threshold is called the *support*.

Algorithm 7.3 outlines the steps needed to mine maximal reference sequences [CPY98]. After the maximal forward references are found, all subsequences of these references that occur greater than the required support are identified. Those large reference sequences that are not subsequences of other large reference sequences are found in step 3 and become the large reference sequences.

ALGORITHM 7.3

```
Input:
    D = {S₁, S₂, ..., Sₖ} //Database of sessions
    s //Support
Output:
    Maximal reference sequences
Maximal frequent forward sequences algorithm:
    find maximal forward references from D;
    find large reference sequences from the maximal ones;
    find maximal reference sequences from the large ones;
```

Maximal Frequent Sequences.   The transformation used to remove backward references also loses potentially useful information; for example, from the two forward sequences $\langle A, B \rangle$ and $\langle A, C \rangle$, we could not tell whether a direct link to page C from page B is needed, as shown in Example 7.2.

With *maximal frequent sequences (MFS)*, all four properties in Table 7.1 are required. Since an MFS could potentially start with any page (click) in any session, the definition of support assumes that the number of clicks is in the denominator. Thus, the support of a sequence X is defined to be

$$\frac{\text{freq}(X)}{\text{len}(D)} = \frac{\text{freq}}{\text{\# clicks}}$$

A sequence X is frequent if its support is above a minimum threshold. An MFS must be maximal. Example 7.8 (from [XD01a]) shows the mining of MFS.

EXAMPLE 7.8

Given $D = \{\langle A, B, C, D, E, D, C, F \rangle, \langle A, A, B, C, D, E \rangle, \langle B, G, H, U, V \rangle, \langle G, H, W \rangle\}$. The first session has backward traversals, and the second session has a reload/refresh on page A. Here $\text{len}(D) = 22$. Let the minimum support be $s_{\min} = 0.09$. This means that we are looking at finding sequences that occur at least two times. There are two maximal frequent sequences: $\langle A, B, C, D, E \rangle$ and $\langle G, H \rangle$. Both sequences occur two times.

Algorithm 7.4 (from [XD01a]) shows the *OAT (Online Adaptive Traversal Patterns)* algorithm designed to find MFS. It utilizes a suffix tree to store patterns. One suffix tree is created for all sessions. Counts of patterns are maintained in the tree. A unique feature of OAT is its ability to adapt to the availabe amount of main memory. If the suffix tree is too big to fit into memory, it is compressed and the algorithm continues. Details concerning the exact techniques used for compression can be found in the literature [XD01a].

ALGORITHM 7.4

Input:
    $S_1, S_2, \ldots, S_n$: sessions
    $s_{\min}$: minimum support threshold
    M: main memory size
Output:
    All maximal frequent sequences (MFSs)
OAT algorithm:

```
        ST = an empty suffix tree;
        //first scan
        for i from 1 to n do
            //if insufficient main memory with inclusion of S_i;
            //compress the suffix tree using frequent sequences;
            if  mem(ST ∪ S_i) > M, then
               ST = OAT_compress(ST);
            endif
            //update the suffix tree with inclusion of S_i
            ST = update(ST, S_i);
            if interrupted by the user, then
                //do a depth-first traversal of ST and output the MFSs.
                MFS_depth_first(ST.root);
            endif
        endfor
        //second scan
    if there are sequences not completely counted, then
        count them in an additional scan,
    endif
    output the MFSs in the suffix tree.
```

7.4.4   Pattern Analysis

Once patterns have been identified, they must be analyzed to determine how that information can be used. Some of the generated patterns may be deleted and determined not to be of interest.

Recent work has proposed examining Web logs not only to identify frequent types of traversal patterns, but also to identify patterns that are of interest because of their uniqueness or statistical properties [WUM00]. Patterns found need not have contiguous page references. A Web mining query language, *MINT*, facilitates the statement of interesting properties. The idea of a sequence is expanded to the concept of what the authors call a g-sequence. A *g-sequence* is a vector that consists not only of the pages visited (events) but also of wildcards. For example, the g-sequence $b * c$ stands for a sequence consisting of b, any number of pages, then c. With the use of wildcards, it is indicated that the events need not be contiguous. More complicated g-sequences can indicate specific constraints on the number of events that replace the wildcard. With MINT, selection of patterns that satisfy a g-sequence template are accomplished. The selection constraints may also include restrictions on support.

Some of the thrust of this work has been in comparing the differences between traversal patterns of the customers of an e-business site and those that are not customers [SPF00]. Visitors to a site have been classified as short-time visitors, active investigators, and customers [BPW96]. Preprocessing first filters out the visitors who are short-time. Using concept hierarchies, the contents of the Web pages are then abstracted to more general concepts. The log is then divided into those for customers and those for noncustomers. Each log is then examined to find patterns based on any desired requirements (such as frequency). The patterns found across the two logs are then compared for similarity. Similarity is determined using the following rule [SPF00]:

- Two patterns are comparable if their g-sequences have at least the first n pages the same. Here n is supplied by the user.

In addition, only fragments of patterns that occur frequently are considered. The goal of this work is to increase the number of customers. Noncustomer patterns with no comparable customer patterns indicate that some changes to the link structure or Web page designs may be in order. The project proposes rules and the use of a proxy server to dynamically change the link structures of pages.

7.5   EXERCISES

1. **(Research)** Find and describe two different approaches used by Web sites to perform personalization. Be as specific as possible.

2. **(Research)** Perform the same Web search using three different search engines. Describe the results. Your description should include the number of documents retrieved. Compare the differences of the five top pages found by each. Hypothesize why these differences exist.

3. Construct a trie for the string $\langle A, B, A, C \rangle$.

4. Construct a suffix tree for the string $\langle A, B, A, C \rangle$.

5. Given the following sessions, $\{\langle A, B, A, C \rangle, \langle C, B, D, F \rangle, \langle A, B, A \rangle\}$, indicate the sequential patterns, forward sequences, and maximal frequent sequences assuming a minimum support of 30%. Assume that each session occurs from a different user.

6. The use of a Web server through a proxy (such as an ISP) complicates the collection of frequent sequence statistics. Suppose that two users use one proxy and have the following sessions:

- User 1: $\langle 1, 3, 1, 3, 4, 3, 6, 8, 2, 3, 6 \rangle$
- User 2: $\langle 2, 3, 4, 3, 6, 8, 6, 3, 1 \rangle$

When these are viewed together by the Web server (taking into account the time-stamps), one large session is generated:

$$\langle 1, 2, 3, 3, 4, 1, 3, 6, 3, 8, 4, 3, 6, 3, 6, 1, 8, 2, 3, 6 \rangle$$

Identify the maximal frequent sequences assuming a minimum support of 2. What are the maximal frequent sequences if the two users could be separated?

7. (**Research**) Perform a literature survey concerning current research into solutions to the proxy problem identified in Exercise 6.

7.6 BIBLIOGRAPHIC NOTES

A recent survey of Web mining has been published [KB00] and contains an excellent bibliography and a survey of hundreds of Web mining publications. This article provides both an information retrieval view and a database view of Web content mining. Both [Zaï99] and [CMS97] contain taxonomies of Web mining activities.

There have been many published articles exploring crawlers. Incremental crawlers were examined in [CGM00]. Focused crawlers are studied in [CDAR98], [CDI98], [CvdBD99], and [DCL+00]. The periodic crawler was investigated in [CGM00]. The context focused crawler was first investigated in [DCL+00]. Harvest and Essence were described in [BDH+95] and [HS93]. The Virtual Web View with the MLDB was proposed in [Zaï99].

An excellent introduction to personalization appeared in a special issue of the *Communications of the ACM* [Rie00]. A special section within this same issue is aimed specifically at personalization using Web usage mining [Spi00]. Firefly's automatic personalization approach was examined in [SM95].

A recent doctoral dissertation has examined many issues associated with Web mining [Zaï99]. In addition to providing an excellent bibliography with comparisons of various Web mining activities, this work also proposes a Web mining query language, *WebML*. WebML accesses the Web data, which have been transformed into a multilayered database. Information about WordNet is available on the Web [Wor00].

The suffix tree data structure is actually a PATRICIA trie [Bay74] constructed for the relevant suffixes. Efficient algorithms for suffix trees were shown in [McC76].

Sequential patterns as applied to Web log were studied in [AS95]. Maximal frequent sequences were studied in [XD01a].

The World Wide Web Consortium (W3C) is a consortium of over 400 member organizations whose purpose is to develop protocols needed to ensure the use and growth of the Web. Various versions of HTML have been proposed. The most recent, XHTML 1.0, uses the syntax of XML. XML is the next-generation markup language to be used by Web documents. The more structured nature of XML facilitates easier access and querying for Web documents. Both XML and HTML are based on *standard generalized markup languaged (SGML)*, which is an ISO standard from 1986.

Recently there have been several proposals for query languages aimed at the Web. Most of these are extensions of SQL (WebSQL, W3QL, WebOQL), while others are based on deductive type rules (WebLog). Instead of using relations, WebSQL uses virtual relations, which are viewed as abstractions of Web documents [MMM96]. When using WebSQL, the actually work of accessing the Web is performed by a traditional search engine. WebSQL queries are converted into search engine queries, and results of these queries are compiled and returned to the user. Similarly, W3QL [KS95] takes advantage of a search engine to access the Web. W3QL, however, allows the use of external code or Unix commands to be embedded within the query. WebLog uses deductive rules rather than an SQL-like syntax [LSS96]. It is considered to be a second-generation language because it actually can generate new Web documents. Based on OQL, WebOQL views data as consisting of trees, while groups of trees are called webs [GM98].

There are several ongoing research prototypes examining Web mining. The *WEB-MINER* system being developed at DePaul University [Mob00] consists of both Web log preparation steps (cleaning, transaction identification, and integration) and mining functions. An ongoing research project at the University of Minnesota, *WebSIFT*, has produced a comprehensive system design, including preprocessing, knowledge discovery, and pattern analysis steps [CTS97]. The data mining functions performed include classification of Web pages, identification of sequential patterns of Web usage data, clustering of both pages and users, generation of association rules, and creation of usage statistics.

IBM has a Web mining product called SurfAid Analytics [IBM00]. SurfAid performs traversal pattern analysis, referral analysis, and other data mining activities. *Referral analysis* determines where visitors came from when they entered a Web page.

CHAPTER 8

Spatial Mining

8.1 INTRODUCTION

Spatial data are data that have a spatial or location component. Spatial data can be viewed as data about objects that themselves are located in a physical space. This may be implemented with a specific location attribute(s) such as address or latitude/longitude or may be more implicitly included such as by a partitioning of the database based on location. In addition, spatial data may be accessed using queries containing spatial operators such as near, north, south, adjacent, and contained in. Spatial data are stored in spatial databases that contain the spatial data and nonspatial data about objects. Because of the inherent distance information associated with spatial data, spatial databases are often stored using special data structures or indices built using distance or topological information. As far as data mining is concerned, this distance information provides the basis for needed similarity measures.

Spatial data are required for many current information technology systems. *Geographic information systems (GIS)* are used to store information related to geographic locations on the surface of the Earth. This includes applications related to weather, community infrastructure needs, disaster management, and hazardous waste. Data mining activities include prediction of environmental catastrophes. Biomedical applications, including medical imaging and illness diagnosis, also require spatial systems.

Spatial mining, often called *spatial data mining* or *knowledge discovery in spatial databases*, is data mining as applied to spatial databases or spatial data. Some of the applications for spatial data mining are in the areas of GIS systems, geology, environmental science, resource management, agriculture, medicine, and robotics. Many of the techniques discussed in previous chapters are applied directly to spatial data, but there also are new techniques and algorithms developed specifically for spatial data mining.

We investigate these issues in this chapter. Before investigating spatial mining, we first provide a brief introduction to spatial data and databases.

8.2 SPATIAL DATA OVERVIEW

Accessing spatial data can be more complicated than accessing nonspatial data. There are specialized operations and data structures used to access spatial data.

8.2.1 Spatial Queries

Because of the complexity of spatial operations, much work has been performed to examine spatial query processing and its optimization.

A traditional selection query accessing nonspatial data uses the standard comparison operations: $>, <, \leq, \geq, \neq$. A *spatial selection* is a selection on spatial data that may use other selection comparison operations. The types of spatial comparators that could be used include near, north, south, east, west, contained in, and overlap or intersect. The following are examples of several spatial selection queries:

- Find all houses near Mohawk Elementary School.

- Find the nearest fire station to 9631 Moss Haven Drive in Dallas.

A special join operation applied to two spatial relations is called a *spatial join*. In some ways, a spatial join is like a regular relational join in that two records are joined together if they have features in common. With a traditional join, two records must have attributes in common that satisfy a predefined relationship (such as equality in an equijoin). With a spatial join, the relationship is a spatial one. The type of relationship is based on the type of spatial feature. For example, the nearest relationship may be used for points, while the intersecting relationship is used for polygons.

In GIS applications, it is common to have different views of the same geographic area. For example, city developers must be able to see where infrastructure facilities are located, including streets, power lines, phone lines, and sewer lines. At another level, they might be interested in actual elevations, building locations, and rivers. Each of these types of information could be maintained in separate GIS files. Merging these disparate data can be performed using a special operator called a *map overlay*.

A spatial object usually is described with both spatial and nonspatial attributes. Some sort of *location* type attribute must be included. The location attribute could identify a precise point, such as a latitude or longitude pair, or it may be more logical such as a street address or zip code. Often, different spatial objects are identified by different locations, and some sort of translation between one attribute and the other is needed to perform spatial operations between the different objects. As in **SAND**, the nonspatial attributes may be stored in a relational database, while each spatial attribute is stored in some spatial data structure. Each tuple in the relationship represents the spatial object, and a link to the spatial data structure is stored in the corresponding position in the nonspatial tuple.

Many basic spatial queries can assist in data mining activities. Some of these queries include:

- A *region query or range query* is a query asking for objects that intersect a given region specified in the query.

- A *nearest neighbor query* asks to find objects that are close to an identified object.

- A *distance scan* finds objects within a certain distance of an identified object, but the distance is made increasingly larger.

All of these queries can be used to assist in clustering or classification.

8.2.2   Spatial Data Structures

Because of the unique features of spatial data, there are many data structures that have been designed specifically to store or index spatial data. In this section, we briefly examine some of the more popular data structures. Many of these structures are based on extensions to conventional indexing approaches, such as B-trees or binary search trees.

Nonspatial database queries using traditional indexing structures, such as a B-tree, access the data using an exact match query. However, spatial queries may use proximity measures based on relative locations of spatial objects. To efficiently perform these spatial queries, it is advisable that objects close in space be clustered on disk. To this end, the geographic space under consideration may be partitioned into *cells* based on proximity, and these cells would then be related to storage locations (blocks on disk). The corresponding data structure would be constructed based on these cells.

A common technique used to represent a spatial object is by the smallest rectangle that completely contains that object, *minimum bounding rectangle (MBR)*. We illustrate the use of MBRs by looking at a lake. Figure 8.1(a) shows the outline of a lake. If we orient this lake in a traditional coordinate system with the horizontal axis representing east–west and the perpendicular axis north–south, we can put this lake in a rectangle (with sides parallel to the axes) that contains it. Thus, in Figure 8.1(b) we show an MBR that can be used to represent this lake. Alternatively, in Figure 8.1(c) we could represent it by a set of smaller rectangles. This option can provide a closer fit to the actual object, but it requires multiple MBRs. An MBR can easily be represented by the coordinates for two nonadjacent vertices. So we could represent the MBR in Figure 8.1(b) by the pair $\{(x_1, y_1), (x_2, y_2)\}$. There are other ways to store the MBR values, and the orientation of the MBRs need not be with the axes.

We use the triangle shown in Figure 8.2(a) as a simple spatial object. In Figure 8.2(b) we show an MBR for the triangle. Spatial indices can be used to assist in spatial data mining activities. One benefit of the spatial data structures is that they cluster objects based on location. This implies that objects that are close together in the

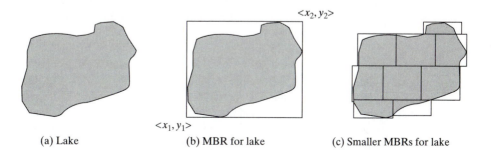

$\langle x_2, y_2 \rangle$

$\langle x_1, y_1 \rangle$

(a) Lake   (b) MBR for lake   (c) Smaller MBRs for lake

FIGURE 8.1: MBR example.

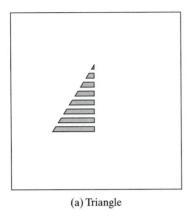

(a) Triangle

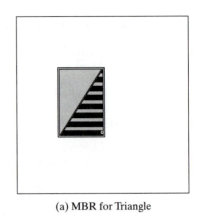

(a) MBR for Triangle

FIGURE 8.2: Spatial object example.

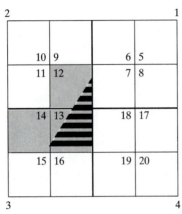

(a) Representing triangle with quadrants

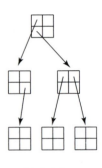

(b) Quad tree

FIGURE 8.3: Quad tree example.

n-dimensional space tend to be stored close together in the data structure and on disk. Thus, these structures could be used to reduce the processing overhead of an algorithm by limiting its search space. In effect, filtering is performed as you traverse down a tree. In addition, spatial queries can be more efficiently answered by use of these structures.

Quad Tree.   One of the original data structures proposed for spatial data is that of a quad tree. A *quad tree* represents a spatial object by a hierarchical decomposition of the space into quadrants (cells). This process is illustrated in Figure 8.3(a) using the triangle in Figure 8.2. Here the triangle is shown as three shaded squares. The spatial area has been divided into two layers of quadrant divisions. The number of layers needed depends on the precision desired. Obviously, the more layers, the more overhead is required for the data structure. Each level in the quad tree corresponds to one of the hierarchical layers. Each of the four quadrants at that layer has a related pointer to a node at the next level if any of the lowest level quadrants are shaded. We label the quadrants at each level in a counterclockwise direction starting at the upper right quadrant (as shown in the figure). Square 0 is the entire area. Square 1 is the upper right at level one. Square 15 is the square in the lower left corner at the second level. In this figure, the triangle is represented by squares 12, 13, and 14 because it intersects these three regions. The quad tree for this triangle is shown in Figure 8.3(b). Only nodes with nonempty quadrants are shown. Thus, there are no nodes for quadrants 1 and 4 and their subquadrants.

MBRs are similar to the quadrants in the quad tree except that they do not have to be of identical sizes. If hierarchies of MBRs exist, they do not have to be regular as in the quadrant decompositions.

R-Tree.   One approach to indexing spatial data represented as MBRs is an R-tree. Each successive layer in the tree identifies smaller rectangles. In an R-tree, cells may actually overlap. An object is represented by an MBR that is located within one cell. Basically, a cell is the MBR that contains the related set of objects (or MBRs) at a lower level of decomposition. Each level of decomposition is identified with a layer in the tree. As spatial objects are added to the R-tree, it is created and maintained by algorithms similar to those found for B-trees. The size of the tree is related to the number of objects. Looking at a space with only the basic triangle, as seen in Figure 8.2, a tree with only a root node would be created. We illustrate a more complicated R-tree in Figure 8.4. Here there are five objects represented by the MBRs D, E, F, G, and H. The entire geographic space is labeled A and is shown as the root of the tree in Figure 8.4(b). Three of the objects (D, E, F) are contained in an MBR labeled B, while the remaining two (G, H) are in MBR C.

Algorithms to perform spatial operators using an R-tree are relatively straightforward. Suppose we wished to find all objects that intersected with a given object. Representing the query object as an MBR, we can search the upper levels of the R-tree to find only those cells that intersect the MBR query. Those subtrees that do not intersect the query MBR can be discarded.

k-D Tree.   A *k-D tree* was designed to index multiattribute data, not necessarily spatial data. The k-D tree is a variation of a *binary search tree* where each level in the

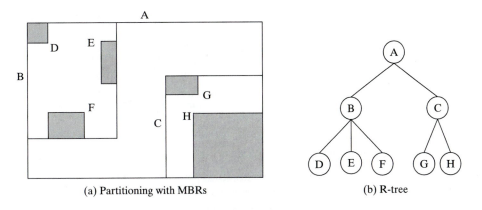

(a) Partitioning with MBRs   (b) R-tree

FIGURE 8.4: R-tree example.

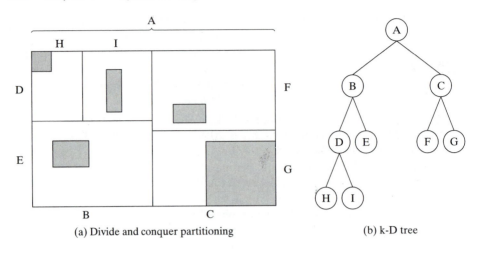

(a) Divide and conquer partitioning   (b) k-D tree

FIGURE 8.5: k-D tree example.

tree is used to index one of the attributes. We illustrate the use of the k-D tree assuming a two-dimensional space. Each node in the tree represents a division of the space into two subsets based on the division point used. In addition, the division alternates between the two axes.

In Figure 8.5 we show a k-D tree using the same data we used for the R-tree. As with the R-tree, each lowest level cell has only one object in it. However, the divisions are not made using MBRs. Initially, the entire region is viewed as one cell and thus the root of the k-D tree. The area is divided first along one dimension and then along another dimension until each cell has only one object in it. In this example, we see that the entire region, A, is first divided into two cells (B, C) along the horizontal axis. Then, looking at B, we see that it is divided into D and E. D is finally divided into H and I.

8.2.3   Thematic Maps

Thematic maps illustrate spatial objects by showing the distribution of attributes or themes. Each map shows one (or more) of the thematic attributes. These attributes describe the important nonspatial features of the associated spatial object. For example, one thematic map may show elevation, average rainfall, and average temperature. *Raster*-based thematic maps represent the spatial data by relating pixels to attribute values of the data. For example, in a map showing elevation, the color of the pixel can be associated with the elevation of that location. A *vector*-based thematic map represents objects by a geometric structure (such as their outline or MBR). In addition, the object then has the thematic attribute values.

8.2.4   Image Databases

In image databases the data are stored as pictures or images. These databases are used in many applications, including medicine and remote sensing.

Some early classification work performed using large image databases looked at ways to classify astronomical objects. One of the applications of this work is to identify volcanos on Venus from images taken by the Magellan spacecraft [FWD93]. This system consisted of three parts: data focusing, feature extraction, and classification. The first component determines which of the areas of the images is the most likely to contain volcanos. Here the intensity of a central point of a region is compared with that of the background. The important features of these areas are extracted and stored in the second part. The focusing portion compares the intensity of a central point of a region with that of the background. During the second phase, interesting features are identified and extracted. Finally, these features are classified based on classifiers built using training data provided by domain experts. The third portion uses a decision tree to perform the actual classification. The tree is created using ID3 and training examples provided by experts. An accuracy of 80% was achieved.

A related work also used decision trees to classify stellar objects [FS93]. As with the volcano work, the first two steps were to identify areas of the images of interest and then to extract information about these areas. Multiple trees were created, and from these sets of rules were generated for classification. Accuracy was found to be approximately 94%. When compared to several neural network approaches, the decision tree/rules approach was found to be much more accurate. Both of these studies found the need to normalize the extracted features to compensate for differences between different images. For example, two images could differ based on the angle at which the image was taken.

8.3   SPATIAL DATA MINING PRIMITIVES

Operations needed to support spatial data mining involve those required for spatial databases. We review some of these in this section. In these discussions, we assume that A and B are spatial objects in a two-dimensional space. Each object can be viewed as consisting of a set of points in the space: $\langle x_a, y_a \rangle \in A$ and $\langle x_b, y_b \rangle \in B$.

As defined in [EFKS00], there are several *topological relationships* that can exist between two spatial objects. These relationships are based on the ways in which two objects are placed in a geographic domain:

- **Disjoint:** A is disjoint from B if there are no points in A that are contained in B.

- **Overlaps** or **intersects:** A overlaps with B if there is at least one point in A that is also in B.

- **Equals:** A equals B if all points in the two objects are in common.

- **Covered by** or **inside** or **contained in:** A is contained in B if all points in A are in B. There may be points in B that are not in A.

- **Covers** or **contains:** A contains B *iff* B is contained in A.

While data mining tasks may not specifically address these relationships, the similarity between spatial objects certainly can be defined based partially on these relationships.

Based on the placement of the objects in the space, relationships with respect to direction may be defined. These usually are defined by adding the traditional map orientations to the space. Thus, we have the relationships such as *north*, *south*, *east*, *west*, and so on. What makes these relationships difficult to identify is the irregular shape of spatial objects and the fact that they may overlap.

As mentioned in Chapter 3, the Euclidean and Manhattan measures are often used to measure the distance between two points. The distance between two spatial objects can be defined as extensions to these two traditional definitions:

- **Minimum:**

$$\text{dis}(A, B) = \min_{(x_a, y_a) \in A, (x_b, y_b) \in B} \text{dis}((x_a, y_a), (x_b, y_b)) \qquad (8.1)$$

- **Maximum:**

$$\text{dis}(A, B) = \max_{(x_a, y_a) \in A, (x_b, y_b) \in B} \text{dis}((x_a, y_a), (x_b, y_b)) \qquad (8.2)$$

- **Average:**

$$\text{dis}(A, B) = \text{average}_{(x_a, y_a) \in A, (x_b, y_b) \in B} \text{dis}((x_a, y_a), (x_b, y_b)) \qquad (8.3)$$

- **Center:**

$$\text{dis}(A, B) = \text{dis}((x_{ca}, y_{ca}), (x_{cb}, y_{cb})) \qquad (8.4)$$

where (x_{ca}, y_{ca}) is a center point for object A and (x_{cb}, y_{cb}) for B.

Note the similarity to distance measures used in clustering. In fact, you can think of the spatial object as a cluster of the points within it. The center points used for the last distance formula can be identified by finding the geometric center of the object. For example, if an MBR is used, the distance between objects could be found using the Euclidean distance between the center of the MBRs for the two objects.

Spatial objects may be retrieved based on selection, aggregation, or join-type operations. A selection may be performed based on the spatial or nonspatial attributes. Retrieving based on spatial attributes could be performed using one of the spatial operators. A spatial join retrieves based on the relationship between two spatial objects.

8.4   GENERALIZATION AND SPECIALIZATION

The use of a concept hierarchy shows levels of relationships among data. When applied to spatial data characteristics, concept hierarchies allow the development of rules and relationships at different levels in the hierarchy. This is similar to the use of roll up and drill down operations in OLAP. We have also seen this idea used in generalized association rules. A similar idea is used in the generalization and specialization concepts found in machine learning. In these cases, however, the hierarchy is not necessarily related to spatial data. Spatial data mining techniques have involved both generalization and specialization type approaches.

8.4.1   Progressive Refinement

Because of the massive amounts of data found in spatial applications, approximate answers may be made before finding more accurate ones. The use of MBRs is a method to approximate the shape of an object. Quad trees, R-trees, and most other spatial indexing techniques use a type of progressive refinement. They estimate the shape of objects at higher levels in the tree structure, and lower-level entries provide more precise descriptions of the spatial objects. *Progressive refinement* can be viewed as filtering out data that are not applicable to a problem.

With progressive refinement, the hierarchical levels are based on spatial relationships. Example 8.1 illustrates the idea of progressive refinement. Here spatial relationships can be applied at a more coarse (move up the hierarchy) or more fine (move down the hierarchy) level.

EXAMPLE 8.1

Suppose that a computer science student wishes to identify apartments close to the SMU Computer Science and Engineering (CSE) Department. A given database listing available apartments in the Dallas metroplex will contain many apartments nowhere near the SMU campus. An initial filtering of the inappropriate elements can be made by finding apartments that are "generalized close" to the CSE Department. This can be performed at any of the levels in the concept hierarchy, Figure 8.6 shows the idea. The closest apartments to SMU probably would be in the Park Cities. By filtering out all apartments in all subtrees other than those for the Park Cities, apartments that are fairly close to SMU would be found. Suppose that a lower level in the concept hierarchy existed that included zip code. If apartments in the same zip code as the CSE Department were found, an even finer estimate of close could be used. This process quickly filters out apartments that could not possibly be used to answer the question. Here a coarser predicate is first used to filter out potential answers. This predicate can be recursively refined until the precise answers are found. Note that when looking at the concept hierarchy, the coarser predicates can be applied to the MBRs at the higher levels, while the finer predicates are applied at the lower levels.

8.4.2 Generalization

As with OLAP, generalization is driven by a concept hierarchy and can be viewed as the process of deriving information at a high level based on information found at lower levels. Concept hierarchies for spatial data can be both spatial and nonspatial. A *spatial hierarchy* is a concept hierarchy that shows the relationships between geographic areas. Figure 8.6 shows a spatial hierarchy. In Chapter 6, Figure 6.7 illustrated a nonspatial

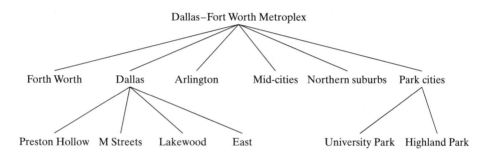

FIGURE 8.6: Illustration of progressive refinement used in Example 8.1.

hierarchy. Generalization can be performed using either of these two hierarchies. When the spatial data are generalized, the nonspatial data must be appropriately changed to reflect the nonspatial data associated with the new spatial area. Similarly, when the nonspatial data are generalized, the spatial data must be appropriately modified. Using these two types of hierarchies, generalization as applied to spatial data can be divided into two subclasses: spatial data dominant and nonspatial data dominant [LHO93]. Both of these subclasses can be viewed as a type of clustering. Spatial data dominant does the clustering based on spatial locations (so that objects close together are grouped), whereas nonspatial data dominant clusters by similarity of nonspatial attribute values. These approaches are referred to as an *attribute-oriented induction* because the generalization process is based on attribute values.

With *spatial data dominant generalization*, generalization is first applied to the spatial data, and then the related nonspatial attributes are modified accordingly. Generalization is performed until a threshold number of regions is reached. For example, determining the average rainfall in the southwestern United States could be done by finding the mean average rainfall for all states shown to be in the Southwest by a spatial hierarchy. Thus, the spatial hierarchy determines which lower-level regions are found in the higher-level region being queried. Determining how to apply the generalization to the nonspatial data is, however, not always a straightforward aggregation operation. Determining the average rainfall in this case actually treats each state the same. However, a weighting by geographic area might be used to provide a more accurate average rainfall for the higher-level region being queried.

An alternative approach is to generalize the nonspatial attribute values as well. Generalization is based on grouping of data. Adjacent regions are merged if they have the same generalized values for the nonspatial data. Suppose that instead of average rainfall values, we simply returned values that represented the southwestern cluster. We could assign values of heavy, medium, light, and so on to describe the rainfall rather than providing actual numeric values. Algorithm 8.1 shows the spatial-dominant approach. A threshold that indicates the maximum number of regions may be given. Based on this threshold, the correct level in the hierarchy is chosen, and thus the number of regions is determined.

ALGORITHM 8.1

```
Input:
    D          //Spatial database
    H          //Spatial hierarchy
    C          //Concept hierarchy
    q          //Query
Output:
    R          //Rule that states the general characteristics requested
SPATIAL-data-dominant algorithm:
    D' = set of data obtained from D based on selection criteria in q;
    Following the structure of H, combine data into regions until
        either the desired threshold number of regions is found
        or the requested level in H is obtained;
    for each region found do
        perform an attribute-oriented induction on the
            nonspatial attributes;
        Generate and output a rule that summarizes the results found;
```

Although not shown here, the *nonspatial-data-dominant generalization* technique works in a similar fashion. The first step in this algorithm is to retrieve the data based on the nonspatial selection criteria stated in the query. Needed attribute-oriented induction is then performed on the retrieved nonspatial data. The nonspatial concept hierarchies are consulted to perform this. During this step, nonspatial attribute values are generalized to higher-level values. These generalizations are higher-level summary values of the lower-level specific values. For example, if average temperature were generalized, several different average temperatures (or ranges) could be combined and labeled "hot." The third step is to perform spatial-oriented generalization. Here neighboring regions with the same (or similar) nonspatial generalized values are merged. This is done to reduce the number of regions returned in response to the query.

A negative of these approaches is that the hierarchy must be predefined by domain experts, and the quality of any data mining requests depends on the hierarchy provided. The complexity to create the hierarchies is $O(n \log n)$.

8.4.3   Nearest Neighbor

We introduced the idea of a nearest neighbor in Chapter 5 with respect to clustering. This idea of identifying objects that are close together is a common query type in spatial databases. The *nearest neighbor distance* is the minimum distance between an object and all other objects in the space.

8.4.4   STING

The *STatistical INformation Grid-based method (STING)* uses a hierarchical technique to divide the spatial area into rectangular cells similar to a quad tree. The spatial database is scanned once, and statistical parameters (mean, variance, distribution type) for each cell are determined. Each node in the grid structure summarizes the information about the items within it. By capturing this information, many data mining requests, including clustering, can be answered by examining the statistics created for the cells. Thus, only clusters with vertical and horizontal boundaries are generated. However, the entire database need not be scanned after this statistical information is captured. This can be quite efficient when several data mining requests may be made against the data. Unlike the generalization and progressive refinement techniques, no predefined concept hierarchy must be provided.

The STING approached can be viewed as a type of hierarchical clustering technique. The first step is to create a hierarchical representation (like a dendrogram). The created tree successively divides the space into quadrants. The top level in the hierarchy consists of the entire space. The lowest level has one leaf for each of the smallest cells. The original proposal was for a cell to have four subcells (grids) at the next lowest level. The division of cells is identical to that performed for quad trees. In general, however, the approach would work with any hierarchical decomposition of the space. Figure 8.7 illustrates the nodes at the first three levels of the constructed tree.

The process to create the tree is shown in Algorithm 8.2. Each cell in the space corresponds to a node in the tree and is described with both attribute-independent (count) data and attribute-dependent (mean, standard deviation, minimum, maximum, distribution) data. As the data are loaded into the database, the hierarchy is created. Placement of an item into a cell is completely determined by its physical position. Algorithm 8.2

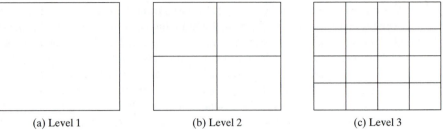

| (a) Level 1 | (b) Level 2 | (c) Level 3 |

FIGURE 8.7: Nodes in STING structure.

is divided into two parts. The first part creates the hierarchy and the second part fills in the values. Since the number of nodes in the tree is less than the number of items in the database, the complexity of STING BUILD is $O(n)$.

ALGORITHM 8.2

Input:
    D //Data to be placed in the hierarchical structure
    k //Number of desired cells at the lowest level
Output:
    T //Tree
STING BUILD algorithm:
    // Create empty tree from top down.
    $T =$ root node with data values initialized; //Initially only
                                                  root node
    $i = 1$;
    repeat
       for each node in level i **do**
          create 4 children nodes with initial values;
        $i = i + 1$;
    until $4^i = k$;
    // Populate tree from bottom up.
    for each item in D **do**
       determine leaf node j associated with the position of D;
       update values of j based on attribute values in item;
    $i := \log_4(k)$;
    repeat
       $i := i - 1$;
       for each node j in level i **do**
          update values of j based on attribute values
             in its 4 children;
    until $i = 1$;

The actual STING algorithm is shown in Algorithm 8.3. The algorithm assumes that a query, q, that can be answered from the stored statistical information in the constructed tree, T, is requested. Such a query might be to find the range of price of apartments near SMU. The statistics (minimum and maximum) of the apartment rental prices for the appropriate cells should be determined. The cell that SMU is in would determine the actual values for those closest to SMU. In addition, the query might retrieve the information for the cells surrounding this cell or perhaps at the next highest level in the tree that contains the cell where SMU is located. The nearby cells could be determined using some distance function. The crucial concept here is that the appropriate cells must be determined and then the information from those cells, in the constructed tree must be retrieved. A breadth-first tree traversal is used to examine the tree. However, a complete traversal of the tree is not performed. Only children of relevant nodes are examined. Here the concept of relevance is much like that with IR queries except that relevance is determined by estimating the proportion of the objects in that cell that meet the query conditions. The complexity of the STING algorithm is $O(k)$ where k is the number of cells at the lowest level. Obviously, this is the space taken up by the tree itself. When used for clustering purposes, k would be the largest number of clusters created.

ALGORITHM 8.3

```
Input:
    T          //Tree
    q          //Query
Output:
    R          //Regions of relevant cells
STING algorithm:
    i = 1
    repeat
        for each node in level i do
            determine if this cell is relevant to q and mark as such;
            i = i + 1
    until all layers in the tree have been visited;
    identify neighboring cells of relevant cells to create
        regions of cells;
```

Calculating the likelihood that a cell is relevant to a query is based on the percentage of the objects in the cell that satisfy the query constraints. Using a predefined confidence interval, if this proportion is high enough, then that cell is labeled as relevant. The statistical information associated with these relevant cells is used to answer the query. If this approximate answer is not good enough, then the associated relevant objects in the database may have to be examined to provide a more exact response. The cells found by STING approximate those found by DBSCAN. Cells that are found to be close enough to relevant cells are included in the regions of cells that are found by the algorithm.

8.5   SPATIAL RULES

Spatial rules can be generated that describe the relationship between and structure of spatial objects. There are three types of rules that can be found during spatial data mining [KAH96]. *Spatial characteristic rules* describe the data. *Spatial discriminant rules* describe the differences between different classes of the data. They describe the features that differentiate the different classes. *Spatial association rules* are implications of one set of data by another. The following examples illustrate these three types of rules:

- Characteristic rule: In Dallas the average family income is $50,000.

- Discriminant rule: In Dallas the average family income is $50,000, while in Plano the average family income is $75,000.

- Association rule: In Dallas the average family income for families living near White Rock Lake is $100,000.

Characterization is the process of finding a description for a database or some subset thereof. All of these rules can be thought of as special types of characterizations. The characteristic rule is the simplest.

Another common approach to summarizing spatial data is that of performing a *trend detection*, which is viewed as a regular change in one or more nonspatial attribute values for spatial objects as you move away from another spatial object [EFKS98]. For example, the average price per square foot of a house may increase as the proximity to the ocean increases. Regression analysis may be used to identify a trend detection.

8.5.1 Spatial Association Rules

Spatial association rules are association rules about spatial data objects. Either the antecedent or the consequent of the rule must contain some spatial predicates (such as near):

- Nonspatial antecedent and spatial consequent: All elementary schools are located close to single-family housing developments.

- Spatial antecedent and nonspatial consequent: If a house is located in Highland Park, it is expensive.

- Spatial antecedent and spatial consequent: Any house that is near downtown is south of Plano.

Support and confidence for spatial association rules is defined identically to that for regular association rules. Unlike traditional association rules, however, the underlying database being examined usually is not viewed as a set of transactions. Instead, it is a set of spatial objects.

The simplest spatial association rule generation algorithm is found in [KH95]. The approach is similar to that discussed earlier for classification in that a two-step approach is used. As with traditional association rule algorithms, all association rules that satisfy the minimum confidence and support are generated by this algorithm. Because of the large number of possibilities for topological relationships, it is assumed that the data mining request indicates what spatial predicate(s) is to be used. Once the relative subset of the database is determined, relationships of this type are identified. It initially is assumed that "generalized" versions of the topological relationships are used. The generalized relationships are satisfied if some objects higher up the concept hierarchy satisfy it. For example, zip codes may be used instead of the exact structure of the house. At this level, a filtering is performed to remove objects that could not possibly satisfy the relationship.

To illustrate the concept of generalization with the spatial relationships, we follow the example found in [Kop99]. Suppose that the topological relationship being examined is "close_to." The GIS system would define precisely what this predicate means. For example, it could define the relationship based on the Euclidean distance between the two spatial objects. In addition, it might be defined differently based on the type of objects in question. The generalization of "close_to" that is written as "g_close_to" may be defined by a hierarchy that shows that g_close_to contains close_to as well as other predicates (such as contains and equal). A first step in determining satisfiability of the close_to predicate would be to look at a coarse evaluation of g_close_to. The coarse evaluation is used as a type of filter to efficiently rule out objects that could not possibly satisfy the true predicate. The coarse predicate coarse_g_close_to is satisfied by objects if their MBRs satisfy g_close_to. Only those objects that satisfy coarse_g_close_to are examined to see if they satisfy g_close_to.

The five-step algorithm is outlined in Algorithm 8.4. It is assumed that a data mining query is input. The query contains selection information that is used to retrieve the objects from the database that are of interest. The topological predicates defining the spatial relationships of interest are also input. Using these predicates, P, an initial table is built, CP, that identifies which pairs of objects satisfy P at a coarse level. The input minimum supports are actually a set of support values to be used at different levels in the processing. $s[1]$ is the support level to be used at the coarse filtering level. After this filtering, the pairs of objects that satisfy the coarse predicates are counted to see if their support is above the minimum. In effect, this frequent coarse predicate (FCP) database is the set of large one-itemsets. The predicates in FCP are then examined to find the frequent predicates at a fine level (FFP). The last step expands these frequent predicates of size 1 to all arbitrary predicate sizes and then generates the rules as with traditional association rules. This is performed similarly to Apriori. By finding the FCRs first, the number of objects to be examined is reduced at the last step.

ALGORITHM 8.4

Input:

D	//Data, including spatial and nonspatial attributes
C	//Concept hierarchies
s	//Minimum support for levels
α	//Confidence
q	//Query to retrieve interested objects
P	//Topological predicate(s) of interest

Output:

R	//Spatial association rules

SPATIAL association rule algorithm:

```
D' = q(D);
CP is built by applying the coarse predicate version of P to D';
//   CP consists of the set of coarse predicates satisfied by
         pairs of objects in D'.
determine the set of frequent coarse predicates FCP by finding
   the coarse predicates that satisfy s;
find the set of frequent fine predicates FFP from FCP;
find R by finding all frequent fine predicates and then
   generating rules;
```

This algorithm works in a similar manner to the Apriori algorithm in that large "predicate sets" are determined. Here a *predicate set* is a set of predicates of interest. A 1-predicate might be {⟨*close_to, park*⟩}, so all spatial objects that are close_to a park will be counted as satisfying this predicate. A 2-predicate could be {⟨*close_to, park*⟩, ⟨*south_of, Plano*⟩}. Counts of 1-predicate sets are counted, then those that are large are used to generate 2-predicate sets, and these are then counted. In actuality, the algorithm can be used to generate multilevel association rules if desired or rules at a coarse level rather than a fine level.

8.6 SPATIAL CLASSIFICATION ALGORITHMS

Spatial classification problems are used to partition sets of spatial objects. Spatial objects could be classified using nonspatial attributes, spatial predicates (spatial attributes), or spatial and nonspatial attributes. Concept hierarchies may be used, as may sampling. As with other types of spatial mining, generalization and progressive refinement techniques may be used to improve efficiency.

8.6.1 ID3 Extension

The concept of neighborhood graphs has been applied to perform classification of spatial objects using an ID3 extension [EKS97]. A *neighborhood graph* is a graph constructed from the objects in the space. Each object becomes a node in the graph. The edges are constructed from the neighbors; that is, two nodes are connected by an edge in the neighborhood graph if one is a neighbor of the other. "Neighbor" can be defined based on any relationship between the spatial objects such as distance less than a particular threshold, satisfiability of a topological relationship between the objects, or direction relationship. Note that some of the relationships are order relationships and others are not.

The idea of the algorithm is to take into account the objects that are near a given object. A max-length indicator is input that specifies the maximum length of a neighborhood path starting at the node. This then identifies a set of nodes that are associated with the target node. ID3 then considers for classification purposes not only the nonspatial attributes of the target object, but also those in neighboring objects.

8.6.2 Spatial Decision Tree

One spatial classification technique builds decision trees using a two-step process similar to that used for association rules [KHS98]. The basis of the approach is that spatial objects can be described based on objects close to them. A description of the classes is then assumed to be based on an aggregation of the most relevant predicates for objects nearby.

To construct the decision tree, the most relevant predicates (spatial and nonspatial) are first determined. It is hoped that this process will create smaller and more accurate decision trees. These relevant predicates are the ones that will be used to build the decision tree. It is assumed that a training sample is used to perform this step and that weights are assigned to attributes and predicates. Initial weights are 0. Two corresponding objects are examined for each object. The *nearest miss* is the spatial object closest to the target object that is in a different class. The *nearest hit* is the closest target in the same class. For each predicate value in the target object, if the nearest hit object has the same value, then the weight of that predicate is increased. If it has a different value, then the weight is decreased. Likewise, the weight is decreased (increased) if the nearest miss has the same (different) value. Only predicates with positive weights above a predefined threshold are then used to construct the tree. It is proposed that, because of the complexity of finding the relevant predicates, relevant predicates be found first at a coarse level and then at a finer level. MBRs, instead of actual objects, and a generalized coarse close_to relationship are first used to find the relevant predicates. Then these relevant predicates and the true objects are used during the second pass.

For each object in the sample, the area around it, called its *buffer*, is examined. A description of this buffer is created by aggregating the values of the most relevant predicates of the items in the buffer. Obviously, the size and shape of the buffer impact the resulting classification algorithm. It is possible, although unrealistic, to perform an exhaustive search around all possible buffer sizes and shapes. The objective would be to choose the one that results in the best discrimination between classes in the training set. This would be calculated using the information gain. Other approaches based on picking a particular shape were examined, and the authors finally used circles (equidistance buffers).

To construct the tree, it is assumed that each sample object has associated with it a set of generalized predicates that it satisfies. Counts of the number of objects that satisfy (do not satisfy) each predicate can then be determined. This is then used to calculate information gain as is done in ID3. Instead of creating a multiway branching tree, a binary decision tree is created. The resulting algorithm to construct the decision tree is shown in Algorithm 8.5.

ALGORITHM 8.5

Input:
```
    D          //Data, including spatial and nonspatial attributes
    C          //Concept hierarchies
```
Output:
```
    T          //Binary decision tree
```
SPATIAL decision tree algorithm:
```
    find a sample S of data from D with known classification;
    identify the best predicates p to use for classification;
    determine the best buffer size and shape;
    using p and C, generalize the predicates for each buffer;
    build binary T using the generalized predicates and ID3;
```

8.7   SPATIAL CLUSTERING ALGORITHMS

Spatial clustering algorithms must be able to work efficiently with large multidimensional databases. In addition, they should be able to detect clusters of different shapes. Figure 8.8 illustrates what we mean. This figure shows clusters in a two-dimensional space. Obviously, by looking at this figure it is easy to see that there are four different clusters, each of a fairly irregular shape. A good spatial clustering algorithm should be able to detect these four clusters even though the shapes are not regular, and some points in one cluster may actually be closer to some points of other clusters rather than to points in its own cluster. An algorithm that works using centroids and simple distance measures probably will not be able to identify the unusual shapes.

Other desirable features for spatial clustering are that the clusters found should be independent of the order in which the points in the space are examined and that the clusters should not be impacted by outliers. In Figure 8.8 the outliers in the lower right part of the figure should not be added to the larger cluster close to them.

Many of the clustering algorithms discussed in Chapter 5 may be viewed as spatial. In the following sections, we evaluate additional algorithms specifically targeted to spatial data.

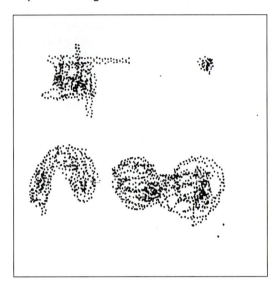

FIGURE 8.8: Different shapes for spatial clusters.

8.7.1 CLARANS Extensions

The main memory assumption of CLARANS is totally unacceptable for large spatial databases. Two approaches to improve the performance of CLARANS by taking advantage of spatial indexing structures have been proposed [EKX95].

The first approach uses a type of sampling based on the structure of an R*-tree (an R-tree variant). To ensure the quality of the sampling, the R*-tree is used to guarantee that objects from all areas of the space are examined. The most central object found in each page of the R*-tree is used to represent that page in the search. The most central object is the object (of all objects stored on that page) with the smallest distance from it to the center of the page. Remember that the page is actually the MBR that contains all the objects in that page. So the center of that MBR can be defined as the geometric center of the bounding rectangle. CLARANS is then used to find clusters for these central objects. The k medoids found in this step represent the k clusters to be found for the database as a whole. Since the R*-tree clusters objects that are spatially near on a node in the tree (and thus page), it is reasonable to believe that this approach to sampling finds good medoids.

The second technique improves on the manner in which the cost for a medoid change is calculated (see Formula 5.10 in Chapter 5.). Instead of examining the entire database, only the objects in the two affected clusters must be examined. A region query can be used to retrieve the needed objects. An efficient technique to retrieve only the objects in a given cluster is based on the construction of a polyhedron around the cluster medoid. The constructed polyhedron is called the *Voronoi polyhedron* or *Voronoi diagram*. This polyhedron is created by constructing perpendicular bisectors between pairs of medoids. This process is illustrated in Figure 8.9. This then defines the cluster. The objectives within a Voronoi diagram are closer to the medoid of that polyhedron than to any other.

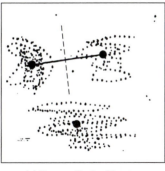

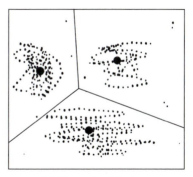

(a) Perpendicular bisector   (b) Voronoi polyhedrons

FIGURE 8.9: Voronoi polyhedron.

8.7.2   SD(CLARANS)

Spatial dominant CLARANS [SD(CLARANS)] assumes that items to be clustered contain both spatial and nonspatial components. It first clusters the spatial components using CLARANS and then examines the nonspatial attributes within each cluster to derive a description of that cluster. For example, clustering of vegetation in remote areas may find that one area (cluster) is predominantly a forest of pine trees, while another contains massive open plains and grassy areas. SD(CLARANS) assumes that some learning tool, such as DBLEARN [HCC92], is used to derive the description of the cluster. This description can be viewed as a generalized tuple; that is, by using a concept hierarchy, the attribute values for the set of tuples in a cluster can be generalized to provide summary values at a higher level in the hierarchy. The learning tool performs this task. Algorithm 8.6 outlines the SD(CLARANS) algorithm. Note that it is a combination of CLARANS, DBLEARN, and the spatial-dominant algorithm discussed earlier in this chapter. It also assumes that in the first step an initial filtering of the data using a relevance based on the nonspatial data is performed. Any clustering algorithm could be used in place of CLARANS in this algorithm. In our algorithm we show that the number of desired clusters is input. However, the authors of the original version propose an approach to determine the "most natural number of clusters" [NH94].

ALGORITHM 8.6

```
Input:
    D          //Data to be clustered
    k          //Number of desired cells at the lowest level
Output:
    K          //Set of clusters
SD(CLARANS) algorithm:
    // Find set of tuples that satisfy selection criteria.
    D' = select tuples from D based on nonspatial selection criteria;
    //Apply CLARANS to D' based on spatial attributes.
    K = CLARANS(D');
    //Perform attribute generalization.
    for each k ∈ K do
        apply DBLEARN to the nonspatial attributes in k;
```

In contrast to SD(CLARANS), *nonspatial dominant CLARANS [(NSD(CLARANS)]* first looks at the nonspatial attributes. By performing a generalization on these attributes, a set of representative tuples, one representing each cluster, can be found. Then the algorithm determines which spatial objects go with which representative tuple to finish the clustering process.

8.7.3 DBCLASD

A recent spatial clustering algorithm based on DBSCAN has been proposed that is called *DBCLASD (Distribution Based Clustering of LArge Spatial Databases)*. DBCLASD assumes that the items within a cluster are uniformly distributed and that points outside the cluster probably do not satisfy this restriction. Based on this assumption, the algorithm attempts to identify the distribution satisfied by the distances between nearest neighbors. As with DBSCAN, a cluster is created around a target element. Elements are added to a cluster as long as the nearest neighbor distance set fits the uniform distribution assumption. Candidate elements are determined and then are added to the current cluster if they satisfy a membership criteria. Candidate elements are determined by executing a region query using a circle of radius m centered around a point p that was just added to the cluster; m is chosen based on the following formula:

$$m > \sqrt{\frac{A}{\pi \, (1 - 1/N^{1/N})}} \tag{8.5}$$

Here N is the number of points in the cluster and A is its area. The added points then become new candidates.

The area of the cluster is estimated by using grids that enclose the cluster with a polygon. When a point is added to a cluster, the grid containing that point is added to the polygon. The closeness of the polygon to the real shape of the cluster depends on the size of the grids. If the grids are too large, the shape may not approximate the cluster well. If they are too small, the cluster could actually be estimated by disconnected polygons. The grid length is chosen to be the largest value in the nearest neighbor distance set.

The algorithm DBCLASD is shown in Algorithm 8.7. Since the χ^2 test usually requires at least 30 elements, the authors assumed that 29 neighboring points are initially added to each cluster [XEKS98]. The last step expands a cluster based on the expected distribution of the nearest neighbor distance set of C using the candidates found in c. Each candidate is added one at a time to C, and the distribution of the nearest neighbor distance set is estimated. If it still has the desired distribution, the points in the neighborhood of this candidate are added to the set of candidates; otherwise the candidate is removed from C. This process continues until c is empty. The points in the neighborhood of a given point are determined based on the radius value stated above.

ALGORITHM 8.7

```
Input:
    D          //Spatial objects to be clustered
Output:
    K          //Set of clusters
DBCLASD algorithm:
    k = 0; //Initially there are no clusters.
```

```
c = Ø;  //Initialize the set of candidates to be empty.
for each point p in D do
    if p is not in a cluster, then
        create a new cluster C and put p in C;
        add neighboring points of p to C;
        for each point q in C do
            add the points in the neighborhood of q that have not
                been processed to c;
        expand C;
```

Performance studies show that DBCLASD successfully finds clusters of arbitrary shapes. Only points on the boundary of clusters are assigned to the wrong cluster.

8.7.4 BANG

The *BANG* approach uses a grid structure similar to a k-D tree. The structure adapts to the distribution of the items so that more dense areas have a larger number of smaller grids, while less dense areas have a few large ones. The grids (blocks) are then sorted based on their density, which is the number of items in the grid divided by its area. Based on the number of desired clusters, those grids with the greatest densities are chosen as the centers of the clusters. For each chosen grid, adjacents grids are added as long as their densities are less than or equal to that of the current cluster center.

8.7.5 WaveCluster

The *WaveCluster* approach to generating spatial clusters looks at the data as if they were signals like STING, WaveCluster uses grids. The complexity of generating clusters is $O(n)$ and is not impacted by outliers. Unlike some approaches, WaveCluster can find arbitrarily shaped clusters and does not need to know the desired number of clusters. A set of spatial objects in an n-dimensional space are viewed as a signal. The boundaries of the clusters correspond to the high frequencies. Clusters themselves are low-frequency with high amplitude. Signal processing techniques can be used to find the low-frequency portions of the space. The authors propose that a *wavelet transform* be used to find the clusters. A wavelet transform is used as a filter to determine the frequency content of the signal. A wavelet transform of a spatial object decomposes it into a hierarchy of spatial images. They can be used to scale an image to different sizes.

8.7.6 Approximation

Once spatial clusters are found, it is beneficial to determine why the clusters exist; that is, what are the unique features of the clusters? *Approximation* can be used to identify the characteristics of clusters. This is done by determining the features that are close to the clusters. Clusters can be distinguished based on features unique to them or that are common across several clusters. Here, features are spatial objects such as rivers, oceans, schools, and so on. For example, some clusters may be unique partly because they are close to the ocean or close to good schools. It usually is assumed that features and clusters are represented by more complex closed polygons than by simple MBRs.

Aggregate proximity is defined as a measure of how close a cluster (or group of elements) is to a feature (or to an object in the space). This is not a measure of distance from the cluster boundary, but rather to the points in the cluster. Traditional data structures, such as R-trees and k-D trees, cannot be used to efficiently find these aggregate proximity relationships because they focus on a cluster (object) boundary as opposed to the objects in the cluster. The aggregate proximity distance may be measured by the sum of distances to all points in the cluster.

The *aggregate proximity relationship* finds the k closest features to a cluster. The *CRH* algorithm has been proposed to identify these relationships [KN96]. C stands for encompassing circle, R for isothetic rectangle, and H for convex hull. These are defined as follows:

- **Isothetic rectangle:** MBR containing a set of points where the sides of the rectangle are parallel to the coordinate axes.

- **Encompassing circle:** Circle that contains a set of points; found by using the diagonal of the isothetic rectangle as its diameter.

- **Convex hull:** Minimum bounding convex shape containing a set of points.

What makes these shapes efficient is that given a set of n points, the first two points can be found in $O(n)$ time and the last in $O(n \lg n)$ time. Each type of geometric shape is viewed as a bounding structure around a feature. These three types of encompassing geometric shapes are used as multiple levels of filtering of the possible close features. These are used in order of increasing accuracy and decreasing efficiency. The concept of using these three types of bounding polygons is shown in Figure 8.10, which illustrates a school. The school is fairly accurately represented by a convex hull, but less accurately represented by a rectangle and a circle. The objective is to obtain a balance between accuracy and efficiency in identifying the relationships.

The first step in CRH is to apply the encompassing circle. The features (using the circular approximation) that are ranked the highest (those that are viewed to be the

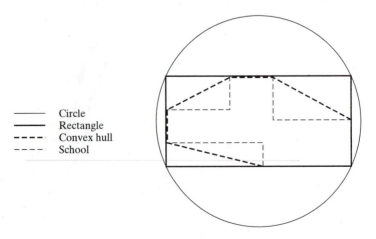

FIGURE 8.10: CRH polygons.

closest) to a given cluster are then sent to the filter at the next level. At this level the isothetic rectangle is used to represent the features, and the features are again ranked based on proximity to the cluster. The highest ranking features at this level are examined at the final level, where a convex hull bounding polygon is used to estimate each feature. This approach is used for each cluster. The desired number of features identified at each level is indicated as input to the algorithm. Although different techniques can be used to rank the features, intersection may be used or actual distances may be calculated. The CRH algorithm uses various optimization features to reduce the overall complexity and to eliminate redundant computation of distances.

8.8 EXERCISES

1. (**Research**) Compare the R-tree to the R*-tree.
2. (**Research**) Another commonly used spatial index is the grid file. Define a grid file. Compare it to a k-D tree and a quad tree. Show the grid file that would be used to index the data found in Figure 8.5.

8.9 BIBLIOGRAPHIC NOTES

Most spatial data structures were proposed many years ago. Quad trees were first introduced to handle queries on composite keys [FB74]. The k-D tree was proposed in [Ben75]. There have been many variation of the k-D tree for use with spatial data data [OSDH93]. The grid file was proposed in [NH84].

There have been many excellent surveys examining spatial data and spatial data structures. A survey of spatial and multimedia data, including indexing, can be found in [ZCF+97]. One unpublished survey of spatial indexing techniques not only provides a taxonomy of the approaches, but also identifies the strengths and weaknesses of the various techniques [OSDH93]. Nievergelt and Widmayer have written an extremely easy-to-read yet thorough survey of spatial data structures with an excellent bibliography [NW97]. Other surveys of spatial data structures are available [Sam95a, GG98]. This last survey [GG98] is an extensive examination of multidimensional indexing techniques, including spatial and nonspatial. It includes a comparison of the various techniques. Additional surveys look at query processing of spatial data [Sam95b]. A more general survey [Güt94] covered spatial data modeling, querying spatial databases, spatial indexing, and architectural approaches. Spatial relationships based on direction are examined in [EFKS00]. The original proposal for R-trees can be found in [Gut84]. The R*-tree is a more efficient improvement on the R-tree [BKSS90]. Many extensions to the basic R-tree have been proposed [OSDH93]. The STING approach was proposed in [WYM97].

There also exist some surveys of spatial data mining. [EFKS00] contains a survey of the algorithms, relationships, and operations needed to support spatial data mining. The concept of progressive refinement has been studied extensively in a recent doctoral dissertation [Kop99]. A recent book [MH01] is a collection of many different spatial data mining articles.

Articles that provide an overview of clustering in spatial databases can be found in [EKSX98], [HKT01], and [NH94]. In fact, many of the clustering techniques introduced in Chapter 5 can be viewed as spatial: K-means and K-medoids and CLARANS. DBCLASD was proposed in [XEKS98]. WaveCluster was examined in [SCZ98]. Aggregate proximity is defined in [KN96]. However, the authors of the original version proposed an approach to determine the "most natural number of clusters" [NH94] based on a concept called *silhouette coefficients* [KR90].

Some of the earliest work on spatial classification was found in [FWD93]. Here decision tree techniques were used to categorize objects in the sky. Specifically, stars and galaxies were identified.

Many traditional clustering and classification algorithms have been modified to perform well for spatial databases. DBSCAN has been generalized into *generalized DBSCAN (GDBSCAN)*, which clusters objects using both spatial and nonspatial attributes [SEKX98]. It was examined in astronomy, biology, earth science, and geography applications.

A spatial data mining query language based on SQL, *GMQL (geo-mining query language)*, has been proposed [Kop99]. This is based on DMQL and is used in DBMiner and GeoMiner.

The SAND approach was initially examined in [AS91].

C H A P T E R   9

Temporal Mining

9.1 INTRODUCTION

Databases traditionally do not contain temporal data. Instead, the data that are stored reflect data at a single point in time. Thus, it may be called a *snapshot* database. For example, an employee database normally contains only the current company employees rather than all employees who have ever worked for the company. However, many questions cannot be answered by this snapshot data. A company CEO might wish to determine trends in the hiring and firing of employees, or he might wish to obtain information about the ethnic diversity of employees and how it has changed over time. These types of data mining questions require temporal data. In a *temporal database*, data are maintained for multiple time points, not just one time point. Example 9.1 illustrates the use of a temporal database that stores employee data. Obviously, storing three separate tuples for one employee with so much redundant information is not efficient, and techniques can be used to eliminate this redundancy. However, this illustrates the concept. Each tuple contains the information that is current from the date stored with that tuple to the date stored with the next tuple in temporal order.

EXAMPLE 9.1

XYZ Corp. uses a temporal database to store employee information. It maintains the Social Security number (SSN), employee name, address, and salary for each employee. When a new tuple is stored in the database, the current date is added to this information. Joe Smith is hired on 2/12/02 at a salary of $50,000. On his six-month performance evaluation, he is given a $2,000 raise and a promotion. On 12/10/02, he moves to a new address. At the end of 2002, there are three tuples in the database for Joe Smith:

Date	Name	SSN	Address	Salary
2/12/02	Joe Smith	123456789	10 Moss Haven	$50,000
8/12/02	Joe Smith	123456789	10 Moss Haven	$52,000
12/10/02	Joe Smith	123456789	13 Chesterton	$52,000

Analysis of temporal (or time-varying) data presents many interesting challenges. For example, there may be many different interpretations for time. In Example 9.1 the date stored in the record is the date representing when that information becomes current. This is often called the valid time. The *valid time* for information is the time during which the information is true in the modeled world. This usually consists of a start time and an end time. The end time in the example is implied by the start time of the next temporal record for the same employee. Another time that could have been used is the transaction time. The *transaction time* is the timestamp associated with the transaction that inserted this record. This could be different from the start time for the valid time interval. The transaction time interval is the time the tuple actually existed in the database. For example, Joe Smith may have indicated on 11/15/02 that he would have the new address effective 12/10/02. The start valid time for the new address was 12/10/02, but the transaction time was 11/15/02. Other types of times may be used as well. When the employee information changes, a new tuple is inserted. Changes and deletes may occur only to change data that was incorrectly inserted.

So far we have seen that temporal data often involve a duration of time; that is, a start time and an end time. In this interpretation, the range of values $[t_s, t_e]$ is associated with each record. Here t_s is the start time and t_e is the end time. Different temporal interpretations may be used. A timestamp of a specific time instance may be used instead of a range. This is common with time series data where specific values are associated with times. For example, a common time series is to show the price of a specific stock at the stock market close each day. This stock quote is the price at that specific point in time.

Many different examples for temporal data exist. Satellites continually collect images and sensory data. This information is temporal and is associated with specific points in time (when the data were obtained). In a hospital, printouts of heartbeats may be kept for patients. This represents a continuous view of temporal data. When an EEG is taken for a patient, several different brain waves are measured in parallel. Each wave represents a continuous set of data over time.

Temporal databases usually do not accept the same types of updates and queries as traditional snapshot databases. The only updates that are allowed are corrections and versions. Actual modifications of tuples usually are not allowed. Instead, a new tuple with a different valid time would be added. Temporal queries may involve fairly complicated temporal selection criteria. For example, it would not make sense to ask for the salaries of all employees. Instead, a temporal value would be needed such as: Find the salaries for all employees on 7/9/01. Or a more complicated range query could be asked: Find the names of all employees who had a salary greater than $100,000 between 1/1/01 and 12/31/01. A temporal query q involves a valid time range $V^q = [t_s^q, t_e^q]$ in the request. Here t_s^q is the start time and t_e^q is the end time of the query's time range. In the last example, these values were 1/1/01 and 12/31/01, respectively. The time range then exists for the query as well as for the data. Suppose that $V^d = [t_s^d, t_e^d]$ is the valid time range for a tuple. Special temporal queries then can involve various combinations of these two ranges:

- **Intersection query:** A tuple is retrieved only if its valid time range intersects that of the query: $V^d \cap V^q \neq \emptyset$.

- **Inclusion query:** A tuple is retrieved only if its valid time range is completely contained in the time range for the query: $t_s^q \leq t_s^d \leq t_e^d \leq t_e^q$.

- **Containment query:** A tuple is retrieved only if its valid time range contains that of the query: $t_s^d \leq t_s^q \leq t_e^q \leq t_e^d$.

- **Point query:** A tuple is retrieved only if it is valid at a particular point in time: $t_s^d = t_s^q = t_e^q = t_e^d$.

When considering time, there are at least four types of databases:

- **Snapshot:** The database system provides no support for any temporal attribute. The stored data usually are assumed to represent data that are valid at the current time.

- **Transaction time:** The only temporal data supported by the database is the time associated with the transaction that inserted the data. This could be a timestamp for when the transaction was committed (or perhaps was requested) or it could be a range.

- **Valid time:** This database supports a valid time range for the data. It may be stored, as with the transaction time, using a unique value or a range. If it is a unique value, this is the start of the time range, and the end is the beginning of the next time range for the data with the same key.

- **Bitemporal:** A bitemporal databases supports both transaction time and valid time.

With temporal data, the concept of a key is complicated as well. In the salary database, the employee SSN can no longer determine a unique tuple. Temporal information is needed as well.

As with spatial mining, several specialized data structures have been proposed to assist in temporal mining. There are many specialized data structures that have been proposed to index temporal databases that we do not discuss here. These usually are generalizations of B$^+$-trees and are similar to those structures we saw with spatial databases. One difference, of course, is that time is usually one dimension where as space may be two or three dimensions. These structures usually assume that a valid time range is associated with each tuple. One complicating factor is the use of the current time. Unlike spatial data, the temporal dimension keeps expanding. Thus, for items that are currently valid, it is not possible to have the current end time for the range. One solution to this problem is to use a special time value called *now*, which is the current time. Thus, a range that ends in "now" means that it is valid up to the current time. The resulting effect is that time ranges that end in "now" actually keep expanding in size.

Mining of temporal data involves many of the conventional data mining activities but, of course, is complicated by the temporal aspect and the more complicated types of queries. For example, time series data may be clustered based on similarities found. However, determining the similarity between two different sets of time series data is difficult, as was shown in Chapter 1. Given a time series, a future value also may be predicted. Association rules may involve temporal aspects and relationships. Web usage mining discussed in Chapter 7 involved temporal data. The combination of spatial and temporal mining also is used.

9.2   MODELING TEMPORAL EVENTS

There have been many different techniques used to model a sequence of temporal events. We briefly examine three of them: Markov models (MMs), hidden Markov models, and recurrent neural networks (NN). Suppose that you are given the problem of recognizing the string of characters "the." This can be viewed as a temporal sequence of events. Each event recognizes one character. One of the earliest techniques used to model a sequence of events was a *finite state recognizer (FSR)* or *finite state machine (FSM)*. Figure 9.1 illustrates an FSR for the sequence "the." The temporal aspect is implied by the arcs. It can be viewed that the individual events (or characters) occur at specific time intervals.

While FSRs can be used to recognize a known sequence, they do not scale well when the vocabulary is large. They also do not work well to model transitions between states that are not precisely defined. Markov models and their variant, hidden Markov models, extend the basic idea of an FSR but scale well and are more general. Figure 9.2 shows a simple Markov model. Notice the similarity and differences between it and the FSR in Figure 9.1. One of the major differences is that the transitions (arcs) are not associated with specific input values. Just as with an FSM, a *Markov model (MM)* is a directed graph that can be used to recognize a pattern. Each node is associated with a state in recognizing a sequence of events (or pattern). Although our example shows a start and end node, these nodes need not be present. One of the major differences is that a transition (arc) is associated with a probability, *transition probability*. The probability, p_{ij}, on an arc $\langle i, j \rangle$ is the probability that a transition will be made from state i to state j. In Figure 9.2, the probability of transitioning from state 1 to state 2 is 0.3, while that of staying in state 1 is 0.7. The sum of the weights on the edges coming out of a node is 1. Any arcs not shown are assumed to have a probability of 0. The probabilities can be combined to determine the probability that a pattern will be produced by an MM. For example, with the MM in Figure 9.2, the probability that the transitions along the

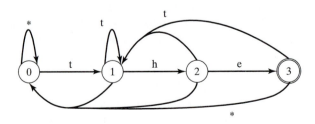

FIGURE 9.1: FSR for sequence "the."

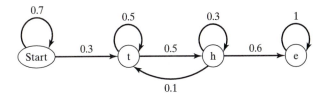

FIGURE 9.2: Simple Markov model.

major horizontal path are all taken is $0.3 \times 0.5 \times 0.6 = 0.09$. As with an FSR, there is always one state that is designated as the current state. A major property of a Markov model is the *Markov property*, which states that, given the current state, the transition probability is independent of any previous states. Thus, an MM is memoryless. A more formal definition of an MM is found in Definition 9.1.

> **DEFINITION 9.1.** A **Markov model (MM)** is a directed graph $\langle V, A \rangle$ with vertices representing states $V = \{v_1, v_2, \ldots, v_n\}$ and arcs, $A = \{\langle i, j \rangle \mid v_i, v_j \in V\}$, showing transitions between states. Each arc $\langle i.j \rangle$ is labeled with a probability p_{ij} of transitioning from v_i to v_j. At any time t, one state is designated as the current state v_t. At time t, the probability of any future transitions depends only on v_t and no other earlier states.

The transition probabilities in an MM are learned during a training phase, where counts are kept for each transition.

Markov models have been used in many different applications. Speech recognition and natural language processing are very common applications for MMs. Suppose that an MM is created to model certain phrases. The individual nodes could represent sounds or words. A sequence of these would be a phrase. Given a phrase, the probability that that phrase occurs is the product of the probabilities from the start state to the end state using the transitions associated with each word in sequence. In this manner, the most likely sequences can be found, and the most likely sequence is the one that is "recognized." Given a model, the probability of the occurrence of a sequence of events can be determined. You also could determine the probability of being in a particular state at a particular time. Another application is in the area of system reliability. Here an MM is used to model the system operation. The transition probabilities can be determined by domain experts or learned from training data. The resulting model can be used to do such things as determine system availability and predict the mean time between failures.

An extension to the MM that still satisfies the Markov property, is the *hidden Markov model (HMM)*. A major difference between the MM and HMM is the fact that the states in an HMM need not correspond to observable states. An HMM models a process that produces as output a sequence of observable symbols. The HMM will actually output these symbols. Given a sequence of symbols, the HMM can be constructed to produce these symbols. What is hidden is the state sequence that produced these symbols. There is no relationship between states and real-world observable values. An observation sequence can be produced by more than one state sequence.

As with the MM, the HMM consists of a set of states with transition probabilities. In addition, the HMM has associated with each state an observation probability distribution.

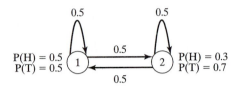

FIGURE 9.3: Simple hidden Markov model (modified from [RJ86]).

An example of an HMM, modified from [RJ86], is found in Figure 9.3. One of the most obvious differences between the HMM and the MM is the presence of the extra probabilities. This represents the hidden part of the model and is associated with the observable output from each state. This example models results that can be found from tossing two coins. The first state is associated with one coin and the second state is associated with the second coin. The first coin is a fair coin in that the probability of obtaining a head or tail is each 0.5. The second coin is biased toward obtaining a tail as that probability is 0.7. The state transitions are all 0.5, which means that after tossing a coin it is equally likely that the next toss will occur with either coin. The hidden probabilities are used to determine what the output from that state will be, while the public (or transition) probabilities are used to determine the next state that will occur.

Notice a major difference between an HMM/MM and an FSR is that the HMM/MM models a system. It is not built simply to recognize a sequence of events. Thus, they have many more applications than an FSR. Not only can they recognize, but also they can forecast (predict). They are much more general, but at the same time they are more complex. Many problems exist when determining what the HMM model should actually look like:

- **Size:** Determining the number of states is not obvious. They need not be associated with a real-world observable event.

- **Transition probabilities:** Determining what the transition probabilities are is difficult. Domain experts and/or learning algorithms can be used to determine the probabilities, much as is done with NNs.

- **Hidden observation probabilities:** As with the transition probabilities, these probabilities can be learned.

A more formal definition of an HMM is found in Definition 9.2. The transition probabilities and observation probabilities are fixed for a given state.

DEFINITION 9.2. A **hidden Markov model (HMM)** is a directed graph $\langle V, A \rangle$ with vertices representing states $V = \{v_1, v_2, \ldots, v_n\}$ and arcs, $A = \{\langle i, j \rangle \mid v_i, v_j \in V\}$, showing transitions between states. Each HMM has the following additional components:

1. Initial state distribution used to determine the starting state at time 0, v_0.
2. Each arc $\langle i.j \rangle$ is labeled with a probability p_{ij} of transitioning from v_i to v_j. This value is fixed.
3. Given a set of possible observations, $O\{o_1, o_2, \ldots, o_k\}$, each state, v_i, contains a set of probabilities for each observation, $\{p_{i1}, p_{i2}, \ldots, p_{ik}\}$.

Given an HMM, an observation sequence is generated based on the algorithm shown in Algorithm 9.1. This algorithm assumes that a sequence of m observations is produced. The variable t represents time.

ALGORITHM 9.1

```
Input:
    H           //HMM
Output:
    S = ⟨s₀, s₁,..., sₘ₋₁⟩        // Output sequence
HMM observation sequence algorithm:
    t = 0
    Based on initial state distribution, determine vₜ;
    repeat
        Output sₜ based on observation probabilities {pₜ₁,pₜ₂,...,pₜₖ};
        Choose vₜ₊₁ based on transition probabilities at vₜ;
        t = t+1;
    until t = k;
```

There are three basic HMM problems [RJ86]:

1. Given a sequence of observed elements and an HMM, what is the probability that the HMM actually produced the sequence? Note that this is associated with the recognition problem. If the probability is low, then this model probably did not produce it. As a result, the system that is modeled by the HMM probably did not produce it.

2. Given a sequence of observed values and an HMM, what is the most likely state sequence that produced this sequence?

3. How can the model parameters (transition probabilities, observation probabilities, and starting state distribution) be improved? This problem is similar to that of how learning is accomplished for a NN.

Relatively efficient algorithms have been proposed to solve all three of these problems.

Traditional feedforward neural networks cannot easily be used to model temporal events because there is no mechanism of time. However, there are advanced neural network (NN) architectures that can be used for both recognition problems and prediction problems. In a *recurrent neural network (RNN)* a neuron can obtain input from any other neuron, including those in the output layer. Specifically, the outputs from nodes in the hidden or output layers are fed back as input to an earlier layer. As RNNs store information about time, they can be used for temporal prediction applications. However, they are quite difficult to use and to train. Unlike traditional feedforward NNs, the time that it takes for a recurrent NN to produce output is not known. This is because the hidden and output layer nodes will continually be activated until the model stabilizes. Recurrence implies that the current state of the network depends not only on the current input values but also on those of the previous cycle (from the previous outputs).

Figure 9.4 shows the basic structure of an RNN. In Part (a), the structure for a feedforward NN is shown. Part (b) shows an RNN. In (b), output from the hidden layer is fed not only to the output layer but also into a new input layer referred to as a *context*

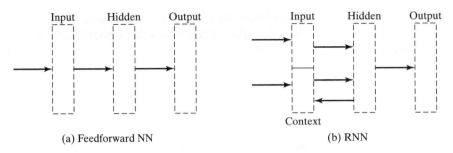

(a) Feedforward NN   (b) RNN

FIGURE 9.4: Recurrent neural network.

layer. In this structure the input to the hidden layer then comes from nodes in the input and context layers.

9.3   TIME SERIES

A time series is a set of attribute values over a period of time. Alternative definitions exist. Some investigators view a time series as consisting only of numeric values. Some investigators assume that the values are at specific, evenly spaced time intervals. Time series data may be continuous or discrete. In this text we take a general view that encompasses all of these. As seen in Definition 9.3, a *time series* is a set of attribute values over a period of time.

> **DEFINITION 9.3.** Given an attribute, A, a **time series** is a set of n values: $\{\langle t_1, a_1 \rangle, \langle t_2, a_2 \rangle, \ldots, \langle t_n, a_n \rangle\}$. Here there are n time values and for each a corresponding value of A. Often the values are identified for specific well-defined points in time, in which case the values may be viewed as a vector $\langle a_1, a_2, \ldots, a_n \rangle$.

> **DEFINITION 9.4.** One time series $Y' = \langle y_{i_1}, \ldots, y_{i_m} \rangle$ is a **subseries** of another $Y = \langle y_1, \ldots, y_n \rangle$ if, $\forall 1 \le j \le m - 1, i_j < i_{j+1}$ and $\forall 1 \le j \le m, \exists 1 \le k \le n$ such that $y_{i_j} = y_k$.

Typical data mining applications for time series include determining the similarity between two different time series and predicting future values for an attribute, given a time series of known values. Obviously, the prediction is a type of classification, while the similarity can be thought of as either clustering or classification. Given several time series, we may want to determine which time series are like each other (clustering). Alternatively, we may be given a time series to find which time series from a set are like this one (classification). A special type of similarity analysis is that of identifying patterns within time series.

9.3.1   Time Series Analysis

Time series analysis may be viewed as finding patterns in the data and predicting future values. Detected patterns may include:

- **Trends:** A trend can be viewed as systematic nonrepetitive changes (linear or nonlinear) to the attribute values over time. An example would be that the value of a stock may continually rise.

- **Cycles:** Here the observed behavior is cyclic.

- **Seasonal:** Here the detected patterns may be based on time of year or month or day. As an example, the sales volumes from department stores always jump around Christmas.

- **Outliers:** To assist in pattern detection, techniques may be needed to remove or reduce the impact of outliers.

Identifying patterns with real-world data may be difficult because of noise, outliers, errors, and missing data. Multiple patterns may be observed in the same data. Looking at gross sales made by retail companies, there usually are large increases around Christmas each year. This seasonal change is independent of the general trend for cost of goods sold to increase (perhaps based on population increase and inflation).

9.3.2   Trend Analysis

Many straightforward techniques can be used to detect trends in time series. *Smoothing* is an approach that is used to remove the nonsystematic behaviors found in a time series. For example, the general trend may be that a time series is increasing in value. However, when the specific attribute values are examined, there are many decreases in value. Smoothing usually takes the form of finding *moving averages* of attribute values. Given a window in time around a particular time point, the local average of all attribute values is used instead of the specific value actually found at this point. Median value, as opposed to mean value, normally is used because it is less sensitive to outliers. Figure 9.5 illustrates the process. Smoothing is used to filter out noise and outliers. It also can be used to predict future values because the resulting data are easier to fit to a known function (linear, logarithmic, exponential, etc.).

Detecting seasonal patterns in time series data is more difficult. One approach is to detect correlations between attributes at evenly spaced intervals. For example, a

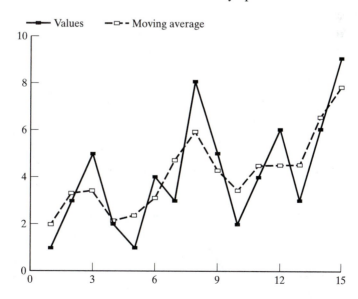

FIGURE 9.5: Smoothing using a moving average.

correlation may be found between every twelfth value (in monthly sales data). The time difference between the related items is referred to as the *lag*. With the sales data, the lag is 12. *Autocorrelation* functions can be generated to determine the correlations between data values at different lag intervals. A *correlogram* graphically shows the autocorrelation values for different lag values.

The *covariance* measures how two variables change together. It can be used as the basis for determining the relationship between either two time series or seasonal trends in one time series. An *autocorrelation coefficient*, r_k, measures the correlations between time series values a certain distance, lag k, apart. Several different approaches have been used for autocorrelation. A *correlation coefficient*, introduced in Chapter 3, measures the linear relationship between two variables (or that between the same variable at a given time lag). Positive values indicate that both variables increase together, while negative values indicate that as one increases the other decreases. A value close to zero indicates that there is little correlation between the two variables. One standard formula to measure correlation is the *correlation coefficient r*, sometimes called *Pearson's r*. Given two time series, X and Y, with means $\bar{X}$ and $\bar{Y}$, each with n elements, the formula for r is

$$\frac{\sum (x_i - \bar{X})(y_i - \bar{Y})}{\sqrt{\sum (x_i - \bar{X})^2 \sum (y_i - \bar{Y})^2}} \tag{9.1}$$

Applying this to find the correlation coefficient with lag of k, r_k, on a time series $X = \langle x_1, x_2, \ldots, x_n \rangle$ is straightforward. The first time series is $X' = \langle x_1, x_2, \ldots, x_{n-k} \rangle$, while the second time series is $X'' = \langle x_{k+1}, x_{k+2}, \ldots, x_n \rangle$. Example 9.2 illustrates the use of autocorrelation coefficients.

EXAMPLE 9.2

By looking at the graph in Figure 9.6, it is obvious that several patterns exist. One is the fact that the values rise linearly for two time units and then drop and restart. Thus, there is an obvious autocorrelation with a lag of 3. In this case we find that $r_k = 1$ because there is a perfect positive relationship.

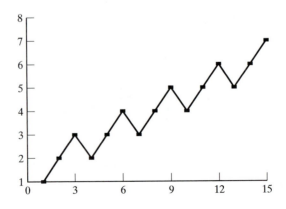

FIGURE 9.6: Correlation with lag $= 3$.

9.3.3 Transformation

To assist in pattern detection, the actual time series data may be transformed in some manner. A logarithmic transformation can be used to stabilize the variance and to make seasonal effects constant over years. Transformation is also used to solve the dimensionality curse. The *dimensionality curse* is the fact that many problems are caused by data sets with many dimensions. Data mining on time series data with many variables is not only difficult but also expensive. Data structures to store high-dimensional data are not very efficient. Transformation can be used to reduce the number of dimensions. Note that feature extraction also reduces the number of dimensions.

9.3.4 Similarity

We saw examples for examining the similarity between patterns in Web usage mining. Indeed, these applications are temporal data mining. Given a target pattern $X = \langle x_1, x_2, \ldots, x_n \rangle$ and a sequence $Y = \langle y_1, y_2, \ldots, y_m \rangle$, the problem is that of determining $\text{sim}(X, Y)$. Here n may or may not be the same as m. Matching may be based on matching the two series completely, matching subseries thereof, or more advanced types of matching. One series may be scaled or shifted to match the other. Gaps or "don't care" values may have to be added to one series to match the second.

Some common distance measures that may be used are Euclidean, linear correlation, and discrete Fourier transform. We have already seen the Euclidean distance metric. There are problems with these common distance measures:

- **Length:** X and Y may be of different lengths but may still be quite similar.

- **Scale:** While the general shape of X and Y may be identical, the scale may be somewhat different. For example, one may use a log scale. Different metrics may be used (Fahrenheit vs. Centigrade).

- **Gaps:** One of the series may be missing some of the values that exist in the other series.

- **Outliers:** This is similar to the problem to gaps, except that it is assumed that the extra values in one series may be due to erroneous readings.

- **Baseline:** The actual baseline values may differ. This means the time between successive values in X and Y may differ.

One similarity approach is to look at the *longest common subseries* between two series [BDGM97]. When looking at X and Y, the idea is to find the longest subseries that they have in common. For example, suppose $X = \langle 10, 5, 6, 9, 22, 15, 4, 2 \rangle$ and $Y = \langle 6, 9, 10, 5, 6, 22, 15, 4, 2 \rangle$. The longest common subseries is $\langle 22, 15, 4, 2 \rangle$. The $\text{sim}(X, Y) = l/n = 4/9$, where l is the length of largest common subseries and n is the length of the largest of the two given series. While this approach handles some of the issues stated above, it does not handle the scale or baseline problem.

A recent similarity measure has been proposed to solve these issues [BDGM97]. The basic idea is to convert one series to the other using a linear transformation function f to convert a value from one series to a value in the next. This function, along with an allowed tolerated difference, ϵ in the results, compensates for the scale and baseline issues. The baseline issue is also addressed by allowing a slight difference, up to δ, in the time values used. The resulting similarity function $\text{sim}_{\epsilon,\delta}(X, Y)$ is shown in Definition 9.5 (modified from [BDGM97]). The maximum is taken over all possible values for f. The closer $\text{sim}_{\epsilon,\delta}(X, Y)$ is to 1, the more similar X and Y are.

DEFINITION 9.5. Given integer value $\delta > 0$, real number $\epsilon < 1$, and linear function function f, and two time series X, Y with the longest one of length n. Let $X' = \langle x_{i_1}, x_{i_2}, \ldots, x_{i_m} \rangle$ and $Y' = \langle y_{j_1}, y_{j_2}, \ldots, y_{j_m} \rangle$ be the longest subseries in X and Y, respectively, where:

- $\forall 1 \leq k \leq m - 1, | i_k - j_k | \leq \delta$ and

- $\forall 1 \leq k \leq m, \frac{y_{j_k}}{(1+\epsilon)} \leq f(x_{i_k}) \leq y_{j_k}(1 + \epsilon)$

Then, $\text{sim}_{\epsilon,\delta}(X, Y) = \max_f (m/n)$

The longest common subseries between two given series can be found in $O(n^2)$. Thus, the most difficult part of finding $\text{sim}_{\epsilon,\delta}(X, Y)$ is finding f. Several algorithms have been proposed to find the function. An exact algorithm is $O(n^3)$, while approximate algorithms with better behavior are also proposed [BDGM97].

9.3.5 Prediction

The *prediction* (or *forecasting*) of time series data can use some of the techniques discussed earlier, such as regression. However, in practice, time series data are replete with errors and noise. Using simple regression often is not sufficient. Given a discrete time series over equally spaced time intervals, the forecasting problem is to predict a value at time t, $\hat{x}_t(l)$, and a lead time of l. It is assumed that previous time series values, $\langle x_1, x_2, \ldots, x_t \rangle$, are known. The objective is to minimize the mean square of the deviations $x_{t+l} - \hat{x}_t(l)$. Various models may be used to represent the time series values and thus predict future values. We briefly review some of these models here.

Studies of time series prediction often assume that the time series is *stationary*. This means that the values come from a model with a constant mean. More complex prediction techniques may assume that the time series is *nonstationary*. A time series usually represents values that are dependent on each other, but they may be viewed as being generated from a series of independent values called *shocks*. The shocks are randomly drawn from a normal distribution with a zero mean. A sequence of these random values is thought of as representing a *white noise* process. This white noise process is transformed into the time series by a *linear filter*, which may be viewed as a simple weighted sum of previous shocks.

A special case of the linear filter model is one that assumes that time series values are dependent on earlier ones. *Autoregression*, then, is a method of predicting a future time series value by looking at previous values. Given a time series $X = \langle x_1, x_2, \ldots, x_n \rangle$, a future value, x_{n+1}, can be found using

$$x_{n+1} = \xi + \phi_n x_n + \phi_{n-1} x_{n-1} + \cdots + \phi_1 x_1 + \varepsilon_{n+1} \qquad (9.2)$$

Here ε_{n+1} represents a random error, at time $n + 1$. In addition, each element in the time series can be viewed as a combination of a random error and a linear combination of previous values. Here the ϕ_i are the autoregressive parameters. Alternatively, the value may be viewed as a weighted sum of previous deviations from the mean. Autoregression models may be stationary or nonstationary.

Another dependency that may exist between values in a time series is that of a *moving average*. Here a future value, x_{n+1}, can be found using a moving average model applied to a set of previous consecutive values. There are many different moving average models, and any model could be used. In addition, there may be a lag between the point where the moving average is applied and the prediction value. For example, a seasonal forecast for sales could be based on an average of the sales for the prior season 12 months earlier. A future time series value, x_{n+1}, can be predicted using:

$$x_{n+1} = a_{n+1} + \theta_n a_n + \theta_{n-1} a_{n-1} + \cdots + \theta_{n-q} a_{n-q} \tag{9.3}$$

where a_i is a shock. For a moving average, then, the time series value is predicted based on a weighted average of a set of previous shock values.

Autoregression and moving average can be combined to created a model of a time series that is called *ARMA (Autoregressive Moving Average)*. In practice, this combined model is sufficient to represent many real-world time series. When the model is not stationary, an extension of ARMA, *ARIMA (Autoregressive Integrated Moving Average)* may be used. The ARIMA model has become quite popular, but it is relative complex and requires an expert to use it effectively.

9.4   PATTERN DETECTION

Given a set of data values $\langle d_1, d_2, \ldots, d_n \rangle$ where d_i is collected at time t_i and $t_i < t_j$ *iff* $i < j$, the *pattern detection* problem is to determine a given pattern that occurs in this sequence. This can be viewed as a type of classification problem where the pattern to be predicted is one found in a given set of patterns. Typical pattern detection applications include speech recognition and signal processing. Spelling correctors and word processors also use simple pattern detection algorithms. Although these simpler cousins of the true data mining pattern detection problems are precise, the more general pattern detection problems are fuzzy with no exact matches. Approximations are needed. While humans are good at detecting such patterns, machines are not.

9.4.1   String Matching

The string matching problem assumes that both a long text document and a short pattern are given. The problem is to determine where the pattern is found in the text. Example 9.3 illustrates the pattern detection problem when it is applied to string matching. This problem is a common one, with many applications in word processing.

EXAMPLE 9.3

Martha Holder is editing her resume using a popular word processor. She has just gotten married and wishes to change the name Holder to her new last name of Laros, where appropriate. Not all occurrences of Holder, however, should be changed. For example, she does not want to change the author's names of previous publications that were made under her maiden name. Using the word processor, she repeatedly finds all occurrences of Holder in the vita. She then must examine the context to determine whether it should be changed to Laros. In this case, the pattern being matched is $\langle H, o, l, d, e, r \rangle$. Only words that are an exact match to this pattern should be found. Note that here each letter is viewed as if it occurred at a later point in time. In actuality, it is a later point in the document.

One of the earliest string matching algorithms is the *Knuth–Morris–Pratt* or *KMP* algorithm. KMP creates a finite state machine (FSM), which is used to recognize the given pattern. The FSM represents all possible states that exist when scanning a string to match the given pattern. Each node in the FSM relates to one of these states. Figure 9.7 shows an FSM created to recognize the pattern "ABAABA." Here there are seven states. State i represents the fact that the first i characters in the pattern match the most recent i characters in the string. State six is designated as the recognizer state with two concentric circles. The arcs in the graph are labeled with the character from the pattern that causes a transition between the two states as indicated. Transitions labeled with "*" indicate that this transition is taken with any other character found in the string. The KMP algorithm creates the FSM for a given pattern. The FSM can then be applied to the string by starting at the first character in the string. From a given state, the next character in the string determines which transition is taken. The accepting state of the FSM is reached only when the pattern is found in the string. The worst-case behavior of the application of the FSM is $O(m + n)$, where m is the length of the pattern and n is the length of the string. The preprocessing phase to create the FSM is $O(m)$ in space and time.

Another algorithm that builds on the KMP approach is called the *Boyer–Moore*, or *BM*, algorithm. The same FSM is constructed to recognize the pattern, but the pattern is applied to the string in a right-to-left pattern. For example, when looking for the string "ABAABA," if the sixth character in the string is not A, then we know that the pattern is not found in the string starting at the first character in the string. We also know that if the sixth character is neither an "A" nor a "B," then the pattern does not exist in the string starting at any of the first six characters. The BM needs only one comparison to determine this, while the KMP would have to examine all of the first six characters. Again, the BM is $O(m + n)$ in the worst-case scenario, but the expected and best cases

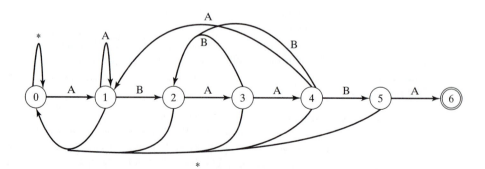

FIGURE 9.7: FSM for string "ABAABA."

are better than this. The actual performance depends (of course) on both the pattern and the string.

Even though KMP and BM are pattern recognition algorithms, they usually are not thought of as data mining applications. The identification of patterns in these earlier techniques is precise. Most data mining pattern matching applications are fuzzy; that is, the pattern being compared to (i.e., the class representative) and the object being classified will not match precisely. However, as we will see, there are more advanced pattern recognition algorithms that are similar in that graphical structures are built to specifically recognize a pattern. In effect, these true data mining applications build on these earlier non–data mining algorithms.

When examining text strings, it often is beneficial to determine the "distance" between one string and another. For example, spelling checkers use this concept to recommend corrections for misspelled words. Again, these usually are not thought of as data mining activities, but the distance measure technique we discuss here is often the basis for more advanced distance measure approaches. Suppose that we wish to convert $A = \langle a_1, a_2, \ldots, a_n \rangle$ to $B = \langle b_1, b_2, \ldots, b_m \rangle$. The basic idea is to determine the minimum cost of steps that are needed to convert one string to another. There are three operations that can be performed to convert string A to string B. Starting at the first character in each string, each operation identifies what operation should be performed on A and B to change A to B. Each operation not only indicates specific functions to be performed but also associates a cost for it. The following assume that we are currently examining a_i in A and b_j in B:

- **Match:** Leave a_i and b_j as they are. New character in A is a_{i+1} and in B is b_{j+1}. The cost of this operation is 0 if $a_i = b_j$; otherwise the cost is ∞.

- **Delete:** Drop a_i from A. The new length of A is $n - 1$. The cost of this operation is 1.

- **Insert:** Insert b_j into A at position a_i. All characters in A following the previous a_i are shifted down one, and the new length of A is $n + 1$. Next character in A is a_{i+1} and in B is b_{j+1}. The cost of this operation is 1.

The distance between string A and B is then determined by the minimum total cost for all operations needed to convert A to B. For example, the distance from *catch* to *cat* is 2 because the c and h have to be deleted. Similarly, the distance from *cat* to *hat* is 2 because c must be deleted and h must be inserted. Example 9.4 illustrates the process.

EXAMPLE 9.4

Suppose that we wish to determine the distance between a string "apron" and "crayon." By looking at the strings, we see that we can match at most three characters: either a, o, n or r, o, n. Figure 9.8 illustrates the use of the first matching. Here the cost is 5 because we have to insert c, r, y and delete p, r. The figure shows that we can view the problem as a shortest path between two points: the top left corner and the bottom right corner.

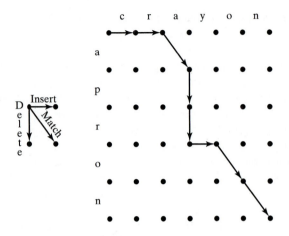

FIGURE 9.8: Convert *apron* to *crayon*.

9.5 SEQUENCES

A *sequence* is an ordered list of itemsets [AS95]. Definition 9.6 gives the definition of a sequence.

> **DEFINITION 9.6.** Let $I = \{I_1, I_2, \ldots, I_m\}$ be a set of items. A **sequence**, S, is: $S = \langle s_1, s_2, \ldots, s_n \rangle$, where $s_i \subseteq I$.

As with a time series, we find that there are many different definitions for a sequence. In Chapter 7 the sequence was a list of web pages. A sequence is sometimes viewed as an ordered list of attribute values from any domain. The individual members of the sequence are sometimes viewed to be sets of items from some underlying domains (alphabets). One common difference is that the sequence may not have explicit relationships with time. The only requirement is that the entries be totally ordered. As a matter of fact, the terms *sequence* and *time series* are often used interchangeably. In this text, we use the two definitions as shown in Definition 9.3 and Definition 9.6. The basic difference between the two concepts, then, is that a series is an ordered list of values, while a sequence is an ordered list of sets of items or values. The *length* of a sequence is the sum of the cardinalities of all itemsets in the sequence. A *subsequence* of a given sequence is one that can be obtained by removing some items and any resulting empty itemsets from the original sequence. We briefly examined the concept of sequential patterns in Chapter 7. These are specific types of subsequences in that they are maximal.

> **DEFINITION 9.7.** Let $I = \{I_1, I_2, \ldots, I_m\}$ be a set of items. One sequence $T = \langle t_{i_1}, \ldots, t_{i_m} \rangle$ is a **subsequence** of another $S = \langle s_1, \ldots, s_n \rangle$ if $\forall 1 \leq j \leq m-1, i_j < i_{j+1}$ and $\forall 1 \leq j \leq m, \exists 1 \leq k \leq n$ such that $t_{i_j} \subseteq s_k$. In this case, S **contains** T.

We assume that items are grouped together into transactions. The temporal feature is added by assuming that a customer may obtain different items at different times. Each set of items purchased at one time by a customer is a *transaction*. Example 9.5

illustrates the concept of a sequence. The sequence of itemsets purchased by a customer is referred to as the *customer-sequence*. Note that customer C_1 has the customer-sequence $\langle\{A, B\}, \{B, C\}, \{C\}\rangle$. $\langle\{A\}, \{C\}\rangle$ is a subsequence of this, but $\langle\{A, C\}, \{B\}\rangle$ is not. To be a subsequence, each itemset must be a subset of an item in the larger sequence. In addition, the larger itemsets must satisfy the ordering indicated.

The use of support and confidence in sequences is defined in Definition 9.8 and Definition 9.9, respectively. Given a minimum support threshold, a sequence is said to be *large* or *frequent* if its support exceeds this threshold.

> **DEFINITION 9.8.** Given a set of customers and transactions for each customer, the **support** of a sequence $s(S)$ is the percentage of total customers whose customer-sequence contains S.

> **DEFINITION 9.9.** The **confidence** (α) for a sequence association rule $S \Rightarrow T$ is the ratio of the number of customers (customer-sequences) that contain both sequences S and T to the number that contain S.

An example of sequences is found in Example 9.5. As with traditional itemsets, a lattice can be constructed to illustrate the sequences. The *sequence lattice*, originally proposed in [PZOD99], uses the subsequence (as opposed to subset) relationship. The data at one level in the lattice are obtained from that at the next lower level by adding one item. This is done either by adding the item to one of the itemsets or by inserting it as a singleton itemset somewhere in the sequence.

EXAMPLE 9.5

Let $I = A, B, C, D$, suppose that there are three customers, C_1, C_2, and C_3, who purchase these items at different times. The following table shows purchases made by these three customers:

Customer	Time	Itemset
C_1	10	AB
C_1	20	BC
C_1	30	D
C_2	15	ABC
C_2	20	D
C_3	15	ACD

(In this table we have removed commas and set notation.) Given $S = \langle\{A\}, \{C\}\rangle$, we see that the support is $s(S) = 1/3$ because it is contained only in the sequential pattern found for customer C_1. A second sequence $T = \langle\{A\}, \{D\}\rangle$ has a support of $s(T) = 2/3$, while $U = \langle\{B, C\}, \{D\}\rangle$ has a support of $s(U) = 2/3$. Figure 9.9 shows the lattice with frequent sequences, assuming a minimum support of $2/3$, only for this data.

As with frequent itemsets, a frequent sequence follows a *large sequence property*. This means that any subsequence of a large (frequent) sequence is also frequent.

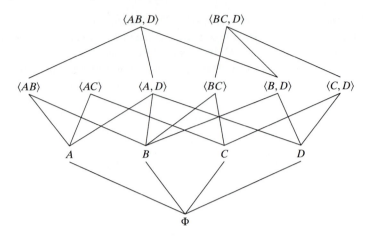

FIGURE 9.9: Frequent sequence lattice for Example 9.5.

9.5.1 AprioriAll

Algorithm AprioriAll in Chapter 7 contained a simple algorithm for finding sequential patterns. AprioriAll works in three parts by first finding all frequent itemsets, then relacing original transactions with frequent itemsets, and finally finding sequential patterns. This algorithm does not scale well, partly because of the transformation step. It also would be difficult to incorporate extensions such as sliding windows.

9.5.2 SPADE

The algorithm that we now introduce, *SPADE (Sequential PAttern Discovery using Equivalence classes)*, identifies patterns by traversing the lattice top-down. To improve processing, SPADE uses an *id-list* that associates the customers and transactions associated with each item. Table 9.1 illustrates this concept for the data in Example 9.5. Here we see the id-lists for sequences of length 1. These can be viewed as the atoms to construct support counts for larger sequences. The support for a k-sequence can be determined by looking at the intersection of any two of its $(k-1)$-subsequences. To accomplish this, temporary id-lists are generated from the starting id-lists. To illustrate this process, look at the sequence $T = \langle \{A\}, \{D\} \rangle$. Looking at Table 9.1, we see that the count for $\langle \{A\} \rangle$ is 3, as is that for $\langle \{D\} \rangle$. As seen in Example 9.5, $T = \langle \{A\}, \{D\} \rangle$ count of 2. To derive this, an id-list for T is created by determining the intersection for the two subsequences:

Customer	Time
C_1	10
C_3	15

Note that intersection must take times into account. Thus, its count is 2 and its support is 2/3. This observation is used in SPADE to count the sequences and determine their support. The lattice can be traversed to construct id-lists for higher-level sequences by intersecting two subsequences at the next lower level. The problem with this is that there may not be enough memory to do this all in memory.

TABLE 9.1: ID-Lists for Sequences of Length 1

A		B		C		D	
Customer	Time	Customer	Time	Customer	Time	Customer	Time
C_1	10	C_1	10	C_1	20	C_1	30
C_2	15	C_1	20	C_2	15	C_2	20
C_3	15	C_2	15	C_3	15	C_3	15

To address the space issue, the lattice is divided into partitions and these partitions are traversed independently. This reduces the memory requirements by reducing the number of id-lists that must be kept at one time. An equivalence class concept is used to accomplish this. A k length *prefix* for a sequence is determined by looking at the first k items (and associated ordering) for the sequence. Given a sequence S, the k length prefix of S is denoted by $p(S, k)$, In Example 9.5, we looked at the sequence $U = \langle \{B, C\}, \{D\} \rangle$. This sequence is a 3-sequence because it is of length 3. It has a length 2 prefix of $\langle \{B, C\} \rangle$, as does another 3-sequence $W = \langle \{B, C, D\} \rangle$. Θ_k is an equivalence relation. As seen in Definition 9.10, two sequences are Θ_k equivalent if they have identical prefixes of length k. Thus, we see that U is equivalent to W, written as $U \equiv W(\text{mod }\Theta_2)$. If we had the id-lists for U and W with their counts, we could determine the count.

DEFINITION 9.10. Two sequences S and T are **equivalent**, $S \equiv T(\text{mod }\Theta_k)$ iff $p(S, k) = p(T, k)$.

To partition the frequent sequence lattice, we look at those sequences in a Θ_k equivalence class. In Figure 9.10 we have identified the equivalence classes $[A]_{\Theta_1}$, $[B]_{\Theta_1}$, $[C]_{\Theta_1}$, and $[D]_{\Theta_1}$. The supports for the sequences in each sublattice can be determined by intersecting the id-lists for two sequences at the lower level. The partitioning of the lattice can be accomplished by any of the Θ_k equivalence classes. If the number of classes for Θ_1 is too large (i.e., the number of id-lists will not fit into memory), then a larger value of k can be used. Figure 9.10 shows the lattice from Figure 9.9 with equivalence classes for Θ_1.

Algorithm 9.2 shows the steps in SPADE. A breadth-first search or depth-first search of the lattice can be performed to enumerate the large sequences within each class. The first step is to find the frequent 1-sequences. This is performed by reading the id-lists into memory and counting the support for each customer. The frequent 2-sequences can then be found by intersecting the id-lists for the frequent 1-sequences. A straightforward approach for this is to look at all ($mover2$) possible combinations. The authors of the algorithm have proposed improvements to this naive technique, which we do not discuss here [Zak98]. The equivalence classes, ϵ, for Θ_1 can then be determined. SPADE successfully finds all frequent sequences in only three database scans and has been shown to outperform other algorithms for identifying frequent sequences.

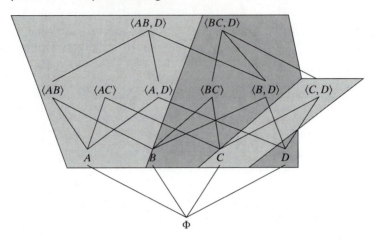

FIGURE 9.10: Θ_1 Equivalence classes for lattice in Figure 9.9.

ALGORITHM 9.2

```
Input:
    D          //ID-lists for customer transactions
    s          //Support
Output:
    F          // Frequent sequences
SPADE algorithm:
    Determine frequent items, F₁;
    Determine frequent 2-sequences, F₂;
    Find equivalence classes ∈ for all 1-sequences [S]Θ₁;
    for each [S] ∈ ∈ do
        Find frequent sequences F;
```

9.5.3 Generalization

The concept of subsequence has been generalized to include concept hierarchies and more temporal information. These generalizations can make the concept of sequences applicable to a wider range of applications. For example, one constraint would be to include a **maximum time** between elements in the sequence. For example, you might want to see customers who purchase a digital camera and then purchase a printer within three months. This also illustrates the concept hierarchy problem. There are many types of digital cameras. This sequence should be for any brand and type. This requires the use of taxonomies as in generalized association rules.

Adding concept hierarchies to sequences is relatively straightforward. The idea is to change the definition of subsequence as seen in Definition 9.11.

DEFINITION 9.11. One sequence $T = \langle t_{i_1}, \ldots, t_{i_m} \rangle$ is a **subsequence** of another $S = \langle s_1, \ldots, s_n \rangle$ if $\forall 1 \leq j \leq m - 1, i_j < i_{j+1}$ and $\forall 1 \leq j \leq m, \exists 1 \leq k \leq n$ such that $t_{i_j} \subseteq s_k$ or $\forall x \in t_{i_j} x$ is an ancestor in a concept hierarchy for some item in s_k.

Another technique that has been proposed is to look at a sliding window around the data [SA96b]. A *sliding window* is a maximum time difference used to group transactions together. When transactions are grouped together, a sequence is said to exist in a customer sequence if it exists in any of the transactions in a window. The effect of this is to increase the support of sequences.

One last extension proposed in [SA96b] is to add a time constraint that indicates the allowed time between successive elements in the sequence. The *time constraint* is a pair $\langle t_{min}, t_{max} \rangle$ that indicates the minimum and maximum distances that are allowed to exist in a sequence. These are allowable time gaps. The time difference between transactions with consecutive elements in the sequence must be greater than t_{min} but no greater than t_{max}.

The three extensions also may be combined. With no concept hierarchy, a window size of 0, and time constraints of $\langle 0, \infty \rangle$, there is the regular concept of sequences.

One algorithm has been proposed specifically to handle generalized sequential patterns. This algorithm *generalized sequential pattern (GSP)* has been shown to outperform an extended version of AprioriAll by up to 20 times [SA96b]. As with Apriori, GSP scans the database several times. The support for all items is determined during the first scan. The input to the next scan is the frequent items (sequences of length one) found during the first traversal. The algorithm works iteratively in this fashion. During each scan, candidate sequences are generated from the frequent sequences of the prior scanned and then counted. As with Apriori, the size of each candidate during a database scan is the same. GSP terminates when no candidates at that pass are found to be frequent.

To assist with the time constraint issue, the concept of contiguous subsequences is used. A sequence will always contain all contiguous subsequences, but with time constraints added, it may not contain noncontiguous subsequences. The definition of *contiguous subsequence* is found in Definition 9.12 [SA96b]. For example, $\langle A, C, DE, D \rangle$, $\langle AB, C, DE \rangle$, and $\langle AB, C, D, D \rangle$ are contiguous subsequences of $S = \langle AB, C, DE, D \rangle$, while $\langle AB, DE, D \rangle$ and $\langle AB, C, D \rangle$ are not. Notice that any time constraints that a sequence satisfy will also always be satisfied by any contiguous sequence.

> **DEFINITION 9.12.** One sequence $T = \langle t_1, \ldots, t_m \rangle$ is a **contiguous subsequence** of another $S = \langle s_1, \ldots, s_n \rangle$ if T is a subsequence of S and one of the following applies:
>
> - $n = m$; $\forall 2 \le i \le n-1 t_i = s_i$; and either $t_1 = s_1$ and $\mid t_m \mid = \mid s_n \mid -1$ or $t_m = s_n$ and $\mid t_1 \mid = \mid s_1 \mid -1$. Note that if the cardinality of either s_1 or s_n is one, when one item is dropped from it then that particular itemset in the subsequence is dropped effectively making the length of T $n - 1$.
>
> - $n = m$; $\exists 2 \le i \le n - 1$ such that $\mid t_i \mid = \mid s_i \mid -1$ and for all other $\forall 1 \le j \le n j \ne i; t_i = s_i$.
>
> - T is a contiguous subsequence of another sequence U, which is a subsequence of S.

The generation of candidate sequences must be handled differently than with candidate itemsets in Apriori. For example, suppose it is found that $\langle \{A\} \rangle$ and $\langle \{B\} \rangle$ are frequent during the first scan. These two sequences can be used to generate three candidates: $\langle \{AB\} \rangle$, $\langle \{A\}, \{B\} \rangle$, and $\langle \{B\}, \{A\} \rangle$. In addition, the generalization constraints must be satisfied. As with candidate generation in Apriori, candidates are generated by joining frequent sequences from the prior scan. Here, however, joining is defined slightly differently. Two sequences $T = \langle t_1, \ldots, t_m \rangle$ and $S = \langle s_1, \ldots, s_n \rangle$ are joined if the subsequence of T obtained by dropping the first item in t_1 is the same as a subsequence of S obtained by dropping the last item in s_n. When T and S are joined, the new sequence obtained is either $U = \langle t_1, \ldots, t_m, x \rangle$ or $U = \langle t_1, \ldots, t_m \cup x \rangle$. The first sequence is obtained if $x = s_n$; otherwise the second sequence is obtained.

9.5.4 Feature Extraction

The feature extraction problem is to extract k features from every sequence and to represent that sequence by those features. This approach may make it easier to perform sequence analysis, and each sequence can be represented as a point in k-dimensional space. R-trees or other multidimensional data structures can then be used to store and search the time series data. The problem, of course, is how to extract the features.

As with time series clustering, identifying features that describe classes of sequences is beneficial. One algorithm, *FEATUREMINE*, has been proposed to extract features for sequences [LZO99]. The approach is to use a preprocessor sequence mining algorithm to extract features. Then classification can be performed on these features. A *sequence classifier* maps each sequence into a class based on features. There are four goals for features [LZO99]:

- Features should occur often in the database.

- Features should be usable to distinguish between classes.

- There should be no redundant features.

- Avoid searching the entire database to find the features.

The last item indicates how the feature extraction should not be performed. FEATUREMINE uses SPADE and integrates a pruning technique into the algorithm. The approach is to traverse the sequence lattice in a depth-first manner to find the frequency sequences. Observe that sequences at the root of the lattice are more general than those beneath it. As with SPADE, to ensure that processing in main memory, the lattice is partitioned into equivalence class sections and the traversal actually is performed in each partition separately.

9.6 TEMPORAL ASSOCIATION RULES

With traditional association rules, a transaction can be viewed as the following:

$$\langle TID, CID, I_1, I_n, \ldots, I_m \rangle$$

where TID is the ID for the transaction, CID is the ID for the customer, and $I_1, \ldots, I_m$ are the items. When considered part of a temporal database, a transaction could be viewed as

$$\langle TID, CID, I_1, I_n, \ldots, I_m, t_s, t_e \rangle$$

where $[t_s, t_e]$ is the valid time range for the transaction. If this were a grocery store transaction, $t_s = t_e$ could be the point in time that the transaction was completed. Alternatively, if the transaction represented products ordered over the Web, t_s might be the time the order was placed and t_e might be the time the actual delivery was made. Thus, $[t_s, t_e]$ would be the range of time the transaction was active. Once time is added to the database, different association rules can be found for different times or time ranges. This is similar to the idea of combining clustering with association rules in the spatial mining area. The analogy in temporal mining is to cluster the data based on time and then determine the association rules. This can be done to examine the change in association rules over time, to detect seasonal association rules, and to identify rules that may not be found if looking at larger sets of data. For example, a grocery store could look at association rules for an entire year. However, this would not identify frequent items sold at particular times of the year. This would not allow the store to take advantage of some of the most frequently sold items over short periods of time. The importance of this concept is demonstrated by the fact that many supermarkets now have aisles dedicated to the sale of seasonal products.

When time is added to the concept of association rules, different types of rules may be generated. We observe several of these different interpretations in this section.

9.6.1 Intertransaction Rules

The basic association rule approaches look only at items occurring together within one transaction. These may be viewed as *intratransaction association rules*. However, there certainly are situations in which rules generated across transactions would be of interest. For example, an electronics store manager might want to know if customers purchase computer software after they purchase a computer. These purchases could occur in transactions at two different times. To define these new rules, the concept of a window is applied to the transaction database. Recall that the basic association rule problem assumes the existence of a set of items $I = \{I_1, I_2, \ldots, I_m\}$ and a database of transactions $D = \{t_1, t_2, \ldots, t_n\}$ where $t_i = I_{i1}, I_{i2}, \ldots, I_{ik}$ and $I_{ij} \in I$. Assume that each transaction t_i has associated with it a value d_i which could be time, location, or other information describing the transaction. We assume here that the value is time, so that d_i is the time that t_i executed. Although the original proposal in [TLHF99] viewed that d could be any ordinal attributes, to simplify discussion here we look at specific integers representing time. A *sliding window* is viewed to be placed on top of D. The interval between two transaction t_j and t_k is $| d_j - d_i |$. The number of transactions to be included in the window, w, is an input parameter.

9.6.2 Episode Rules

An *episode rule* is a generalization of association rules applied to sequences of events. An *event sequence* S is an ordered list of events, each one occurring at a particular time. Thus, it can be viewed as a special type of time series. An *episode* is a set of event predicates, A, and a partial order, $\leq$, on the events in A: $\{A, \leq\}$. An event predicate is a predicate that can be evaluated as true or false when applied to an actual event occurrence. It could be as simple as to check the type or severity of an event. An episode can be viewed as a directed graph where the vertices are the events and the arcs represent the partial order. An episode B is a *subepisode* of an episode A if the graph of B is a subgraph of the graph of A. A sequence of events, S, *contains* an episode if all the alarm predicates are satisfied in S and these events satisfy the partial order. A formal definition for episode rule is found in Definition 9.13. As with association rules, we may also define support and confidence.

DEFINITION 9.13. An **episode rule** is an implication of the form $B \Rightarrow A$ where B and A are episodes and B is a subepisode of A.

An important application in networks is to predict the failure of a switching node. Episode rules can be used to help solve this problem. If a failure can be accurately predicted, then the node can be taken offline and replaced before the occurrence. When viewed as a temporal data mining problem, it becomes one of predicting an event (failure) based on a sequence of earlier events. These events can be viewed as the amount of traffic passing through a node or alarms (messages generated by a network entity usually describing a problem). An alarm can be viewed as a triple $\alpha = \langle t, s, m \rangle$, where t is the time the alarm occurred, s is where this alarm message came from, and m is the alarm message itself [Kle99b]. The sequence of alarms could be viewed as a time series.

The following preprocessing techniques may be used to perform some of the following functions [Kle99b]:

- Remove redundant alarms.

- Remove lower priority alarms if higher alarms also exist.

- Replace some alarms by either new information or perhaps higher-level alarms.

A *correlation pattern* is then used to match to the sequences that have been found in the alarm data. This pattern may be compared to alarms that have occurred in a recent time window. If the sequence of alarms that have occurred matches a correlation pattern, then the associated *correlation action* is taken.

Two different approaches have been proposed to find episode rules. One approach, WINEPI, applies a window to the events. Given an event sequence, S, the window is a time span $\langle t_s, t_e \rangle$ that defines a subseries of S, namely, those events (in order) that occur in the window. Given an episode B, the subseries of B that occur in all windows of size W is referred to as B_W. The window can be used to define support and confidence as seen in Definition 9.14 and Definition 9.15. The support is the percentage of windows in which the target episode occur.

DEFINITION 9.14. Given a set of subseries, S_W, of an episode, S, as defined by a window W the **support** of a episode B, $s(B)$ is the percentage of total subseries in B_W that have S as a subepisode.

DEFINITION 9.15. The **confidence** (α) of an episode rule $B \Rightarrow A$ is the ratio of the support of A to the support of B: $\frac{s(A)}{s(B)}$.

9.6.3   Trend Dependencies

Trend dependencies are like association rules in that they compare attribute values, but they do so over time [WM97]. For example, we might observe that an employee's salary always increases over time. A formal definition (as found in [WM97]) is found in Definition 9.18. Note that the definition does not explicitly indicate that the two database states must differ in time. Of course, this is our assumption here, but in general it is not necessary. To add this temporal aspect to it, we assume that the pattern on the left-hand side is from a relation state valid at an earlier time than the pattern on the right-hand side of the trend dependency.

DEFINITION 9.16. Let R be a schema containing attributes $A_1, A_2, \ldots, A_m$. The domain for each attribute A_i must be a totally ordered set. A **pattern** over R is a set $\{(A_1, \theta_1), (A_2, \theta_2), \ldots, (A_m, \theta_m)\}$ where $\forall 1 \leq i, j \leq m, A_i \neq A_j$ and $\theta_i \in \{<, =, >, \leq, \geq, \neq\}$.

DEFINITION 9.17. Let R be a schema containing attributes $A_1, A_2, \ldots, A_m$. A pair of tuples t_1, t_2 **satisfy** a pattern $\{(A_1, \theta_1), (A_2, \theta_2), \ldots, (A_m, \theta_m)\}$ iff $t_1(A_i)\theta_i t_2(A_i) \forall 1 \leq i \leq m$.

DEFINITION 9.18. A **trend dependency** is an implication of the form $X \Rightarrow Y$ where X and Y are patterns over schema R.

A trend dependency, just as an association rule, is also subject to a support and a confidence. For example, we would not be interested in the trend dependency concerning salaries if it rarely were true.

DEFINITION 9.19. Given two relations, I_1, I_2 over schema R, the **support (s)** for a trend dependency $X \Rightarrow Y$ is the percentage of tuple pairs in $I_1 \times I_2$ that satisfy both patterns X and Y. If $\mid I_1 \times I_2 \mid = 0$, then $s = 0$.

DEFINITION 9.20. Given two relations, I_1, I_2 over schema R, the **confidence (α)** for a trend dependency $X \Rightarrow Y$ is the ratio of the number tuple pairs in $I_1 \times I_2$ that satisfy both patterns X and Y to the number that satisfy X. If the number that satisfy X is 0, then $\alpha = 0$.

Example 9.6, which is adapted from [WM97], illustrates a trend dependency. In this example, there are two database states: $\mid I_1 \mid = 6$ and $\mid I_2 \mid = 6$. Thus, $\mid I_1 \times I_2 \mid = 36$. Here $X = (SSN, =)$ AND $Y = (Salary, \leq)$. The number of tuple pairs in $I_1 \times I_2$ that satisfy both patterns is 4. The number that satisfies X is 5. Thus, the $\alpha = 4/5 = 80\%$ and $s = 4/36 = 11\%$.

EXAMPLE 9.6

Imagine having the data in Example 9.1 for all employees at XYZ. Instead of viewing it as one table, however, we want to look at it as three different instances: I_1, I_2, and I_3. I_1 contains the valid data at time 2/12/02, I_2 has the valid data for 8/12/02, and I_3 has the valid data for 12/10/02. A trend that can be observed (at least for Joe Smith) is that an employee's salary always increases with time. This trend detection can be stated as

$$(SSN, =) \Longrightarrow (Salary, \leq)$$

Given two tuples $t_1 \in I_1$ and $t_2 \in I_2$, if $t_1(SSN) = t_2(SSN)$ then $t_1(Salary) \leq t_2(Salary)$. This holds for any two database states where the second state is at a later time. The following tables show I_1 and I_2.

Name	SSN	Address	Salary
Joe Smith	123456789	10 Moss Haven	50,000
Mary Jones	111111111	10 Main	75,000
Bill Adams	222222222	215 North	100,000
Selena Shepherd	876543298	25 Georgetown	15,000
Paul Williams	908734124	13 East	250,000
Martha Laros	873659365	1010 Fox	150,000

Name	SSN	Address	Salary
Mary Jones	111111111	10 Main	85,000
Joe Smith	123456789	10 Moss Haven	52,000
Bill Adams	222222222	215 North	90,000
Selena Shepherd	876543298	25 Georgetown	15,000
Paul Williams	908734124	13 East	270,000
Bob Holder	838383838	22 South	20,000

Given these two states, the confidence and support of $X \Rightarrow Y$ is $\alpha = 4/5 = 80\%$ and $s = 4/36 = 11\%$.

Trend dependencies are defined over only two database states. They are not easily generalized to more states. As with association rules, we can state a trend dependency problem as that of finding all trend dependencies with a given minimum support and confidence over two identified database states. The complexity of this problem in the worst-case scenario is quite high. There are $| \Theta |^D$ possible combinations of attributes and operations. Here Θ is the set of operators (we assume there are six in this case), and D is the number of possible attribute pairs. In the example this becomes 6^{16}. Obviously, an exhaustive search is not advisable. In fact, it has been shown that the general problem is NP-complete [WM97]. When the set of operators is restricted to $\{<, =, >\}$, it becomes polynomial and an efficient algorithm has been proposed [WM97].

9.6.4 Sequence Association Rules

We can use sequences in rules, which we call *sequence association rules*.

DEFINITION 9.21. Given a set of items $I = \{I_1, I_2, \ldots, I_m\}$ and a set of transactions grouped by customer in customer-sequences, a **sequence association rule** is an implication of the form $S \Rightarrow T$, where S and T are sequences.

DEFINITION 9.22. The **support** for a sequence association rule $S \Rightarrow T$ is the percentage of customers (customer-sequences) that contain S and T.

DEFINITION 9.23. The **confidence** (α) for a sequence association rule $S \Rightarrow T$, is the ratio of the number of customers (customer-sequences) that contain both sequences S and T to the number that contain S.

As with conventional association rules, we can state the *sequence association rule problem* to be that of finding sequence association rules with minimum support and confidence. There are many applications that could use sequence association rules. In the market basket area, the buying behavior over time can be used to predict future buying behavior. This could be used to do targeted advertising to customers with the first type of buying behavior. Note that we are predicting buying patterns over time, not just within one transaction. An example of sequence association rules is found in Example 9.7. The SPADE algorithm discussed earlier can be used to find frequent sequences, and these sequences can then be used to solve the sequence association rule problem.

EXAMPLE 9.7

Using the data introduced for Example 9.5, we can construct the following sequence association rules:

Rule	Support	Confidence
$\langle\{A\},\{C\}\rangle \Rightarrow \langle\{A\},\{D\}\rangle$	1/3	1
$\langle\{B,C\},\{D\}\rangle \Rightarrow \langle\{A\},\{C\}\rangle$	1/3	1/2

9.6.5 Calendric Association Rules

Calendric association rules, as defined in Definition 9.24, assume that each transaction, t_i, is associated with a timestamp, t_{is}, when it was executed. In addition, time is assumed to be divided into predefined units, t. A time interval, k, is defined by the range $[kt, (k+1)t)$. A transaction occurs in a time interval k, which is defined by $[kt, (k+1)t)$, if $kt \leq t_{is} < (k+1)t$. $D[k]$ is the subset of transactions that occur in time interval k. The *support* of an itemset, X in $D[k]$, is the percentage of transactions in $D[k]$ that contain X. The *confidence* of $X \Rightarrow Y$ in $D[k]$, is the ratio of the number of transactions in $D[k]$ that contain $X \cup Y$ to the number that contain X. Example 9.8 illustrates use of a calendric association rule. Here the time unit is a day. Notice, however, that the same data could have been evaluated for calendric association rules where the time unit was a different granule: hour, month, year, etc.

> **DEFINITION 9.24.** Given a set of items $I = \{I_1, I_2, \ldots, I_m\}$, a set of transactions $D = \{t_1, t_2, t_n\}$, a time unit k, and a calendar $C = \{(s_1, e_1), \ldots, (s_k, e_k)\}$, a **calendric association rule** is an association rule, $X \Rightarrow Y$ that occurs in $D[k]$.

EXAMPLE 9.8

Suppose that a grocery store wishes to obtain information about purchases for a particular day. In this case, the time unit is a day (24-hour period). The manager is interested in finding all association rules in this time frame that satisfy a given minimum support and confidence. The manager also is interested in association rules that satisfy the support and confidence for all but five days in a given season. During the year 2001, the manager defines two time intervals by looking at days in winter as defined by the calendar:

{(1, 79), (355, 365)}. There are 90 time units, or days, in this calendar. With a mismatch threshold of 5, he is then interested in only association rules that satisfy the support and confidence on at least 85 of the days.

One could imagine a regular association rule algorithm, such as Apriori, applied to a subset of D created by finding all transactions that occur in the given time interval. However, the problem may be more general, such as finding all calendric association rules that occur over any time interval (or some set of intervals). This could be used to determine important association rules over any day or period of time (not just one). It is assumed that a particular calendar is defined with potentially many different time granularities. The more general problem, then, is to find all calendric association rules that hold given this calendar. Given a calendar of time intervals and a time unit, various occurrences of the time unit can be defined in each. In Example 9.8, the time unit is a day, but the intervals are the seasons consisting of days in the four seasons. An association rule may satisfy the support and confidence for some of the time units. Thus, an additional threshold, m, is used to indicate the number of time units in the intervals of the calendar in which the association rule does not hold. A calendar *belongs* to a rule $X \Rightarrow Y$ if there are at most m mismatches. A calendric association rule algorithm has been proposed that is given as input a set of possible calendars and a time unit [RMS98]. It first finds large itemsets over all time units and then determines which calendars belong to which association rules.

9.7 EXERCISES

1. Using the time series data in Example 9.2, determine the autocorrelation with a lag of 4. Explain what this value indicates.
2. Assume that you are given the following temperature values, z_t, taken at 5-minute time intervals: {50, 52, 55, 58, 60, 57, 66, 62, 60}. Plot both z_{t+2} and z_t. Does there appear to be an autocorrelation? Calculate the correlation coefficient.
3. Plot the following time series values as well as the moving average found by replacing a given value with the average of it and the ones preceding and following it: {5, 15, 7, 20, 13, 5, 8, 10, 12, 11, 9, 15}. For the first and last values, you are to use only the two values available to calculate the average.
4. Using the MM in Figure 9.2, determine the probability that the model is in the state labeled 't' after 3 characters.
5. Determine the probability that the sequence "ththe" is recognized by the MM in Figure 9.2.
6. (**Research**) Investigate and describe two techniques which have been used to predict future stock prices.

9.8 BIBLIOGRAPHIC NOTES

The original string matching algorithms, KMP and BM, were proposed over 20 years ago [BM77] [KMP77]. A variation on KMP proposed by Aho and Corasick constructs an FSM that can recognize multiple patterns [AC75].

One recent text has examined the impact of time on databases, logic, and data mining [BJW98]. There are several excellent surveys and tutorials concerning temporal data mining, including a recent textbook that examines sequential patterns [Ada00] [HLP01].[1]

Markov models and hidden Markov models have been extensively studied. An excellent introduction to the topic of HMM can be found [RJ86].

Time series have been extensively studied in the literature with several introductory books and surveys. One online statistics textbook contains a survey, [Sta01] that is quite simple to understand and very complete. Many time series textbooks are available, including [And71], [BJR94], and [BD96]. A recent dissertation examined the telecommunication network alarm issues in detail [Kle99b]. One of the earliest proposals for a recurrent network was by Jordan in 1986 [Jor86]. Jordan proposed feedback from output units to special context input nodes. Note that this allows conventional NN back-propagation learning techniques. Elman proposed that RNNs allow a feedback form the hidden layer to a separate context input layer [Elm90]. Recurrent neural networks have been proposed to detect automobile emission problems that occur over time. One recent dissertation has studied the temporal NNs [II98].

The various applications of time to association rules is becoming quite popular in the research community. Intertransaction association rules were introduced in [TLHF99]. Calendric association rules were proposed in [RMS98] as an extension to the earlier proposed *cyclic association rules* [ÖRS98]. The authors propose a calendar algebra to manipulate time intervals using a predefined calendric system.

SPADE was first introduced in 1998 [Zak98]. The concept of subsequence generalization was examined in [SA96b] The approach of applying windows to events in WINEPI was proposed in [MTV95].

---

[1]Eamonn Keogh, "A Tutorial on Indexing and Mining Time Series Data," The 2001 IEEE International Conference on Data Mining.

APPENDIX A

Data Mining Products

A.1 BIBLIOGRAPHIC NOTES

The following paragraphs provide a superficial overview of data mining tools on the market. Links are provided to resources where more detailed information can be found.

4Thought
- Product: 4Thought
- Vendor: Cognos Inc.
- URL: www.cognos.com/products/4thought
- Functions: Prediction
- Techniques: Neural networks (MLP)
- Platforms: Windows

4Thought supports decision support applications, including forecasting. A spreadsheet interface is provided. Data can be accessed as text files, Excel, Lotus, dBase, Impromptu, Powerplay, and Scenario files.

AC^2
- Product: AC^2
- Vendor: ISoft
- URL: www.alice-soft.com/html/prod_ac2.htm
- Functions: Clustering, classification, prediction, segmentation
- Techniques: Decision trees
- Platforms: Unix, Windows

AC^2 is a complete data mining toolkit designed for knowledgeable users. AC^2 has a graphical object-oriented modeling language and C/C++ libraries. Interactive editing of trees is supported. It behaves as a multiplatform library of data mining functions.

Affinium Model
- Product: Affinium Model
- Vendor: Unica Corporation
- URL: www.unicacorp.com
- Functions: Classification, segmentation
- Platforms: Unix, Windows

Affinium Model provides CRM applications with segmentation capabilities.

AI Trilogy

- Product: AI Trilogy
- Vendor: Ward Systems Group, Inc.
- URL: www.wardsystems.com
- Functions: Classification, forecasting, prediction
- Techniques: Genetic algorithms, jackknife estimation, neural networks
- Platforms: Windows

AI Trilogy is a suite of three products: *NeuroShell Predictor, Neuroshell Classifier* and *GeneHunter*. Ascii, CSV, and Excel files are supported. The *NeuroShell Run-Time Server* is also included as a utility for trained neural networks to run in Excel and user programs.

Alice

- Product: Alice d'ISoft & Alice Server
- Vendor: ISoft
- URL: www.alice-soft.com/html/prod_alice.htm
- Functions: Clustering, correlation, segmentation
- Techniques: Decision trees
- Platforms: Metaframe, TSE, Windows, Unix

Alice d'ISoft is an interactive data mining tool that covers all aspects of the KDD process. Alice can access data in many different formats, including relational databases via both ODBC and OLE DB drivers. Alice integrates decision tree techniques with an OLAP engine. A companion tool, *Amadea*, supports data transformation and cleansing. The *Alice Server* version supports a client/server architecture.

AnswerTree

- Product: AnswerTree 3.0
- Vendor: SPSS Inc.
- URL: www.spss.com/answertree
- Functions: Classification
- Techniques: Decision trees [CHAID, Exhaustive CHAID, C&RT (a variation of CART), QUEST]
- Platforms: Client (Windows), Server (Solaris, Windows)

AnswerTree is an SPSS product used to create decision trees. As a data mining tool it targets profiling groups for marketing and sales. Four basic decision tree algorithms are used. Included are two CHAID algorithms, both of which SPSS has extended to handle nominal categorical, ordinal categorical, and continuous dependent variables.

Braincel

- Product: Braincel
- Vendor: Jurik Research and Consulting
- URL: www.jurikres.com/catalog/ms_bcel.htm
- Functions: Forecasting
- Techniques: Neural networks (back-percolation)

Braincel is an Excel add-in that uses neural networks to perform forecasting. An improved version of backpropagation called back-percolation is used. Promised Land Technologies developed Braincel, and Jurik Research developed the back-percolation approach.

BrainMaker

- Product: BrainMaker
- Vendor: California Scientific Software
- URL: www.calsci.com
- Functions: Forecasting
- Techniques: Neural networks
- Platforms: Macintosh, Windows

BrainMaker is neural network software that can be used with many different data sources, including Lotus, Excel, dBase, ASCII, or binary. It is one of the most popular NN software tools. A companion product, *NetMaker*, is included to assist in the construction of the neural networks. An optional package, *Genetic Training Option (GTO)*, uses a genetic algorithm to create several possible neural nets. Through several iterations of training and genetic evolution, the best network can be chosen. This process also helps to choose the best training data.

CART

- Product: CART
- Vendor: Salford Systems
- URL: www.salford-systems.com
- Functions: Classification
- Techniques: Decision tree (CART)
- Platforms: CMS, MVS, Unix (Linux), Windows

CART is a decision tree tool that uses the CART algorithm and boosting. Missing data are handled through specialized backup rules that do not always assume that all values for a missing attribute are the same. Seven different splitting criteria (including Gini) are used. Through the use of a data-translation engine, *DBMS/Copy*, data from over 80 different file formats (including Excel, Informix, Lotus, Oracle) may be used. An optional product, *TreeCoder*, allows the use of CART directly in SAS. *TreeViewer* allows trees created on a Unix platform to be viewed on Windows.

Clementine

- Product: Clementine
- Vendor: SPSS Inc. (formerly Integral Solutions, Ltd.)
- URL: www.spss.com/clementine
- Functions: Association rules, classification, clustering, factor analysis, forecasting, prediction, sequence discovery discovery
- Techniques: Apriori, BIRCH, CARMA, Decision trees (C5.0, C&RT a variation of CART), K-means clustering, neural networks (Kohonen, MLP, RBFN), regression (linear, logistic) rule induction (C5.0, GRI)
- Platforms: HP/UX, IBM AIX, Sun Solaris, Windows NT

Perhaps the most unique feature of *Clementine* is its GUI approach to data mining, which Clementine pioneered in 1994. Through the use of descriptive icons, a user creates a data flow description of the functions to be performed. Each icon represents a step in the overall KDD process. Included are icons for such functions as accessing data, preparing data, visualization, and modeling. By dragging and dropping the icons onto the Clementine desktop, a stream of functions is created. Through the use of predefined templates of streams, Clementine provides support for common Web usage mining applications. To assist in the creation of sequences, Clementine uses Capri.

Clementine mines large data sets using a client/server model. When applicable, the server converts data access requests into SQL queries, which can then access a relational database. Clementine supports a wide variety of data formats. Clementine solutions are exported and deployed outside of Clementine using Clementine Solution Publisher.

Cubist

- Product: Cubist 1.10
- Vendor: RuleQuest Research Pty Ltd
- URL: www.rulequest.com/cubist-info.html
- Functions: Numerical modeling
- Techniques: Regression, rules
- Platforms: Windows, Unix (Linux, Irix, Solaris)

As a companion product to See5/C5.0, *Cubist* generates actual prediction values with the rules. Source code in C is provided so that models generated by Cubist can be embedded in applications.

Darwin

- Product: Darwin
- Vendor: Oracle Corporation
- URL: www.oracle.com/ip/analyze/warehouse/datamining/content.html
- Functions: Clustering, prediction, classification, association rules
- Techniques: Decision trees (CART), K-means, K-nearest neighbors, neural networks, regression (linear, logistic)
- Platforms: Windows, Sun Solaris, HP-UX

Darwin, or *Oracle Data Mining Suite*, provides a simple-to-use Windows-based GUI interface and parallel implementations of various data mining algorithms. It implements a complete KDD process model. Through OCI direct data access and ODBC, access to many relational systems is facilitated. Access to text and SAS files is also supported. Oracle Data Mining uses a client–server approach. C, C++, or Java code can be exported.

DataEngine

- Product: DataEngine
- Vendor: Management Intelligenter Technologien GmbH
- URL: www.dataengine.de
- Functions: Classification, clustering, decision trees, time series analysis
- Techniques: Decision trees, fuzzy rules, K-means, neural networks (MLP, Kohonen), regression (linear)
- Platforms: Windows

DataEngine supports many different data mining tasks as well as statistical methods. DataEngine supports many methods for data cleansing, data transformation, and handling missing data. Many types of data are supported via an import–export interface. With DataEngine ADL you can generate C code or produce DLLs, which can be incorporated in application code for subsequent use of a generated model.

Data Mining Suite

- Product: Data Mining Suite
- Vendor: Information Discovery, Inc.
- URL: www.datamining.com/dmsuite.htm
- Functions: Association rules, forecasting, prediction, rules
- Techniques: Rule induction

The Data Mining Suite is designed to mine large relational databases. The suite of tools actually consists of six different modules, each targeted to different data mining functions. Incremental data mining is supported, as are multidimensional mining and ROLAP. The results of all data mining are viewed as patterns or rules. The most unique feature of the Data Mining Suite is the fact that generated patterns are stored and are accessible using the *Pattern Query Language (PQL)*.

DataMite

- Product: DataMite
- Vendor: Logic Programming Associates Ltd.
- URL: www.lpa.co.uk/ind_pro.htm
- Functions: Rules
- Techniques: Decision trees, rule induction
- Platforms: ODBC, Windows

DataMite performs mining against relational databases, which can be accessed via ODBC. If-then rules are generated based on outcomes desired by the user.

DBMiner

- Product: DBMiner Analytical System
- Vendor: DBMiner Technologies Inc.
- URL: www.dbminer.com
- Functions: Association rules, classification, clustering
- Techniques: Decision trees, K-means
- Platforms: Windows

DBMiner accesses data from many sources, including Microsoft SQL Server, Excel, OLEDB, and other relational databases through ODBC. Users can use either a DMSQL interface or a GUI interface. Interface through MS SQL server's OLAP allows a cube view of data. There actually are three different products: *DBMiner AX 2000* targets association rules, *DBMiner SX 2000* performs sequential mining, and *DBMiner GX 2000* targets OLAP mining.

Decider

- Product: Decider and Decider-Online
- Vendor: Neural Technologies
- URL: www.neuralt.com
- Functions: Classification, prediction, rules
- Techniques: Neural networks

Decider and *Decider-Online* are DSS tools that incorporate data mining functionality to identify credit risks and fraud.

DecisionTime

- Product: DecisionTime and WhatIf
- Vendor: SPSS Inc.
- URL: www.spss.com/decisiontime
- Functions: Time series forecasting and analysis
- Techniques: ARIMA, exponential smoothing
- Platforms: Windows

DecisionTime is a time series forecasting tool. Through user interaction, Decision-Time chooses the best of the included models via a wizard to perform the forecasting or allows the more sophisticated user to build his or her own models. Input is accepted from many different types of files, including Excel, SPSS, ASCII, and an ODBC source. The *WhatIf?* part of the solution allows the user to change ARIMA model predictor variables to create various scenarios of the forecasts generated in DecisionTime.

Enterprise Miner

- Product: Enterprise Miner
- Vendor: SAS Institute Inc.
- URL: www.sas.com/products/miner
- Functions: Association rules, classification, clustering, prediction, time series
- Techniques: Decision trees (CART, CHAID), K nearest neighbors, regression (linear, logistic), memory-based reasoning, neural networks (Kohonen, MLP, RBF, SOM)
- Platforms: Client(Windows), Server (Unix, Windows)

Enterprise Miner from SAS implements the complete KDD process using their own process model called *SEMMA (Sample, Explore, Modify, Model, Assess)*. An icon-based, point and click GUI (not unlike Clementine) creates a process flow to be performed by the data mining task. In addition, Enterprise Miner contains many tools for bagging and boosting, sampling, visualization, imputation, filtering, transformations, and model assessment. An experiment text mining feature is also available. Enterprise Miner generates the complete scoring formula for all stages of model development in the form of SAS, C, and Java for subsequent model deployment and scoring.

GainSmarts

- Product: GainSmarts
- Vendor: Urban Science
- URL: www.urbanscience.com/main/gainpage.htm
- Functions: Classification, clustering, prediction
- Techniques: Bayesian classification, decision trees (AID, CHAID), genetic algorithms, K-means, neural networks, regression (linear, logistic)
- Platforms: SAS, Windows

GainSmarts is a comprehensive product that supports all steps in the KDD process. It is flexible in the data sources that are supported, including any supported by SAS or ACCESS. Collaborative filtering and survival analysis are also supported.

HNC Risk Suite

- Product: HNC Risk Suite
- Vendor: HNC Software
- URL: www.hnc.com
- Functions: Prediction
- Techniques: Neural networks, rules

HNC's *Risk Suite* actually is a set of tools targeting risk analysis and prediction. The *Falcon Fraud Manager* is an integral part of this suite.

Intelligent Miner

- Product: Intelligent Miner
- Vendor: IBM Corporation
- URL: www.software.ibm.com/data/iminer
- Functions: Association rules, clustering, classification, prediction, sequential patterns, time series
- Techniques: Decision trees (modified CART), K-means, neural networks (MLP, back-propagation, RBF), regression (linear)
- Platforms: Windows, Solaris, AIX, OS/390, OS/400

DB2 Intelligent Miner for Data performs mining functions against traditional DB2 databases or flat files. It also has capabilities to access data in other relational DBMSs using ODBC. However to do this IBM's DataJoiner must be used. It is implemented using a client–server approach with a straightforward GUI interface provided to assist the user in choosing data mining functions. Several visualization techniques are used.

There are two other products in the IBM Intelligent Miner family. *Intelligent Miner for Text* performs mining activities against textual data, including e-mail and Web pages. It consists of text analysis tools, a search engine, *NetQuestion Solution*, and a Web crawler package. The text analysis tools include the ability to cluster, classify, summarize, and extract important features from a document. NetQuestion Solution is a set of tools to facilitate indexing and searching Web documents. *DB2 Intelligent Miner Scoring* allows SQL applications the ability to request data mining applications against a DB2 or Oracle database. It is a user-defined extension to DB2. It can be used to determine the actual score that a record has with respect to user-defined ranking criteria.

JDA Intellect

- Product: JDA Intellect (formerly Decision Series)
- Vendor: JDA Software Group, Inc.
- URL: www.jda.com/jdad/ProductsServices/Intellect_facts.htm
- Functions: Association rules, classification, clustering, prediction
- Techniques: Naive Bayes, decision trees, K-means, K nearest neighbors, neural networks (back-propagation, RBF)
- Platforms: Solaris, Windows

JDA purchased NeoVista in June 2001. The new *JDA Intellect* product is based on Neovista's *Decision Series* data mining suite. JDA Intellect actually is a set of KDD and data mining tools. *Seasonal Profiling Intellect* can be used to extract and describe profiles reflecting seasonal sales trends. *Channel Clustering Intellect* is targeted to the clustering of retail stores based on products sold. The Decision Series consists of many different data mining engines, including DecisionNet, DecisionCubist, DecisionTree, DecisionBayes, DecisionCluster, DecisionKmean, and DecisionAR. Each of these engines implements one or more of the data mining techniques. A GUI interface facilitates creation of data flow designs by naive users. More experienced users can use a command line and programming interface.

JDBCMine
- Product: JDBCMine
- Vendor: Intelligent Systems Research
- URL: www.intsysr.com/JDBCMine.htm
- Functions: Classification
- Techniques: Decision trees (C4.5)
- Platforms: Windows, Java

JDBCMine performs classification against JDBC and ODBC databases using C4.5. The decision trees created can be visually browsed, printed, or saved as JPEG files.

Kaidara Advisor
- Product: Kaidara Advisor (formerly KATE)
- Vendor: Kaidara
- URL: www.kaidara.com
- Functions: Classification, clustering, prediction
- Techniques: Case-based reasoning, decision trees

Kaidara Advisor (formerly *KATE*) is a data mining tool targeted to support CRM applications. Kaidara Advisor supports sales automation and intelligent catalogs.

KnowledgeSTUDIO
- Product: KnowledgeSTUDIO
- Vendor: ANGOSS Software Corporation
- URL: www.angoss.com/ProdServ/AnalyticalTools/index.html
- Functions: Classification, clustering, prediction, rules
- Techniques: Decision trees (CHAID), expectation-maximization, K-means, neural networks (MLP, RBF), regression (linear, logistic)
- Platforms: Windows, Server (Solaris, Windows)

KnowledgeSTUDIO is a complete data mining workbench that performs many different tasks. It reads data from all major statistical packages and can import data from relational databases using ODBC. The optional *KnowledgeSTUDIO Software Development Kit* can be used to create in-house data mining applications. Application code can be generated for Visual Basic, PowerBuilder, Delphi, C++, and Java and then embedded into user code. *KnowledgeSERVER* can be used to create a client–server architecture. It also can be used to access data directly in relational databases.

KnowledgeSEEKER
- Product: KnowledgeSEEKER
- Vendor: ANGOSS Software Corporation
- URL: www.angoss.com/ProdServ/AnalyticalTools/index.html
- Functions: Classification
- Techniques: Decision trees (CHAID, XAID, entropy-based algorithms)
- Platforms: Windows, Unix (AIX, HP-UX, IRIX, Digital Alpha, Sinux, Solaris, SCO, LINUX)

KnowledgeSEEKER has a graphically based GUI and supports decision tree classification algorithms.

LOGIT
- Product: LOGIT
- Vendor: Salford Systems
- URL: www.salford-systems.com
- Functions: Forecasting, hypothesis testing
- Techniques: Regression (logistic)
- Platforms: DOS, MacOS, Unix

LOGIT is a logistic regression tool. As with MARS, DBMS/Copy allows the use of many different data formats.

Magnify
- Product: Magnify
- Vendor: Magnify
- URL: www.magnify.com
- Functions: Prediction
- Platforms: Unix

Magnify offers complete solutions (technology suite, consulting) for customer-related prediction problems. Magnify targets the insurance, direct marketing, and government industries. The technology used is designed to be scalable to any size dataset.

Magnum Opus
- Product: Magnum Opus 1.3
- Vendor: RuleQuest Research Pty Ltd
- URL: www.rulequest.com/MagnumOpus-info.html
- Functions: Association Rules
- Techniques: Opus
- Platforms: Windows, Unix (Solaris, Linux)

Magnum Opus generates association rules using the measures of leverage, lift, strength, coverage, and support. Only rules that satisfy the desired measurement constraints are generated. Filtering of rules is also performed. Association rules can be generated for market basket–type data as well as other attribute values. Numeric attributes are automatically partitioned into subranges.

Mantas
- Product: Mantas
- Vendor: Mantas, Inc.
- URL: www.mantas.com
- Functions: Association rules, classification, clustering, link analysis, prediction, sequence analysis, time series
- Techniques: Decision trees, neural networks
- Platforms: Unix, Windows

Mantas, Inc., a spin-off from SRA International in May 2001, provides knowledge discovery solutions for the global financial services industry. The *Mantas Knowledge Discovery Platform* provides an extensible foundation that proactively collects, analyzes, highlights, and disseminates relevant, actionable information. The Mantas product suite includes five products. *Mantas Best Execution* is used to analyze brokerage trading and identify opportunities to improve execution quality. *Mantas Equities Trading Compliance* monitors trading behaviors to ensure adherence to industry rules and regulations. *Mantas Brokerage Fraud and Anti-Money Laundering* monitors security and monetary transaction for potential fraud and money laundering activities. *Mantas Brokerage and Investor Protection* monitors broker and investor behavior and trading activity to identify potential risks to both the investor and the firm. *Mantas Enterprise Anti-Money Laundering* is used to identify potential money laundering risks relating to enterprise products and transaction services.

MarketMiner
- Product: MarketMiner
- Vendor: MarketMiner Inc.
- URL: www.marketminer.com
- Functions: Classification, pattern recognition, prediction, segmentation
- Techniques: Decision trees (C4.5), KNN, regression (linear, logistic), statistical techniques
- Platforms: Windows

MarketMiner is a set of marketing analysis tools designed to automate the data mining and analysis process for a business user without advanced statistics knowledge.

MARS
- Product: MARS
- Vendor: Salford Systems
- URL: www.salford-systems.com
- Functions: Forecasting
- Techniques: Regression
- Platforms: Unix (Linux, Solaris), Windows

MARS performs forecasting via the *Multivariate Adaptive Regression Splines* technique. It fits separate splines to different intervals for the predictor variables. Automatic selection of predictor variables is performed. As with, CART, DBMS/COPY allows access to many different formats of data. A graphical GUI is provided.

Minotaur
- Product: Minotaur and Minotaur Transcure
- Vendor: Neural Technologies
- URL: www.neuralt.com
- Functions: Classification, prediction, rules
- Techniques: Neural networks

Minotaur and *Minotaur Transcure* are neural network products targeted to support financial applications. Minotaur is aimed at fraud detection analysis in the telecommunications industry. Minotaur Transcure targets improving the efficiency of credit card transaction processing.

Net Perceptions Retail Analyst
- Product: Net Perceptions Retail Analyst (formerly KD1)
- Vendor: Net Perceptions, Inc.
- URL: www.netperceptions.com
- Functions: Association rules, clustering

Net Perceptions Retail Analyst is a retail analysis and report tool targeted toward retail sales applications. It supports OLAP functions.

Oracle9i Database
- Product: Oracle9i Database
- Vendor: Oracle Corporation
- URL: www.oracle.com/ip/deploy/database/oracle9i/bi_dm.html
- Functions: Association rules, classification, prediction
- Techniques: Naive Bayes
- Platforms: All platforms on which Oracle9i runs

Oracle9i Database has a data mining component embedded within it. The API used is based on a Java data mining approach called *Java Data Mining (JDM)*.

Partek
- Product: Partek
- Vendor: Partek Incorporated
- URL: www.partek.com
- Functions: Clustering, prediction
- Techniques: Genetic algorithms, neural networks, regression
- Platforms: Unix, Windows

Partek actually consists of several companion products designed to perform pattern recognition, exploratory data analysis, statistical inference, and predictive modeling. The pattern recognition product, *Partek Pro*, contains over 20 predefined similarity measures. Partek can access data imported from flat files, ODBC databases, and Web servers. Many normalization and scaling transformation techniques are supported. The *Pattern Visualization System* contains many tools to graphically view the data mining results.

PolyAnalyst
- Product: PolyAnalyst 4.4
- Vendor: Megaputer Intelligence Inc.
- URL: www.megaputer.com/products/pa/index.php3
- Functions: Association rules, classification, clustering, prediction
- Techniques: Decision trees, neural networks
- Platforms: Windows, Unix

PolyAnalyst can access data stored in relational databases using the ODBC interface. In addition, it can process flat files, MS Excel, and DBF files. A point and click object-oriented GUI is provided to facilitate use. Many different visualization tools are included.

Quadstone
- Product: Quadstone System
- Vendor: Quadstone
- URL: www.quadstone.com
- Functions: Prediction, profiling, segmentation
- Techniques: Decision trees, regression
- Platforms: Unix (Solaris, HP, IBM AIX) and Windows NT

Quadstone System is a comprehensive analytical CRM software tool that includes tools to create customer-oriented datasets; segment, profile, and model customer data with advanced data mining algorithms; and deploy customer selections, models and scores in real-time or batch modes. A sophisticated GUI interface and graphical visualization tools are provided.

Re:order
- Product: Re:order (formerly Capri)
- Vendor: Lumio Limited
- URL: www.lumio.com/products.reorder
- Functions: Sequential patterns

The *Re:order* software product targets the efficient discovery of sequences. Sequences may or may not be required to be contiguous in time. Through the use of templates, users indicate the type of sequences to be detected. Templates may include temporal constraints as well as information about required or optional items to appear in the sequence. Capri uses the *Predictive Modeling Mark-Up Language (PMML)* to represent sequences.

Scenario
- Product: Scenario
- Vendor: Cognos Inc.
- URL: www.cognos.com/products/scenario
- Functions: Classification, clustering, outlier detection
- Techniques: Decision trees
- Platforms: Windows

Scenario provides support for clustering and classification applications. Data may be input from various sources, including Excel, Lotus 1-2-3, and from relational databases using ODBC.

See5
- Product: See5/C5.0 1.15
- Vendor: RuleQuest Research Pty Ltd
- URL: www.rulequest.com/see5-info.html
- Functions: Classification
- Techniques: Decision trees, rules
- Platforms: Windows, Unix(Linux, Solaris, Irix)

The classification algorithm C5.0 is implemented in these two products: *See5* runs on Windows machines and *C5.0* runs on Unix. Source code in C is provided so that classifiers generated by See5/C5.0 can be embedded in applications.

S-Plus
- Product: S-Plus
- Vendor: Insightful Corporation
- URL: www.insightful.com
- Functions: Classification, clustering, hypothesis testing, prediction, time series analysis

- Techniques: ARIMA, correlation (Pearson), decision trees, hierarchical clustering (agglomerative, divisive), K-means, regression (linear, logistic, nonlinear, polynomial), statistical techniques (Jackknife, Monte Carlo),
- Platforms: Unix, Windows

The *S-Plus* data mining tool has versions for Unix (including Linux) and Windows, as well as client–server versions. S-PLUS can import or export data from ASCII, SAS, SPSS, Matlab, Excel and Lotus spreadsheets, and other formats. S-PLUS can also import data from databases via ODBC or directly from Oracle on Solaris. S-PLUS is extensible: analytics are created using the object-oriented "S" language, and user-defined C, C++, Fortran, or Java code can be incorporated into S routines. A GUI is provided on both Windows and Unix, and S-PLUS supports over 80 different charting types. Techniques are provided to handle missing data and for analysis of data with outliers.

STATISTICA Data Miner
- Product: STATISTICA Data Miner
- Vendor: StatSoft, Inc.
- URL: www.statsoft.com/dataminer.html
- Functions: Classification, clustering, prediction
- Techniques: ARIMA, decision trees (CART, CHAID), exponential smoothing, neural networks (Back-propagation, MLP, RBF, SOM), regression
- Platforms: Windows

STATISTICA Data Miner provides a comprehensive set of statistical methods to solve data mining problems. It offers a point and click iconic-based GUI to create a workflow description of the KDD and data mining tasks to be performed. Created Visual Basic code can be used to update or modify the tasks at a later date. Extended versions of traditional neural network techniques, association rule algorithms, CART and CHAID, and a wide variety of other techniques are included. The application offers options to process remote databases "in place" (without creating local copies), which greatly increases the performance when data repositories are very large.

SuperQuery
- Product: SuperQuery
- Vendor: AZMY Thinkware, Inc.
- URL: www.azmy.com
- Functions: Rules
- Techniques: Rule induciton
- Platforms: Windows

There are two main versions of *SuperQuery*. The Office edition is designed to work with Excel and Access data files, whereas the Discovery edition can be used to access many different types of data sources, including Acces, xBASE, Borland Paradox, Excel, text files, and ODBC databases.

SurfAid Analytics

- Product: SurfAid Analytics
- Vendor: IBM Corporation
- URL: www.ibm.com/surfaid
- Functions: Web mining

SurfAid Analytics is an IBM e-business service offering that provides Business Intelligence for Web sites. SurfAid identifies visitor attributes that directly relate to customer retention, navigation patterns, and buying habits. SurfAid is compatible across all servers and platforms, requires no software installation or prerequisite hardware, and is serviced entirely on SurfAid machines by SurfAid consultants. Customers send their Web logs to the IBM SurfAid facility for processing.

Visualizer Workstation

- Product: Visualizer Workstation
- Vendor: Computer Science Innovations, Inc.
- URL: www.csi-inc.com
- Functions: Classification, clustering, correlations, prediction, rules
- Techniques: Neural networks(RBF)
- Platforms: Windows

Visualizer Workstation facilitates the process of identifying trends and correlations in data, as well as outliers and exceptions thereto. It is a module of CSI's *Advisor Toolkit*, which includes software to build predictive models and perform additional data mining functions. CSI supports its own KDD development process called the *Cognitive Engineering Methodology*, which closely matches the CRISP-DM, with an extension to address ROI analysis.

WebAnalyst

- Product: WebAnalyst
- Vendor: Megaputer Intelligence Inc.
- URL: www.megaputer.com/products/wa/index.php3
- Functions: Web mining (prediction, patterns)
- Platforms: Windows

WebAnalyst provides Web usage mining functions in a client–server architecture. WebAnalyst not only analyzes Web usage logs, but also can be used to make real-time predictions as to the future behavior of a Web site visitor. These can then be used to dynamically personalize pages for the user.

WebMiner ASP

- Product: WebMiner ASP
- Vendor: Webminer
- URL: www.webminer.com
- Functions: Prediction, web mining

WebMiner ASP is a subscriber-based data mining tool for e-commerce Web sites. By evaluating both customer databases and clickstream data, rules are generated that are used to segment users allowing customization for future Web site visitors.

WizWhy
- Product: WizWhy
- Vendor: WizSoft
- URL: www.wizsoft.com/Why.html
- Functions: Prediction, rules (if-then and if-and-only-if)
- Techniques: Rule induction
- Platforms: Windows

WizWhy is a rule induction data mining tool that can be used for (1) analyzing the data, (2) issuing predictions, and (3) revealing unexpected cases that deviate from the rules. WizWhy accesses many different types of data, including dBase, MS Access, MS SQL, Oracle, OLE databases, ODBC, and ASCII.

XpertRule Miner
- Product: XpertRule Miner
- Vendor: Attar Software Ltd.
- URL: www.attar.com
- Functions: Association rules, classification, clustering
- Techniques: Decision trees, rules
- Platforms: ODBC, Windows

XpertRule Miner supports the complete KDD process through the use of an iconic click and drag GUI interface. It supports the CRISP DM KDD development process. Visualization of results includes various 2D and 3D graphs and figures. XpertRule Miners supports a multitier client–server architecture. Access to any database supported by an ODBC connection is allowed.

Attar provides a companion product to XpertRule Miner. *XpertRule Knowledge Builder* provides a data flow development environment for KDD applications. The output from XpertRule Miner can be exported to a Knowledge Builder application.

A.1   BIBLIOGRAPHIC NOTES

Several surveys of data model software tools have been published, including [GG99]. An extensive list of data mining software products is found at the *St@tServ* home page: http://www.statserv.com/datamsoft.html. The *DBMS Online* page also provides a list of data mining vendors at: http://www.dbmsmag.com/9807mbg.html as does the KDnuggets homepage: http://www.kdnuggets.com/software/index.html. A recent tutorial provided an overview of data mining tools [IA98]. This tutorial contained a complete comparison of the 17 covered products, including a discussion of algorithm approaches used, input and output techniques, usability, and automation and bundling techniques included. A tutorial comparing leading data mining tools was presented at KDD in 1998 [IA98]. This appendix is kept up-to-date at www.engr.smu.edu/~mhd/book.

APPENDIX B

Bibliography

AC75.   Alfred V. Aho and Margaret J. Corasick. Efficient string matching: An aid to bibliographic search. *Communications of the ACM*, 18(6):333–340, 1975.

Ada00.   Jean-Marc Adamo. *Data Mining for Association Rules and Sequential Patterns*. New York: Springer-Verlag, 2000.

Agr94.   Rakesh Agrawal. Tutorial database mining. *Proceedings of the ACM International Conference on Management of Data*, pages 75–76, 1994.

Agr95.   Rakesh Agrawal. Data mining: The quest perspective. Tutorial presented at EDBT Summer School Advances in Database Technology, September 1995.

AIS93.   Rakesh Agrawal, Tomasz Imielinski, and Arun N. Swami. Mining association rules between sets of items in large databases. *Proceedings of the ACM International Conference on Management of Data*, pages 207–216, 1993.

And71.   T. W. Anderson. *The Statistical Analyis of Time Series*. New York: John Wiley & Sons, 1971.

AS91.   Walid G. Aref and Hanan Samet. An approach to information management in geographical applications. *Proceedings of the 4th International Symposium on Spatial Data Handling*, pages 589–598, July 1991.

AS94.   Rakesh Agrawal and Ramakrishnan Srikant. Fast algorithms for mining association rules in large databases. *Proceedings of the International Very Large Databases Conference*, pages 487–499, 1994.

AS95.   Rakesh Agrawal and Ramakrishnan Srikant. Mining sequential patterns. *Proceedings of the IEEE International Conference on Data Engineering*, pages 3–14, 1995.

AS96.   Rakesh Agrawal and John C. Shafer. Parallel mining of association rules. *IEEE Transactions on Knowledge and Data Engineering*, 8(6):962–969, December 1996.

ASY98.   Charu C. Aggarwal, Zheng Sun, and Philip S. Yu. Online algorithms for finding profile association rules. *Proceedings of the ACM CIKM Conference*, Pages 86–95, 1998.

BA96.   Ronald J. Brachman and Tej Anand. The process of knowledge discovery in databases. In Usama M. Fayyad, Gregory Piatetsky-Shapiro, Padhraic Smyth, and eds. Ramasamy Uthurusamy, eds., *Advances in Knowledge Discovery and Data Mining*, pages 37–57. Cambridge; Mass.: AAAI/The MIT Press, 1996.

Bay63.   T. Bayes. An essay towards solving a problem in the doctrine of chances. *Philosophical Transactions of the Royal Society of London*, 53:370–418, 1763.

Bay74.   J. C. Bays. The complete patricia. Technical report, The University of Oklahoma, PhD Dissertation, 1974.

BD96.   Peter J. Brockwell and Richad A. Davis. *Introduction to Time Series and Forecasting*. New York: Springer-Verlag, 1996.

BDGM97.   Béla Bollobás, Gautam Das, Dimitrios Gunopulos, and Heikki Mannila. Time-series similarity problems and well-separated geometric sets. *Proceedings of the 13th Annual Symposium on Computational Geometry*, pages 454–456, 1997.

BDH⁺95.   C. Mic Bowman, Peter B. Danzig, Darren R. Hardy, Udi Manber, Michael F. Schwartz, and Duane P. Wessels. Harvest: A scalable, customizable discovery and access system. Technical report, Department of Computer Science, University of Colorado–Boulder, Technical report CU-CS-732-94, March 1995.

BdVS91.   D. Biggs, B. de Ville, and E. Suen. A method of choosing multiway partitions for classification and decision trees. *Journal of Applied Statistics*, 18:49–62, 1991.

BE97.   Ramon C. Barquin and Herbert A. Edelstein, eds., *Building, Using, and Managing the Data Warehouse*. Englewood Cliffs, NJ: Prentice Hall PTR, 1997.

Ben75.   J. L. Bentley. Multidimensional binary search trees used for associative searching. *Communications of the ACM*, pages 509–517, 1975.

BFOS84.   Leo Breiman, Jerome H. Friedman, Richard A. Olshen, and Charles J. Stone. *Classification and Regression Trees*. Belmont, Calif.: Wadsworth International Group, 1984.

BFOS98.   Leo Breiman, Jerome H. Friedman, Richard A. Olshen, and Charles J. Stone. *Classification and Regression Trees*. New York: Chapman & Hall/CRC, 1998.

BFR98.   Paul Bradley, Usama Fayyad, and Cory Reina. Scaling clustering algorithms to large databases. *Proceedings of the International Conference on Knowledge Discovery and Data Mining*, pages 9–15, 1998.

BH65.   G. H. Ball and D. J. Hall. Isodata, a novel method of data analysis and classification. Technical report, Technical Report, Stanford University, 1965.

Bis95.   Christopher M. Bishop. *Neural Networks for Pattern Recognition*. New York: Oxford University Press, 1995.

BJR94.   George E. P. Box, Gwilym M. Jenkins, and Gregory C. Reinsel. *Time Series Analysis: Forecasting and Control, 3rd ed.* Englewood Cliffs, N.J.: Prentice Hall, 1994.

BJW98.   Claudio Bettini, Sushil Jajodia, and Sean Wang. *Time Granularities in Databases, Data Mining, and Temporal Reasoning*. New York: Springer-Verlag, 1998.

BKKS01.   Markus M. Breunig, Hans-Peter Kriegel, Peer Kröger, and Jörg Sander. Data bubbles: Quality preserving performance boosting for hierarchical clustering. *Proceedings of the ACM International Conference on Management of Data*, pages 79–90, 2001.

BKSS90.   N. Beckmann, H. Kriegel, R. Schneider, and B. Seeger. The R* tree: An efficient and robust access method for points and rectangles. In *Proceedings of the ACM International Conference on Management of Data*, pages 322–331, May 1990.

BL88.   D. S. Broomhead and D. Lowe. Multivariate functional interpolaiton and adaptive networks. *Complex Systems*, 2:321–355, 1988.

BL94.   V. Barnett and T. Lewis, eds., *Outliers in Statistical Data, 3rd ed.* New York: John Wiley & Sons, 1994.

BM77.   R. S. Boyer and J. S. Moore. A fast string searching algorithm. *Communications of the ACM*, 20(10):762–772, October 1977.

BMS77.   Sergey Brin, Rajeev Motwani, and Craig Silverstein. Beyond market baskets: Generalizing association rules to correlations. *Proceedings of the ACM International Conference on Management of Data*, pages 265–276, 1977.

BMUT77.   Sergey Brin, Rajeev Motwani, Jeffrey D. Ullman, and Shalom Tsur. Dynamic itemset counting and implication rules for market basket data. *Proceedings of the ACM International Conference on Management of Data*, pages 255–264, 1977.

BP99.   D. Billsus and M. Pazzani. A hybrid user model for news story classification. *Proceedings of the Seventh International Conference on User Modeling*, June 1999.

BPW96.   Pierre Berthon, Leyland F. Pitt, and Richard T. Watson. The World Wide Web as an advertising medium. *Journal of Advertising Research*, pages 43–54, 1996.

BRE91.   Jay N. Bhuyan, Vijay V. Raghavan, and Venkatesh K. Elayavalli. Genetic algorithms for clustering with an ordered representation. *Proceedings of the Fourth International Conference on Genetic Algorithms*, pages 408–415, 1991.

BS97.   Alex Berson and Stephen J. Smith. *Data Warehousing, Data Mining, and OLAP*. McGraw-Hill, 1997.

BYRN99.   Ricardo Baeza-Yates and Berthier Ribeiro-Neto. *Modern Information Retrieval*. Reading, MA: Addison Wesley, 1999.

Cat91.   Jason Catlett. Megainduction: Machine learning on very large databases. Technical report, University of Sydney, PhD Dissertation, 1991.

CDAR98.   Soumen Chakrabarti, Byron Dom, Rakesh Agrawal, and Prabhakar Raghavan. Scalable feature selection, classification and signature generation for organizing large text databases into hierarchical topic taxonomies. *VLDB Journal*, 7(3):163–178, August 1998.

CDI98.   Soumen Chakrabarti, Byron Dom, and Piotr Indyk. Enhanced hypertext categorization using hyperlinks. *Proceedings of the ACM International Conference on Management of Data*, 1998.

CDK^{+}99.   Soumen Chakrabarti, Byron E. Dom, S. Ravi Kumar, Prabhakar Raghavan, Sridhar Rajagopalan, Andrew Tomkins, David Gibson, and Jon Kleinberg. Mining the web's link structure. *Computer*, 32(8):60–67, August 1999.

Cen87.   J. Cendrowska. Prism: An algorithm for inducing modular rules. *International Journal of Man-Machine Studies*, 27(4):349–370, 1987.

CGM00.   Junghoo Cho and Hector Garcia-Molina. The evolution of the web and implications for an incremental crawler. *Proceedings of the International Very Large Databases Conference*, pages 200–209, 2000.

Cha97.   J. Chattratichat. Large scale data mining: Challenges and responses. *Proceedings of the Third International Conference on Knowledge Discovery and Data Mining*, pages 143–146, 1997.

Cha98.   Surajit Chaudhuri. Data mining and database systems: Where is the intersection? *Bulletin of the IEEE Computer Society Technical Committee on Data Engineering*, 21(1):4–8, March 1998.

Che76.   P. P. Chen. The entity-relationhsip model: Toward a unified view of data. *ACM Transactions on Database Systems*, 1(1):9–36, March 1976.

CHN^{+}96.   David Wai-Lok Cheung, Jiawei Han, Vincent Ng, Ada Wai-Chee Fu, and Yongqian Fu. A fast distributed algorithm for mining association rules. *Proceedings of the Parallel and Distributed Information Systems Conference*, 1996.

CHNW96.   D. W. Cheung, J. Han, V. T. Ng, and C. Y. Wong. Maintenance of discovered association rules in large databases: An incremental updating technique. *Proceedings of the IEEE International Conference on Data Engineering*, pages 106–114, 1996.

CHY96.   Ming-Syan Chen, Jiawei Han, and Philip S. Yu. Data mining: An overview from a database perspective. *IEEE Transactions on Knowledge and Data Engineering*, 8(6):866–883, December 1996.

CLK97.   David Wai-Lok Cheung, Sau Dan Lee, and Benjamin C. M. Kao. A general incremental technique for maintaining discovered association rules. *Proceedings of the DASFAA*, 1997.

CMS97.   R. Cooley, B. Mobasher, and J. Srivastava. Web mining: Information and pattern discovery on the World Wide Web. *Proceedings of the IEEE International Conference on Tools with Artificial Intelligence*, 1997.

CMS99.   Robert Cooley, Bamshad Mobasher, and Jaideep Srivastava. Data preparation for mining World Wide Web browsing patterns. *Knowledge and Information Systems*, 1999.

CNT96.   David W. Cheung, Vincent T. Ng, and Benjamin W. Tam. Maintenance of discovered knowledge: A case in multi-level association rules. *Proceedings of the Second International KDD Conference*, pages 307–310, 1996.

Cod70.   E. F. Codd. A relational model of data for large shared data banks. *Communications of the ACM*, 13(6):377–387, June 1970.

Com01.   International Standards Organization/Internation Electrotechnical Commission. Iso/iec fcd 13249-6 information technology—database languages—sql multimedia and application packages—part 6: Data mining, final committee draft. Technical report, International Standards Organization, 2001.

Cor99.   Two Crows Corporation. *Introduction to Data Mining and knowledge Discovery, 3rd ed.* Two Crows Corporation, 1999.

CP95.   L. Catledge and J. Pitkow. Characterizing browsing behaviors on the World Wide Web. *Computer Networks and ISDN Systems*, pages 1065–1073, 1995.

CPY98.   Ming-Syan Chen, Jong Soo Park, and Philip S. Yu. Efficient data mining for path traversal patterns. *IEEE Transactions on Knowledge and Data Engineering*, 10(2):209–221, March/April 1998.

CS93.   Philip K. Chan and Salvatore J. Stolfo. Experiments on multistrategy learning by metalearning. *Proceedings of the Second International Conference on Information and Knowledge Management*, pages 314–323, 1993.

CTS97.   Robert Cooley, Pang-Ning Tan, and Jaideep Srivastava. Websift: The web site information filter system. *Proceedings of the Web Usage Analysis and User Profiling workshop (WEBKDD'99)*, August 1997.

CvdBD99.   Soumen Chakrabarti, Martin van den Berg, and Byron Dom. Focused crawling: A new approach to topic-specific web resource discovery. *Proceedings of the WWW8 Conference*, 1999. Also available at http://http.cs.berkeley.edu/ soumen/doc/www1999f/html/.

Dat00.   C. J. Date. *An Introduciton to Database Systems, 7th ed.* Addison Wesley, 2000.

DCL+00.   M. Diligenti, F. M. Coetzee, S. Lawrence, C. L. Giles, and M. Gori. Focused crawling using context graphs. *Proceedings of the International Very Large Databases Conference*, pages 527–534, 2000.

DD97.   Hugh Darwen and Chris J. Date. *A Guide to the SQL Standard: A User's Guide to the Standard Database Language SQL.* Addison Wesley, 1997.

Def77.   D. Defays. An efficient algorithm for a complete link method. *The Computer Journal*, 20(4):364–366, 1977.

DHS00. Richard O. Duda, Peter E. Hart, and David G. Stork. *Pattern Classification*. New York: Wiley-Interscience, 2000.

DLR77. A.P. Dempster, N.M. Laird, and D.B. Rubin. Maximum likelihood from incomplete data via the EM algorithm. *Journal of the Royal Statistical Society*, B39:1–38, 1977.

DXGH00. Margaret H. Dunham, Yongqiao Xiao, Le Gruenwald, and Zahid Hossain. A survey of association rules. Technical report, Southern Methodist Univeristy, Department of Computer Science, Technical Report TR 00-CSE-8, 2000.

EFKS98. Martin Ester, Alexander Frommelt, Hans-Peter Kriegel, and Jörg Sander. Algorithms for characterization and trend detection in spatial databases. *Proceedings of the Fourth International Conference on Knowledge Discovery and Data Mining*, pages 44–50, 1998.

EFKS00. Martin Ester, Alexander Frommelt, Hans-Peter Kriegel, and Jörg Sander. Spatial data mining: Database primitives, algorithms and efficient dbms support. *Data Mining and Knowledge Discovery*, 4(2/3):193–216, 2000.

EKS97. Martin Ester, Hans-Peter Kriegel, and Jörg Sander. Spatial data mining: A database approach. *Proceedings of the Fifth International Symposium on Large Spatial Databases (SSD)*, pages 47–66, 1997.

EKSX96. Martin Ester, Hans-Peter Kriegel, J. Sander, and Xiaowei Xu. A density-base algorithm for discovering clusters in large spatial databases with noises. *Proceedings of the International Conference on Knowledge Discovery and Data Mining*, pages 226–231, 1996.

EKSX98. Martin Ester, Hans-Peter Kriegel, Jörg Sander, and Xiaowei Xu. Clustering for mining in large spatial databases. *KI-Journal*, 1:18–24, 1998.

EKX95. Martin Ester, Hans-Peter Kriegel, and Xiaowei Xu. Knowledge discovery in large spatial databases: Focusing techniques for efficient class identification. *Proceedings of the Fourth International Symposium on Large Spatial Databases (SSD)*, pages 67–82, 1995.

Elm90. Jeffrey L. Elman. Finding structure in time. *Cognitive Science*, 14:179–211, 1990.

EN00. Ramez Elmasri and Shamkant B. Navathe. *Fundamentals of Database Systems, 3rd ed.* Addison Wesley, 2000.

Fay98. Usama Fayyad. Mining databases: Towards algorithms for knowledge discovery. *Bulletin of the IEEE Computer Society Technical Committee on Data Engineering*, 21(1):39–48, March 1998.

FB74. R. A. Finkel and J. L. Bentley. Quad trees: A data structure for retrieval on composite keys. *Acta Informatica*, 4(1):1–9, 1974.

FF63. E. A. Feigenbaum and J. Feldman, eds., *Computers and Thought*. New York: McGraw-Hill, 1963.

Fif92. D. J. Fifield. Distributed tree construction from large data-sets. Technical report, Bachelor's Honors Thesis, Australian National University, 1992.

Fis21. R. A. Fisher. On the probable error of a coefficient of correlation deduced from a small sample. *Metron International Journal of Statistics*, 1(4):3–32, 1921.

FJ51. E. Fix and J. L. Hodges Jr. Discriminatory analysis; non-parametric discrimination: Consistency properties. Technical report, Technical report 21-49-004(4), USAF School of Aviation Medicine, Randolph Field, Texas, 1951.

FLP+51. K. Florek, J. Lukaszewicz, J. Perkal, H. Steinhaus, and S. Zubrzycki. Taksonomia wroclawska. *Przeglad Antropologiczny*, 17(4):93–207, 1951.

For65.   E. Forgy. Cluster analysis of multivariate data: Efficiency versus interpretability of classification. *Biometrics*, 21:768, 1965.

FPSM91.   William J. Frawley, Gregory Piatetsky-Shapiro, and Christopher J. Matheus. Knowledge discovery in databases: An overview. In *Knowledge Discovery in Databases*. Cambridge, Mass.: AAAI Press, 1991.

FPSS96a.   Usama Fayyad, Gregory Piatetsky-Shapiro, and Padhraic Smyth. The kdd process for extracting useful knowledge from volumes of data. *Journal of the ACM*, 39(11):27–34, November 1996.

FPSS96b.   Usama Fayyad, Gregory Piatetsky-Shapiro, and Padhraic Smyth. Knowledge discovery and data mining: Towards a unifying framework. *Proceedings of the International Conference on Knowledge Discovery and Data Mining*, pages 82–88, 1996.

FPSS96c.   Usama M. Fayyad, Gregory Piatetsky-Shapiro, and Padhraic Smyth. From data mining to knowledge discovery: An overview. In Usama M. Fayyad, Gregory Piatetsky-Shapiro, Padhraic Smyth, and Ramasamy Uthurusamy, eds., *Advances in Knowledge Discovery and Data Mining*, pages 1–34. AAAI/MIT Press, 1996.

FS93.   U. M. Fayyad and P. Smyth. Image database exploration: Progress and challenges. *Proceedings of the Knowledge Discovery in Databases Workshop*, pages 14–27, 1993.

Fuk90.   Keinosuke Fukunaga. *Introduction to Statistical Pattern Recognition, 2nd ed.* Boston: Academic Press, 1990.

FWD93.   Usama M. Fayyad, Nicholas Weir, and S. George Djorgovski. Automated analysis of a large-scale sky survey: The skicat system. *Proceedings of the Knowledge Discovery in Databases Workshop*, pages 1–13, 1993.

GG98.   Volker Gaede and Oliver Günther. Multidimensional access methods. *ACM Computing Surveys*, 30(2):170–231, June 1998.

GG99.   Michael Goebel and Le Gruenwald. A survey of data mining and knowledge discovery software tools. *SIGKDD Explorations*, 1(1):20–33, 1999.

GGR99a.   Venkatesh Ganti, Johannes Gehrke, and Raghu Ramakrishnan. Mining very large databases. *Computer*, 32(8):38–45, August 1999.

GGR99b.   Venkatesh Ganti, Johannes Gehrke, and Raghu Ramakrishnan. Cactus—clustering categorical data using summaries. *Proceedings of the International Conference on Knowledge Discovery and Data Mining*, pages 73–84, 1999.

GJJ96.   Earl Gose, Richard Johnsonbaugh, and Steve Jost. *Pattern Recognition and Image Analysis*. Englewood Cliffs, N.J.: Prentice Hall, 1996.

GM98.   O. Gustavo and Alberto O. Mendelzon. Weboql: Restructuring documents, databases and webs. *Proceedings of the IEEE International Conference on Data Engineering*, 1998.

GM99.   Amy E. Graham and Robert J. Morse. How *U.S. News* ranks colleges. *U.S. News & World Report*, pages 84–87, August 1999.

GMPS96.   Clark Glymour, David Madigan, Daryl Pregibon, and Padhraic Smyth. Statistical inference and data mining. *Journal of the ACM*, 39(11):35–34, November 1996.

GMUW02.   Hector Garcia-Molina, Jeffrey D. Ullman, and Jennifer Widom. *Datbase Systems: The Complete Book*. Upper Saddle River, N.J.: Prentice Hall, 2002.

Gol89.   D. E. Goldberg. *Genetic Algorithms in Search, Optimization, and Machine Learning*. Reading, Mass.: Addison Wesley, 1989.

Goo00.   Google. www.google.com, 2000.

Goo01.   Google. www.google.com/press/pressrel/3billion.html, December 2001.

GRG98.   J. Gehrke, R. Ramakrishnan, and V. Ganti. Rainforest—a framework for fast decision tree construction of large datasets. *Proceedings of the International Very Large Databases Conference*, pages 416–427, 1998.

GRS98.   Sudipto Guha, Rajeev Rastogi, and Kyuseok Shim. Cure: An efficient clustering algorithm for large databases. *Proceedings of the ACM International Conference on Management of Data*, pages 73–84, 1998.

GRS99.   Sudipto Guha, Rajeev Rastogi, and Kyuseok Shim. Rock: A robust clusteirng algorithm for categorical attributes. *Proceedings of the IEEE International Conference on Data Engineering*, pages 512–521, 1999.

Gut84.   A. Guttman. R-trees: A dynamic index structure for spatial searching. In *Proceedings of the ACM International Conference on Management of Data*, pages 47–57, June 1984.

Güt94.   Ralf Hartmut Güting. An introduction to spatial database systems. *VLDB Journal*, 3:357–399, 1994.

Han96.   Kiawei Han. Data mining techniques. Technical report, ACM SIGMOD Tutorial, 1996.

Har72.   Frank Harary. *Graph Theory*. Reading, Mass.: Addison Wesley, 1972.

Har75.   John A. Hartigan. *Clustering Algorithms*. New York: John Wiley & Sons, 1975.

Has95.   Mohamad H. Hassoun, ed., *Fundamentals of Artificial Neural Networks*. Cambridge, Mass.: The MIT Press, 1995.

Haw80.   D. Hawkins, ed., *Identification of Outliers*. New York: Chapman & Hall, 1980.

Hay99.   Simon Haykin. *Neural Networks—a Comprehensive Foundation, 2nd ed.* Upper Saddle River, N.J.: Prentice Hall, 1999.

HCC92.   Jiawei Han, Yandong Cai, and Nick Cercone. Knowledge discovery in databases: An attribute-oriented approach. *Proceedings of the International Very Large Databases Conference*, pages 547–559, 1992.

HF95.   Jiawei Han and Yongjian Fu. Discovery of multiple-level association rules form large databases. *Proceedings of the International Very Large Databases Conference*, pages 420–431, 1995.

HFW+96.   J. Han, Y. Fu, W. Wang, K. Koperski, and O.R. Zaïane. DMQL: A data mining query language for relational databases. *Proceedings of Workshop on Research Issues in Data Mining and Knowledge Discovery (DMKD'96)*, pages 27–34, June 1996.

Hid99.   Christian Hidber. Online association rule mining. *Proceedings of the ACM International Conference on Management of Data*, pages 145–156, 1999.

HK98.   A. Hinneburg and D. A. Keim. An efficient approach to clustering in large multimedia databases with noise. *Proceedings of the International Conference on Knowledge Discovery and Data Mining*, pages 58–65, 1998.

HK99.   Alexander Hinneburg and Daniel A. Keim. Clustering methods for large databases: From the past to the future. Technical report, ACM SIGMOD Tutorial, 1999.

HK01.   Jiawei Han and Micheline Kamber. *Data Mining: Concepts and Techniques*. San Francisco: Morgan Kaufmann, 2001.

HKK97.   Eui-Hong Hand, George Karypis, and Vipin Kumar. Scalable parallel data mining for association rules. *Proceedings of the ACM International Conference on Management of Data*, pages 277–288, 1997.

HKMT95.   Marcel Holsheimer, Martin Kersten, Heikki Mannila, and Hannu Toivonen. A perspective on databases and data mining. *Proceedings of the International Conference on Knowledge Discovery and Data Mining*, pages 150–155, 1995.

HKT01.   Jiawei Han, Micheline Kamber, and Anthony K. H. Tung. *Spatial Clusteirng Methods in Data Mining: A Survey.* Philadelphia: Taylor & Francis, 2001.

HLP01.   Jiawei Han, Laks V.S. Lakshmanan, and Jian Pei. Scalable frequent-pattern mining methods: An overview. Technical report, ACM SIGKDD Tutorial, 2001.

HMS66.   E. B. Hunt, J. Martin, and P. J. Stone. *Experiments in Induction.* Boston: Academic Press, 1966.

HMS01.   David Hand, Heikki Mannila, and Padhraic Smyth. *Principles of Data Mining.* Cambridge, Mass.: The MIT Press, 2001.

Hol75.   J. H. Holland. *Adaptation in Natural and Artificial Systems.* Ann Arbor.: University of Michigan Press, 1975.

Hol93.   R. C. Holte. Very simple classification rules perform well on most commonly used datasets. *Machine Learning*, 11:63–91, 1993.

HS93.   Darren R. Hardy and Michael F. Schwartz. Essence: A resource discovery system based on semantic file indexing. *Proceedings of the Winter USENIX Conference*, pages 361–374, January 1993.

HS95.   M. Houtsma and A. Swami. Set-oriented mining for association rules in relational databases. *Proceedings of the IEEE International Conference on Data Engineering*, pages 25–34, 1995.

HTF01.   T. Hastie, R. Tibshirani, and J. H. Friedman, eds., *The Elements of Statistical Learning: Data Mining, Inference, and Prediction* (Springer Series in Statistics). New York: Springer-Verlag, 2001.

IA98.   John F. Elder IV and Dean W. Abbott. A comparison of leading data mining tools. Technical report, Proceedings of the International Conference on Knowledge Discovery and Data Mining, 1998.

IBM00.   IBM. Surfaid analytics. www.surfaid/dfw.ibm.com/web/index.html, 2000.

II98.   Neil R. Euliano II. Temporal self-organization for neural networks. Technical report, University of Florida, PhD Dissertation, 1998.

IM96.   Tomasz Imielinski and Heikki Mannila. A database perspective on knowledge discovery. *Communications of the ACM*, 39(11):58–64, November 1996.

Inm95.   W. H. Inmon. What is a data warehouse? *www.cait.wustl.edu/papers/prism/vol1_no1/*, 1995.

Inm96.   W. H. Inmon. The data warehouse and data mining. *Communications of the ACM*, 39(11):49–50, November 1996.

IP96.   John F. Elder IV and Daryl Pregibon. A statistical perspective on knowledge discovery in databases. In Usama M. Fayyad, Gregory Piatetsky-Shapiro, Padhraic Smyth, and Ramasamy Uthurusamy, eds., *Advances in Knowledge Discovery and Data Mining*, pages 83–113. Cambridge, Mass.: AAAI/The MIT Press, 1996.

JB91.   Donald R. Jones and Mark A. Beltramo. Solving partitioning problems with genetic algorithms. *Proceedings of the Fourth International Conference on Genetic Algorithms*, pages 442–449, 1991.

JD88.   Anil K. Jain and Richard C. Dubes. *Algorithms for Clustering Data.* Englewood Cliffs, N.J.: Prentice Hall, 1988.

JFM97.   T. Joachims, D. Freitag, and T. Mitchell. Webwatcher: A tour guide for the World Wide Web. *Proceedings of the 15th International Joint Conference on Artificial Intelligence*, pages 770–775, 1997.

JLN00.   Theodore Johnson, Laks V. S. Lakshmanan, and Raymond T. Ng. The 3W model and algebra for unified data mining. *Proceedings of the International Very Large Databases Conference*, pages 21–32, 2000.

JMF99.   A. K. Jain, M. N. Murty, and P. J. Flynn. What is a data warehouse? *ACM Computing Surveys*, pages 264–323, September 1999.

Jor86.   M. I. Jordan. Attractor dynamics and parallelism in a connectionist sequential machine. *Proceedings of the Eighth Annual Conference of the Cognitive Science Society*, pages 531–546, 1986.

JS71.   N. Jardine and R. Sibson. *Mathematical Taxonomy*. New York: John Wiley & Sons, 1971.

KAH96.   Krzysztof Koperski, Junas Adhikary, and Jiawei Han. Spatial data mining: Progess and challenges survey paper. *Proceedings of the ACM SIGMOD Workshop on Research Issues in Data Mining and Knowledge Discovery*, 1996. Also available at http://db.cs.sfu.ca/GeoMiner/survey/html/survey.html.

Kas80.   G. V. Kass. An exploratory technique for investigating large quantities of categorical data. *Applied Statistics*, 29:119–127, 1980.

Kas96.   Nikola K. Kasabov. *Foundations of Neural Networks, Fuzzy Systems, and Knowledge Engineering*. Cambridge, Mass.: The MIT Press, 1996.

KB00.   Raymond Kosala and Hendrik Blockeel. Web mining research: A survey. *SIGKDD Explorations*, pages 1–15, July 2000.

Kei97.   Daniel A. Keim. Visual data mining. Technical report, VLDB Tutorial, 1997.

KFW98.   Chan Man Kuok, Ada Fu, and Man Hon Wong. Mining fuzzy association rules in databases. *Proceedings of the International Very Large Databases Conference*, 1998.

KH95.   Krzysztof Koperski and Jiawei Han. Discovery of spatial association rules in geographic information databases. *Proceedings of the Fourth SSD Symposium*, pages 47–66, 1995.

KHK99.   George Karypis, Eui-Hong Han, and Vipin Kumar. Chameleon: Hierarchical clustering using dynamic modeling. *IEEE Computer*, 32(8):68–75, 1999.

KHS98.   Krzysztof Koperski, Jiawei Han, and Nebojsa Stefanovic. An efficient two-step method for classification of spatial data. *Proceedings of the International Symposium on Spatial Data Handling*, pages 45–54, 1998.

Kle99a.   Jon M. Kleinberg. Authoritative sources in a hyperlinked environment. *Journal of the ACM*, pages 604–632, September 1999.

Kle99b.   Mika Klemettinen. A knowledge discovery methodology for telecommunication network alarm databases. Technical report, University of Helsinki, PhD Dissertation, 1999.

KLKF98.   Flip Korn, Alexandros Labrinidis, Yannis Kotidis, and Christos Faloutsos. Ratio rules: A new paradigm for fast, quantifiable data mining. *Proceedings of the International Very Large Databases Conference*, 1998.

KLR⁺98.   Ruby L. Kennedy, Yuchun Lee, Benjamin Van Roy, Christopher D. Reed, and Richard P. Lippman. *Solving Data Mining Problems Through Pattern Recognition*. Englewood Cliffs, N.J.: Prentice Hall, 1998.

KMP77.   D. E. Knuth, J. H. Morris, and V. R. Pratt. Fast pattern matching in strings. *SIAM Journal on Computing*, 6(1):323–350, 1977.

KN96.   E. Knorr and R. Ng. Finding aggregate proximity relationships and commonalities in spatial data mininng. *IEEE Transactions on Knowledge and Data Engineering*, 8(6):884–897, December 1996.

KN98.   Edwin M. Knorr and Raymond T. Ng. Algorithms for mining distance-based outliers in large datasets. *Proceedings of the International Very Large Databases Conference*, pages 392–403, 1998.

Koh82.   T. Kohonen. Self-organized formation of topologically correct feature maps. *Biological Cybernetics*, 43:59–69, 1982.

Kol57.   A. N. Kolmogorov. On the representation of continuous functions of many variables by superposition of continuous functions of one variable and addition. *Doklady Akademii Nauk SSR*, 114:953–956, 1957.

Kop99.   Krzysztof Koperski. A progressive refinement approach to spatial data mining. Technical report, Simon Fraser University, 1999.

KR90.   L. Kaufman and P.J. Rousseeuw. *Finding Groups in Data: An Introduction to Cluster Analysis*. New York: John Wiley & Sons, 1990.

KS95.   David Konopnicki and Oded Shmueli. W3qs: A query system for the world-wide web. *Proceedings of the International Very Large Databases Conference*, pages 54–65, 1995.

KY95.   George J. Klir and Bo Yuan. *Fuzzy Sets and Fuzzy Logic: Theory and Applications*. Englewood Cliffs, N.J.: Prentice Hall, 1995.

LD98.   Jun-Lin Lin and Margaret H. Dunham. Mining association rules: Anti-skew algorithms. *Proceedings of the IEEE International Conference on Data Engineering*, pages 486–493, 1998.

LHM99.   Bing Liu, Wynne Hsu, and Yiming Ma. Mining association rules with multiple supports. *Proceedings of KDD*, pages 337–341, 1999.

LHO93.   W. Lu, J. Han, and B. C. Ooi. Discovery of general knowledge in large spatial databases. *Proceedings of Far East Workshop on Geographic Information Systems*, pages 275–289, 1993.

Liu95.   H. Liu. X2R: A fast rule generator. *Proceedings of the IEEE International Conference on Systems, Man and Cybernetics*, 1995.

LJ98.   Y. H. Li and A. K. Jain. Classification of text documents. *The Computer Journal*, pages 537–546, 1998.

LS97.   W. Y. Loh and Y. S. Shih. Split selection methods for classification trees. *Statistica Sinica*, 7:815–840, 1997.

LSL95.   Hongjun Lu, Rudy Setiono, and Huan Liu. Neurorule: A connectionist approach to data mining. *Proceedings of the International Very Large Databases Conference*, pages 478–489, 1995.

LSL96.   Hongjun Lu, Rudy Setiono, and Huan Liu. Effective data minng using neural networks. *IEEE Transactions on Knowledge and Data Engineering*, 8(6):957–961, 1996.

LSS96.   L. Lakshmanan, F. Sadri, and I. Subramanian. A declarative language for querying and restructuring the web. *Proceedings of the Sixth International Workshop on Research Issues in Data Engineering*, 1996.

LZO99.   Neal Lesh, Mohammed J. Zaki, and Mitsunori Ogihara. Mining features for sequence classification. *Proceedings of the International Conference on Knowledge Discovery and Data Mining*, pages 342–346, 1999.

Man96.   Heikki Mannila. Data mining: Machine learning, statistics, and databases. *Proceedings of the Eighth International Conference on Scientific and Statistical Database Management*, pages 1–8, June 1996.

Man97.   Heikki Mannila. Methods and problems in data mining. *Proceedings of International Conference on Database Theory*, 1997.

Man98.   Heikki Mannila. Database methods for data mining. *Proceedings of the KDD Conference*, 1998.

MAR96.   Manish Mehta, Rakesh Agrawal, and Jorma Rissanen. Sliq: A fast scalable classifier for data mining. *Proceedings of the Fifth International Conference on Extending Database Technology (EDBT)*, 1996.

MBK99.   Ryszard S. Michalski, Ivan Bratko, and Miroslav Kubat. *Machine Learning and Data Mining Methods and Applications*. New York: John Wiley & Sons, 1999.

McC76.   E. M. McCreight. A space economical suffix tree construction algorithm. *Journal of the ACM*, pages 262–272, 1976.

McQ67.   J. McQueen. Some methods for classificaiton and analysis of multivariate observations. *Proceedings of the Fifth Berkeley Symposium on Mathematical Statistics and Probability*, pages 281–297, 1967.

MCS00.   Bamshad Mobasher, Robert Cooley, and Jaideep Srivastava. Automatic personalization based on web usage mining. *Communications of the ACM*, pages 142–151, August 2000.

MH01.   Harvey J. Miller and Jiawei Han, eds., *Geographic Data Mining and Knowledge Discovery*. Philadelphia: Taylor & Francis, 2001.

Mit97.   Tom M. Mitchell. *Machine Learning*. New York: McGraw-Hill, 1997.

Mit99.   Tom M. Mitchell. Machine learning and data mining. *Communications of the ACM*, 42(11):31–36, November 1999.

MMM96.   Alberto Mendelzon, George Mihaila, and Tova Milo. Querying the World Wide Web. *Proceedings of the PDIS Conference*, December 1996.

Mob00.   Mobasher. http://maya.cs.depaul.edu/ mobasher/Research00.html, 2000.

MP43.   W. S. McCulloch and W. Pitts. A logical calculus of the ideas immanent in nervous activity. *Bulletin of Mathematical Biophysics*, 5:115–133, 1943.

MPR00.   Udi Manber, Ash Pater, and John Robison. Experience with personalization on yahoo! *Communications of the ACM*, 43(8):35–39, 2000.

msn00.   msnbc. http://msnbc.com, 2000.

MTV94.   Heikki Mannila, Hannu Toivonen, and A. Inkeri Verkamo. Efficient algorithms for discovering associaton rules. *Proceedings of the AAAI Workshop on Knowledge Discovery in Databases (KDD-94)*, pages 181–192, July 1994.

MTV95.   Heikki Mannila, Hannu Toivonen, and A. Inkeri Verkamo. Discovering frequent episodes in sequences. *Proceedings of the KDD Conference*, pages 210–215, 1995.

NH84.   J. Nievergelt and H. Hinterberger. The grid file: An adaptable, symmetric multikey file structure. *ACM Transactions on Database Systems*, 9(1):38–71, 1984.

NH94.   Raymond T. Ng and Jiawei Han. Efficient and effective clustering methods for spatial data mining. *Proceedings of the International Very Large Databases Conference*, pages 144–155, 1994.

Nil65.   N. J. Nilsson. *Learning Machines*. New York: McGraw-Hill, 1965.

NW97.   Jürg Nievergelt and Peter Widmayer. *Spatial Data Structures: Concepts and Design Choices*, pages 153–197. New York: Springer Verlag, 1997.

NW99.   Hung T. Nguyen and Elbert A. Walker. *A First Course in Fuzzy Logic*. Boca Raton: CRC Press, 1999.

OO01.   Patrick O'Neil and Elizabeth O'Neil. *Database Principles, Programming, and Performance, 2nd ed.* San Francisco: Morgan Kaufmann, 2001.

Orr96.   Mark J. L. Orr. Introduction to radial basis function networks. Technical report, www.anc.ed.ac.uk/ mjo/rbf.html, 1996.

ÖRS98.   Banu Özden, Sridhar Ramaswamy, and Abraham Silberschatz. Cyclic association rules. *Proceedings of the IEEE International Conference on Data Engineering*, pages 412–421, 1998.

OSDH93.   Beng Chin Ooi, Ron Sacks-Davis, and Jiawei Han. Indexing in spatial databases. www.comp.nus.edu.sg/ ooibc/papers.html, 1993.

ÖV99.   Tamer Özsu and Patrick Valduriez. *Principles of Distributed Database Systems*. Englewood Cliffs, N.J.: Prentice Hall, 1999.

PB99.   Gregor Purdy and Stephen Brobst. Perfect dimensions. *Intelligent ENTERPRISE*, 2(8):48–53, June 1999.

PBMW98.   Lawrence Page, Sergey Brin, Rajeev Motwani, and Terry Winograd. The PageRank citation ranking: Bringing order to the web. http://google.stanford.edu/ backrub/pageranksub.ps, 1998.

PCY95.   Jong Soo Park, Ming-Syan Chen, and Philip S. Yu. An effective hash based algorithm for mining association rules. *Proceedings of the ACM International Conference on Management of Data*, pages 175–186, 1995.

PG98.   Witold Pedrycz and Fernando Gomide. *An Introduction to Fuzzy Sets: Analysis and Design (Complex Adaptive Systems)*. Cambridge, Mass.: The MIT Press, 1998.

PKB98.   Vidette Poe, Patricia Klauer, and Stephen Brobst. *Building a Data Warehouse for Decision Support, 2nd ed.* Englewood Cliffs, N.J.: Prentic Hall PTR, 1998.

PZOD99.   S. Parthasarathy, M. J. Zaki, M. Ogihara, and S. Dwarkadas. Incremental and interactive sequence mining. *Proceedings of the CIKM Conference*, 1999.

Qui86.   J. R. Quinlan. Induction of decision trees. *Machine Learning*, 11(1):81–106, 1986.

Qui93.   J. R. Quinlan. *C4.5: Programs for Machine Learning*. San Francisco: Morgan Kaufmann, 1993.

Res01.   RuleQuest Research. Data mining tools see5 and c5.0. www.rulequest.com/see5-info.html, 2001.

RG99.   Naren Ramakrishnan and Ananth Y. Grama. Data mining: From serendipity to science. *Computer*, 32(8):34–37, August 1999.

Rie00.   Doug Riecken. Personalized views of personalization. *Communications of the ACM*, 43(8):26–28, 2000.

RJ86.   L. R. Rabiner and B. H. Juang. An introduction to hidden Markov models. *IEEE ASSP Magazine*, pages 4–16, January 1986.

RM86.   D. E. Rumelhart and J. McClelland, editors. *Parallel Distributed Processing, Vol. 1.* Cambridge, Mass.: The MIT Press, 1986.

RMS98.   Sridhar Ramaswamy, Sameer Mahajan, and Avi Silberschatz. On the discovery of interesting patterns in association rules. *Proceedings of the International Very Large Databases Conference*, pages 368–379, 1998.

Ros58.   M. Rosenblatt. The perceptron: A probabilistic model for information storage and organization in the brain. *Psychological Review*, 65:386–408, 1958.

RS99.   Rajeev Rastogi and Kyuseok Shim. Scalable algorithms for mining large databases. Tutorial presented at the CIKM Conference, August 1999.

SA95.   Ramakrishnan Srikant and Rakesh Agrawal. Mining generalized association rules. *Proceedings of the International Very Large Databases Conference*, pages 407–419, 1995.

SA96a.   Ramakrishnan Srikant and Rakesh Agrawal. Mining quantitative association rules in large relational tables. *Proceedings of the ACM International Conference on Management of Data*, pages 1–12, 1996.

SA96b.   Ramakrishnan Srikant and Rakesh Agrawal. Mining sequential patterns: Generalizations and performance improvements. *Proceedings of the Fifth International Conference on Extending Database Technology*, pages 3–17, 1996.

Sal71.   G. Salton. *The SMART Retrieval System—Experiments in Automatic Document Processing*. Englewood Cliffs, N.J.: Prentice Hall, 1971.

Sam95a.   Hanan Samet. Spatial data structures. In Won Kim, ed., *Modern Database Systems*, pages 361–385. New York: ACM Press, August 1995.

Sam95b.   Hanan Samet. Spatial data structures. In Won Kim, ed., *Modern Database Systems*, pages 338–360. New York: ACM Press, August 1995.

SAM96.   J. Shafer, R. Agrawal, , and M. Meha. Sprint: A scalable parallel classifier for data mining. *Proceedings of the International Very Large Databases Conference*, pages 544–555, 1996.

San98.   Arturo Sangalli. *The Importance of Being Fuzzy*. Princeton: Princeton University Press, 1998.

SCDT00.   Jaideep Srivastava, Robert Cooley, Mukund Deshpande, and Pang-Ning Tan. Web usage mining: Discovery and applications of usage patterns from web data. *SIGKDD Explorations*, pages 12–23, January 2000.

SCZ98.   Gholamhosein Sheikholeslami, Surojit Chatterjee, and Aidong Zhang. Wavecluster: A multi-resolution clustering approach for very large databases. *Proceedings of the International Very Large Databases Conference*, pages 428–439, 1998.

SEKX98.   J. Sander, M. Ester, H. P. Kriegel, and X. Xu. Density based clustering in spatial databases: The algorithm gdbscan and its applications. *Data Mining and Knowledge Discovery*, 2(2):169–194, 1998.

Sib73.   R. Sibson. Slink: An optimally efficient algorithm for the single link cluster methods. *The Computer Journal*, 16(1):30–34, 1973.

Sim96.   Patrick K. Simpson, ed., *Neural Networks Theory, Technology, and Applications*. IEEE Technical Activities Board, 1996.

Sin98.   Harry Singh. *Data Warehousing Concepts, Technologies, Implementations, and Management*. Englewood Cliffs, N.J.: Prentice Hall PTR, 1998.

Sin99.   Harry Singh. *Interactive Data Warehousing*. Englewood Cliffs, N.J.: Prentice Hall PTR, 1999.

SK96.   Takahiko Shintani and Masaru Kitsuregawa. Hash based parallel algorithms for mining association rules. *Proceedings of the Parallel and Distributed Information Systems Conference*, 1996.

SM83.   Gerald Salton and Michael J. McGill. *Introduction to Modern Information Retrieval*. New York: McGraw-Hill, 1983.

SM95.   U. Shardanand and P. Maes. Social information filtering: Algorithms for automating 'word of mouth.' *Proceedings of CHI'95 Conference on Human Factors in Computing Systems*, 1995.

SON95.   Ashoka Savasere, Edward Omiecinski, and Shamkant B. Navathe. An efficient algorithm for mining association rules in large databases. *Proceedings of the International Very Large Databases Conference*, pages 432–444, 1995.

SP00.   Deborah J. Smith and James E. Pricer. Sessioninzing clickstream data. *Teradatareveiw*, pages 8–9, Fall 2000.

SPF00.   Myra Spiliopoulou, Carsten Pohle, and Lukas C. Faulstich. Improving the effectiveness of a web site with web usage mining. *Proceedings of the WEBKDD'99 Workshop*, pages 139–159, 2000.

Spi00.   Myra Spiliopoulou. Web usage mining for web site evaluation. *Communications of the ACM*, pages 127–134, August 2000.

Sri96.   Ramakrishnan Srikant. Fast algorithms for mining association rules and sequential patterns. Technical report, PhD Dissertation, University of Wisconsin, 1996.

SS73.   P. H. A. Sneath and R. R. Sokal. *Numerical Taxonomy*. San Francisco: W. H. Freeman and Company, 1973.

Sta01.   StatSoft. *Electronic Statistics Textbook*. StatSoft, Inc., 2001. http://www.statsoft.com/textbook/stathome.html.

TB70.   R. C. Tryon and D. E. Bailey. *Cluster Analysis*. New York: McGraw-Hill, 1970.

TBAR97.   Shiby Thomas, Sreenath Bodagala, Khaled Alsabti, and Sanjay Ranka. An efficient algorithm for the incremental updation of association rules in large databases. *Proceedings of the Third International Conference on Knowledge Discovery and Data Mining (KDD)*, page 263, 1997.

TF82.   Toby J. Teorey and James P. Fry. *Design of Database Structures*. Englewood Cliffs, N.J.: Prentice Hall, 1982.

TK98.   Sergios Theodoridis and Konstantinos Koutroumbas. *Pattern Recognition*. Boston: Academic Press, 1998.

TLHF99.   Anthony K. H. Tung, Hongjun Lu, Jiawei Han, and Ling Feng. Breaking the barrier of transactions: Mining inter-transaction associaton rules. *Proceedings of the International Conference on Knowledge Discovery and Data Mining*, pages 297–301, 1999.

Toi96.   Hannu Toivonen. Sampling large databases for association rules. *Proceedings of the International Very Large Databases Conference*, pages 134–145, 1996.

TS93.   G. G. Towell and J. W. Shavlik. Extracting refined rules from knowledge-based neural networks. *Machine Learning*, 13(1):71–101, 1993.

Web00.   Geoffrey I. Webb. Efficient search for association rules. *Proceedings of the International Conference on Knowledge Discovery and Data Mining*, 2000.

WF00.   Ian H. Witten and Eibe Frank. *Data Mining Practical Machine Learning Tools and Techniques*. San Francisco: Morgan Kaufmann, 2000.

WI98.   Sholom M. Weiss and Nitin Indurkhya. *Predictive Data Mining*. San Francisco: Morgan Kaufmann, 1998.

WM97.   Jef Wijsen and Robert Meersman. On the complexity of mining temporal trends. *Proceedings of the Workshop on Research Issues in Data Mining and Knowledge Discovery*, 1997.

Wor00.   WordNet. Wordnet—a lexical database for English. www.cogsci.princeton.edu/ wn, 2000.

WTMSW72.   Jr. W. T. McCormick, P. J. Sweitzer, and T. W. White. Problem decomposition and data reorganization by a clustering technique. *Operations Research*, 20(5):993–1009, September–October 1972.

WUM00.   WUM. http://wum.wiwi.hu-berlin.de/wumDescription.html, 2000.

WYM97.   Wei Wang, Jiong Yang, and Richard Muntz. Sting: A statistical information grid approach to spatial data mining. *Proceedings of the International Very Large Databases Conference*, pages 186–195, 1997.

XD01a.   Yongqiao Xiao and Margaret H. Dunham. Efficient mining of traversal patterns. *Data and Knowledge Engineering*, 39(2):191–214, November 2001.

XD01b.   Yongqiao Xiao and Margaret H. Dunham. Interactive clustering for transaction data. *Proceedings of the International Conference on Data Warehousing and Knowledge Discovery*, 2001.

XEKS98.   X. Xu, M. Ester, H.-P. Kriegel, and J. Sander. A distribution based clustering algorithm for mining in large spatial databases. *Proceedings of the IEEE International Conference on Data Engineering*, pages 324–331, 1998.

Yah00.   Yahoo. http://my.yahoo.com, 2000.

YM98.   Clement T. Yu and Weiyi Meng. *Principles of Database Qeury Processing for Advanced Applications*. San Francisco: Morgan Kaufmann, 1998.

Zad65.   Lotfi Zadeh. Fuzzy sets. *Information and Control*, 8:338–353, 1965.

Zaï99.   Osmar Rachid Zaïane. Resource and knowledge discovery from the internet and multimedia repositories. Technical report, PhD Dissertation, Simon Fraser University, March 1999.

Zai01.   Osmar R. Zaiane, *Building Virtual Web Views*, 39(2):143–163, 2001.

Zak98.   Mohammed J. Zaki. Efficient enumeration of frequent sequences. *Proceedings of the ACM CIKM Conference*, pages 68–75, 1998.

Zak99.   Mohammed Javeed Zaki. Parallel and distributed association mining: A survey. *IEEE Concurrency*, October–December 1999.

ZCF+97.   Carlo Zaniolo, Stefano Ceri, Christos Faloutsos, Richard T. Snodgrass, V. S. Subrahmanian, and Roberto Zicari. *Advanced Database Systems*. San Francisco: Morgan Kaufmann, 1997.

ZH00.   Mohammed J. Zaki and Ching-Tien Ho, eds., *Lecture Notes in Artificial Intelligence 1759; Large-Scale Parallel Data Mining*. New York: Springer-Verlag, 2000.

Zha71.   C. T. Zhan. Graph-theoretical methods for detecting and describing gestalt clusters. *IEEE Transactions on Computers*, C(20):68–86, 1971.

ZHLH98.   Osmar R. Zaïane, Jiawei Han, Ze-Niam Li, and Joan Hou. Mining multimedia data. Technical report, Technical Report Intelligent Database System Research Laboratory, School of Computer Science, Simon Fraser University, 1998.

ZOPL96.   Mohammed Javeed Zaki, Mitsunori Ogihara, Srivivasan Parthasarathy, and Wei Li. Parallel data mining for association rules on shared-memory multiprocesors. Technical report, Technical Report TR 618, University of Rochester, Computer Science Department, May 1996.

ZPOL97.   Mohammed Javeed Zaki, Srinivasan Parthasarathy, Mitsunori Ogihara, and Wei Li. New parallel algorithms for fast discovery of association rules. *Data Mining and Knowledge Discovery*, 1(4):343–373, December 1997.

ZRL96.   Tian Zhang, Raghu Ramakrishnan, and Miron Livny. Birch: An efficient data clustering method for very large databases. *Proceedings of the ACM International Conference on Management of Data*, pages 103–114, 1996.

Index

About the Author

Margaret H. Dunham received the B.A. and the M.S. in mathematics from Miami University in Oxford, Ohio. She earned the Ph.D. degree in computer science from Southern Methodist University. Professor Dunham's research interests encompass main memory databases, data mining, temporal databases, and mobile computing. She is currently an Associate Editor for IEEE *Transactions on Knowledge and Data Engineering*. She has published numerous technical papers in such research areas as database concurrency control and recovery, database machines, main memory databases, and mobile computing.